BRITISH GARDENERS

A BIOGRAPHICAL DICTIONARY

FIRST PUBLISHED 1980
BY A. ZWEMMER LTD., 26 LITCHFIELD STREET, LONDON W.C.2.
COPYRIGHT © 1980 THE CONDE NAST PUBLICATIONS LTD

British gardeners
1. Gardeners - Great Britain - Biography
I. Hadfield, Miles
II. Harling, Robert
III. Highton, Leonie
635'.092'2   SB61

ISBN 0302-00541-2

Made and printed in Great Britain by
Hazell Watson and Viney Ltd., Aylesbury

BRITISH GARDENERS

A BIOGRAPHICAL DICTIONARY

Miles Hadfield·Robert Harling·Leonie Highton

A.Zwemmer Ltd London

in association with

The Condé Nast Publications Ltd

*A discursive note on Diderot,
Dr Johnson, Larousse, Professor Colvin
and the pictorial as well as
lexicographical aspects of*

GARDENERS
AND GARDENING

Unlike the French who seem to have revelled in illustrating their dictionaries for a couple of centuries, the English have remained stolidly textual in their lexicographical exercises.

The seventeen volumes of the *Encyclopedie, ou Dictionnaire Raisonné des Sciences, des Arts et Métiers*, published by that versatile if wayward genius, Denys Diderot, between 1751 and 1765, were augmented, for example, by eleven volumes of illustrations. And the various *dictionnaires illustrés* issued by the publishing house (which, happily, still vigorously survives) founded by that nineteenth-century protean, Pierre Athanase Larousse, have enthralled many a child, enriched the cuisine of innumerable chatelaines, and encouraged the studies of youthful academic aspirants far beyond the boundaries of France.

English lexicographers are different. Dr Johnson had no time for any graphical supplement to his enquiries. Neither, in our time, have the many lexicographers who have contributed their etymological learning to *A New English Dictionary on Historical Principles*, later and better known as *The Oxford English Dictionary*. None of the thirteen volumes, plus supplements, abridgements and the rest carries an illustration. And when we come to more specialized dictionaries, the story is the same. Professor Howard Colvin's invaluable *Biographical Dictionary of British Architects* (1660–1840) has no reproductions of portraits or buildings. Even the *Penguin Dictionary of Art and Artists* manages to eschew graphic references. That notable literary tradition which put down such deep roots in Victorian England certainly continues to flourish. English lexicographers apparently deprecate pictures. And for students of gardening history the equally invaluable *Dictionary of English and Irish Botanists and Horticulturists*, by James Britten and George Boulger, originally published in 1893 (revised by Ray Desmond in 1977) is also without representation of relevant faces or places.

Yet we live, we are told, in a world in which images are rapidly replacing alphabets. All newspapers – Western newspapers, anyway – spend hundreds of thousands of pounds and millions of francs and lira on manning and equipping their picture-desks. Their cameramen cover the waterfronts and warfronts of the world. The coming of international television programmes, bounced off obliging satellites, has made no difference to these newspaper practices and conventions. The frozen frames of newspaper pictures still compete with the moving images of the screen, and, curiously enough, seem to be holding their own. Pictures are clearly still quite important.

Thus it seemed to the editors of *House & Garden*, which owes its sales basically to its illustrations (mostly taken by half-a-dozen supremely competent photographers of the indoor and outdoor scene) that an illustrated *Biographical Dictionary of Gardeners* would be an interesting successor to our completed and published *Dictionary of Design and Decoration*. Whenever, in the past, we had consulted other rigidly textual works to check dates and/or publications of botanists, plant-collectors, horticulturists and gardeners, we were invariably forced to ponder, without satisfaction, that elusive conundrum which so fascinated President Kennedy: 'What's he like?'

When I learned in due course that Miles Hadfield had been compiling, over several years, entries for a projected biographical dictionary of British gardeners (which, he had dolefully decided would never be published) I was immediately interested. But here again I

(Opposite) Temple of the Winds, Castle Howard, Yorkshire, built 1725–28 to the designs of Vanbrugh. From a painting by Felix Kelly.

was defeated, for his notes lacked illustrations. He had regretfully decided that the search for portraits, prints and photographs would prove far too lengthy, expensive and extensive a project for anyone other than an enthusiastic and philanthropic publisher with a lively team of researchers. Fortunately, we were able to assure him that *House & Garden* could supply the necessary seekers after this graphic impedimenta. He said snap and we quickly decided to underwrite the project as a monthly feature in the magazine. (Curiously enough, Britten and Boulger began their *Dictionary* as a part-work, as it were, in the *Journal of Botany* between 1888 and 1891.)

The search has proved as absorbing a task as any gardening enthusiast could hope for. Many of the finds were more surprising and interesting than those apt to reward most questors after similar hidden or forgotten treasures and pleasures. Batty Langley's engraved design for the 1743 invitation to the Society of Gardeners and Florists was found on a stall in a junk market. A 1972 catalogue of rare books from Traylen of Guildford offered for sale a rare contemporary oil painting (artist unknown) of John Gerard, the noted seventeenth-century herbalist. (The buyer generously allowed *House & Garden* to reproduce the portrait.) Another junk-shop find was the engraving of the Camberwell house and garden of Dr John Lettsom, patron of the early American plant-hunters.

Rediscovering and photographing little-known original paintings was another pleasure. The exquisite paintings of the flowers of the Falkland Islands made on the spot by Elinor Vallentin for her botanist husband in the early years of this century were photographed at Kew. Water-colours commissioned from Chinese artists by Sir Stamford Raffles, whilst acting as a colonial governor in the Far East, were located and photographed in the East India Office Library by Blackfriars Bridge. A more up-to-date discovery was that Edward Bawden, the Royal Academician and also a skilful lifelong gardener, had designed a coloured lino-cut which showed how he thought Francis Bacon's ideal garden might have looked. He was delighted for the design to be reproduced in these pages. Selections from the incomparable collection of paintings of exotic plants by Marianne North (for which she provided the funds for her own gallery at Kew) were also photographed *in situ*.

Portraits were fairly easily come by in most cases. A surprising number of engraved portraits of the early gardeners and plant-collectors are still extant. Family photographic albums supply the answers to queries concerning more recent gardeners and others; occasionally, however, off-beat enquiries were employed. Thus a call-by-call to the *Rohde* entries in the London telephone directory brought to light an unknown photograph of Eleanour Sinclair Rohde, Edwardian author of several books on the early history of English gardening. The most resolutely elusive of all portraits which we sought – and never found – was that of John James, the architect of St George's Hanover Square, and of his own house, Warbrook at Eversley in Hampshire and, more to our point, translator of Dezallier d'Argenville's important book *The Theory and Practice of Gardening*, published in England in 1712. We had to admit defeat, despite much searching and a final desperate appeal in the editorial notes of *House & Garden*. The search continues. On the other hand, a print of Sir Thomas Lawrence's enchanting portrait of Lady Amherst (now in Amherst College, Massachusetts, USA) arrived too late for publication in the magazine, but is shown here.

The compilation, once started, considerably expanded the scope of Miles Hadfield's original notes and references. At an early stage he became, alas, seriously indisposed and virtually all the editorial work from that time on was undertaken by Leonie Highton, deputy editor of *House & Garden*, and myself. Miles Hadfield was unfailingly generous, cooperative and encouraging in this unavoidable switch of direction and emphasis.

As in all such exercises a single entry frequently sponsored further entries. Our researchers became increasingly knowledgeable concerning possible sources and increasingly uxorious concerning the value of their pictorial discoveries.

Certain botanists, plant-hunters and gardeners emerged as quite exceptional human beings. Plant-collectors appealed on every count, of course. In a world of materialism and money-making, particularly during their Victorian hey-dey, they appear supremely superior to such mundane considerations as personal renown and worldly success, oblivious (or perhaps contemptuous) of the profit and glory nurserymen and plutocrats were deriving from their discoveries. They were a special breed: courageous, resolute, enterprising, dedicated to their quest, devoted to their plants. Foremost amongst our favourites in this group were David Douglas; the Hookers, father and son; William Purdom; George Forrest; John Gibson; Frank Kingdon Ward.

The artists were another appealing group, for they

included a remarkable group of women, mostly young, frequently forced to learn their craft against man-made odds; frequently, too, intrepid travellers. Two, previously mentioned, were Marianne North, daughter of a well-heeled Liberal MP for Hastings, who travelled the world over a century ago with the sangfroid of a jetting lady executive of our own day, and Elinor Vallentin, who painted the flowers of the Falkland Island for her botanist husband. But the stay-at-home Victorians were also unusually emancipated ladies, well-ahead of their time as workers and bread-winners: Clara Leigh supported four young daughters by her botanical paintings – and continued her work after marrying her Mr Pope; Anne Pratt even got a grant from the Civil List for her botanical drawings.

Our month-by-month compilation of the *Dictionary* matched an ever-increasing interest in the history of gardening on the part of the British public. More and more popular histories as well as books on specialist aspects of the subject are now being published. An increasing number of television programmes is devoted to this notable heritage we too often take for granted. Sir John Gielgud has been co-opted for an Independent Television programme on the history of the English garden. The success of the 1979 exhibition of *The Garden*, at the Victoria & Albert Museum, organized by Dr. Roy Strong and John Harris, Curator of the Prints and Drawings Collection of the Royal Institute of British Architects, underlined this growing interest in the history of gardening as emphatically as the annual Chelsea Show underlines the English passion for the hard graft of gardening. Indeed, as more and more facts become known, it could be said that interest in gardening history is fast catching up with the now well-established non-specialist interest in architectural history.

Inevitably, more and more information about the history of gardens, gardeners and gardening was published during the course of compilation. When the *Dictionary* was begun, little was known, for example, about Charles Bridgeman. But in 1977, Professor Peter Willis published his biographical study* of the gardener to George II, considerably extending our knowledge of the man and his influence. Again, facsimile copies of *Humphry Repton's Red Books for Sheringham Hall, Attingham and Antony* were published in a limited edition by the Basilisk Press in 1977. Admittedly, the price of the book would have daunted all but a gardening millionaire but the publication was yet another sign of the times.

Here and there the names of botanists and others not born in Britain have been slipped into the entries – Bartram, Ehret, Solander and a few more. These deliberate infiltrations were deemed necessary and logical due to the intricate, even inextricable involvement of these men with the history of English gardening. Above all, we thought that some reference should be made to the great Carolus Linnaeus, whose influence on the nomenclature of English botanical studies was so emphatic, decisive, if occasionally controversial. We trust that these few borrowings will be readily forgiven by their latterday gardening compatriots.

There are, we realize, many omissions. But even the *Oxford* admits to omissions and needs supplements from time to time. Discovering details about every important gardener, horticulturist or plant-collector is every bit as difficult as discovering a new word and then establishing its derivation. No doubt this *Dictionary*, too, will need a supplement.

Finally, any compilation of this kind owes much to well-wishers. Our aiders and abettors have ranged from horticultural scholars to riders of hobby-horses, from energetic enthusiasts and obsessionists to altruistic collectors. We extend our gratitude to all, whether they amended our entries by telephone or criticized our efforts by postcard.

More specifically we should like to thank others for more specialized help. Peter Coats, gardening editor of *House & Garden*, exercised a pervasive interest in the increasing data of the *Dictionary* between travels, inseparable from an international garden-designing practice and photographic assignments. (From which, incidentally, the *Dictionary* has pictorially profited to a high degree). Peter Barnes, botanist at Wisley, checked the plant names. Three successive *House & Garden* art editors, Peter Holdsworth, Neville Poulter and John Bridges, took a particular interest in assembling into agreeable *mises en page* the material collected for the numerous entries, while Pedro Prá-Lopez translated the monthly features into book format. Onetime editorial assistant, Corinne Page, was of inestimable help in the early stages of the compilation. In preparing all the material for publication in book form, Penny Carmichael has been responsible for the inordinate and demanding programme of checking and indexing. To all these we offer thanks.

ROBERT HARLING

* *Charles Bridgeman* by Peter Willis (Zwemmer)

Aberconway, Charles Melville McLaren, 3rd Baron of Bodnant (1913–). President of the Royal Horticultural Society since 1961 and the inheritor of the notable gardens at Bodnant, Tal-y-cafn, Denbighshire, North Wales, established by his great-grandfather, Henry Pochin, who bought the estate in 1875, and his grandmother, Laura McLaren, the first Lady Aberconway, who inherited the property on her father's death.

Bodnant is situated high up on the banks of the River Conway in Caernarvonshire, with spectacular views over the river towards Snowdonia.

In 1894, in collaboration with her son, Henry McLaren, the 2nd Baron (1879–1953), Laura McLaren began to transform Bodnant into gardens of outstanding beauty and wide botanical repute, the last great British garden combining formality, natural planting and horticultural interest of great style and scale.

In his remarkable development of Bodnant, Henry McLaren took advantage of the site on an axis running roughly north and south and protected from the east by high ground behind, with a steep slope to the west. He was aided by an abundance of water.

Between 1905 and 1914, a lawn, which sloped from the house to the west, was converted into a magnificent series of terraces in the Italian style. These terraces made use of existing features and each was given its own character: viz, rose terrace, croquet terrace, lily terrace, pergola and lower rose terrace and canal terrace. They overlook the river below and the Snowdonian range beyond, embellished and loosely unified by fountains, statuary, urns. Most noteworthy of all additions is the charming, gabled 1730 Pin Mill which stands at the southern end of the Canal Terrace and once stood as a garden-house to an Elizabethan house in Gloucestershire. When threatened by decay and demolition, the building was removed to Bodnant in 1938.

From the south flows the small River Hiraethlyn, and the river valley more or less forms the lower

(Opposite) The gardens at Bodnant in Wales, home of Lord **Aberconway**. *The 1730 pin mill (top left) was brought from Gloucestershire in 1938.*

Henry McLaren of Bodnant, father of the 3rd Lord **Aberconway**.

boundary of the garden. At its head is a mill-pond, from which the river and the mill-race flow downwards until the old mill is reached. This site, including an area called the Dell, is dominated by gigantic conifers and other trees, some planted by Pochin during the earlier stage of

Charles Melville McLaren, the 3rd Lord **Aberconway** *(1913–).*

the garden's development when the landscape designer Edward Milner, who had worked with Sir Joseph Paxton (qv), was asked to advise on planting projects. Today, a wide range of rhododendrons grows beneath the trees. Here, as throughout the garden, the revolutionary

developments, brought about by the plants introduced soon after the beginning of the new garden, are admirably exploited. The 2nd Lord Aberconway was an outstanding supporter of several notable plant-collecting expeditions which were undertaken during the early years of this century.

The coherence and success of the variegated plantings at Bodnant owed much to the bold and imaginative manner in which the 2nd Lord Aberconway's maxim, 'Find out which plants grow well for you and plant a lot of them', has been followed.

The making of Bodnant was not his only horticultural activity. In cooperation with F. C. Puddle (qv), who joined Bodnant as head gardener after the 1914–18 war, he bred plants, particularly rhododendrons, with remarkable success. He was also an outstanding grower and raiser of greenhouse plants, including hippeastrums and paphiopedilums. The garden also made a fine home for the gentians, meconopsis, primulas and other smaller plants

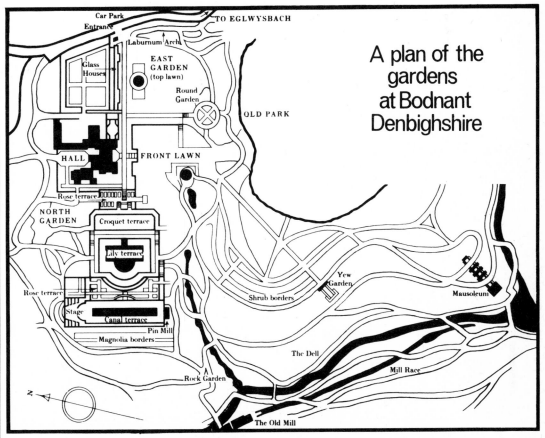

A plan of the gardens at Bodnant Denbighshire

Plan of the gardens at Bodnant, Denbighshire, North Wales, home of Lord **Aberconway**.

Title-page from Every Man his own Gardener, *first published in 1767 by John* **Abercrombie.**

The island pagoda designed by Robert **Abraham** *for Lord Shrewsbury at Alton Towers, Staffordshire.*

which were coming into cultivation from Western China.

The gardens were endowed to the National Trust in 1949. The 3rd Baron and his wife have continued to live at Bodnant and to maintain, supervise and even extend the great gardens.

Abercrombie, John (1726–1806). Horticulturist. Abercrombie was born at Prestonpans, East Lothian, Scotland, and educated at the local grammar school. He entered his father's market-gardening business, which supplied vegetables to the Edinburgh market, but after family disagreements, he moved south to seek work as a journeyman gardener. He was employed at the Royal Gardens at Kew and by a Dr Munro at Sunning Hill, before establishing his own garden and nursery at Hackney. A misty legend persists that a bookseller proposed that Abercrombie should write a book on popular gardening which would be revised by Oliver Goldsmith. Nothing came of this project (even, indeed, if it was ever mooted) but in 1767 Abercrombie did publish a book entitled *Every Man his own Gardener.* For some reason, said

to have been Abercrombie's excessive diffidence, the title-page claimed that the book was the work of one Thomas Mawe, gardener to the Duke of Leeds, in Yorkshire. The book was an immediate success and went through many editions. Although Abercrombie eventually disclaimed that Mawe had any connexion with the book, the attribution was maintained. Even as late as 1829, when the twenty-third edition was published, the title-page announced that the work had been 'brought down to the present state of horticultural knowledge by James Maine, ALS' but still announced the authors to have been Thomas Mawe and John Abercrombie. By then *Every Man his own Gardener* contained 688 pages of small print. Abercrombie wrote a number of other books on almost every aspect of gardening, including *The Universal Gardener and Botanist* (1778) and *The Gardener's Pocket Journal* (1791).

Abraham, Robert (1774–1850). Architect, landscape gardener. Abraham was the son of a builder and trained as a surveyor. His early career was much occupied in settling contractual disputes but, following the end of the Napoleonic wars, he set up as an architect and quickly established a successful practice, particularly amongst aristocratic Roman Catholic families. He carried out much work for the Duke of Norfolk at Arundel, Worksop and at Norfolk House in London.

Although primarily known as an architect, Abraham was also commissioned by the Earl of Shrewsbury to design various buildings for the vast and fantastic gardening projects he sponsored at Alton Towers in Staffordshire. These were begun in about 1814. Abraham's most remarkable work at Alton is the Chinese pagoda fountain which, although never completed to its intended height, still throws its jet of water high amongst the surrounding trees.

John Loudon (qv), who visited Alton Towers in 1826, commented on 'a range of architectural conservatories, with seven elegant glass domes, designed by Mr Abraham, richly gilt. Farther on and placed on a high and bold naked rock, is a lofty gothic tower or temple, on what is called Thomson's rock, also designed by Mr Abraham, consisting of several tiers of balconies round a central staircase and rooms; the exterior ornaments numerous and resplendent with gilding. Near the base of the rock is a corkscrew fountain of a peculiar description which is amply supplied from an adjoining pond.' Loudon also mentions a Grecian temple and second terrace containing conservatories. Loudon's description of the foun-

Alton Towers (drawn by the son of Robert **Abraham**), *showing the position of the pagoda as originally planned by Abraham.*

John **Abercrombie** *(1726–1806).*

Sir Thomas Dyke **Acland** *(1787–1871).*

Joseph **Addison** *(1672–1719).*

Queen **Adelaide** *(1792–1849).*

tain continues as follows: 'This pagoda was intended to be eighty-eight feet high. It is placed on an island in the centre of a small pond, and was to have been approached by a Chinese bridge richly ornamented. The diameter of the base of the pagoda is forty feet and there were to have been six stories, the lower one of stone, and the others of cast iron. From the angles were to have been suspended forty highly enriched Chinese lamps and these were to be lighted by a gasometer fixed in the lower story. Besides the lamps, there were to have been grotesque figures of monsters projecting over the angles of the canopies, which were to spout water from their eyes, nostrils, fins, tails, etc; a column of water was also to have been projected perpendicularly from the terminating ornament on the summit of the structure, which, from the loftiness of the source of supply, would have risen to the height of seventy or eighty feet. This fountain was designed by Mr Abraham; but only the lower story has been executed.'

In these projects Robert Abraham was assisted by his son, H. R. Abraham, one of several of Abraham's pupils who later gained some success as architects.

Acland, (Sir) Thomas Dyke (Bt) (1787–1871). Politician, landowner, philanthropist, planner and developer of the notable gardens at Killerton, Broadclyst, South Devon. The Aclands moved from Landkey in North Devon to the southern part of the county in the early fifteenth century, first at Culm John, and, from the beginning of the eighteenth century, at Killerton House. In 1778 the house was rebuilt, over the old cellars, to the designs of John Johnson, a Leicestershire architect. Acland began to lay out the present gardens at Killerton after the Napoleonic Wars. His plans envisaged largely informal gardens devoted to

trees, newly-introduced plants and shrubs. In this considerable enterprise he was aided by John Veitch, a tenant on the Killerton estate. Veitch (qv) was a Scotsman, who came to the West Country from Jedburgh in Northumberland and set up as nurseryman and landscape gardener at Budlake, near Killerton, the origin of the famous Exeter Nursery.

Many of the trees and shrubs were grown from seed, brought back from expeditions abroad, partly underwritten by Acland. The large wellingtonia is said to have been grown from the first seeds introduced into Britain in 1853. This tradition has been continued by the family, and a number of the younger rhododendrons were grown from seed brought by F. Kingdon Ward (qv) during this century. The fine plants and shrubs, especially rhododendrons, at Killerton thrive in the mild air, sheltered conditions and acid soil of the gentle slope of the volcanic hill which forms the contours of the garden. Acland's work in creating the garden is commemorated by a cross in the gardens at Killerton, extended by the 12th baronet from 1900 onwards. In 1944, Sir Richard Acland, and present baronet, gave Killerton, with its now historic collection of plants to the National Trust.

Addison, Joseph (1672–1719). Essayist, poet, statesman. Despite the fact that in his writings Addison was a pioneer of the new landscape style, he seems to have had little practical interest in gardening. A century after his death, his garden at Bilton near Rugby was still described as 'preserving all the formality of the old taste'. And in his published correspondence, unlike that of his near-contemporary Alexander Pope, there is scarcely a reference to the practice of horticulture.

Yet Addison's influence on the history of gardening was consider-

able, for he was the first English writer to attack publicly the formal style of Le Nôtre, which was still almost exclusively practised by serious gardeners in England. As early as 1699 he had written to Congreve saying that he preferred the rocks and woods of Fontainebleau, with its fine variety of savage prospects, to other French gardens. This was an unusual preference at that time. In his *Remarks on Several Parts of Italy in the Years 1701, 1702, 1703*, he wrote that he had seen nothing so worthy of admiration as Vesuvius 'smoking with sulphur in several places'. Of the Italian gardens he had visited, he affirmed that he had seen none worthy of notice, adding that it must be said 'to the honour of the Italians that the French took from them the first plans of their gardens, as well as of their waterworks; so that the surpassing of them at present is to be attributed to their riches than to the excellence of their taste'.

All this was written when, in England, the vogue for formal gardens in the French manner was still at its height. Indeed, Canons, in Middlesex, which was to become the most ornate and elaborate of them, was not begun until 1713.

In an essay published by *The Spectator* in 1712, Addison wrote 'Our British gardeners . . . instead of humouring nature, love to deviate from it as much as possible. Our trees rise in cones, globes and pyramids. We see the marks of the scissors on every plant and bush. I do not know whether I am singular in my opinion, but, for my part, I would rather look upon a tree in all its luxuriancy, than when it is cut and trimmed into a mathematical figure . . . but as our great modellers of gardens have their magazine of plants to dispose of, it is very natural of them to . . . contrive a plan that may most turn to their own profit, in taking off their evergreens and the like movable plants, with which their shops are plentifully

stocked.' (He was attacking the Brompton Park nurseries of London and Wise, whose stock of plants, largely evergreens, was at that time estimated to be worth over £40,000.)

In the same year, he published his celebrated essay on *An Humorist in Gardening*. In this he refers to the confusion in his garden which a foreigner would look upon 'as a natural wilderness and one of the uncultivated parts of our country.' Whether his garden was indeed so carefree is irrelevant: his writings indicated the coming of the English informal landscape style of gardening which replaced French formality and, within a few decades, had recrossed the Channel as the popular *jardin anglais*.

Adelaide, Queen (1792–1849). Landscape gardener, patroness. Daughter of the Duke of SaxeCoburg Meiningen, she married William Duke of Clarence in 1818. They first lived at Bushy House, where he was Ranger of the Park. On his accession to the throne in 1830 they moved to Windsor Castle where the gardens had recently been modernized. There she grew fashionable florist's flowers—those kinds, such as tulips, auriculas, and carnations which were cultivated to carefully laid down rules. Augusta Withers (qv), an outstanding botanical artist, was her Flower Painter in Ordinary.

The Queen was the first patroness of the Metropolitan Society of Florists and Amateurs, founded in 1832. Such societies were usually small groups of enthusiasts holding their shows in local taverns, but the new society was on a grander scale. The Queen provided a ten-guinea plate for tulips and received the winning flowers.

Her patronage was clearly of considerable benefit to the new society. At its highly successful show on June 10th, 1834, at the Crown and Anchor Tavern, a Mr Davis showed

Zamia pungens (*a tropical American fern*) *at Kew Gardens, as depicted in 1839 by Mrs Withers, Flower Painter in Ordinary to Queen* **Adelaide**.

Twin fishing-lodges by the lower lake at Fountains Abbey, an extension of Studley Royal, Yorkshire, designed by John **Aislabie**.

a pelargonium named in her honour. A year later the society had become so prosperous that its show, held at the Surrey Zoological Society's gardens, was one of the first staged on the lavish scale that later became the vogue. There were several tents, a band played and as an incidental, the spectators had a view of the animals. This attracted the previously undreamed of attendance of some 11,000 people.

A scarlet flake carnation and a pink were also named after her.

Aislabie, John (1670–1742). Politician, landowner, landscape artist. Aislabie was born near York but little is known of his early life, except that he inherited the Studley Royal estates in the West Riding of Yorkshire. In 1718 he became Chancellor of the Exchequer and, in 1719, sponsored what became known as the South Sea Bubble. After that vast financial operation collapsed, Aislabie was found guilty of 'most notorious, dangerous and infamous corruption with a view to his own exorbitant profit'. Although substantially fined, he was able to retain his Studley Royal property, to which he retired. There, in the steep-sided and sequestered valley of the little River Skell, he made, with the help of several outstanding craftsmen, the magnificent garden, much of which still exists.

Before political disgrace overtook him, he had been keenly interested in gardening, as were several of his 'Bubble' colleagues, including Sir John Fellowes at Carshalton in Surrey; Robert Chester of Briggins, Hertfordshire; Sir William Gore at Tring Park, Hertfordshire and Francis Hawes at Purley, Berkshire. Aislabie's own garden was at that time Hall Barn, Buckinghamshire. All these gardens are associated with the name of Charles Bridgeman (qv), the most imaginative designer of his day. Yet Studley shows no sign of Bridgeman's influence.

Aislabie was also one of the subscribers to John James's *Theory and Practice of Gardening* published in

William **Aiton** (1731–1793) *and the title page of his three-volume* Hortus Kewensis *or a* Catalogue of Plants cultivated in the Royal Gardens at Kew, *which listed some 5,600 species. The Catalogue was enlarged by his son, from 1810–1813.*

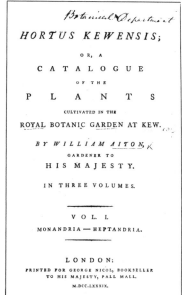

1712. This was a translation of Dezallier d'Argenville's important work of 1709, describing the principles of the great French school of Le Nôtre (who had died nine years previously). Aislabie's Studley design, entirely formal and geometric though it was, bears no general resemblance to the plans published by d'Argenville, an essential feature of which is a main axis usually centred on the house. Nor does Studley Royal resemble typical garden layouts by London and Wise, the English formalists of this period. At Studley the house (long ago burned down) played no part in the design. Instead, the main axis is the river emerging from sombre woodland and confined to a straight canal lying close to one bank for its whole length until it splashes down a cascade, bordered by two fishing lodges, into the lake spreading out in the park, with its famous oaks (many of which were destroyed in the gale of 1962). Between this canal and the other steep wooded bank is a large circular pond with circumfer-

ential pools and statuary, centred on the axis of a building based on an old engraving of the classical Temple of Jupiter, now usually called the Temple of Piety, the façade of which emerges from the umbrageous trees. On the hillsides are other ornamental buildings, both of this and later periods, each commanding wide vistas.

Higher up the valley is an extension to John Aislabie's design. At its extremity lies the magnificent ruin of Fountains Abbey. Aislabie had always wished to acquire the Abbey but was unable to do so, although after his death it came into the hands of his son, William. By then taste was changing. The Picturesque and medieval ruins had come into fashion. William Aislabie therefore made the abbey the climax of an irregular landscaped scene, the river first swelling out into a curving lake and then winding its way towards the astonishing 'eye catcher' that is Huby's 170ft. tower, still dominating the Cistercian ruins. Although the younger Aislabie spoilt the dig-

nity of the scene by inappropriate additions, these no longer exist. The two Aislabies must be credited with one of the most prodigious formal garden designs still in existence in Britain.

Aiton, William (1731–1793). Gardener and horticultural cataloguer. Aiton was born at Hamilton, Lanarkshire, and trained as a gardener before moving to London in 1754 to work under Philip Miller at the Chelsea Physic Garden. In 1759 the Earl of Bute engaged Aiton to manage the Dowager Princess Augusta's botanic garden at Kew. After her death, George III, a keen gardener, bought the adjoining estate of Richmond, and, in 1783, Aiton was placed in charge of both, the king building him a house at Kew. Aiton is today remembered by his *Hortus Kewensis*, a catalogue of some 5,600 species growing at Kew, in the preparation of which he had the help of others. The catalogue is still widely accepted as establishing the dates at which many garden plants were first cultivated in Britain. In his day Aiton was much respected for his 'benign disposition'. One son, William Townsend (qv), succeeded him at Kew. Another, John Townsend, became royal gardener at Windsor.

Aiton, William Townsend (1766–1849). Gardener, horticulturist. Aiton was the son of William Aiton (qv) and was born at Kew. As a youth, he was assistant to his father. Later he became a garden designer working for the Duke of Kent, father of Queen Victoria, and other patrons. He returned to succeed his father at Kew in 1793. In 1804 he was one of the seven men who met at Hatchard's book shop in Piccadilly for the purpose of forming a Society for the Improvement of Horticulture, the origin of the Royal Horticultural Society. In that year,

(Opposite) 'Temple of Piety' and lake at Studley Royal, Yorkshire, landscaped by John **Aislabie**.

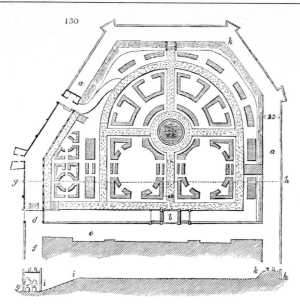

William Townsend **Aiton** *(1766–1849) and the plan and section of the garden at Windsor Castle, designed by Aiton for George IV. The letter-forms indicate the lines through which the contours of the site are taken from the Castle.*

Prince **Albert** *(1819–1861), patron of botany and horticulture.*

he also received some early introductions of the tiger lily (*Lilium lancifolium*) sent from Canton by William Kerr (qv), a collector despatched by Kew. Realizing the value of this remarkable importation, he set to work propagating it and, by 1812, had distributed over ten thousand bulbs. Between 1810–1813, he published a second and enlarged edition of his father's *Hortus Kewensis*, listing over 11,000 species.

With the accession of George IV royal interest in the remarkable botanical and horticultural activities of Kew, still royal property, lapsed, and the gardens were largely used merely to supply plants and flowers to decorate the royal establishments. Aiton was then employed on designing the somewhat unimaginative gardens at the Brighton Royal Pavilion and making considerable alterations to the gardens at Windsor Castle, typical of the uninspired formal style then coming into fashion.

Meantime, the standards of Kew Botanic Gardens had also declined, together with its international renown. In 1838, following a public outcry, the Lords of the Treasury appointed a committee to enquire into the state of the gardens. The enquiry eventually resulted in the garden becoming national instead of royal property. The committee was at pains to state that Aiton, now an aging man, had done well in his attempt to keep up Kew's traditional standards in difficult circumstances.

Albert, Francis Charles Augustus Emmanuel (1819–1861). Patron. On his arrival in England, in 1840, to become Prince Consort to Queen Victoria, Albert displayed the type of interest in botany and horticulture that was soon expected of him in all the arts and sciences. Quite soon after his marriage· he was responsible for preventing the fell-ing of some fine trees in order to enlarge Kew Gardens. He is commemorated botanically by a strange monotypic genus of conifer, introduced by William Lobb (qv) from south Chile in 1846, and named by Professor John Lindley (qv) *Saxegothea conspicua*. At Osborne House in the Isle of Wight, Prince Albert was much concerned with planting the gardens and was personally responsible for the large shrubberies of cherry laurel (*Prunus laurocerasus*), ensuring, as has since been written, 'the popularity of the unhappiest features of nineteenth-century gardening'. There, too, he grew a rare, almost hardy, fern sent to him from

Countess **Amherst** *(1762–1838), from a portrait by Sir Thomas Lawrence. Her name is commemorated by the spectacular tree,* Amherstia nobilis.

Some White Flowers of New Zealand, by the Hon Alicia **Amherst** *(later The Lady Rockley) for her* Wild Flowers of the Great Dominions of the British Empire. *Legend: (1) Mount Cook Lily (Ranunculus Lyallii). (1a) Mount Cook Lily (the leaf). (2) Mountain Daisy (Celmisia coriacea). (2a) Mountain Daisy (the leaf). (3) Pua-wananga (Clematis indivisa). (3a) Pua-wananga (the seed). (4) New Zealand Edelweiss (Leucogenes Leontopodium).*

China by its discoverer, Robert Fortune (qv), through Sir William Hooker (qv) of Kew.

In 1861 he opened the Royal Horticultural Society's new garden at Kensington, claiming that it was an 'attempt to reunite the science and art of gardening to the sister arts of architecture, sculpture and painting'. The garden at Kensington is no longer extant.

Allen, James (d. 1906). Horticulturist. Allen was an outstanding amateur gardener of Shepton Mallet, Somerset, of whose early life little is known, but whose paper read to the Royal Horticultural Society's Snowdrop Meeting in 1891 was followed up in William Robinson's (qv) *English Flower Garden* and was thus largely responsible for the enthusiasm that has since developed for the cultivation of the many kinds of snowdrop. He is remembered by *Galanthus allenii* which he discovered in a parcel of mixed bulbs received from an Austrian nurseryman in 1883. He also collected daffodils, particularly early-flowering kinds of *Narcissus pseudonarcissus*. One, highly praised in its day, was a dwarf which he named 'Allen's Beauty', a variety scarcely ever grown today.

Amherst, Countess (née Sarah Thynne) (1762–1838). Botanist. Wife of Earl Amherst of Arracan, Lady Amherst was a keen gardener, botanist and ornithologist (as was her daughter, Alicia). While her husband was Governor-General of India (1823–8) she collected and introduced numerous plants into Britain, notably the now widely grown *Clematis montana*, as well as *Anemone vitifolia*. These collections were made during a tour, begun in 1826, through the then remote Northern Provinces. The spectacular tree *Amherstia nobilis*, introduced in 1837 by Dr Nathaniel Wallich (qv), Superintendent of Calcutta Botanical Garden, was named in honour of Lady Amherst.

Amherst, (the Hon.) Alicia (1865–1941). Writer. Alicia Amherst was known as 'citizen and gardener of London.' She was the daughter of the first baron Amherst of Hackney. Her *History of Gardening in England*, originally published in 1895, showed both a mastery of the subject and of practical gardening. In 1898, by her marriage, she became the Hon. Mrs Evelyn Cecil and under that name published *Children's Gardens* and *London Parks and Gardens*. After her husband had become Lord Rockley in 1934 she published, as The Lady Rockley, a number of books: *Wild Flowers of the Great Dominions of the British Empire*, *Some Canadian Wild Flowers* and, finally, in 1938, *Historic Gardens of England*.

*Thomas **Anderson** (1832–1870), botanist working in India.*

Anderson, Thomas (1832–1870). Botanist. Anderson was born in Edinburgh and was educated at Edinburgh Institution and the University, where he studied medicine, graduating MD in 1853. Whilst still an undergraduate his herbarium specimens, collected within ten miles of the city centre, gained him a gold medal, and his doctoral thesis was on the therapeutic qualities of *Atropa belladonna*.

In 1854 he joined the Bengal Medical Service and after a spell as medical officer to a native regiment on the North-West frontier he moved to Lucknow, where he compiled notes on local flora before using his leave to go plant-hunting in the Himalayan passes.

Due to ill-health he had to leave India but, at Aden, during a stopover, he was enabled to make a collection of plants on which he based his *Florula Adenensis*, published in 1860.

In 1860 he returned to take temporary charge of the Calcutta Botanic Garden, becoming superintendent in the following year. He introduced several medicinal plants to India. He also began work on a flora of India. Recurrent ill-health, due to his intense exertions in all conditions, caused him to return to Edinburgh, where he died at the early age of thirty-eight.

Anderson, William (1766–1846). Horticulturist. Anderson was born in Edinburgh. After travelling to England he was, in 1793, appointed botanic gardener to James Vere, a wealthy silk merchant with a celebrated garden in Kensington Gore. After remaining in Vere's employment for over twenty years he left to become curator of the Chelsea Physic Garden, a post he held until his death. Unfortunately, during Anderson's tenure the garden's renown, which had previously been

*Isaac **Anderson-Henry** (1800–1884), horticulturist and hybridizer.*

internationally acknowledged, sharply declined. Anderson, a sound botanist, but no administrator, and undoubtedly conservative in his outlook concerning scientific advances in horticultural practice, seems to have been unwilling to move with the times. He became a Fellow of the Linnean Society.

Anderson-Henry, Isaac (1800–1884). Hybridist. Anderson—the Henry was required by a deed of entail—was born in Perthshire, and educated for the law, later practising as a solicitor for some years. He early established a reputation as an authoritative horticulturist, specializing in hybridizing, particularly in exotics from South America, India and New Zealand. Primulas and veronicas were his two main interests and he published many papers on these flowers. He also published an important paper on the necessity of the free access of air to the roots of plants. He was a correspondent of Charles Darwin (qv) and Sir Joseph Hooker (qv). His home and gardens

*Pavilion at Wrest Park, Bedfordshire, designed by Thomas **Archer**.*

were open to horticulturists from all countries and his expertise was widely consulted.

Archer, Thomas (c. 1668–1743). English architect. Archer was born in Umberslade in Warwickshire and educated at Trinity College, Oxford, afterwards travelling abroad for four years. His chief renown rests upon the highly individual buildings he designed in the so-called English Baroque manner, influenced by the work of Borromini. His buildings included St John's Church, Smith Square, Westminster (1714–28) and St. Philip's Church in Birmingham (1710–15). Thomas Archer finds a place in this DICTIONARY on account of two highly distinguished garden structures that still exist. In about 1705 he designed the domed building that houses the fountains from which arises the cascade at Chatsworth (of which great house, in 1704, he had previously designed the north front for William, Duke of Devonshire). Less widely known, perhaps, is the

*Domed pavilion at Chatsworth in Derbyshire, designed by Thomas **Archer** in 1705 to house the fountains which feed the cascade.*

Engraved view of the canal and gothick tower in the garden of the 3rd Duke of **Argyll** at Whitton, Middlesex, one of the many gardening projects carried out by the Duke there and at Inverary, in Scotland.

Archibald Campbell, 3rd Duke of **Argyll** (1682–1761).

Inverary Castle, where the 3rd Duke of **Argyll** introduced many foreign trees.

The approach to Inverary Castle, Scottish home of the Dukes of **Argyll**.

'banqueting house', placed at the termination of the long canal at Wrest Park, Bedfordshire, designed for the Duke of Kent in 1711.

Argyll, (3rd Duke of) Archibald Campbell (1682–1761). Landscape gardener, arboriculturist. In about 1720 the Duke began planting and making a garden around his villa at Whitton near Hounslow, in Middlesex. He introduced, and grew from seed, many plants, particularly trees. In 1748, after visiting Whitton, Pedre Kalm, the Finnish pupil of Linnaeus (qv), wrote that, though Argyll was very interested in botany he was most keenly interested in dendrology (Gk: dendron = tree), planting many trees with his own hands, 'diligence and art' not being spared. He added that the house was pretty though somewhat smaller than conventional

(Opposite) Osborne House in the Isle of Wight, built as a Marine Residence by Queen Victoria, and designed by Prince **Albert**, with Thomas Cubitt, about 1848. The gardens were planned mainly by the Consort.

houses of great nobles, a fact that was explained by the duke's determination to complete his garden: the house would come later. Long after his death, many of the trees Argyll had planted still stood in the district, notably the Lebanon cedars he raised from seed in 1720.

Although trees were his first love, the duke was markedly successful with plants in his stove. A celebrated specimen of the tropical genus *Annona* was recorded. His oranges, lemons, limes and citrons, grown against a wall and merely covered by glass in winter, were the finest in the country, and it is probable that he and not the Earl of Rochford at St Osyth's Priory or Henry Conway (qv) at Park Place (as is often claimed) was the first to grow the Lombardy poplar in England.

After Argyll's death a number of trees still of a size small enough to be moved were lifted, transported and transplanted in the Dowager Princess of Wales's garden at Kew, now forming part of the Royal Botanic Gardens.

Argyll's gardener, Daniel Crofts, received a legacy in his will and was

responsible for preparing a catalogue of the plants at Whitton that were eventually put up for sale.

Argyll was also a considerable planter on his Scottish estates. His influence on the English landscape is indicated by Horace Walpole in his *Anecdotes on Planting in England*: 'The introduction of foreign trees and plants, which we owe principally to Archibald, Duke of Argyle, contributed essentially to the richness of colouring so peculiar to our modern landscape. The mixture of various greens, the contrast between our forest trees and the northern and West Indian firs and pines, are improvements more recent than Kent, or but little known to him. The weeping willow, and every florid shrub, each tree of delicate or bold leaf, are now tints in the composition of our gardens. The last century was certainly acquainted with many of those rare plants we now admire. The Weymouth pine has long been naturalized here; the patriarch plant still exists at Longleat. The light and graceful acacia was known early; witness those ancient stems in the

court of Bedford-house in Bloomsbury Square; and in the Bishop of London's garden are many exotics of very ancient date. I doubt, therefore, whether the difficulty of preserving them in a climate so foreign to their nature did not convince their ancestors of their inutility in general; unless the shapeliness of the lime and horse-chestnut, which accorded so well with established regularity, and which thence and from their novelty, grew in fashion, did not occasion the neglect of the more curious plants.'

Arnott, Samuel (1852–1930). Horticulturist and writer. Provost of Dumfries where his garden was noted for snowdrops and colchicums. He is commemorated by *Galanthus nivalis* 'S. Arnott'.

Atkins, James (1804–1884). Gardener. Atkins lived at Painswick, Gloucestershire, and was a noted grower of snowdrops. He is remembered by the large, slender-flowered *Galanthus nivalis* 'Atkinsii', of unknown origin, which he received from a friend in the 1860s.

*Engraving from William Chambers' book of views of Kew Gardens (1763), dedicated to Princess **Augusta**, showing the pagoda, lake and island, as seen from the lawn.*

*Princess **Augusta's** Palace at Kew (no longer in existence), from an engraving in William Chambers'* Plans, Elevations, Sections and Perspective Views of the Gardens and Buildings at Kew in Surrey, *published in 1763.*

*Princess **Augusta** (1719–1772). (Detail from painting by C. Philips.)*

Augusta, Princess of Saxe Gotha (1719–1772). Patroness. In 1736, Princess Augusta was married to Frederick, Prince of Wales, patron of William Kent. The latter was commissioned to modernize the White House set in the now famous royal garden at Kew. In 1759, due largely to his enthusiasm for winter gardening and lack of care, Frederick died from pneumonia. He left his widow with eight small children. She continued his gardening interests at Kew, with Sir William Chambers (qv) as her architectural adviser. Little seems to be known about her abilities as a botanist or horticulturalist, but after her husband's death, Princess Augusta initiated a botanical garden of about nine acres (on singularly infertile soil) and her enterprise was the beginning of the Royal Botanic Gardens, the most famous botanical gardens in the world. Between 1757 and 1763, Chambers added numerous garden buildings to Kew, notably the Pagoda, the Orangery, three temples which survive and the Roman arch. In a large folio edition, published in 1763, dedicated to the Princess, 'by Royal Command and nobly paid for by Royal Bounty', William Chambers provided a series of *Plans, Elevations, Sections and Perspective Views of the Gardens and Buildings at Kew in Surrey*. The White House was demolished by order of George III, son of Augusta, in 1802.

Austen, Ralph (d. 1676). Writer. Born in Staffordshire, became Proctor of Oxford University. He has some reputation as the author of an early book on fruit, *A Treatise on Fruit Trees* (1653). It is, however, much concerned with moral matters and of little practical use.

Austin, Felix (fl. 1828–1850). Nurseryman. In about 1828, Austin acquired the firm called Van Spangen and Powell, which manufactured artificial stone at Bow. He moved the firm to a factory at New Road, Regent's Park, which he then renamed Austin and Seeley. Among its productions the firm included garden ornaments. Some of these were based on classical prototypes, but Austin also commissioned original designs for ornaments from contemporary artists, including Sidney Smirke and J. B. Papworth (qv). In 1835 tiles brought from China by John Reeves (qv), who was concerned with early plant introductions from that country, were being imitated in 'hard and durable material'. In 1842 ornaments, such as pineapples, gothic work in great variety, chimney-pots from one foot ten inches to ten feet high, and fountains from six pounds upwards, were being advertised. In 1852 an 'immense stock' of garden ornaments was being offered. The firm of Austin and Seeley was still in existence in 1872. The artificial stone which was used for the manufacture of these ornaments was exceptionally hard and durable, for examples of the objects are still occasionally found in old gardens.

Ayres, — (fl. 1800–1820) of Duffield, Derbyshire. In the early part of the nineteenth century, Ayres advertised with a handsome trade-card as a landscape gardener, designer and constructor.

*Typical fountain by Felix **Austin**.*

*Trade card used by Mr **Ayres**.*

B

Backhouse, James (1794–1869). Nurseryman. Born in Darlington, he was a member of the Society of Friends and a keen botanist devoting much time to the study of local plants. In 1816, with his brother Thomas, he acquired the old York Friars Gardens from the long-established Telford family. This became known as James Backhouse & Son of York (and, later, Leeds) which long continued, the notable rockery at the Edgbaston Botanic Gardens, Birmingham, remaining a good example of their work carried out during the early years of the present century.

In 1831 Backhouse set out as a missionary preaching the Quaker faith and urging teetotalism. His tour took in Australia, Mauritius and southern Africa. He combined his spiritual enthusiasm with botanizing and plant collection. (A manuscript devoted to the Flora of New South Wales exists at Kew, unpublished.) Backhouse also collected plants from those areas, such as Mount Wellington, with climates comparable with that of the British Isles. He was particularly interested in the genus *Eucalyptus*, measuring notable specimens, and sending home seed of several kinds which were successfully raised in the York nursery by his brother, Thomas, who expressed a hope to prove their hardiness, for 'as they are all evergreens, they will be valuable auxiliaries to our park scenery'. Backhouse also botanized in Norway (1851) with his son, also James (1825–90), the pair penetrating the Arctic circle.

Backhouse, Robert Ormston (1854–1940). Hybridist. Son of William Backhouse (qv) of Walsingham, Durham, Backhouse moved from Durham to Sutton Court, Hereford, where, with his wife Sarah Elizabeth (1857–1921) he showed similar skills to those of his father in hybridizing plants, notably daffodils, lilies and colchicums. At the Daffodil Show of 1920 a group of hybrid daffodils raised by Mrs Backhouse caused considerable interest, but even greater interest was aroused by her husband's exhibit in 1923 of the first daffodil with a pink trumpet which he named in her honour, 'Mrs R. O. Backhouse'. Mrs Backhouse is herself best remembered in the so-called Backhouse

William Ormston **Backhouse** *(1885–1962), son of Robert Backhouse.*

hybrid lilies which she initiated in 1890 by crossing the various forms of *Lilium martagon* with *L. hansonii*.

Backhouse, William (1807–1869). Horticulturist. Backhouse was a banker, of Walsingham, Durham, and was an early pioneer in daffodil breeding. He was the father of Robert Backhouse (qv) and possibly the family was related to the Backhouses of nursery fame. Backhouse *père* produced two famous 'trumpet' varieties of daffodils, still sometimes grown, 'Emperor' and 'Empress'. Ill-health caused him to cease his experiments and his stock was acquired by Peter Barr (qv).

Backhouse, William Ormston (1885–1962). Botanist. William Backhouse was the son of Robert Ormston Backhouse (qv). After studying agriculture and forestry at Trinity College, Cambridge, he worked at the Cambridge Plant Breeding Station and the John Innes Horticultural Institute. He then went to the Argentine and was highly successful as a breeder of new types of wheat and as a developer of scientific methods of other types of farming, becoming agricultural adviser to the Argentine Railways.

Francis **Bacon** *(1561–1626), from an early engraving.*

While in America, he obtained daffodils from his Herefordshire home from which he continued to breed, aiming particularly at strong, red-cupped early-flowering kinds for the markets. He returned to Sutton Court in 1940 and continued successful breeding of the bulbs which his parents had developed. He recorded that neither his father nor mother kept records of their crossings and he had had no more than suppositions as to how they achieved their remarkable results.

The first red-trumpet daffodil hybridized by Robert **Backhouse.**

Backhouse's 'MA38' wheat, which revolutionized wheat growing in South America, remains his most outstanding achievement.

Bacon, Francis, 1st Baron Verulam and Viscount St Albans (1561–1626). Statesman, essayist and gardener. Although appointed Lord Chancellor, in 1618, Bacon is now mostly remembered for his philosophical works, and particularly his essays, published from 1597 onwards. Their extraordinary range, thought and display of knowledge left scarcely any subject untouched. Possibly his most quoted phrase today is 'God almightie first planted a garden. And indeed it is the purest of Humane pleasures. It is the greatest refreshment to the spirits of man; without which, buildings and pallaces are but grosse handiworks: and a man shall ever see, that when ages grow to civility and elegancie, men come to build stately, sooner than to garden finely, as if gardening was the greater perfection'. This introduces his essay *Of Gardens*, published in 1625. Little else of the essay is remembered today. Yet at times, particularly in the early stages of the English landscape movement in the eighteenth century, his views have had considerable influence.

Bacon himself was concerned with the making of a garden at Gray's Inn, and in 1608 he began the restoration of his father's garden at Gorhambury, near St Albans, which he inherited and which had been badly neglected. He therefore wrote with some practical knowledge.

Very briefly summarised, his views, almost exclusively concerning large and grandiose gardens, were as follows:

The first part is a green at the entrance of four acres. There is 'nothing more pleasant to the eye, than green grasse kept finely shorne. Then comes a heath or a desert as you proceed, with the main garden in its midst (twelve acres). On either side are alleys.' Other alleys, one 'on a frame work' give shade on a hot day.

Over the hedges are built arches and turrets, each containing a cage of birds. Between the turrets are 'broad plates of round coloured glasse, gilt, for the sunne to play upon'.

In the hedges, 'images cut out in

juniper, or other garden stuff, they be for children.'

'Pretty pyramids' are considered permissible.

A mount, thirty foot high, reached by a path to enable four to walk abreast, should be built from which to survey the garden. And there should be a banqueting house.

'For fountaines, they are a great beauty and refreshment; but pooles marre all, and make the garden unwholesome and full of flies and frogs.'

The heath is to be a natural wilderness, without trees, but with thickets of sweet briar and honeysuckle, the ground set with violets, strawberries and 'primeroses'. The ground should be scattered, not in any order, with 'little heaps in the shape of molehills', which must be set with a variety of plants.

The side grounds are to be filled with a variety of private alleys, some planned to give shade and others shelter 'when the winde blows sharp'. Some alleys are to be grassed, others finely gravelled 'because of going wet'. Fruit trees, and some, but not too many, flowers ('lest they decive the trees') should be incorporated in the hedges. In these side grounds mounts should be raised from which to observe the surrounding fields.

Francis Bacon's ideas were, to say the least, varied and they can be quoted as sound, authoritative precepts for almost every style of gardening that has been followed since his time.

Baker, John Gilbert (1834–1920). Botanist. Baker was born in Yorkshire and educated at Quaker schools in Ackworth and York. During his schooling, he became fascinated by plants, made frequent plant-collecting outings and was appointed curator of the school herbarium. In 1863 he published *A Supplement to Baine's Flora of Yorkshire*, which was the result of his prodigious field-work in his native county. In 1866, he became First Assistant in the Kew Herbarium, being made Keeper twenty-four years later. He wrote extensively on botanical subjects, and made a particular study of the genus Rosa. His books include, *Flora of Mauritius and the Seychelles* (1877); *Handbook of the Fern-allies* (1887); *Amaryllideae* (1888) and *Irideae* (1892). Baker also contributed to several periodicals, including the *Botanical Magazine*, then under the editorship of Sir Joseph Hooker (qv). In 1866, he was elected a Fellow of the Linnean Society, and in 1897 he received the Victoria Medal of Honour from the RHS.

(Opposite) Wooded area and (inset) a view of the rock-garden at the Edinburgh Botanic Garden, laid out by John Hutton Balfour (1808–1884).

*An artist's interpretation of Francis **Bacon's** ideal garden. (Drawing, circa 1953, by Edward Bawden, RA.)*

Baker, Richard (fl. 1706). Gardener. Baker was engaged at the beginning of the eighteenth century to serve the Earl of Dorset and Middlesex at Knole in Kent, and may be taken as a typical representative of a head gardener working on a large estate at this time.

Baker was required to keep all the fruit for his lordship's use; look after all trees and evergreens, pruning, trimming and dunging them; provide all the herbs and other things necessary for the kitchen; maintain all the walls; preserve all flowers and plants in the garden; repair all the glass frames, and provide for the present use of the garden fifty loads of dung. For this he was paid thirty pounds a year, and was provided with rooms and conveniences in the house for his business.

Short of what he had to supply for the garden, Baker had the right to all the dung produced about the house and the right of disposing of all peas, beans, cabbage and other herbs not required in the kitchen.

Balfour, (Sir) Andrew (1630–1694). Botanist. Balfour was born in Fife, and trained in medicine at Caen in Normandy, France. He was one of those responsible for founding the Edinburgh Botanical Garden in 1670. In common with others who began what was to become a world-famous institution, his continental training had convinced him of the backwardness of scientists and medical men among his compatriots in the study of botany, particularly as applied to medicine.

John Hutton **Balfour** *(1808–1884).*

Picea breweriana (Brewer's spruce) with which Frederick **Balfour** *is associated.*

Sir Isaac **Balfour** *(1853–1922).*

Balfour, Frederick Robert Stephen, CVO (1873–1945). Arborologist and horticulturist. Balfour first became associated with an already-famous garden at Dawyck, near Peebles, after his widowed mother acquired the estate in 1897, which passed to him in 1920. Earlier, Dawyck had been in the hands of two old families: the Veitches (no connexion with the nurserymen of that name), who planted what were probably some of the earliest horse chestnuts in Britain in about 1650, and the Naesmiths. A member of the latter family raised, in 1725, some of the first larches grown in Scotland. They also raised many of the plants sent by David Douglas, William Lobb (qv), and others from north-west America in the early nineteenth century. The remarkable, erect-growing form of the common beech was also found growing there: now known as *Fagus sylvatica 'Dawyck'*, it has been widely propagated.

Balfour spent four years in California on behalf of his family business—a firm of merchants—and whilst there was able to study in their natural habitat many of the trees already planted at Dawyck. Then, and on subsequent visits, he collected more tree seeds, often planting them in forest conditions. He is particularly associated with the rare and difficult Brewer's spruce (*Picea breweriana*), successfully lifting and establishing at Dawyck a number of living specimens in 1908. He also visited the Arnold Arboretum near Boston and, as a friend of its enterprising director, Charles Sprague Sargent, acquired many of the rare plants growing then arriving from Western China, Japan and elsewhere, during an era of plant introduction. His friendship with Professor Isaac Bayley Balfour (no relative) also brought him much that was passing through the Edinburgh Botanic Garden.

Of these new species he was a remarkably successful cultivator. He replaced the massive plantings of older rhododendrons with newly-introduced kinds, eventually growing about 250 different species. This pioneering enterprise, undertaken in a cold and difficult climate, provided many outstanding lessons. In 1915 a number of enthusiasts formed the Rhododendron Society, with Frederick Balfour as an original member.

Balfour took an active part in the affairs of the Royal Horticultural Society (which awarded him the Victoria Medal of Honour in 1927), the Roads Beautifying Association and other institutions concerned with forestry, horticulture and arboriculture.

Balfour, (Sir) Isaac Bayley (1853–1922). Botanist. Isaac Balfour was the son of John Hutton Balfour (qv) and was born in Edinburgh. He was educated at Edinburgh Academy and Edinburgh University. Although he qualified as a doctor, his botanical interests, which had been fostered by his father and maintained throughout his school and university career, caused him to be appointed as botanist and geologist to an astronomical expedition sent to Rodriguez in Mexico in 1874, which was sponsored by the Royal Society.

After serving as deputy-professor of natural history at Edinburgh University, and continuing his laboratory studies at Strassburg and Würzburg, Balfour was appointed Professor of Botany at Glasgow University in 1879. In the same year he went on a second expedition, this time to Socotra in the Indian Ocean, to study the geology and botany of the island. Balfour remained at Glasgow for six years and was then appointed Sherardian Professor of Botany at Oxford, given charge of the Botanic Garden there and made a Fellow of Magdalen College. One popular change which marked his tenure was the admission of the public to the garden on Sundays. He also helped in the publishing of the *Annals of Botany*, started in 1887 by the Clarendon Press.

In 1887, Balfour was recalled from Oxford to fill the three posts his father had held at Edinburgh. By coincidence he also occupied these for the same span of thirty-four years. Balfour, a man of considerable charm and energy, at once set out to make the Royal Botanic Garden of interest to the general public. The site had first been acquired in 1820. John Balfour had added a wooded area, experimental garden, conservatories and palm-house, rock garden and a lecture-theatre. Bayley Balfour greatly enlarged the garden; reconstructed the somewhat unnatural rock-garden—made from stones and salvaged from old walls—into one of the finest natural rock gardens in the British Isles, the stones being brought from Callender in Perthshire. He also reconstructed the woodland garden, showing no hesitation in transplanting mature trees to new sites. He also greatly enriched the Edinburgh collection of hardy plants and shrubs, including an enormous influx of Western Chinese plants resulting from various expeditions sponsored during the early years of this century.

Balfour visited Japan in 1909 and China in 1909 and 1910 to gain first-hand knowledge of Eastern Asiatic conditions. The Edinburgh Royal Botanic Garden today is largely Balfour's conception and of great interest to gardeners as well as botanists. He was knighted in 1920, retired to Haslemere and died on St Andrew's Day, 1922.

*Planting machine, designed by the McNabs, used by the **Balfours** at Edinburgh.*

*Exhibition Hall of the Royal Caledonian Horticultural Society which served as the Herbarium of the Edinburgh Botanic Garden 1864–1964, where both John and Isaac **Balfour** were Regius Keepers.*

*Palm House, at the Botanic Garden, Edinburgh, where John **Balfour** was Keeper.*

*Ernest **Ballard** amongst Michaelmas daisies raised at Colwall, Herefordshire.*

*Charles Frederick **Ball** (1879–1915).*

Balfour, John Hutton (1808–1884). Botanist. Balfour, the son of an army doctor turned publisher, was educated at the Edinburgh High School and Edinburgh University. He was intended for the Church, but despite academic successes in philosophical studies and mathematics, plus a post-graduate apprenticeship to the professor of military surgery, his keen interest in botany caused him to help found the Botanical Society of Edinburgh in 1836 and to accept the appointment of Professor of Botany at Glasgow University in 1841. Four years later he was appointed to the equivalent chair at Edinburgh University. In the same year he was appointed Regius Keeper of the Edinburgh Botanic Garden, a post he was to retain for thirty-four years. He was also dean of the medical faculty in the University for thirty years and secretary to the Edinburgh Royal Society for over ten.

In 1850, John Balfour was concerned with the formation of the Oregon Association ('of gentlemen interested in the promotion of arboriculture and horticulture of Scotland'), which financed a plant-collecting expedition to western North America by John Jeffrey, a collector recommended by Hutton. After a successful beginning, Jeffrey disappeared without trace. According to a notice in the *Proceedings of The Royal Society*, Balfour 'was more interested in observing facts than in discussing theories. This checked his scientific use of the imagination, but safeguarded him against the effects of somewhat austere convictions.'

Ball, Charles Frederick (1879–1915). Anglo-Irish horticulturist and journalist. C. F. Ball was born at Loughborough, Leicestershire, and after working in nurseries at Elvaston, Derbyshire, and Long Ditton in Surrey, entered the Royal Botanical Garden at Kew in 1900, being seconded to the herbaceous and alpine department. He left Kew to join his brother in a market gardening project, but returned to Kew after a year.

In 1906 Charles Ball was appointed assistant keeper at the Glasnevin Botanical Gardens in Dublin. On behalf of the gardens he went several times to Switzerland to collect plants. He also visited Bulgaria (thanks to the encouragement of King Ferdinand), who loaned his gardener, and the Maritime Alps. Ball was interested in hybridization and conducted many successful experiments, some of which resulted in plants being named after him. He was also editor of the periodical, *Irish Gardening*. On the outbreak of World War I, he joined the Royal Dublin Fusiliers. Charles Ball was killed in the Dardenelles Campaign in 1915.

Ballard, Ernest (1870–1952). Specialist grower and author. Ballard, who lived at Colwall in Herefordshire, first became widely known in 1907 when he showed the Michaelmas daisy at the Royal Horticultural Society. This was a fully double form of *Aster novi-belgii*, called 'Beauty of Colwall', which was followed by many more of the same species, mostly bearing family or localized names. These introductions were outstanding among those raised in the first half of this century. Ballard's experiments considerably changed the status and scope of these flowers which, although long introduced, had been relatively neglected until the Society had held a conference upon them in 1891. Ballard also raised a number of other attractive and interesting hybrids, notably of dianthus and hepatica. He was one of the few growers to succeed in crossing the Christmas rose (*Helleborus niger*) with the plant long known as *H. corsicus* to produce the remarkable *H.* 'Nigricors'—still a great rarity. In 1919 he published *Days in My Garden*, which was illustrated with his own photographs.

Balls, Edward Kent (1892–   ). Plant collector. Balls was born in Essex. During and after World War I, he was a relief worker with the Quakers in France, the Balkans and Russia, being invalided home in 1925. In the following year he joined the Six Hills Nursery at Stevenage in Hertfordshire, founded by Clarence Elliott (qv) and renowned for alpine plants. In 1932, after designing and planting a number of gardens, he engaged on the first of his plant-collecting expeditions, travelling to Persia with Dr Paul Giuseppi (later President of the Alpine Garden Society of England). He remained in Persia for six months. Between 1932 and 1938 he was involved in several other expeditions, including three to Turkey, accompanied on different occasions by W. Balfour-Gourlay, Charles Bird and Dr Richard Seligman. In 1939 he was sent to South America by the Imperial Agricultural Bureau to collect wild and cultivated potatoes, and various plants. He was responsible for discovering twenty new species, including the *Verbascum ballsii*, a member of the mullein family, and *Verbena ballsii* (from the North Argentine), a tall herbaceous plant, growing from two to two and a half feet tall, with a flower-head about two inches across, cream in colour with red on the outside of the petals, almost like an apple blossom, and sweet-scented.

During a lecture tour of the USA in 1939–40, World War II broke out, and Balls, unable to return to London, worked for the British Purchasing Commission in Washington and New York. In the post war years, he returned to relief work in Yugoslavia and China.

In 1947, he joined the Rancho Santa Ana Botanic Garden in California, for which organization he made a number of plant-collecting expeditions. He has also written a handbook *Early Uses of California Plants* (University of California Press) and contributed to many horticultural journals.

Balls retired in 1960.

Banister, (Reverend) John Baptist (1650–1692). Horticulturist, plant-collector and natural historian. Banister had shown a deep interest in natural history whilst an undergraduate at Oxford. These interests, combined with his theological studies, brought him to the notice of

*The Corsican Hellebore, raised by Ernest **Ballard** at Colwall, Herefordshire.*

Henry Compton, Bishop of London, whose garden at Fulham Palace was famous for the numerous plants and trees which the Bishop had been amongst the first to introduce from abroad and cultivate with considerable skill.

As the Church for the American Colonies came under Compton's jurisdiction, and as Banister was a talented artist as well as an enthusiastic naturalist, Compton selected him as one of the chaplains to be sent first to the West Indies, thence to Virginia. Banister spent some time studying and making drawings of natural objects in the West Indies before proceeding to Charles Court County where he arrived in 1678. He sent home material, not only to his bishop but also to John Ray, the great systematist, who records that

*Edward Kent **Balls** (1892–   ).*

Banister had proposed a natural history of his wide parish. Drawings which he sent (together with dried specimens) to the botanist, James Petiver, were probably intended for this projected work. Meantime, his catalogue of American plants was incorporated and published in the second volume of Ray's *Historia Plantarum*.

Banister died as a result of a fall during a plant-collecting expedition, probably the first plant-collector to sacrifice his life in pursuit of his vocation. Among the plants which Banister sent home were, *Echinacea purpurea, Magnolia virginiana* (the sweet bay), *Mertensia virginica* and an early example of the American azalea, the swamp honeysuckle, *Rhododendron viscosum*.

Banks, (Sir) Joseph (1743–1820). Scientific patron and plant-collector; President of the Royal Society, 1778–1820. Joseph Banks, the son of a Lincolnshire landowner, was born in London, educated first at Harrow, transferring to Eton at thirteen, and entering Christ Church, Oxford, at eighteen. An early interest in botany was furthered by finding a copy of Gerard's *Herball* in his mother's dressing-room, and these interests were continued at the University. Finding that no lectures on botany were available at Oxford, he caused Israel Lyons, a Cambridge astronomer, botanist and author of a book on Cambridge flora, to be brought to Oxford to instruct undergraduates interested in the subject. Years later, Banks enabled Lyons to join exploratory voyages towards the North Pole.

Banks' father died in 1761, leaving his son a wealthy man. In 1766 Banks was elected Fellow of the

Royal Society, and made the first of his plant-collecting expeditions—with Constantine Phipps to Newfoundland. On his return, he established a lifelong collaboration with Dr Daniel Solander (qv), an assistant in the British Museum Library and one-time pupil of Linnaeus. Later, Solander was Banks' companion on his world voyages and, finally, his librarian.

By the influence of Lord Sandwich, First Lord of the Admiralty, Banks was enabled to accompany Captain Cook on his expedition in 1768 in the *Endeavour*. Banks was accompanied by a personal party of five, including Solander and Sydney Parkinson, a draughtsman responsible for objects of natural history. The voyage (1768–1771) was a great success in every way and Banks was invited by Lord Sandwich to participate in a second journey. Due to various problems in the provision of accommodation, Banks did not make this second voyage, but proceeded instead to plan an expedition to Iceland in 1772.

Banks' worldly talent for gaining and using the friendship of men in the highest positions was well demonstrated by his virtual direction of Kew Gardens, thanks to the high regard in which he was held by King George III. The fact that the study of plant life had played so significant a part in his own three long voyages—with Phipps to Newfoundland, round the world with Cook, and to Iceland with Solander—undoubtedly coloured Banks' decision to send Kew's first plant collector overseas. Francis Masson, a Kew gardener, was sent to the Cape in 1772. Banks was also one of the seven men who met on 7th March, 1804, at Hatchard's book shop in Piccadilly, to institute what is now the Royal Horticultural Society.

Banks was a man of strong, even imperious, will and the somewhat autocratic manner in which he carried out his duties at the Royal Society and at Kew made him a number of enemies. Yet, amongst those with whom he worked closely, he was greatly admired. In a posthumous eulogy, Georges Cuvier, the French botanist, spoke of Banks' generosity towards foreign naturalists. When the results of a notable French plant-collecting expedition fell into British hands by fortune of war, Banks forwarded

(Opposite) Genus Banksia, *the Australian honeysuckle, which is only found in that country, commemorating Sir Joseph **Banks** (1743–1820), English scientific patron and plant-collector, who made the first scientific study of the Australian continent when he accompanied Captain Cook's expedition in the* Endeavour, *1768–1771. He also helped to found the Royal Horticultural Society in 1804.*

Dr Daniel Solander, colleague, friend and librarian to Sir Joseph **Banks**.

Peter **Barr** (1825–1909), specialist in bulbs, particularly daffodils.

Topiary work at Elvaston Castle, near Derby, designed by William **Barron** for the Earl of Harrington.

them to France without examination. He would not, said another French naturalist, steal a single botanic idea from those who had hazarded their lives to gain them.

Towards the end of his life, he was severely troubled by gout and, at times, was lamed. He died at his house in Isleworth and was buried in the parish church. He left his extensive library for the use of the British Museum.

Botanically, he is particularly associated with the Australian continent of which, with Cook's party, he made the first scientific study. He is commemorated by the genus *Banksia*, Australian honeysuckle, which is restricted to that country. Horticulturally, he is probably best

described as an *entrepreneur* on the grandest scale. His own garden at Revesby in Lincolnshire was of no consequence.

Barr, Peter (1826–1909). Bulb specialist. Although Barr was born in Scotland, his career, which was almost wholly concerned with the cultivation and improvement of the daffodil, was concentrated on Covent Garden. He was at first an amateur, travelling on the Continent and collecting those plants which interested him. He then became a nurseryman at Worcester, but apparently without any notable success. In 1862, however, he founded, with a partner, the firm of Barr and Sugden, of King Street, Covent

Garden. He published in 1884 *Ye Narcissus or Daffodyl Flowre*. The archaically self-conscious title belies the importance of the book, one of the earliest and the most authoritative on the cult of the narcissus. Barr was in touch with other pioneer breeders, including Edward Leeds (1802–1877) of Pendleton and William Backhouse (1807–1869). The bulbs he acquired from Backhouse came to be known as the 'Barrii' daffodils. He was largely instrumental in bringing about a meeting of the early daffodil enthusiasts at the first Daffodil Conference, held in 1884.

The firm was later renamed Barr & Son, with nurseries at Surbiton. Later members of the family contin-

ued to take an influential interest in bulbs, particularly daffodils.

Barron, William (1800–1891). Gardener. Barron was first a gardener and later a nurseryman who became particularly associated with evergreens and their use. He was concerned, as gardener to the Earl of Harrington, with the plantations of numerous species of conifer at Elvaston Hall in Derbyshire, including the Japanese *Cephalotaxus harringtonia*, named after his employer. Barron's own name was attached to the yew, *Taxus baccata* 'Barroni', described as 'one of the most showy of the golden-leaved varieties, the habit being dense and the colour very rich.' In 1852 he

Sir Joseph **Banks** (1743–1820), patron and plant-collector, from the portrait painted in 1810 by Thomas Philips.

Urn and fountain on the formal terrace at Harewood House, Yorkshire, designed by Sir Charles **Barry** for the Earl of Harewood, 1843–1850.

The Buckland yew near Dover, transplanted in 1880 under the supervision of William **Barron**, *in order to prevent damage to the church.*

Sir Charles **Barry**, *architect and landscape designer (1795–1860).*

published *The British Winter Garden: A Practical Treatize on Evergreens.* He later founded the firm of William Barron and Son of Elvaston Nurseries, Borrowash, Derbyshire, gaining a reputation for the successful transplanting of large trees, such as the ancient and famous Buckland yew near Dover which in 1880 had spread so widely that it was pressing against, and damaging, the church—a successful operation on a scale probably never repeated.

Barry, (Sir) Charles (1795–1860). Architect. Charles Barry was born in London, the son of a well-to-do stationer, and at the age of fourteen was articled to a London surveyor. The completion of his articles coincided with his majority and the death of his father. He thereupon determined to use his inheritance on an architectural tour of Europe.

From 1817 he travelled, studying buildings and drawing extensively in France, Italy, Greece, Turkey, Egypt and Syria. Having thus accumulated a detailed knowledge of many styles, he became the most scholarly and eclectic architect of his time. On his return to London in 1819 he set up in private practice in Holborn, and having assimilated the necessary knowledge of Gothic won competitions which caused him to be particularly active in designing churches and public buildings in and around Manchester. In London his designs included those for the Travellers' and Reform Clubs and for Bridgewater House. He was elected a member of the Royal Academy. From 1840 until his death he was mainly occupied (greatly helped by Pugin) with the building of the Houses of Parliament in the Gothic style, although most of his work had followed the classical manner. Barry makes his appearance in this DICTIONARY because he was one of the earliest practitioners of the Victorian style of landscaping, designing elaborate flower-gardens and terraces which were the antithesis of the Georgian ideal of a natural-looking landscape.

An early work was the garden front at Trentham Hall, Staffordshire, carried out between 1830–40, set in a 'Capability' Brown landscape and connecting the house with Brown's artificial lake. The main house has now gone, and Barry's garden has also been much simplified.

Barry's most important design of the early 1850s is at Shrubland Park in Suffolk, which remains largely unchanged. The fall of some seventy feet from the house to the gardens is encompassed by a magnificent stone stairway.

Barry was also responsible for the terraced garden linking Harewood House in Yorkshire to another of Brown's landscapes, and also for the garden front at Holkham in Norfolk. Both these projects included fountains in an appropriate style designed by Raymond Smith. Other examples of Barry's work are to be seen at Duncombe in Yorkshire and Bowood, Wiltshire.

In 1850–51 at Cliveden, Buckinghamshire, now a National Trust property, Barry rebuilt the house on the top of William Winde's existing seventeenth-century terraces and it seems probable that Barry was also concerned with the design of the formal garden.

Apart from the problem of providing the labour for its proper maintenance—Shrubland in its heyday needed forty gardeners—Barry's work has now lost most of its original horticultural connotation. Not many decades after it had been finished, William Robinson wrote that 'Shrubland Park . . . was the great bedding-out garden, the "centre" of the system in England. The great terrace garden in front of the house was laid out in scrolls and intricate beds, all filled with plants of a few decided colours, principally yellow, white, red and blue, and edged with box . . . When some particular colour was wanted in a certain spot, coloured stones were freely used—yellow, or red and blue . . . there were no flowers in this large garden to cut for the house.' Even Barry's close friend, J. L. Wolfe, admitted that Barry 'seemed to think that enrichment could never be over done.'

Barry's limitations as a landscape architect are now obvious and have probably been exaggerated by a number of minor architects, lacking his qualifications, who designed gardens for municipal buildings, often in the Barry style, in the latter part of the nineteenth century.

Bartram, John (1699–1777). Botanist. Although Bartram was the first of a long line of eminent American plant-collectors, he finds a place in this DICTIONARY as having been born under the British flag and as one of the most important collectors on behalf of seventeenth-century English patricians, nurserymen and gardeners. Bartram was born at Darby, in Pennsylvania, the son of a farmer, and at an early age showed, he

Victorian engraving showing the garden terrace at Trentham Hall, Staffordshire, designed in 1838 by Sir Charles **Barry** *for the Duke of Sutherland. The house was demolished in 1910; the gardens remain.*

recalled, 'a great inclination to Botany and Natural History', even though, for a time, he seriously studied medicine. He began to farm on his own account, converting marshy land into productive use by skilful drainage. As an adjunct to his farming he established a garden where he cultivated many indigenous North American plants. In about 1734, the London merchant and avid plant-cultivator, Peter Collinson (qv), was put in touch with John Bartram as 'a very proper person' to collect and despatch plants to British gardeners. Bartram agreed to collect for Collinson who in turn arranged a consortium of British patrons, including various ducal landowners (Richmond, Norfolk, Argyll and Bedford), Philip Miller (qv), compiler of *The Gardener's Dictionary*, Sir Hans Sloane (qv) and others.

John Bartram is credited with the introduction of over one hundred American species to Europe. He made several botanical expeditions to various parts of North America, from Virginia to Delaware, and his account of a journey to Onondago was published in London in 1751. He was one of the most persistent, courageous and single-minded of all plant-collectors. In 1765 Bartram was named King's Botanist.

Bartram, William (1739–1823). Botanist, plant-collector, artist. William was the third son of John Bartram and his second wife, Ann, and was born at Kingsessing, Philadelphia. He studied at the Academy of Philadelphia, but, in the words of his father, 'botany and drawing were his darling delight'. He accompanied his father on his later botanizing trips in 1753 and 1755. He began to make drawings for Peter Collinson (qv) and later for Dr John Fothergill (qv). After various false starts as merchant and planter, he set out through the Southern States, living off the land and studying the Indians, amongst whom he was known as Puc-Puggy, 'The Flower Hunter'. His account of his four-year experiences was published in America in 1791 and in London in 1792, influencing Coleridge and the other poets and writers of the Romantic Movement. In 1782, he declined the offer of the professorship of botany at the University of Pennsylvania. He spent the remaining years of his life on the farm on which he had been born, and, like his father, was frequently consulted by scientists and naturalists.

Bateman, James (1811–1897). Landowner and gardener. James Bateman was a typical representative of a

---

(Opposite) The stairway at Shrubland Park, Suffolk, designed by Sir Charles **Barry** *in the early 1850s.*

Magnolia grandiflora, *a plant sent to Britain by John* **Bartram** *(1699–1777).*

James **Bateman** *(1811–1897).*

Bridge spanning a stream in the Chinese garden at Biddulph Grange, Staffordshire, designed by James **Bateman**.

nineteenth-century type of amateur gardener, who was enabled by his wealth, aided by taste and knowledge, to create a garden in the grand manner.

Bateman was born at Redivals, near Bury in Lancashire, and completed his formal education at Magdalen College, Oxford. In his youth, the family moved to Knypersley Hall, in Staffordshire, an uninviting spot in which to practise horticulture. Here, however, the young Bateman registered his first success in fruiting for the first time in England, the Carambola tree (*Averrhoa carambola*), which had been cultivated in tropical Asia from ancient times for its acid fruit, but had resolutely failed to fruit since its introduction in 1793.

At Oxford, Bateman became something of a rich dandy. He also became interested in tropical orchids, then little grown in England. (The first English catalogue of these exotics was not issued by Lod-

A corner of the Egyptian garden at Biddulph Grange, Staffordshire, designed by James **Bateman** *in the nineteenth century.*

diges of Hackney until 1839.) A former gardener to Sir Joseph Banks, named Fairbairn, had set up as a nurseryman in Oxford and grew the orchid *Renanthera coccinea*, introduced in 1816, and illustrated in the Botanical Register after Joseph Paxton (qv) had flowered it at

*William Jackson **Bean** (1863–1947), arboriculturist and author.*

radially arranged leaflets. Leaflets glabrous, oblong or obovate, distinctly notched at the apex, 1½ to 3 in. long, with stalks about ½ in. long. Flowers produced on slender, pendent racemes, very fragrant; males ⅓ in. across, with pale purple, reflexed sepals, and occupying the terminal part of the raceme; females

AKEBIA QUINATA

(usually two) 1 to 1½ in. across, dark chocolate-purple, the sepals broadly elliptical and concave. Fruit 2½ to 4 in. long, in shape like a thick sausage, greyish violet or purplish in colour, containing numerous seeds immersed in white pulp. *Bot. Mag.*, t. 4864.

First introduced in 1845 from the Island of Chusan by Robert Fortune, this

found it near Ningpo, China, in 1850. Although allied in a botanical sense to *C. patens* and *C. florida*, it is amply distinct in its dwarfer habit, large flowers with overlapping sepals, and the very woolly, often simple leaves and woolly flower-stalks. Also, it bears its flowers successively from late spring into the autumn,

CLEMATIS × JOULINIANA

in contrast to the other two Asiatic allies, which, if left unpruned, bear their main crop before midsummer. Although the species is very rare in cultivation, if not extinct, there must be few large-flowered garden clematises that do not have its blood in them. The first crosses using it as a parent were made by Isaac Anderson-Henry and of these two, 'LAWSONIANA' and 'HENRYANA',

Typical pages from a recent edition of Trees and Shrubs Hardy in the British Isles, *a comprehensive survey by William Jackson **Bean** (published by John Murray).*

Chatsworth in 1827. Bateman saw this rare plant and purchased it, proceedings which delayed his return to college. As a consequence (so the story goes) he was compelled to write out half the Book of Psalms. The influential botanist, gardener and draughtsman, John Lindley (qv), an early authority on the Orchidaceae was so impressed by Bateman's ability and knowledge that he overcame his well-known dislike of precocious undergraduates and an enduring friendship was established.

Helped by his wealthy father, Bateman was able to expand his cultivation of, and enthusiasm for, the Orchidaceae. In 1833 he engaged a collector named Thomas Colley to bring back orchids from British Guiana. The names of both patron and collector were commemorated by Lindley in *Batemannia colleyi*. This expedition was the forerunner of a far more influential venture which arose out of Bateman's friendship with George Ure Skinner (1804–67), a merchant from Leeds trading in South America, who was also a capable botanist and knowledgeable concerning orchids. During his travels Skinner obtained for Bateman a considerable number of new and rare kinds. Incongruously, the orchid houses in the bleak air of North Staffordshire soon contained what was probably the finest collection of tropical orchids in England.

This and Bateman's wealth resulted in the publication of the *Orchidaceae of Mexico and Guatemala* between 1837 to 1843. This

ranks literally as one of the biggest garden books ever published. The plates, mainly reproduced from paintings by Mrs Withers and Miss Drake, measure 30 by 20 inches and are printed by lithography. The book was further enlivened by a series of amusing vignettes by George Cruickshank. Other outstanding books for which Bateman was responsible were *A Second Century of Orchidaceous Plants* (1867), a sequel to W. J. Hooker's *A Century of Orchidaceous Plants*, and *A Monograph of Odontoglossum* (1864–1874). Both these books were superbly illustrated by Walter Hood Fitch (qv), draughtsman and lithographer.

In 1838 Bateman married Maria Warburton, the sister of a distinguished civil servant and explorer in Australia. She was an ardent amateur botanist and grower of hardy plants. Under her guidance, Bateman took an interest in these with an enthusiasm equal to that which he displayed in the cultivation of orchids. In the early 1840s he acquired a farmhouse on Biddulph Moor, near Knypersley, an inhospitable site for a garden, but with plenty of water and a variable terrain. Here he built an impressive mansion, Biddulph Grange, and made one of the most remarkable gardens in England.

Biddulph Grange has now been converted to a hospital, but many traces remain to evoke something of the quality of the remarkable garden Bateman designed and made. The 'Chinese' garden with its light-hearted bridges now contains many

mature trees and shrubs introduced from China. There is also an extraordinary Egyptian tomb chamber guarded by sphinxes and clipped yews, and rockwork on an almost cyclopean scale—despite the lack of a local quarry. There are avenues of deodars and red horse chestnuts, many gnarled rhododendrons—often original introductions—as well as several kinds of holly and, finally, nine miles of hedges to be clipped!

With his publications, he remains one of the foremost of English gardeners both in theory and practice. He was elected a Fellow of the Linnean Society in 1833 and of the Royal Society in 1838. He moved to Kensington in 1860 and died at Worthing.

Bean, William Jackson (1863–1947). CVO, ISO. Gardener and horticultural lexicographer. William Bean was born into a family of gardeners at Leavening in Yorkshire. His father died when he was young, and he left Archbishop Holgate's Grammar School in York to work in the gardens at Belvoir Castle, Leicestershire, the seat of the Duke of Rutland. In 1883 he became a student gardener at the Royal Botanic Gardens, Kew, where he worked until his retirement forty-six years later. At Kew his worth was soon appreciated and he passed through the Palm, Orchid and Temperate Houses as sub-foreman. In 1892 he became foreman of the Arboretum, and his continuing renown is based on a remarkable knowledge of trees

and shrubs acquired in the Arboretum and in his extensive planting experience in the gardens. In 1908 he published *The Royal Botanic Gardens Kew: Historical and Descriptive*, a standard work.

Bean was appointed Assistant Curator of the Arboretum in 1900, a particularly felicitous instance of the right man in the right place, at the right moment, for in that year Ernest Wilson's (qv) arrival at Ichang signalled the start of introductions from Western China of trees and shrubs which were to continue during the next forty years, significantly changing the practice of tree and shrub cultivation in the British Isles. Bean studied these introductions as they were planted in one of the greatest collections in the temperate world. He published early descriptions of some in the *Botanical Magazine*. He also travelled widely, visiting in particular the famous Arnold Arboretum of Harvard University in the USA and its director, Charles Sprague Sargent.

In 1908 he began his definitive work, *Trees and Shrubs Hardy in the British Isles* (now in its eighth edition). The first two volumes of this great work were published in 1914. Bean's many official activities delayed the publication of a third volume, dealing with recent introductions, until 1933, following his retirement from Kew in 1929.

Bean also published slighter yet still-authoritative books on trees and shrubs and contributed important articles to many journals. He also contributed to the Royal Horticultural Society's *Dictionary of Gardening* (1951).

He was also a member of the committee that advised on the trees at Windsor Park and worked with the Roads Beautifying Association. For his work in the former capacity he was made a Companion of the Royal Victorian Order in 1936. His career at Kew brought him membership of the Imperial Service Order in 1924. His interest in the work of the Royal Horticultural Society was rewarded by honorary fellowship, the Victoria Medal of Honour (1918) and Veitch Memorial Medal (1923).

Beaton, Donald (1802–1863). Gardener, hybridist and writer. Donald Beaton was born at Urray, Ross-shire. He travelled south and was clearly an outstandingly good gardener and contributor to the gardening press. In the latter role, he had a tendency to be controversial and argumentative. We first know of him from an interesting account he contributed, in 1836, to the *Gardener's Magazine* concerning the garden in which he worked near Ledbury, Herefordshire. The estate had been acquired in 1817 by William Gordon, a kinsman of Lord Biddulph, who by 1819 had built Haffield House in Herefordshire (designed by Sir Robert Smirke). Beaton went there in 1829. The estate had consisted of several small properties, one of which (still called the Vineyard) had been bought in 1720 by Jacob Tonson, publisher of Milton's *Paradise Lost*, as well as works by Addison, Dryden and Pope. Tonson grew fruit as well as vines. Beaton's researches uncovered much about Tonson's activities. He learned, for example, that the vines had been grown on the steep bank as espaliers in what had been called locally 'diamond palisading'. Beaton also measured and described the ornamental trees which Tonson had planted: Scots pines, spruce, yews, variegated hollies and limes. All had made unusual growth. Two trees of great size still growing—a tulip tree (*Liriodendron*) and holm oak (*Quercus ilex*)—he does not mention, and although they look older than a century-and-a-half, it is possible that they were Beaton's contribution to the present garden. Nearby, at Eastnor, there was mistletoe growing on oak—as indeed there still is. When the council of the Horticultural Society of London (now the Royal Horticultural Society) concluded, after due deliberation, that this parasite was no longer to be found on oaks in Britain, Beaton sent members of the council a specimen to prove them wrong.

After the death of his employer and patron in 1837, Beaton moved to a garden at Kingsbury, near Kilburn, and began to write on the

The tulip trea (Liriodendron) *at Haffield House, Somerset, possibly planted by* Donald **Beaton** *in the eighteen-thirties.*

The Duchess of **Beaufort** *(1630–1714) by Sir Peter Lely.*

subject which became his principal interest: hybridity in garden plants. He had unorthodox views and expressed them with didactic firmness. A comment on this aspect of his work is to be found in the correspondence of Charles Darwin (1861) where Beaton is described as 'a clever fellow and a damned cocksure man'. Against this, the great authority on the Iris family, the Hon. Rev. William Herbert (qv), named a whole genus *Beatonia* in his honour, though this name is no longer in use.

One suggestion that Beaton made in the *Gardener's Magazine* of 1837 was that there should be a method of distinguishing what he called 'home made' plants from mere varieties by a special term, thus anticipating the present use of the word cultivar.

Beaufort, Mary Somerset, Duchess of (1630–1714). In 1730 The Society of Gardeners, 'consisting of all the principal nurserymen and florists about London', published a *Catalogue of Trees and Shrubs, both Exotic and Domestic, which are propagated for sale in the Gardens near London*. Among the 'generous procurers of plants' from overseas 'Her Grace the Duchess of Beaufort did also collect a numerous quantity of rare plants into those famous gardens of Badmington, where she preserved and maintained them with great care in wonderful beauty for many years; but this collection also consisted chiefly of the most tender exotic plants.'

There is not much detailed information about the plants the Duchess introduced, though the zonal 'geranium' (*Pelargonium zonale*) in 1710 was one of them. It has been said that she introduced many more than she has since been credited with in horticultural literature.

Stephen Switzer in his *The Nobleman, Gentleman and Gard'ner's Recreation* (1715) includes among those who were enthusiasts for horticulture 'the Dowager Duchess of Beaufort (very lately deceas'd).' It was at Badminton in Gloucestershire that 'this noble Lady us'd to spend those momenta that many other ladies devote to the tiresome pleasure of the town. What a progress she made in exoticks, and how much of her time she virtuously and busily employed in the garden is easily observable from the thousands of those foreign plants (by her as it were made familiar to this clime) there regimented together, and kept in a wonderful deal of health, order and decency, if they are now the same as about seven or eight years ago, when I had the happiness of seeing them, with some others. Besides, her servants assured us, excepting the times of her devotions, at which she was a constant attendant, gard'ning took up two thirds of her time. The great favour she held towards virtuoso's in her

own way, I have in several instances heard from Monsieurs the Bobarts, both very eminent in "botanick amusements."—their "amusements" being the management of the Oxford Botanic Garden.'

Beaumont, Guillaume (fl. 1680s–1720s). Although of French origin, Beaumont figures in this DICTIONARY as a practitioner in his adopted country, England. Beaumont remains a rather shadowy figure, but he is said to have worked under Le Nôtre in France and later undoubtedly for Colonel Graham, first at Bagshot and then at Levens Hall in Westmorland, where he went in 1689. He seems to have been *persona grata* and respected as an adviser on gardening matters among Graham's aristocratic friends. At Levens he is particularly associated with the topiary garden (which was, however, re-constructed by the gardener there in 1808) as well as the fine avenues. Those of lime planted in 1697 do not justify the claim of being early examples in the north, as this tree was planted in Scotland long before, while the rather unusual and very fine oak avenue is comparable with the much earlier example at Croft Castle. He had a house at Levens. It seems that he was finally overcome by the effects of drink. More about this remarkable man may remain to be uncovered in the archives at Levens.

Beckford, William (1760–1844). Dilettante, writer, traveller. Although Beckford is chiefly known as the builder of the fantastic but short-lived pseudo-gothic pile, Fonthill Abbey, in Wiltshire, he has a right to a place in the history of British gardening as a pioneer in the kind of prose which was subsequently to be written about mountain plants and the construction of alpine gardens.

Of the former we have an example written on the Cintra Mountains of Portugal in 1787: 'I noticed . . . on a little flat space before the convent a numerous tribe of pinks, gentians and other alpine plants, fanned and invigorated by the pure mountain air. These refreshing breezes, impregnated with the perfume of innumerable aromatic herbs and flowers, seemed to infuse new life into my veins, and, with it, an almost irresistible impulse to fall down and worship in this vast

Lime avenue at Levens Park, Westmorland, designed by Monsieur **Beaumont**.

Monsieur **Beaumont** *(fl. 1689–1699).*

William **Beckford** *(1760–1844).*

A view of Fonthill Abbey, designed by James Wyatt for William **Beckford**.

temple of Nature the source and cause of existence.'

It is known that among his other considerable gardening activities he constructed a rockery in a quarry at Fonthill, but no detailed records of this extravagance exist. Beckford's gardener, Vincent, was certainly a man out of the ordinary as his correspondence with Sir J. E. Smith (qv), to be found in The Smith Papers of the Linnean Society, amply confirms.

The grounds of Fonthill Abbey were a magnificent essay in the Picturesque manner, enclosed within a wall twelve miles long and twelve feet high. The Abbey was surrounded by lawns, with a 100-foot-wide avenue over a mile in length. There was also an American plantation filled with rhododendron, magnolia and azalea. An artificial lake was the haunt of water fowl, and from the lake wooded slopes rose to a high hill. Estimates claimed that a guest could drive for twenty-two miles without retracing his steps. The gardens inevitably included a huge grotto, alpine gardens and a quarry, apart from the ruins of Beckford's family house, Splendens. Beckford maintained the eight-acre kitchen-garden there

until the collapse of his house and his family fortune.

Bedford, Dukes of:
Since Restoration times the Russell family has been actively concerned with gardening in all its aspects, especially at Woburn Abbey in Bedfordshire. Those who were prominent in this sphere include in historical order:

WILLIAM RUSSELL, 5th Earl and 1st Duke (1613–1700). At his London residence, Bedford House, in Bloomsbury, the Earl had a typical town garden of the period. The gardener in charge (at £40 a year) was Thomas Gilbank who was succeeded by Thomas Todd. Both these men also acted as purchasing agents for supplies at Woburn Abbey, then being built. The walled London garden lay behind the house and was of simple design. Near to the house was a terrace, below which a broad gravelled walk divided the area into two parts. In one were smaller paths dividing it into beds of geometrical shapes filled with a considerable variety of plants and decorated by stone ornaments. On the other side was a wilderness consisting of an elaborate

pattern of paths running among trees and shrubs. This, we learn, needed much attention. There was no room for a kitchen garden, although there was a plot for herbs—doubtless for the kitchen.

In 1660 William Russell began a new house at Thorney Abbey in Cambridgeshire, but this did not compare with Woburn. At that time the Woburn garden was a typical, but not outstanding formal garden of the period, lying on three sides of the house, with the kitchen garden and orchards beyond. In about 1663 John Field was appointed to take charge. He was, as was then apparently the practice, on the regular pay-roll of the house, whereas all other gardening labour was casual. In due course Field and his wife, a good sick-nurse, became much more than mere employees of the Russell family.

Soon after his arrival, Field began to buy all the newest plants. The orchards and kitchen garden were increased in size and scope; the latest kinds of fruit were planted. There were fifteen kinds of plum, twelve of peach, eight of pear, seven of cherry, two of nectarine and apricot, one of quince, but, surprisingly, only three of apple. The

Engraving showing the landscaped park and west front of Woburn Abbey, Bedfordshire, home of the Dukes of **Bedford**.

Francis Russell, 5th Duke of **Bedford** *(1765–1802).*

John Russell, 6th Duke of **Bedford** *(1766–1839).*

runner-bean, originally grown not many years previously as a decorative climber, was now grown as a vegetable, while nasturtiums, marigolds, and gillyflowers were planted for preserving and using in salads.

Celia Fiennes wrote of the garden in 1697: 'The house (still the old Tudor building) stands in a fine park full of deer and wood, and some of the trees are kept cut in works and the shape of several beasts . . . the gardens are fine, there is a large bowling-green with eight arbours kept cut neatly, and seats in each. There is a seat up in a high tree that ascends fifty steps that commands the whole park round to see the deer hunted, as also a large prospect of the country. There are three large gardens, fine grand walks and full of fruit. I ate a great quantity of the red Carolina (?) gooseberry which is a large, thin-skinned sweet gooseberry. The walks are above one another with stone steps. In the square just by the dining room window is all sorts of pots of flowers and curious evergreens—fine orange, citron and lemon trees and myrtles, striped phillyrea and a fine aloes plant. On the side of this you pass under an arch into a cherry garden, in the midst of which stands a figure of stone resembling an old weeder woman used in the garden, and my Lord would have her effigy done so like and her clothes so well that at first I took it to be the real living body.

'On the other side of the house is another large garden with several gravel walks one above another, and on the flats are fishponds the whole length of the walk. Above that on the next flat are two fish ponds. And here are spreading dwarf trees of great bigness.'

Tree, fruit and plants were purchased from the leading nurserymen of the day—Mordan, Gurle and Ricketts among them—and there was clearly much exchanging of plants with other gardens.

In 1681 Field joined, presumably as a part-time partner, the influential group of nurserymen headed by George London (qv). He died in 1687, but Woburn, as can be seen from its description by Miss Fiennes, continued in its glory.

JOHN RUSSELL, 4th Duke (1710–1771), was the next outstanding patron of botany, horticulture and arboriculture. Through his connexion with the naturalist Peter Collinson (qv) of Mill Hill, who obtained plants from John Bartram (qv) in North America, he became one of the small group which, from 1740 on, entered into an arrangement to finance Bartram in his plant-collecting and surveying expeditions, receiving his share of what was received and distributed by Collinson. Bartram's most consequential patron was Lord Petre (qv) of Thorndon Hall, where he raised and planted 40,000 trees. Petre died prematurely in 1743, and from the sale of plants that followed, many went to Woburn. A certain Dr Lumley Loyd of Cheam presented the Duke with his notable collection of plants. The original pinetum was apparently made on the advice of Philip Miller of the Chelsea Physic Garden. We can also assume that the duke was one of the influential people who obtained for John Bartram the post of Botanizer Royal for America in 1765.

FRANCIS RUSSELL, 5th Duke (1765–1802), who is best known as an agricultural pioneer. He was the first to open his gardens to the public—on Mondays. During his era the structure now used as a sculpture gallery was built as an orangery. Henry Holland's Chinese dairy also belongs to this period. J C Loudon wrote an account of Woburn shortly after the 5th Duke's death, and this was published in his *Encyclopaedia of Gardening*: 'From the duke's apartments a covered way leads to a greenhouse, 140 feet in length; and from the end of the greenhouse a piazza of nearly a quarter of a mile leads along the margin of a flower garden to a dairy, a handsome Chinese building, ornamented in stained glass. The park is very extensive, varied in surface, and abundantly clothed with trees, but it wants one feature of essential importance, water. This might be

The Great Ash at Woburn Park, from J. G. Strutt's Sylva Britannica *(1830) and (right) Woburn Abbey seen across the lake, home of the Dukes of* **Bedford**.

*The ballustraded, triple-arched bridge in the park at Woburn Abbey designed by Sir William Chambers for the 4th Duke of **Bedford**.*

*The small pale-flowered daffodil named in honour of John Thomas **Bennett-Poë**.*

*The Reverend Henry Jardine **Bidder** (1847–1923), alpine gardener.*

given, but it would be at considerable expense. At present there are several small pieces or lakes; but they have no effect in a general point of view, though some of them are pleasantly picturesque as recluse scenes. One of them, contrived to fall in the way of the approach, is crossed by a viaduct designed by Repton. There are many fine old cedars, silver firs, and pines in one part of the park, which were planted under the direction of Miller. The gardens are extensive, and abundant in everything.'

Loudon, a pioneering sociologist, also paid tribute to the Duke's work in improving agriculture, adding that 'the present duke (John) has not the same taste as his late brother,' an opinion that he was later to revise.

JOHN RUSSELL, 6th Duke (1766–1839). He was presumably little known to Loudon at that time, but was, in fact, greatly interested in botany and botanical exploration, becoming a Fellow of the Linnean Society in 1816. His contribution to Woburn was made in conjunction with his remarkable gardener, James Forbes (1773–1861). Their additions to the already considerable collections of willows and conifers, resulted in the volumes *Salicetum Woburnense* (1829) and *Pinetum Woburnense* (1839). They were never published for sale but privately printed with hand-coloured illustrations by an accomplished but little-known artist named Weddell. By this time, Loudon had so altered his opinion of the duke that his review of the book on conifers in his *Gardener's Magazine* occupied many euologistic pages, while in his own *Arboretum et Fruticetum Britannicum* of 1838 there are over a hundred references to specimens at Woburn. This 6th Duke also played an important part in the history of Kew when the future of the gardens was in dispute. In the reign of William IV, it was proposed to abandon the use of what was still royal property as a botanic garden

and, giving the plants to learned societies, turn the place into a private royal demesne where fruit would be grown in the glass houses. The Duke used his influence behind the scenes against this proposal, urging that it should become a national garden. This he did not live to see as it came about in the year following his death.

HERBRAND, 11th Duke from 1893 (1858–1940). He was an outstanding forester. Woburn owes to him the planting of many of the new ornamental trees that arrived in Britain in the opening decades of the present century.

The interest of the Bedford family in horticulture and botany is also displayed in the remarkable collection of outstanding books on these subjects, which have been collected over a long period.

Bennett-Poë, (Reverend) John Thomas (1846–1926). Horticulturist. Bennett-Poë was one of the outstanding horticultural parsons of the second half of the last century. He was born in County Tipperary and privately educated, graduating MA at Trinity College, Dublin. He was somewhat frail and devoted much of his time to out-of-door gardening, seeking good health. In the process he gained an extensive knowledge of plants and their ways and treatment. In 1889 he moved to London and became an active member of the Royal Horticultural Society. His decided views caused him to resign from Council in 1902, at the time of a proposal to acquire a site for a hall, on the grounds that a site for a new garden was more important than a new hall. Appropriately, when Wisley gardens passed into the management of the Society in 1903, Bennett-Poë was appointed one of the three trustees.

He took a lively part on several committees of the Royal Horticultural and the Royal Botanic Societies, travelling to judge at Dublin, Cork and Scarborough.

The extent of his enthusiasms as a practical gardener are suggested in the citation of the award to him of the Horticultural Society's Victoria Medal of Honour in 1902 as 'a fine cultivator of uncommon plants, an enthusiast for daffodils, florists auriculas and Old English tulips'. He also had a remarkable collection of forms of the Christmas rose (*Helleborus niger*). A small pale-primrose-flowered daffodil was named in his honour.

Bentham, George (1800–1884). Botanist. Bentham was born at Stoke, near Plymouth, Devonshire, the son of Sir Samuel Bentham, naval architect to Catherine II of Russia, and only brother of Jeremy Bentham, the noted philosopher. Bentham was educated at Cambridge, but also spent much time in the parental home at Montpellier in Southern France, where his early interest in botany was expressed in the compilation of his *Catalogue des plantes indigènes des Pyrénées et des Bas Languedoc,* published in 1826. He was for a time secretary to his uncle, but in 1829 became secretary to the Horticultural Society. His herbarium and library were incorporated in the Kew Collections.

In 1858 he published his *Handbook of the British Flora*, which went into several editions. He was also responsible for various volumes in the Government-sponsored series on the flora of British colonial possessions, notably *Flora Hongkongensis* (1861) and the seven-volume *Flora Australiensis* (1863–78). His most notable achievement, however, was the three-volume *Genera Plantarum* (1862–1883) produced in conjunction with Sir Joseph Hooker (qv), and completed the year before his death.

Bidder, (Reverend) Henry Jardine (1847–1923). Alpine gardener. Bidder was a Fellow of St John's College, Oxford, and persuaded his colleagues to appoint him *custos*

*George **Bentham** (1800–1884).*

*Corner of the rock garden designed by the Reverend Henry Jardine **Bidder** at St. John's College, Oxford.*

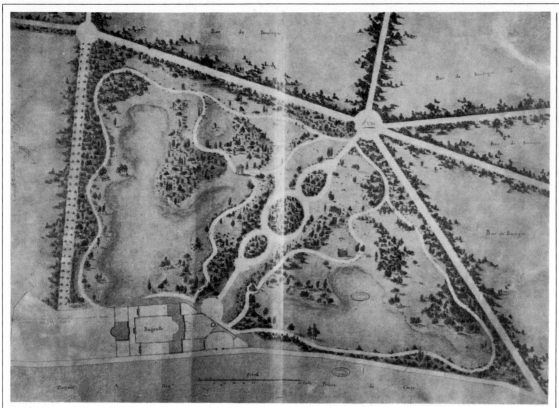

*The original design for the garden of Bagatelle, in France, with which Thomas **Blaikie** was associated.*

*Marquis of **Blandford** (1776–1840).*

sylvarum. He was a clever, knowledgeable gardener but, it seems, of a particularly forthright personality likely to daunt those without comparable knowledge. In 1893 he designed and built in the grounds of the college a rock garden. His purpose was the growing of true alpine plants, not, apparently, a natural alpine garden in the present manner, but, nevertheless, of considerable interest and inspiration to Bidder's friends, such as Reginald Farrer (qv), Ellen Willmott (qv), and no doubt to others who were pioneering the spirit of rock gardening, now an essential feature in the Alpine Garden Society's activities.

Blaikie, Thomas (1750–1838). Landscape gardener. Blaikie does not enter directly into the history of gardening in the British Isles itself, but he is representative of those British (particularly Scots) gardeners who worked in many overseas countries as exponents of the late-eighteenth and early-nineteenth century *le jardin anglais.*

Blaikie was well enough known to appear in J. C. Loudon's *Encyclopaedia* as an outstanding gardener in France: 'A number of gardens in the English style were laid out just before the French revolution, by Mr Blaikie, a British landscape-gardener. He was born in the neighbourhood of Edinburgh, and continued till his death, the proprietor of a large market garden, which belonged to his father in the parish of Corstorphine. He went to France first as a botanical collector and walked in that capacity through the greater part of Switzerland. Mr

Blaikie entered upon the profession of a landscape gardener in Paris in 1776; and died there in 1838, aged eighty-nine'.

Loudon also records that Blaikie was associated with such gardens as Bagatelle, Monceau and le Petit Trianon. Subsequently, during the Consulate, he altered Malmaison in cooperation with an Englishman, called Hudson. Little else would be known about this remarkable man had not Francis Birrell published in 1931 *The Diary of a Scotch Gardener at the French Court at the End of the Eighteenth Century.* As far as the interests of British botany were concerned, Blaikie's early life was of far greater significance than his work for the French aristocracy, particularly on account of his alpine travels and collections, and his connexion with two remarkable amateur botanists, Dr. John Fothergill (1712–1780) (qv) and Dr. William Pitcairn (1711–1791) (qv).

In the seventeenth and early eighteenth centuries, mountainous landscapes were generally regarded with apprehension, even horror. In the eighteenth century this attitude changed, sponsored by such books as Haller's *Die Alpen,* published in 1732, Saussure's *Voyages dans les Alpes Prédé d'un Essai Sur l'Histoire Naturelle des Environs de Geneve,* published in 1749.

The plant life of the mountains became a novel and important interest to botanists and gardeners such as Fothergill and Pitcairn, who jointly engaged Blaikie 'to undertake a journey to the Alps in Switzerland in search of rare and curious plants.'

Why they chose a young man of twenty-five and how and when he came south from Edinburgh, already knowing a number of important people in the British botanical and horticultural world, is not known, but many entries in William Aiton's *Hortus Kewensis,* which attributed the introduction of certain mountain plants to the two doctors, were due to Blaikie, who left London in 1775.

His entertaining diary, one of the best of the many epics written by plant-collectors searching the mountains, is the record of an observant and lively character who made friends easily among all classes as he travelled in a new country. A typical despatch was 440 packets of 'specimints and seeds sent together in one box directed to Dr Pitcairn Warwick court Warwick Lane London' from Bourdigny the 25 November, 1775.

Blaikie's invaluable mission ended on December 31, 1775 when, he records, 'I dined at Dr Fothergills where I was well received by him and all the family; here ended a long and troublesome journey accompanied with many hardships.'

On the next day he breakfasted with Sir Joseph Banks (qv), an indication of his standing, before proceeding to Upton to find that his introductions were doing well, except that the warmth of a greenhouse drew the silkworms out of their nests prematurely so that they had all died.

In September, 1776, Blaikie's whole career was changed, thanks to an introduction by James Lee

(1715–95), another Scot, who had with Lewis Kennedy, once gardener to Spencer Compton, Speaker of the House of Commons and a prominent arboriculturist, set up the Hammersmith Nursery, one of the leading establishments of its kind in England with wide continental contacts. Blaikie was engaged by the Comte du Lauragais, a versatile French intellectual, to work on the laying out of his estates in Normandy. Although Lauragais was quite unreliable financially—much to Blaikie's disadvantage—he did introduce the Scot to a brilliant social set, with whose frequently grandiose garden schemes Blaikie later became involved.

The rest of Blaikie's diary is concerned with his work closely connected with notable garden-makers, designers and architects of the French court and their rivalries. Of greater interest to British gardening history would be to pursue in detail Blaikie's continuing connexions with prominent British nurserymen and horticulturists, a task awaiting, perhaps, some future historian.

Blaikie's opinion of most French architects and garden designers was poor, though, he said, they had great taste in their buildings. The French, he wrote, bragged about Le Nôtre, whose plans were the reverse of nature, with stiff terraces and extravagant stairs as if they imagined nothing could be 'noble without statues, terraces etc.'

We gain a good idea of Blaikie's interests and activities after the Revolution from his contributions to Loudon's *Gardener's Magazine.*

Blandford, George Spencer (Marquis of) (1766–1840). Landscape gardener, plant-collector. Blandford was one of the foremost planters of the early nineteenth century and became widely known when he lived

*(Opposite) Garden at Athelhampton, Dorset, showing formal elements attributed to Sir Reginald **Blomfield** (1856–1942).*

Whiteknights, Berkshire, engraved from drawing by T. C. Holland, early home of the Marquis of **Blandford**.

Captain William **Bligh** *(1754–1817)*.

at Whiteknights, near Reading, before moving to Blenheim on succeeding to the dukedom of Marlborough in 1817. In about 1800 he began practising gardening in all its forms, collecting plants of all descriptions, building numerous hot-houses for his tender exotics, and growing a collection of hardy

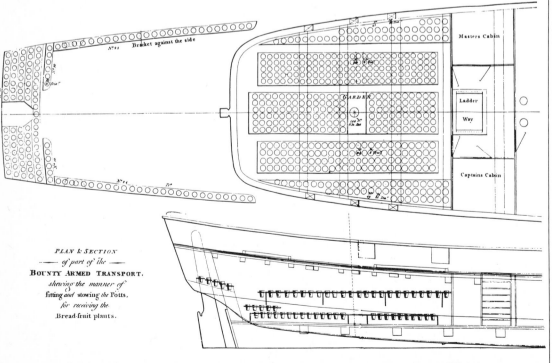

Thatched arbour at Whiteknights, home of the Marquis of **Blandford**.

herbaceous plants and the choicest shrubs within a large walled garden. Finding these activities too limiting he planted many trees throughout his parkland, including collections of whole large genera such as the thorns, *crataegus*, which were then fashionable.

The most famous feature at Whiteknights was the magnolia wall, 145 feet long and 24 feet high, the upper part of *treillage*. On this trellis the upper branches of the trees terminated, and by their projection, protected all those beneath from perpendicular rain and snow, an unnecessary extravagance, as magnolias, a fact known, of course, to the Marquis, flower freely without any such protection! The garden was surrounded by a hedge and sunk fence, laid out in the ancient style, and abounding with curious seats and rustic huts.

Subsequent to 1816, 'in view of his extravagant mode of proceeding in his transactions generally' the Marquis found himself involved in

debt and law suits. On succeeding to the dukedom he showed the same taste for planting in the pleasure grounds at Blenheim.

White Knights (as it is now termed) is today occupied by the University of Reading. Some of the original trees remain.

Bligh, William (1754–1817). Navigator. Bligh was born in Cornwall, the only child of Francis Bligh, a customs officer, and his wife Jane. He appears in this DICTIONARY as the commanding officer of what has been termed 'the first floating garden', the legendary *Bounty*.

In 1787, in conjunction with the Government, Sir Joseph Banks (qv), deputed the *Bounty* to transport the bread plant, indigenous to the South Sea Islands, from Tahiti to the West Indies, where it was hoped that the plant would provide an adequate and cheap diet for the thousands of slaves working on the plantations of Jamaica and other islands. The botanist-gardener

appointed by Sir Joseph was David Nelson (qv) who had sailed with Captain Cook (qv) (and with Bligh as sailing-master) in the *Resolution* on Cook's ill-fated third voyage.

Although the *Bounty*, including Bligh's Great Cabin, was transformed virtually into a plant-collector's conservatory, Bligh was agreeable to these arrangements and the *Bounty* sailed in December 1787 for the South Seas, reaching Tahiti in October the following year. After a stay of almost six months, the *Bounty* sailed for the West Indies with over a thousand breadfruit trees. *En route*, however, the mutiny on the *Bounty* occurred and Nelson was cast adrift with Bligh and others, to undergo much privation and hardship before they reached Timor after a voyage of over 4,000 miles.

Bligh returned to England and, in 1791, commanding the *Providence*, voyaged to Tahiti to collect breadfruit plants which he then transhipped to St Vincent in the West Indies. Although it had been voted a substantial sum by the Jamaican planters, the breadfruit project proved a failure.

The remainder of Bligh's career was equally controversial and stormy. The full story of his extraordinary life is told in *Captain Bligh* by Richard Humble (1976).

Blomfield, (Sir) Reginald Theodore (1856–1942). Architect. Blomfield was born in Devon, the son of a clergyman. After leaving Oxford he was articled to his uncle, the well-established ecclesiastical architect, Sir Arthur Blomfield. His energies and interests extended to both gardening and literature, and the two interests were combined in his first book, *The Formal Garden in England*, published in 1892, followed, five years later, by *A History of Renaissance Architecture*. These publications consolidated his growing practice in both architecture and landscape gardening, and he was responsible for remodelling not only a number of large houses—

Diagram showing how the breadfruit plants were stored on board the Bounty *under the command of Captain* **Bligh**.

Apethorpe, Northants; Chequers, Bucks; Athelhampton, Dorset; and Mellerstain, Berwickshire, among them—but also their settings, making a high reputation as a designer of formal gardens.

His predelection for an architectural style combining a latterday English baroque with French Renaissance overtones was well-suited to Edwardian taste. As a garden designer, he was also well-suited to express the ambitions of Edwardian nobilities and plutocrats wishful to demonstrate their wealth and taste by building vast houses set within magnificent formal gardens, the last flowering of such ostentation before the more manageable cult of the wild or natural garden promulgated by William Robinson (qv) and Gertrude Jekyll (qv) was taken up.

Blomfield was highly successful as an urban architect, designing The Quadrant, Regent Street; Lambeth Bridge; the United Universities Club, etc. He also published a four-volume *History of French Architecture 1494–1774* in addition to a biography of his architectural hero, Norman Shaw.

Bobart (or **Bobert**), Jacob (1599–1680). Bobart was born in Brunswick. His early history is obscure, although he is known to have served as a soldier. When he came to England is not recorded, but in 1642 he was appointed, in curious circumstances, as the first *Horti Praefectius* or superintendent of the Oxford Physic Garden, founded in 1621 by Henry Danvers, First Earl of Danby (qv). Danvers, having overspent on the construction of the garden, seems to have lacked funds to appoint a horticulturist of any known eminence. Bobart, a local innkeeper, was also a successful gardener, and in the event got the appointment. Bobart amplified his income by selling the fruit and other produce that he grew in the Botanic Garden. He was undoubtedly a man of energy and

Sir Reginald **Blomfield** *(1856–1942).*

accomplishment. Contemporary records speak of him as a huge man with a long black beard, which, on holy days, he tricked out with silver. He was followed about by a tame goat. He was also a man of some academic intention and application, for in 1648 he published *Catalogus Hortus Botanicus Oxoniensis*, listing 1,600 plants. Ten years later, with assistance from others, a revised edition was issued. Bobart kept the garden going throughout the difficult times prior to the restoration of Charles II.

Bobart, Jacob (the younger) (1641–1719). The son of the above. He was born in Oxford and succeeded his father as superintendent of the Oxford Botanic Garden in 1680. Four years later he was appointed Professor of Botany at Oxford. In 1699 he completed and published the third volume of Robert Morison's important *Plantarum Historiae Universalis Oxoniensis*, Morison, the first Professor of Botany at Oxford, having died in an accident in 1683.

The younger Bobart began an exchange of seeds and plants with other botanic gardens and private patrons. Interesting instances of

Jacob **Bobart** *the elder (1599–1679).*

these exchanges are recorded in correspondence of the period. The virtuoso Charles Hatton, for example, wrote in 1688 of having received from 'Mr Bobart seeds of very curious plants.' The earliest record of the London plane being grown is in Bobart's garden as *Platanus inter orientalum et occidentalum media* (the

Jacob **Bobart,** *the younger (1641–1719).*

plane between the oriental and western—i.e. North American—kinds). This hybrid is said to have arisen in seed sent to him from Montpellier Botanic Garden, in southern France.

Bobart, Tilleman (fl. 1650s–1724). Brother of the foregoing, who worked as a young man in the

Botanic Garden, Oxford, of which both Jacob **Bobart** *and son were superintendents.*

Two illustrations from The Formal Garden in England *by Sir Reginald* **Blomfield,** *one of the chief exponents of this Edwardian style of landscaping.*

Part of Charles **Bridgeman's** *garden design at Stowe in Buckinghamshire, as illustrated in* Views of Stowe, *drawn and engraved by Jacques Riegaud and Bernard Baron and published by Sarah Bridgeman in 1739. The gardens at Stowe were altered by Bridgeman's successors.*

of Rousham before it was altered by William Kent, shows a marked breaking-away from strict formality in an imaginative style, suggesting Vanbrugh rather than later versions of the natural landscape garden. Horace Walpole, in his celebrated description of the introduction of the landscape style of gardening, wrote: 'But the capital stroke, the leading step to all that has followed, was (I believe the first thought was Bridgeman's) the destruction of walls for boundaries, and the invention of fosses—an attempt then deemed so astonishing that the com-

Part of the garden at Ebberstone Hall, Yorkshire, one of the few designs by Charles **Bridgeman** *which are still in existence.*

mon people called them Ha! Ha's! to express their surprise at finding a sudden and unperceived check to their walk.'

The ha-ha, so important to the English landscape garden, was surprisingly a device used and named by the French during the great days of their formal style. D'Argenville in *La Théorie et la Pratique du Jardinage* published in France, in 1709, writes of a terrace *'terminé par une claire voie, qu'on appelle autremont un ah, ah, avec un fosse sec au pied.'* An English translation by John James (qv) was published in 1712, with over 200 subscribers, including most of the consequential garden owners of the day.

Bridgeman cannot, therefore, be credited with the invention of the ha-ha, but he may have introduced it into England at Stowe in 1719, as a fortress-like 'stockade ditch' under the enthusiastic encouragement of his military-minded employer, later Viscount Cobham. Subsequently, Bridgeman certainly used the ha-ha in the simpler and more extensive form that we know today.

Very little of Bridgeman's work remains. Most of it, such as his magnificent creation at Stowe, was amended or destroyed by his successors. He worked largely for members of the same political party, and particularly for those concerned in what is popularly known as the 'South Sea Bubble'.

Some of the gardens he was associated with were Amesbury House, Wiltshire; Down Hall, Essex; Marble Hill, Middlesex; Purley Hall, Berkshire and Wimpole Hall, Cambridgeshire. There were many others.

Bright, Henry Arthur (1830–1884). Amateur gardener and writer. Bright's book *A Year in a Lancashire Garden* (first published in 1879 and three times reprinted) was a collection of garden notes written month by month in 1874 for *The Gardener's Chronicle*. Intended for those who 'love gardens, but not for those who have a professional knowledge of the subject; they are written in the hope that it may not be quite impossible to convey to others some little of the delight which grows . . . from the possession and management of a garden.' The book amply illustrates the wide knowledge of a cultured gardener and the manner of his gardening a century ago. The book was influential and typical in its period and is of interest today. Bright also published *The English Flower Garden* in 1881. He was a partner in a Liverpool shipping firm and a member of the Roxburghe Club and Philobiblon Club, for both of which he edited publications.

Brookes, John (1933–   ). Garden and landscape designer. Brookes was born in Durham and educated at Durham School and the Durham County School of Agriculture. Then followed a three-year apprenticeship with the Nottingham Corporation Parks Department, after which he worked for a year as assistant to Brenda Colvin. After gaining a diploma in landscape design at University College London, he worked as assistant to Sylvia Crowe before becoming assistant editor of *Architectural Design*. Since 1964 he has been in private practice. He also lectures on landscape design at various schools and institutes, including the Royal Botanical Gardens, Kew.

His practice ranges from commissions for private clients to larger works for public bodies.

Brookes has written extensively on the design of gardens, particularly on the problems attending small town gardens. His designs invariably show considerable ingenuity and imaginative scope. He has published the following books: *Room Outside* (Thames & Hudson, 1969), *Gardens for Small Spaces* (Pan, 1970), *Garden Design &*

(Left) Formal pool with stepping-stones in the garden adjoining the offices of Penguin Books, Harmondsworth, Middlesex, landscaped by John **Brookes** *(right), who has written extensively on garden design, particularly in relation to town sites.*

Layout, and *Living in the Garden* (Queen Anne Press, 1970).

Brotherston, Robert Pace (1848–1923). Gardener and writer. Brotherston was born at Ednam in Berwickshire, and in his mid-twenties was appointed head gardener to the Earl of Haddington of Tyninghame, East Lothian, Scotland, remaining there for the rest of his life. He combined this practical experience with a literary career which began with contributing to the garden press, continued with the *Book of the Carnation* and culmi-nated in publication in 1906 of *The Book of Cut Flowers*, subtitled *A Complete Guide to the Preparing, Arranging and Preserving of Flowers for Decorative Purposes*. At the time it was issued, little serious attention had been given to flower decoration. Indeed, the book was written because of the very low standard in flower arrangement classes which were mostly held at flower shows. People of sensibility were beginning to realize the aesthetic and imaginative possibilities of the craft, particularly following the publication in 1899 of Josiah Conder's *The* *Flower Art of Japan*. With knowledge of the innate qualities of plants of very many kinds, allied with his understanding of practical requirements, this book was the first really authoritative study of a craft, which has now become widely popular, and is more reliable than many of its now numerous successors.

Brotherston's brother, Andrew (1834–91), was also a gardener and Scottish botanist of some repute.

Brown, Lancelot (1716–1783). Landscape gardener and architect. Brown, known as 'Capability'

Glasses for arranging flowers, shown in The Book of Cut Flowers *by Robert Pace* **Brotherston** *(1906).*

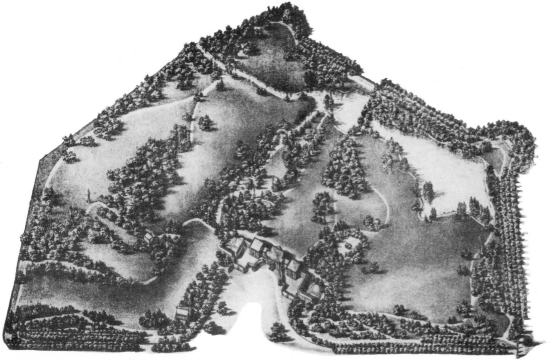

Bird's eye view by Desmadryl of the naturalistic design by Lancelot **Brown** *for the gardens at Stowe, Northamptonshire, which supplanted (and destroyed) the earlier layout. (Right) Detail of a portrait of 'Capability' Brown by Sir Nathaniel Dance-Holland.*

Weston Park, Staffordshire, seen from the Temple of Diana against the woodlands planted by Lancelot **Brown** *for the Earl of Bradford.*

Park at Bowood, Wiltshire, planned by 'Capability' **Brown** *from 1761 onwards for Lord Shelburne.*

Brown from his reputed habit of assuring potential clients that their estates had 'capabilities' for improvement, is probably the best known of all English landscape gardeners.

He was born at Kirkharle, Northumberland, of a family in modest circumstances. He was educated at the village school at Cambo and afterwards employed on the garden staff of Sir William Loraine on his nearby estate. Brown was thus, unlike most of the enthusiasts for the new, more naturalistic fashion in

gardening—such as Addison, Pope and Kent—professionally trained, a background he shared with Charles Bridgeman.

In 1739 he went south to Wotton in Buckinghamshire, to the estate of Sir Richard Grenville. This was a significant move, for Grenville was brother-in-law to Lord Cobham at Stowe, only fourteen miles away. Cobham's garden had already undergone some of the transformations which were to make Stowe so influential in the history of garden design. Brown joined the garden

staff at Stowe in the following year.

He began work in the kitchen garden but his character and ability, allied with his practical skills, were so readily evident that he was soon made head gardener. He remained at Stowe for eleven years, working with Bridgeman and several architects, including William Kent and James Gibbs. Brown was, therefore, working, as executant under the influence of the innovators of the English landscape movement.

Yet he was also evolving his own style and it has been suggested that

some of the wide unimpeded sweeps of gently curving grass and woodland at Stowe, so typical of Lancelot Brown's later work, may be attributed to Brown.

In 1749 Cobham died and two years later Brown moved to London. He was now 'Capability' Brown, the landscape designer, living at Hammersmith, and was already designing for other estates, including Warwick Castle and Packington.

He also began the practice of architecture, his style being essentially Burlingtonian. He took into partnership Henry Holland, son of a neighbouring builder. Holland later married Brown's daughter.

As usual, political allegiance had considerable effects in patronage.

Brown himself was a close friend and confidant of many politicians, but his party allegiance delayed his receiving the appointment of royal gardener, for which he was anxious, until the accession of George III. Probably his connexion with the Whigs was at least partially due to the important part Cobham had played in his early career.

Although Brown suffered from asthma and was the object of a thinly disguised attack from Sir William Chambers in *A Dissertation on Oriental Gardening* in 1772 (because

---

(Opposite) View from the roof of Longleat in Wiltshire, showing the landscape setting designed by Lancelot ('Capability') **Brown** *for the Marquis of Bath. The park, though somewhat altered, includes typical features of Brown's naturalistic style: large areas of grass, clumps of irregularly-planted trees and a glittering, informal expanse of water.*

Chatsworth House, Derbyshire, seen against a background of woodlands which were planted by 'Capability' **Brown** *from 1761 onwards for the 4th Duke of Devonshire.*

A view of the park at Chatsworth, Derbyshire, showing the River Derwent, widened by 'Capability' **Brown** *to give the effect of an informal, lake-like sheet of water, as part of his general plan for landscaping the gardens. The river is crossed by a handsome, arched bridge, designed by James Paine, 1761–2.*

Column at Wrest Park, Bedfordshire (left), designed by Lancelot **Brown** *and inscribed 'These gardens were begun in the year 1706 by the Duke of Kent, who continued to beautify them until his death.' (Right) Garden-house at Burghley, Northamptonshire, designed by 'Capability' Brown (1756–8).*

Robert Clive had preferred Brown to Chambers at Claremont, his estate in Surrey), his life was harmonious and successful.

This sense of security and assurance is reflected in his work. Smooth gradients, gently serpentining paths, natural-seeming groupings of trees, the park brought right up to the house by means of the ha-ha and an entire absence of any rigidity or formality are the pivotal points of Brown's designs. All exotic plants were secreted in splendid walled gardens, themselves tactfully placed so as not to interfere with Nature. But his genius undoubtedly lay in his masterly management of water.

Attempts have been made to estimate the number of gardens designed by Brown, but the task is difficult. His assistants, pupils and imitators were many; documentary evidence is often essential to distinguish his work from that of such lesser-known designers as John Spyers, Lapidge, Richard Woods, William Eames, Sandys and Webb, whilst Humphry Repton, after Brown's death, had access to his plans and, for a time, continued in the Brown style before developing his own individual manner as a landscape designer.

Brown worked on a different system from that of his predecessors,

such as George London and Henry Wise. He had no nursery, but subcontracted the supply of trees and so on, supervising the work and checking the costs. The economics of his designs were also sound, for much of his planting provided valuable timber. And he designed for the future, as we can still see. Brown had, and continues to have, his critics, as does any artist with so resolute and personal a style. And his activities undoubtedly destroyed hundreds of Britain's then-finest gardens. To design gardens and parks in Brown's naturalistic manner demanded the obliteration of the formalism of earlier times. On the

other hand, the Brown landscapes have stood the test of time and remain a majestic yet seemingly natural feature of the English countryside today.

In 1764, when nearing fifty, Brown was appointed to his long-desired post of Surveyor to His Majesty's Garden and Waters at Hampton Court, for which the salary was £2,000 a year with an official residence, Wilderness House, where Brown lived until his death nearly twenty years later. No other landscape gardener has had so profound an influence on the English landscape, an influence which is, in many instances, even more impressive now than when the boldly imaginative and far-sighted 'Capability' Brown drew up his sketch-plans for his many projects.

A few of Brown's typical landscapes, the main features of which are still identifiable, would include: AUDLEY END, ESSEX. Brown worked here from 1763 onwards. This still-huge house lies on the eastern bank of a quite broad, shallow valley, up which runs the main road to Cambridge and down which flows an insignificant stream (though the visitor does not notice this).

Turning into the park, we cross over a large sheet of water by means of a three-arched bridge (by Robert Adam). Winding up to the house, we can stop and look back over a very wide expanse of undisturbed, shortly cut grass, an example of his 'shaven lawn'. This was a feature of the 'Capability' Brown landscape which we seldom see now, for an area such as this must today normally be used for some more economic purpose.

Far away, on the opposite bank, beyond the road (concealed by hedges) gleams a circular Adam temple. Nearer, well to the right, embowered in trees, is another feature—the stables, probably Jacobean. The scene is one of great simplicity and, particularly when the thorn hedges are in flower, of singular beauty.

On the slope behind the house, other buildings, in Sir Nikolaus Pevsner's words, are 'scattered about, exquisitely hidden, half concealed, or thrown into relief by planting'.

It is entertaining to walk along the lake-side until we find its true nature, a small stream disappearing under a narrow bridge among giant plane trees.

BERRINGTON HALL, HEREFORDSHIRE. Apart from visiting the house, much of Brown's Berrington landscape can be seen from the A49 road. This is of particular interest as the house was built by his son-in-law, Henry Holland, and there is every reason to believe that Brown chose the site as he was working at Eywood, not far away. The house is on fairly level ground, with (though now rather obscured by trees) exceptionally wide views over the county into the border mountains of Wales. From a small tributary of the little River Lugg, Brown engineered a pool of some fourteen acres. Scattered, massive oak trees form the majestic planting. His plan is dated 1780, when he was growing old, and the total cost was £1,600.

BLENHEIM PALACE, OXFORDSHIRE. The landscaping of Blenheim is undoubtedly Brown's most powerful achievement. Its principal feature was the lake, conjured out of the little River Glyme, so causing Vanbrugh's triumphal arch to arise from a good sheet of water rather

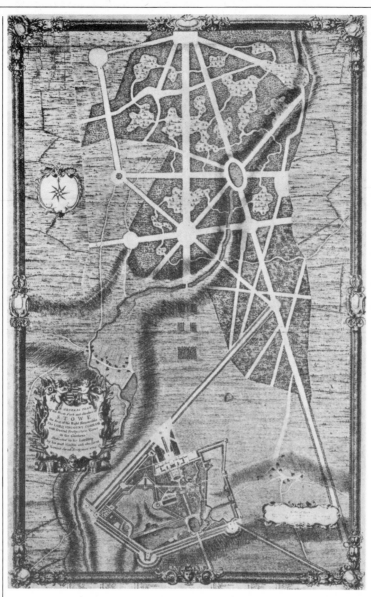

Plan showing the gardens in the formal manner at Stowe in Buckinghamshire, designed by Vanbrugh, Bridgeman and Kent, with whom Lancelot **Brown** worked.

Robert **Brown** (1773–1858).

than span a trickle inconsequently. The formal gardens we now see so suitably set around the palace are the work of Achille Duchene from 1925 to 1932 to replace the original and exceptionally fine garden created by Henry Wise, which Brown obliterated when he created his new Blenheim landscape in 1764–74.

CHARLECOTE, WARWICKSHIRE, through which flows Shakespeare's Avon. The member of the Lucy family, owners of Charlecote, who commissioned Brown, insisted that the elm avenue from the road to the gatehouse should not be destroyed. But what was obliterated we can see from a painting of 1696 which is hanging in the house and shows, among other delightful features, a long, formal canal parallel with the river, and gay parterres dropping down to it. (The present formal gardens are nineteenth century).

HAREWOOD, YORKSHIRE. A fine example of Brown's work, although the trees were badly damaged some years ago in a devastating gale. From Charles Barry's fine terrace

one now sees down towards the lake and then upwards on the far side beyond it. Likewise, when one descends to the bottom of the valley one has fine views up and down the lakeside (the lake was first made in about 1750 but Brown enlarged and re-designed it). Brown was employed in 1772 and worked for nine years, being paid £6,000. It is an imaginative design conceived on a magnificent scale.

LONGLEAT, WILTSHIRE. This most popular of English parks has a Brown setting, somewhat altered, and lake.

MOCCAS, HEREFORDSHIRE. The grounds here lie on the level beside a winding stretch of the River Wye, the plan being dated 1778. The Moccas design is of particular interest because Foxley, the home of Uvedale Price (1747–1829), the strongest of all Brown's critics, is only five miles away. It is possible that Brown supplied plans only, for which he was paid £100.

NUNEHAM, OXFORDSHIRE. This was one of the last of Brown's landscapes, completed in 1782, just

before he died. It lies quietly beside the Thames, designed to give carefully and partially concealed glimpses of the river. Nuneham also has a flower garden designed by the Rev William Mason (qv), who poetically defended Brown from attacks by Sir William Chambers.

PACKINGTON, WARWICKSHIRE. Brown's plan, which included a new serpentined pool and a band of trees with typical Brown 'bays', is dated 1751, the year he left Stowe and set up on his own in London. Today, numerous Lebanon cedars and other ornamental conifers planted subsequently somewhat alter the appearance of the place.

PETWORTH HOUSE, SUSSEX, still has the park and pleasure grounds much as they were when Brown worked for the second Lord Egremont between 1753 and 1763. Beyond his usual contouring and tree-planting he enlarged the pond in front of the house and gave it a serpentine shape. Petworth is a particularly good place to study the form and use of the ha-ha.

WESTON PARK, STAFFORDSHIRE. Brown's landscape, with its massive trees and lake, is exceptionally well maintained, dying trees being carefully replaced by the present Lord Bradford.

Brown, Robert (1773–1858). Botanist. Brown, who has been nominated as 'perhaps the greatest figure in the history of British botany', was born in Montrose in Angus, Scotland, and educated at the grammar school in that town and afterwards at the Marishal College, Aberdeen. He studied medicine at Edinburgh University. In 1801 he was appointed naturalist to the expedition under Matthew Flinders commissioned to survey the coasts of Australia. After adventurous and frequently hazardous experiences he returned in 1805

Buddleia globosa, *introduced 1734, named after Adam* **Buddle**.

with some four thousand plants, many new to Britain. In the same year he was appointed librarian of the Linnean Society, a position he retained for some seventeen years. In 1810 he published *Prodromus Florae Novae Hollandiae et Insulae Van Diemen*, followed twenty years later by a supplement. Also in 1810, Brown became librarian to Sir Joseph Banks (qv) and on being bequeathed both library and collec-

tions on Banks' death, in 1820, Brown made an arrangement with the trustees of the British Museum whereby he became Keeper of a new Botanical Department. Brown was a dedicated scientific botanist and a leading protagonist on behalf of the natural classification sponsored by de Jussieu, the French botanist, as opposed to the Linnean System.

Brydges, James (later Duke of Chandos, Earl of Caernarvon and Viscount Wilton) (1673–1744). Brydges' renown derives chiefly from the garden he made at Canons, near Edgware, on land acquired in 1713. This was the last English formal garden on a lavish scale, constructed at a time when the new fashion of informal landscape design had the support of the intelligentsia of the day. Brydges' essay in formality upset the poet, Alexander Pope, who, in his *Moral Essays*, contrasted Canons with Lord Cobham's Stowe. Brydges and his work were savagely attacked, thinly disguised as

Greatness, with Timon dwells in such a draught
As brings all Brobdidnag before your thought.

Pope, continuing in the same vein, concludes:

Another age shall see the golden ear
Imbrown the slope and nod on the parterre,
Deep harvest bury all his pride has plann'd,
And laughing Ceres reassume the land.

This, indeed, happened in 1747, only three years after Pope died, yet the task undertaken by Brydges had been formidable in the extreme.

The estate was without water, which was brought in pipes (made of timber from elm trees) from Stanmore, two miles away, to fill the rigidly formal canals and to supply the numerous fountains. The longest avenue that Brydges planted—there were others—was a thousand yards. There was an abundance of statues 'big as life'. Trees, shrubs and plants were brought from many parts of the world. The turf was scythed two or three times a week and weeded daily during the season. There were ostriches from Africa, tortoises from Majorca, flamingos from Antigua, as well as blue macaws, Virginia fowl, and even eagles which drank out of special stone basins. Even this ornithological profusion did not exhaust the exotic pleasures of Canons. In his *Journey Through England* (1728) J. Macky describes the gardens:

There is a large terrace walk from whence you can descend to the parterre; this parterre has a row of gilded vases on pedestals on each side down to the great canal, and in the middle, fronting the canal, is a gladiator, gilded also, and through the whole parterre an abundance of statues as big as life, regularly disposed.

The canal runs a great way and indeed one would wonder to see such a vast quantity of water in a country where there are neither rivers, nor springs. But they tell me that the Duke has his water in pipes from the mountains of Stanmore about two miles off.

The gardens are very large and well-disposed, but the greatest pleasure of all is that the divisions of the whole are only made by ballustrades of iron and not by walls; you can see the whole at once, be you in what part of the garden or parterre you will.

In his large kitchen garden there are beehives of glass, very curious; and at the end of each of his chief avenues he has neat lodgings for eight old sergeants of the Army, whom he took out of Chelsea College, who guard the whole; and go their rounds at night and call the hours as the watchmen do at London to prevent disorders, and wait upon the Duke to chapel on Sundays.

It is incredible the iron work about this noble palace, more, I must say, than I ever saw about any.

Buddle, (Rev) Adam (c. 1660–1715). Botanist-gardener. Buddle was born at Deeping St James, Lincolnshire, and was educated at Cambridge University, graduating in 1681. He lived at Henley in Suffolk, becoming rector of Great Fambridge, Essex, in 1703, and finally Reader

at Gray's Inn. He was well known in a small circle as an outstanding authority on the botany of mosses and grasses. Even the great Linnaeus thought he was worthy of commemoration and honour by using his name for a new shrub, *Buddleja globosa*, which was introduced from Peru in 1774 by the nurserymen Kennedy and Lee of Hammersmith. This, with its golden balls in June and July, is still grown. The long, purple spikes of *B. davidii* (introduced in 1896) are even better known and give due honour to one of those numerous botanist-gardeners of the seventeenth and eighteenth centuries, now mostly forgotten, yet to whom the richness of the gardening scene owes so much.

Bulley, Arthur Kilpin (1861–1942). Natural historian and botanist. Bulley was born at New Brighton, Cheshire, one of fourteen children of a successful cotton broker. He was educated at Marlborough College and then entered the family business, retiring in 1922.

He was a successful and enterprising businessman. During a period when his cotton-broking business was quiescent, he turned part of his garden into a commercial nursery which later developed into the successful firm of Bees Ltd.

In 1898 he began making an extensive garden in an ideal position at West Kirby on the Wirral peninsula, looking across the Dee estuary towards the mountains of North Wales. The garden soon became celebrated and, as an ardent Fabian, Bulley gave the public access. In 1912 he engaged as his head gardener, John Hope, a foreman at the Edinburgh Royal Botanic Garden. The two made a skilful combination in cultivating a great variety of rare plants. Arthur Bulley became an outstanding authority on the natural history, particularly the flora, of the district and was keenly interested in its preservation.

Bulley had long been interested in the acclimatization of plants from temperate climates not already cultivated in the British Isles and, from time to time, had attempted, usually unsuccessfully, to obtain these through local organizations, such as missions. He decided, therefore, to employ his own collectors. He approached Professor Isaac Bayley Balfour of Edinburgh (qv), who suggested George Forrest (qv) would

James **Brydges**, *later Duke of Chandos (1673–1744).*

(Opposite) The landscaped park at Harewood House, Yorkshire, laid out by Lancelot **Brown** *from 1772 onwards.*
(Top) Looking across Charles Barry's nineteenth-century terrace garden to Brown's naturalistic park beyond.
(Centre) Looking along the lake formed by damming a stream. (Below) General view of the park.

*Recent views of the gardens at Hidcote Manor, Gloucestershire, for many years in the charge of George Henry **Burrows**. They show (left) clipped hedges forming garden 'compartments' and (right) grass walk leading to twin pavilions.*

be a good choice. Thus it was that this then unknown young man set out in 1904 under Bulley's auspices on the first of those journeys to Western China which made him famous. Francis Kingdon Ward (qv), also made his first of many journeys to the same region, working for Bulley. In 1911–13, R. E. Cooper's lesser-known work in Sikkim and Bhutan was also undertaken personally for Arthur Bulley, who later had shares in other joint plant-collecting expeditions.

In 1948 his house and garden were endowed by his daughter, Miss A. L. Bulley, and given to Liverpool University as a botanic garden on the condition that the public had access to it.

Bunyard family:

GEORGE BUNYARD (1841–1919). Horticulturist. Bunyard was the head of a family nursery business founded at Maidstone, Kent, in 1796. Several members of the family have played an outstanding part in British gardening, of whom three are mentioned here.

The firm became important following its move in 1889 to a nursery at Allington, near Maidstone, which eventually covered 165 acres. The conditions at Allington well-suited the cultivation of fruit, and the place-name is recalled in the apple 'Allington Pippin', introduced in 1896, while 'Gasgoyne's Scarlet' (1871) and 'Lady Sudeley' (1885)

were other introductions which brought renown to the firm. George Bunyard had wide and practical experience and a prodigious knowledge of all kinds of fruit. In 1883 he played an outstanding part in the Royal Horticultural Society's influential Apple Conference, and in 1897 he was awarded the Royal Horticultural Society's Victoria Medal of Honour. He served on its Fruit Committee for thirty-four years and was also a member of its Council. The Fruiterer's Company made him a Freeman of the City.

EDWARD ASHDOWN BUNYARD (1878–1939). Horticulturist and author. Edward Bunyard, son of George, became known to a wider

public by his writings in which he displayed a remarkable knowledge, practical and historic, of flowers, fruit, food and wine. Apart from many contributions of a learned nature to various journals, he also published books, including his important *Handbook of Hardy Fruits*, the first volume of which was published in 1920. This placed him in the great tradition of British pomologists. *The Anatomy of Dessert* (1933) and *The Epicure's Companion* (1937), which he edited with Lorna Bunyard and which was illustrated by Francis Bunyard, were typical examples of his style. *Old Garden Roses*, the result of cultivation and historical study over many years, was published in 1936.

*Arthur Kilpin **Bulley** (1861–1942), early patron of George Forrest.*

Two illustrations by Frances Bunyard for The Epicure's Companion *(1937), edited by Lorna and Edward **Bunyard** and typical of the latter's authoritative writing.*

Engraving from The Chrysanthemum *by Frederick **Burbidge** (1884).*

George Henry **Burrows** *(1917–   ), who worked at Hidcote, Gloucestershire.*

Recent view of the Palm House at the Royal Botanic Gardens, Kew (left), a soaring glass-and-iron structure designed by Decimus **Burton**, *and (right) portrait of Burton (1800–1881).*

GEORGE NORMAN BUNYARD (1886–1969). Hybridizer. In 1920 the Bunyard firm turned its attention to the developments in the tall bearded irises following new lines in the practice of hybridization. In 1922, on the formation of the British Iris Society, George Bunyard became its first secretary, resigning in 1927 to become a member of its committee, on which he served for many years. He raised a number of varieties which received high awards.

Burbidge, Frederick William (1847–1905). Gardener, botanist, artist, plant-collector, author. In all these activities Burbidge showed outstanding practical skill. He was born at Wymeswold, Leicestershire, and first worked in the Horticultural Society's garden at Chiswick before moving on to Kew. He wrote for various horticultural journals, particularly William Robinson's *The Garden*, and quite early in life he published several outstanding books, including *The Art of Botanical Drawing* (1873), a sound and reliable manual, followed in 1875 by *The Narcissus: Its History and Culture*, an important contribution to the rising cult of the daffodil, illustrated by his own drawings. He published *The Chrysanthemum* in 1884.

In 1877 he set out for a year of exploration in British North Borneo, where he was joined by Peter Veitch of the celebrated firm of nurserymen. This adventurous and successful undertaking resulted in a considerable number of valuable orchids and tropical ferns being brought back to Britain, notably the giant pitcher plant of Kina Balu (*Nepenthes rajah*), which, although known for some years, had defied all attempts to introduce living specimens. In 1880 Burbidge published an account of the journey, *Gardens of the Sun*. He spent his later years in Ireland. In 1879 he became Curator of the gardens of Trinity College, Dublin, and in 1894 Keeper of the College Park.

At the Royal Horticultural Society's Daffodil Conference of 1890 he read an important paper on the history of the daffodil, and in 1897 he was awarded the Society's Victoria Medal of Honour.

Burrows, George Henry (1917–   ). Gardener. Burrows was born at Pontefract, Yorkshire, and is an outstanding post-war example of the professional gardener whose success derives from great practical experience in the old tradition of private gardening. In 1945 he went to Maesfron, Trewern, near Welshpool, thence to Powis Castle, Montgomeryshire, in 1947. After a spell at Waterer's Nursery in Surrey, he worked for Earl Howe at Chipstead in the same county and, from 1952, for Sir Denys Lowson at Brantridge Park, Balcombe, Sussex. His first position as head gardener was with Col. Pike at Dale Park, Madehurst, Arundel, Sussex. From there, he moved to take charge of Lord Dulverton's Batsford Park garden for four years.

In 1959 the famous gardens of Hidcote Manor, which had been designed and cultivated by an American, Major Johnston, during thirty years of residence, were found to be rapidly deteriorating. He had died two years previously and the gardens had passed into the care of the National Trust. Burrows was appointed to take charge of the Hidcote gardens. In addition to horticultural skills, a full and sensitive understanding of Johnston's objectives was essential if the task were to be carried out successfully. That Burrows was possessed of these qualities, amongst many others, has been made abundantly clear to those who have known Hidcote over many years.

Burton, Decimus (1800–1881). Architect. Burton was the tenth son of a successful London builder. He received an early training in building techniques in his father's office before entering the Royal Academy Schools. Thanks to the influence of his father and John Nash, a family friend, he set up in private practice at an early age, and his designs for the Colosseum in Regent's Park ('a Greek version of the Pantheon') were accepted when he was only twenty-three. Two years later he was appointed to carry out improvements in Hyde Park. In 1828 he began to design the Calverley Park estate at Tunbridge Wells, a congenial essay in the suburban Picturesque. He was also in great demand as an architect of country houses and plant-houses, including the Palm and Temperate Houses at Kew. He was also the architect for buildings in the Royal Botanic and Zoological Gardens in Regent's Park. He undoubtedly found such projects far more to his taste than the design of public buildings, for which he was also in high demand. He retired to live at St Leonard's-on-Sea in 1869 and died, unmarried, in 1881. Decimus Burton was a man of reliable and amiable character and one of the most successful and generally admired architects of the Regency and Victorian eras.

Bushell, Thomas (1594–1674). Gardener and inventor. Bushell had the good fortune to learn from Francis Bacon, to whom he acted as page, something of his master's cyclopaedic knowledge. This expertise enabled him to mine and speculate in minerals as well as to engage in other successful speculative ventures as varied as soap-making and minting. He also had a bizarre tendency to immure himself as a hermit on several islands, including those of Man and Wight.

In 1629 he went to live at Neat Enstone in Oxfordshire. There he made a garden of an extraordinary kind. In his book *The Natural History of Oxfordshire* (1677), Robert Plot wrote that Neat Enstone was 'a place of itself to take up a volume, for the naturalness thereof, and the art and industry that the ingenious owner hath added thereto, makes the same unparalleled.'

There was, for instance, next to a hill, a rock some twelve feet high. On turning a cock, a stream of water shot up beside this, bearing a silver ball. As the stream rose and fell, so did the ball, playing and tossing. And after it had reached its maximum height, instead of meekly descending, ball and all vanished behind the rock. And there was that well known continental feature, a

*Two views showing the exterior and interior of the waterworks at Neat Enstone, Oxfordshire, built to the designs of Thomas **Bushell** (1594–1674). The chief features of the waterworks are shown by numerals on the engraving of the exterior. Thus: (6) is 'a canopy of water cast over the rock by (7) an instrument of brass for that purpose'; whilst (8) is 'a column of water rising about 14 foot, designed to toss a ball'.*

hedge of water about a man's height. Sometimes, 'when fair ladies passed, they might be suddenly enclosed within it, the water flashing and dashing their smooth, soft and tender thighs.'

Above the rock was an artificial chamber, in which a man might stand dry though surrounded by sprays which, when the sun shone, would enclose him within rainbows.

Elsewhere there were pleasant walks, bordered with fruit trees or flowers and several 'curious pools and rare waters.'

While at Enstone Bushell did not 'encumber himself with a wife'. In fine weather he would spend the night walking round the garden with his servants.

The garden was visited by the King, Charles I, in 1636. He was received by Bushell disguised as a hermit, who spoke an address of welcome in extremely bad poetry which he had himself composed. The Queen in turn graciously presented him with an 'entire mummy from Egypt'.

---

*(Opposite) Stewartia Malacodendron (virginica), a plant of great beauty and rarity, the first species of a genus of shrubs named by Linnaeus to commemorate (though his name was mis-spelt) John Stuart, 3rd Earl of **Bute**. (Drawn with Carolina Pigeon, or Turtle Dove, by John Audubon, 1785–1851.)*

*John Stuart, 3rd Earl of **Bute** (1713–92), Prime Minister from 1762–63.*

Bute, John Stuart, 3rd Earl of (1713–1792). Landscape gardener, botanist, patron. Though generally known as a politician of considerable unpopularity—he was Prime Minister 1762–63—history shows Bute to have been of more lasting consequence as a patron of botany and horticulture. He is to be remembered, above all, for his intimate connexion with the inception of the internationally-famous Royal Botanic Gardens at Kew.

In 1730, the equally unpopular, but aesthetically discerning, Frederick Prince of Wales, leased Kew House and engaged William Kent to improve the gardens. In 1736, the Prince married Princess Augusta of Saxe Gotha, who was keenly interested in gardening. Following the death of the Prince in 1751, his close friend, Bute, became botanical adviser to the widowed Princess. Supported by her knowledgeable enthusiasm and with William Aiton as gardener and Sir William Chambers as architect, Bute was virtually the first director of Kew—the garden then covering about nine acres.

Bute had previously proved himself an amateur botanist of persistence and enthusiasm, and a patron of scientific botanical enquiry. He had spent the first nine years of his married life studying the natural history of the island of Bute, and was later concerned with supporting botanical publications of varying merit. These ranged from the £12,000 he spent on Philip Miller's useless *Botanical Tables*, of which only twelve copies were printed, to his help with William Curtis's invaluable *Flora Londinensis*.

Bute had his own botanical garden in the grounds of his house at Luton Hoo, Bedfordshire, and 'Capability' Brown landscaped the setting of his house at Highcliffe in Hampshire.

He is commemorated by the genus of shrubs named by Linnaeus *Stewartia*, the great naturalist misspelling the name, which, under botanical rules, cannot be corrected. The first species, *S. malacodendron* (*virginica*), a plant of exceptional beauty and rarity, was introduced to England from the south-eastern USA by Mark Catesby (qv) in about 1742.

Camelford, (Lord). Thomas Pitt. (1737–1793). Dilettante, landscape gardener. He was a nephew of William Pitt (qv), 1st Earl of Chatham, and spent much of his life as a Parliamentarian. After refusing the Leadership of the House of Commons in 1783 he was raised to the peerage in the following year.

He had a great interest in architecture and was accustomed and encouraged to advise friends and relatives on the design of their gardens. He was friendly with Horace Walpole and went to live at Twickenham in 1762. As an acknowledged authority on the gothic style, Camelford soon became a member of the Walpole coterie which expended much time and thought in discussion upon the nature of true gothic and the gradually-emerging complex of Strawberry Hill. As befitted a true amateur of his time, Camelford was also interested in landscape design, and among his known garden works were the Palladian-type bridge at Hagley (long destroyed) for his cousin, Lord Lyttelton (qv), and the Corinthian arch at Stowe. Both

these were designed in the seventeen-sixties. Camelford was also a friend of Mrs Delany (qv), the inventor of cut-out 'flower mosaics'.

Cameron, David (c. 1787–1848). Gardener and innovator. Cameron was a scientifically inclined botanist. He worked as gardener for Robert Barclay in his famous garden at Buryhill, Surrey. Among Barclay's enthusiasms was the introduction of new stove and greenhouse plants which were in Cameron's charge and some of which were described in *The Gardener's Magazine* in 1832. On his employer's death, Cameron became the first curator of the Birmingham Botanical and Horticultural Society's gardens at Edgbaston. J. C. Loudon had prepared imaginative plans for these gardens, but, owing to lack of funds, these were only partly carried out, much to Loudon's chagrin and expressed annoyance. ('We only regret that the committee have adopted our circuitous line of main walk—which, indeed, we staked out when on the spot—because we dislike exceedingly the idea of having our name

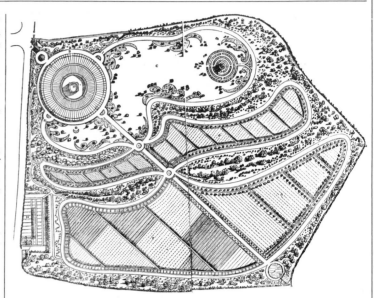

Projected plan by John Claudius Loudon for the Birmingham Botanical Horticultural Gardens, afterwards in the charge of David **Cameron**.

associated in any degree, however slight, with a garden which, though it might have been one of the most perfect in its kind existing anywhere, and altogether unique in some of its arrangements, is now bungled, and never likely to reflect credit on anyone connected with it.') Cameron wrote accounts of the planting and development of the garden which Loudon published in his magazine, at the same time praising Cameron's contribution to the gardens in warm terms. Cameron remained at the Edgbaston garden until he retired to Shrawley in Worcestershire.

Cane, Percy S. (1881–1976). Gardener and horticultural writer. Cane was born at Bocking Mill, Braintree, Essex, and was educated locally and then at Chelmsford School of Science and Art (now the Mid-Essex Technical College). In 1919 he enrolled in the School of Horticulture, later the East Anglian Institute of Agriculture, as well as studying architecture privately.

Subsequently he operated principally from London, editing and owning *My Garden Illustrated* and a quarterly magazine, *Garden Design* (1930–39).

Among the gardens which he designed are Dartington Hall, Totnes, for Mr and Mrs Leonard Elmhirst; Monteviot, Jedburgh, for the Marquis of Lothian; Hascombe Court, Godalming, for Sir John Jarvis; The King's House, Burhill, a gift to HM King George V by the Royal Warrant Holders in Commemoration of his silver jubilee; Hungerdown House, Wiltshire for Mr and Mrs Egbert Barnes; Falk-

Palladian Bridge at Hagley, Worcestershire, built for Lord George Lyttleton after designs by his nephew Thomas Pitt, later Lord **Camelford**, *shown in a watercolour by the Reverend Thomas Streatfield (1777–1848).*

land Palace, Fife, for Major Michael Crichton-Stuart; Rothesay, Isle of Bute, for Lord Colum Crichton-Stuart; Milton, Peterborough, for the Earl Fitzwilliam; The Imperial Palace, Addis Ababa, for HIM Hailie Selassie; Westfield, Oakley, for Mr and Mrs E F Davison; the garden for the British Pavilion, World's Fair, New York, 1939; Llanerch Park, North Wales, for Captain Piers Jones; for Mr and Mrs Clifford Curzon at the White House, Highgate, at Glenridding, Cumberland, and Litzelberg, Austria; plans for a formal garden at Woburn Abbey for the Duke of Bedford; Pilgrim's Cottage, Itchenor, for Mr and Mrs Leslie Goldsmith.

For his exhibits of gardens at the Chelsea show, the Royal Horticultural Society awarded Cane eight gold and three silver-gilt medals; a Coronation cup in 1937 and a silver cup in 1939. In 1963 he was awarded the Society's Veitch Memorial medal in gold for his work as a garden designer and landscape architect.

His principal publications have included *Modern Gardens: British and Foreign* (1926–7) covering British, American, European and Japanese gardens, freely illustrated; *Garden Design for Today* (1934); *The Earth is my Canvas* (1956) and *The Creative Art of Garden Design* (1967).

Capel, (Sir) Henry, Baron Capel of Tewkesbury (d. 1696). Gardener. Capel had a garden at Kew which, although of no great size, was visited by most of his contemporaries interested in horticulture. A number of his visitors recorded impressions and descriptions of the garden, particularly of the plants that he grew. John Evelyn wrote that Capel had the best fruit in England, also imported new varieties from France,

Percy Stephen **Cane** *(1881–1976) and (right) illustration from* The Creative Art of Garden Design *by Cane.*

and was extremely knowledgeable concerning their management. By 1683 Capel had constructed two greenhouses for oranges and myrtles; their novelty caused considerable interest because they connected directly with the rooms of the house. A form of summer-house—or, as he termed it, a cupola—built between two elms at the termination of a walk, delighted Evelyn who, however, objected to the large number of firs (*Abies alba*) Capel had planted. A later account suggests that they were grown to protect Capel's orange trees from winter cold and summer scorching.

The wide variety of 'curious greens' in Capel's garden was also noteworthy, for at that time the number of evergreens available in England was limited. Among them he had the finest mastic trees (*Pistacia lentiscus*) in the country. These

strange mastic-producing shrubs had only been introduced in 1664. Capel paid Vesprit, the London nurseryman, £40 for them. Four white-striped hollies attracted attention and the flower-bosses in winter on his laurustinus shrubs were greatly admired. The yew hedges were also something of a novelty, for clipped yew was a recent introduction. They were evenly trimmed, but at regular intervals one was allowed to grow tall and kept 'in a pretty shape with tonsure.'

Henry's elder brother, Arthur, Earl of Essex, had a garden on a much grander scale at Cassiobury.

Carew, (Sir) Francis (c. 1530–1611). Gardener. Carew, of Beddington in Surrey, had one of the most original gardens during the Elizabethan era and was noted for his importation of plants from abroad. He is often

credited with being the first gardener to grow the orange in England, a claim put forward for him both by John Aubrey and John Evelyn, the latter having seen the trees in 1658, when, he tells us, they were planted in the open ground covered with a wooden 'tabernacle' heated by a stove in the winter. A letter written by Lord Burghley, however, to Sir Thomas Windebank in Paris about a joint order with Carew states that he does not, unlike Carew, want an orange as he already has one, thus suggesting that these claims on Carew's behalf were perhaps overstated.

Sir Hugh Platt (1552–1608) described Carew's triumph in front of his queen. This was in the nature of a successful scientific experiment. In August, 1599, the Queen visited Beddington and Carew picked for her, doubtless to royal amazement,

(Left) Pistacia lentiscus, *or the mastic tree, of which Sir Henry* **Capel** *had the finest examples in the country at his garden in Kew. (Right) Sir Henry Capel and his family, with a glimpse of their formal garden seen in the background of the painting.*

freshly ripened specimens of that then much-admired fruit, the cherry. He had skilfully kept the tree retarded by covering it with canvas which had been kept continually sprayed wth cold water.

Carlisle, Charles Howard, 3rd Earl of (1669–1738). Carlisle appears in this DICTIONARY, as do several others, more as a *deus ex machina* than an active gardener. Carlisle engaged George London (qv) to design the garden for Castle Howard, the house which Vanbrugh had built for Carlisle. In *Ichnographia Rustica* (1718), Stephen Switzer (qv) records, 'In Wray Wood where Mr London design'd a star, which would have spoil'd the wood, but that his Lordships superlative genius prevented it and to the great advancement of the design has given it that labyrinth-diverting model we now see it; and it is at this time a proverb at that place, York against London, in allusion to the design of a Londoner and Mr London the designer'.

There is now no trace of this labyrinth, which must have been amongst the first of the influences which ended the domination of France and the school of Le Nôtre with its rigidly geometric designs. Apart from these innovations, Carlisle's support during the following years of the two geniuses, Sir John Vanbrugh and Nicholas Hawksmoor, was of great significance in the history of landscape design

Catesby, Mark (1682–1749). Plant-collector. Catesby was born at Sudbury in Suffolk. His interest in natural history was encouraged by John Ray, the author of *Historia Plantarum* (1686–1704), who lived in the neighbouring county of Essex. Left with a modest income at the age of twenty-three, Catesby visited his married sister in Virginia in 1712. Though then not primarily concerned with plant collecting, he sent seeds to Bishop Compton (qv) at Fulham Palace and to Thomas Fairchild (qv), of Hoxton, who was a close friend, as well as to Samuel Dale, apothecary and physician of Braintree.

In 1714 Catesby sailed in a cargo vessel to Jamaica, whence he sent further specimens. In 1719 he returned to England with some reputation as an authority on North American natural history and with a considerable collection of notes and drawings.

As a consequence, Catesby was supported and financed by a syndicate to undertake a further collecting trip to America. He arrived at Charleston in 1722 and, in spite of

(Opposite) Plates drawn and engraved by Mark **Catesby** *for his edition of* The Natural History of Carolina, *published between 1730 and 1747.*

Views of the landscaped park of Castle Howard, Yorkshire, originally planned at the behest of the 3rd Earl of **Carlisle**. *The pictures show (top) the Mausoleum designed by Nicholas Hawksmoor (1729–36) and (below left) the view from the Temple of the Four Winds. (Below right) Portrait of the 3rd Earl of Carlisle.*

many difficulties, including the problems of obtaining suitable containers and packing materials in so sparsely inhabited and uncivilized a place, and his own ill-health, he travelled over a wide area collecting and observing. Unfortunately, his detailed itinerary is not known. Afterwards, needing fresh territory in which to work, he journeyed to the Bahamas in 1725, returning to England in the following year.

During his travels he was not only interested in natural history but in the less academic and more felicitous aspects of gardening, distributing plants from Britain to his friends in America. Although he was concerned largely with plant-collecting

while he was in America, he was also a knowledgeable naturalist, covering a wide field, making notes on, and sketches of, many subjects.

After his return to England he spent a major part of the rest of his life working on *The Natural History of Carolina, Georgia, Florida and the Bahama Isles* (1730–47). Apart from drawing the magnificent plates, mostly combining birds and plants, he also engraved the plates after learning that the expense of engaging professionals for this process was beyond his means. He also supervised the superb hand-colouring after printing.

Apart from this notable work he published in 1767, *Hortus Europæ*

Engraving of the Dahoon Holly from A Collection of 85 Curious Trees and Shrubs, the Produce of North America *(1767), by Mark* **Catesby**.

Dogwood Tree from Collection of . . .
Trees and Shrubs *by Mark* **Catesby**.

Americanus or a Collection of 85 Curious Trees and Shrubs, the Produce of North America adapted to The Climates and Soils of Great Britain, Ireland and most Parts of Europe, etc, engraving the copper plates himself.

Many of the plants he introduced were propagated by the nurserymen Thomas Fairchild and Christopher Gray. Curiously, he introduced some American wild plants, now well known, which he discovered in the gardens of his American friends who were unaware of their existence. His most noteworthy introduction was the extremely rare *Stewartia malacodendron.*

Cattley, William (d. 1832). Gardener. Cattley lived at Barnet, Hertfordshire, where he had a notable garden and was one of the first gardeners to make a collection of tropical orchids. William Cattley was a man of substance and was an early patron of the young John Lindley (qv) when he was no more than a clerk at the Horticultural Society's Garden at Chiswick. In 1819, Cattley was one of those who helped to finance the purchase of the Society's first premises, contributing £200.

In 1823, the Society's collector, John Forbes, died whilst making his way up the Zambesi, but he had already collected a number of plants in Brazil, including an orchid which Lindley named *Cattleya.* This, the first of a new genus, later became widely popular, as well as taking a memorable place in the novels of Proust. From the introduction of *Cattleya* were bred many new varieties, and it is now one of the most famous forms of orchid in cultivation. Cattley was also a distinguished botanist in his own right, and made a very fine collection of plant drawings.

Chambers, (Sir) William (1726–96). Landscape architect. Although Chambers is known chiefly as an outstanding architect in the classical style, as the author of the magisterial and influential *Treatise on Civil Architecture,* and as designer of Somerset House, he must also rank high in any history of English landscape architecture on account of his

HORTUS EUROPÆ AMERICANUS:

OR, A

Collection of 85 Curious Trees and Shrubs,

The Produce of NORTH AMERICA;

ADAPTED TO

The CLIMATES and SOILS of GREAT-BRITAIN,
IRELAND, and most Parts of EUROPE, &c.

TOGETHER WITH

Their BLOSSOMS, FRUITS and SEEDS;

OBSERVATIONS on their CULTURE, GROWTH, CONSTITUTION and VIRTUES.

WITH

DIRECTIONS how to COLLECT, PACK UP, and SECURE them in their PASSAGE.

Adorn'd with 63 FIGURES on 17 COPPER-PLATES, large IMPERIAL Quarto.

By MARK CATESBY, F.R.S.

LONDON:
Printed for J. MILLAN, near Whitehall. M DCC LXVII. Price colour'd 1L : 11s. 6d.

The title-page from A Collection of 85 Curious Trees and Shrubs, the Produce of North America, *by Mark* **Catesby**, *published in 1767.*

achievements at Kew.

Chambers was born of Scottish parents in Gothenburg, Sweden. The family had long been involved in the Swedish mercantile trade. Although he was educated at Ripon in Yorkshire, Chambers returned to Sweden to become an administrative officer with the Swedish East India Company, and in that capacity took part in the company's Far Eastern trading voyages.

Being strongly inclined towards architecture, he spent much time studying Chinese buildings and gardens, and whilst still in his twenties

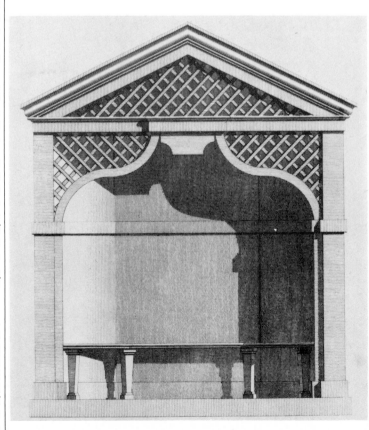

Garden seat designed by Sir William **Chambers** *for the gardens at Kew.*

had gained some renown in Sweden for his expertise in oriental subjects.

By 1749 he was possessed of sufficient funds to be able to set himself up in London, afterwards enrolling as a student at the Ecole des Arts in Paris, then the leading architectural school in Europe. Back in London, an introduction by the Earl of Bute led to Chambers becoming architectural tutor to the Prince of Wales, and later architectural adviser to his widow, the Princess Augusta. For her, he designed, between 1757 and 1763, the ornamental buildings in Kew garden, his first commission of consequence.

Horace Walpole, in one of his more dyspeptic moods, was airily disparaging of Chambers' efforts at Kew, writing, in 1760, that 'there is little invention or taste shown. Being on a flat, Lord Bute raised hillocs to diversify the ground and carried Chambers the architect thither, who built some temples, but they are all of wood and very small. Of his design was the round temple in the middle, with a circular portico, called the Temple of Victory on the battle of Minden; another with a Doric portico; the Corinthian semi-circular arcade, a little round temple in the recess on the left hand, the Roman ruin, an aviary, and a Chinese building in the menagerie. The bridge and the round temple were each erected overnight to surprise the Princess.'

In 1761, Chambers designed the largest stove-house then known, an interesting technical achievement and in sharp contrast to his classical temples and retreats.

Of the other buildings designed by Chambers at Kew, the most impressive is undoubtedly the Chinese pagoda, 163 feet high, set at the heart of several vistas. This exotic structure originally had dragons dangling from its ascending eaves, and despite its apparent lightness and gaiety was well built, its solidity being tested during the war when it withstood the blast effects of German bombs that fell nearby.

Of other buildings at Kew designed by the architect, there remain the temple of Bellona with its Doric columns; the severely simple, classical temple of Aeolus on its 'hilloc' not far from the Cumberland Gate; the Roman arch, no longer spanning its road; and the orangery, now a museum, one of Chambers' masterpieces.

Chambers' further claim to a place in garden history was established by the publication of his fantasia, entitled *A Dissertation on Oriental Gardening,* in 1772. This book, by the 'Comptroller General of His Majesty's Works' (with a most inappropriate engraving of a classical allegory by Cipriani on the title page) was widely influential, particularly as the author had published, in 1775, *Designs of Chinese*

Engraving showing the lake, island, orangery, the temples of Aeolus and Bellona, etc, from the Gardens and Buildings at Kew *(1763) by Sir William* **Chambers**.

Sir William **Chambers** *(detail) by Francis Cotes (1764) and (right) the aviary and flower garden at Kew from an engraving in Chambers'* Gardens and Buildings at Kew.

Buildings, an authoritative study based on his earlier visits to the Far East and which had a considerable influence on the developing cult of Chinoiserie in Britain and also in France. The *Dissertation*, however, was written so that Chambers could give publicity to his personal views of gardening, by foisting them on to the innocent Chinese, and thereby indulge his venom towards 'Capability' Brown, who had been preferred by Lord Clive for the design of Claremont in Surrey—to Chambers' chagrin. Although written with this dubious intention, the book is interesting and has proved curiously prophetic in several of its claims and assertions.

Chambers' innuendoes directed at the homespun Brown are subtle, sophisticated and spiteful as, for example, this comment:

'Amongst the Chinese . . . their gardeners are not only botanists, but also painters and philosophers, having a thorough knowledge of the human kind, and of the arts by which its strongest feelings are excited. It is not in China, as in Italy and France, where every petty architect is a gardener . . . In China, gardening is a distinct profession, requiring an extensive study; to the perfection of which few arrive.' Further reference to the fact that the Chinese never situate roads at the foot of rising ground without contriving drains to receive the waters was probably another quip at 'Capability' Brown's expense, no doubt pointing to some technical shortcoming on Brown's part and clear enough to the *cognoscenti* of the time.

In the context of Walpole's precepts, reinforced by Brown's practice, that landscape scenes should not be differentiated from nature itself, it is amusing to read the pseudo-Sino-Chambers view that 'the scenery of a garden should differ as much from common nature as an heroic poem doth from a prose relation; and gardeners, like poets, should give a loose to their imagination, and even fly beyond the bounds of truth, whenever it is necessary to elevate . . . to enliven, or to add novelty to their subject'.

Chambers was equally dismissive of Brown's tendency to make his gardens tree-and-shrub-studded versions of the open countryside: 'Such is the favourite plan of our smaller gardens; and our larger works are only repetition of our small ones; more green fields, more shrubberies, more serpentine walks, and more seats; like the honest batchelor's seat, which consisted in nothing but a multiplication of his own dinner; three legs of mutton and turneps, three roasted geese and three buttered apple-pies.

'As yet our many handbooks on how to make gardens have not advised us to have among thickets many secret recesses, in each of which is an elegant pavilion, consisting of one state apartment, with outhouses, with proper conveniences for women servants. These are inhabited, during the summer, by their fairest and most accomplished concubines.'

Another notion which Chambers so blandly foisted on the innocent Chinese was that by skilfully camouflaging of their ancient industrial enterprises they added to the awesome sublimity of their landscapes. They concealed, he asserted, 'in cavities on the summits of the highest mountains, founderies, lime-kilns, and glass-works, which send forth large volumes of flame, and continued columns of thick smoke, that give to these mountains the appearance of volcanoes'. He also tells of strong wire fences, painted green, only too accurately anticipating the plastic-covered wire-work of modern suburbia.

Needless to say, in the interesting lists he provides in the *Dissertation* concerning plants chosen and grown in China, many were completely unknown in that country. To the propagandist truth has always been a relative and subsidiary quality.

The book, one of the more imaginative fantasies on the possibilities of garden-making, was, nevertheless, taken seriously enough by numerous so-called authorities, then and later; and it has been suggested that some of the ideas adumbrated in the book were taken up by Gertrude Jekyll (qv).

That any well-read person of the time failed to see that Chambers' Orient was a masterly tongue-in-the-cheek send-up of current ideas and an imaginative *tour de force*, is difficult to believe, for in 1765 J. Dodsley had published *A Particular account of the Emperor of China's*

Engraving showing the Menagerie and Pavilion at Kew, from Gardens and Buildings at Kew *by Sir William* **Chambers** *(1763).*

View of the south side of the ruins at Kew, from Gardens and Buildings at Kew *by Sir William* **Chambers** *(1763).*

Gardens near Peking: in a letter from F. Attiret, a French Missionary, now employed by that Emperor to paint the Apartments of those gardens, to his friend at Paris. The translation of the letter, written in 1743, was by 'Sir Harry Beaumont, the Rev. Joseph Spence'.

But Chambers, well-known for his earthy humour, took his joke to its audacious limit by quoting from that same book.

Chambers' knighthood—of the Polar Star—was a Swedish, not an English honour, although he was allowed to use the title in this country. (He was knighted by the King in 1770.) John Harris, his biographer (1970), has succinctly summed up the personality of this paradoxical man. 'He was respected by the *beau monde* but was never of it; was a friend of blue stockings, writers and artists, yet his shadow barely darkens their memoirs; he is the father of his profession in the modern sense, yet long remained unacknowledged; and he gave fêtes and dances at his great Palladian house at Twickenham where he lived a grandee's life, yet such events have passed from social memory . . . In dealing with his craftsmen, his army of men, Chambers is the champion of the underdog. In all his correspondence his transparency shines forth. Such men were rare.'

Although he held various official sinecures and was the first Surveyor-General and Comptroller (1782) and built up a considerable private practice, Chambers gradually retired from public duties. Sir William Chambers was buried in Westminster Abbey.

Chandler, Alfred (1804–1896). Hybridist and artist. Chandler was the 'Son' in Chandler and Son (originally Napier and Chandler, then Chandler and Buckingham), nurserymen of Vauxhall. They specialized in camellias, chrysanthemums and hollies, particularly the first, of which they raised a number of hybrids. Alfred Chandler was a talented artist and became known through his depiction of Veitch's orchids, although he achieved renown as a painter of camellias.

In 1825 was published *Camellia Britannica*, with text by E. B. Buckingham, describing hybrids produced by the firm in 1819, and lithographs of high quality by Chandler. In 1831 came his forty-four plates for *Illustrations and Descriptions . . . of Camelliae* with a text by William Beattie Booth (qv).

In the mid-nineteenth century a visit to Chandler's Vauxhall ground in the camellia season was a fashionable jaunt, but Chandler lived to see his beloved flower disregarded.

Charlotte Sophia (Queen), Princess of Mecklenberg-Strelitz (1744–1818). Patroness of botany and horticulture. Princess Charlotte married George III in 1761. She was closely connected with what are now the Royal Botanic Gardens at Kew when she was granted Richmond Lodge, and later while the royal family lived at Kew House, demolished in 1802, when their majesties moved to Kew Palace. A souvenir of this period is the rustic cottage set in The Wilderness, said to have been

The rustic cottage set in the Wilderness at Kew, commissioned, according to legend, by Queen **Charlotte** *in 1772.*

built by the queen in about 1772 and decorated with a series of fine prints, some of a comic nature.

She was frequently visited by the Rev. John Lightfoot (1735–88) who discoursed to her on the principles of botany. His herbarium was subsequently bought for the Queen by the King at a cost of one hundred guineas.

An interesting, if misguided, example of her patronage was the support she gave to the unfortunate plant-collector, John Fraser, in his attempt to establish the manufacture of hats 'all in one piece without sewing' that was carried out in Cuba from a silver-leaved palm which he had discovered in that island.

Queen Charlotte was particularly interested in the cultivation of apples and her name is mentioned by pomologists of her time, particularly in connexion with the introduction into England of an Old German variety known as Borsdorfer. Indeed, legend has it that the dish Apple Charlotte commemorates the Queen. There is no doubt, however, that the genus *Strelitzia*, the Bird of Paradise flower from South Africa, honours her name, the famous species *Strelitzia reginae* being introduced to Kew in 1773.

Portrait of Queen **Charlotte** *(1744–1818) from Allan Ramsay's studio, c. 1762.*

Frederich **Chittenden** *(1873–1950).*

Chittenden, Frederick James, OBE (1873–1950). Horticulturalist and lexicographer. Chittenden was born at West Ham and much of his early life was spent at and botanizing in Epping Forest. In 1900, after a spell as schoolmaster he was appointed as lecturer in biology in the Essex County Council's East Anglian School of Horticulture at Chelmsford. His subjects were horticulture and bacteriology. Two years later he was appointed a member of the Royal Horticultural Society's Scientific Committee, and in 1904 became the Committee's secretary, a position he retained until his death. In 1907 he was appointed director of the Society's first laboratory which was built at Wisley, and also head of

the School of Horticulture. In 1908 he took over the editorship of the Society's *Journal*. In 1919 he accepted the directorship of the gardens at Wisley, then at an important stage of development, and was a guiding force in the training and examination of students for the National Diploma of Horticulture. In 1950 he was awarded the OBE for these activities.

From early days he had initiated experiments in solving a number of seemingly intractable horticultural problems, such as pollination in orchards and eelworm in daffodils. With the help of his staff at Wisley, several of these problems were

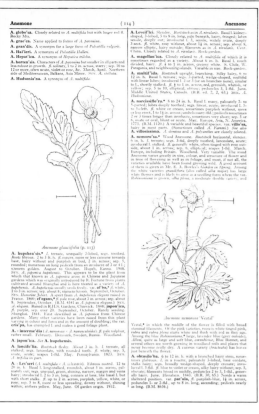

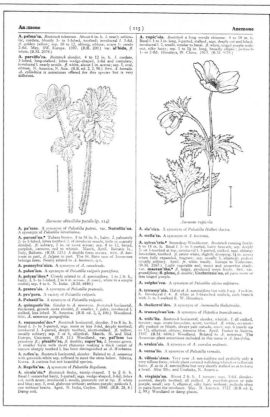

Herbert Francis **Clark** *(1902–71).*

Typical pages from the Royal Horticultural Society's Dictionary of Gardening *edited by Frederich James* **Chittenden.**

solved. He was also an authority on botanical nomenclature, and represented the Society in conferences at New York, Berlin, Vienna and Cambridge. The first edition of the invaluable *Some Good Garden Plants* in 1929 was his work.

In 1931 he left Wisley, becoming the Society's technical adviser, editor of its publications and keeper of the Lindley Library. During this period he became even more widely known to the Fellows, from beginners to experts. He answered their queries with care and consideration; and, as one distinguished gardener said, he had the rare quality of frankly admitting ignorance.

From 1939 he devoted himself to preparing the Royal Horticultural Society's magisterial four-volume *Dictionary of Gardening*, 'a practical and scientific encyclopaedia of horticulture'. Working from his home at Dedham in Essex, coping with wartime difficulties, Chittenden nevertheless delivered 'the first batch of manuscript' to the Clarendon Press, Oxford in December 1945. Unhappily, he died before the completion of the project. Nothing comparable had been published since George Nicholson's massive *Dictionary of Gardening* in 1884–8.

Chittenden was awarded the RHS Victoria Medal of Honour in 1917 as a notable servant of horticulture and the Society in almost every single capacity. In 1947 he was awarded the Veitchian Gold Medal for his outstanding service to horticultural education and literature.

Christian, John (fl. 1724). Gardener. Christian represents those countless forgotten, yet vitally important, gardeners largely responsible for the continuity of the native genius for garden design. In the grass around the ruins of Sutton Scarsdale, Derbyshire, was found a lead plate on which was inscribed: 'This house was begun to be rebuilt in the year 1724 by the Right Honourable Nicholas, Earl of Scarsdale.' The plate includes Christian's name and describes him as 'gentleman gardener'. Apart from this, his achievements are unrecorded—and precisely what position a 'gentleman gardener' held in the aristocratic household remains obscure.

Clark, Herbert Francis (1902–1971). Horticulturalist, teacher, writer. Clark has been aptly described as one of the 'best liked, most distinctive and influential figures in the world of landscape design and history—a practitioner, writer and impresario of the art'.

He was born in Manila in the Philippines, was educated at Marlborough College and briefly at Cambridge. He returned to Manila, but finding life there uncongenial, returned to England for a brief period and then spent seven years in America doing a variety of jobs. Returning once more to England he articled himself to Percy Cane, there meeting another of Cane's pupils, Christopher Tunnard. The two adopted a radical outlook on garden design, which was expressed in Tunnard's book, *Gardens in the Modern Landscape* (1938) to which Clark gave some assistance.

During the war Clark was a full-time Civil Defence rescue worker. Between long shifts he read widely in the British Museum, studies which led to the publication in 1948 of *The English Landscape Garden*. That work, together with the prominent part he played in the Institute of Landscape Architects, from the early nineteen-thirties, attracted him to teaching.

In 1947 he was appointed consultant landscape architect to Stevenage New Town, and in 1951 consultant landscape architect to the Festival of Britain, South Bank site. In 1947, too, he had begun teaching at Reading University and at the University of Liverpool's Department of Civic Design.

The old Fish Pond at Heslington Hall, York University, transformed by the landscape designs of Herbert Francis **Clark.**

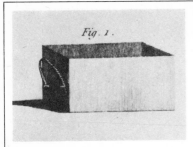
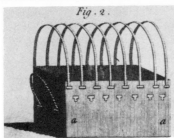
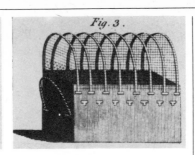

Typical plant containers carried by eighteenth-century botanists and plant-collectors, such as Captain Clerke.

Walcot House, Shropshire, designed by Sir William Chambers, c. 1764, for Edward Clive, a noted tree-cultivator.

Clark was not a man possessed of great self-confidence and despite his successes at the Festival and the subsequent possibility of being Director of the London County Council Parks Department, he went back to the much less remunerative appointment of part-time lecturer at the University of Reading where he ran the three-year diploma course in landscape architecture. The intake was seldom more than a handful of students each year. He taught there three days a week, was consultant at Stevenage for one day, taught at the Institute of Park Administration on another, and from his homes at Woodley and Pyrton, Oxfordshire, ran a small, private practice. In addition he wrote for various journals and gave much of his time to the Institute's affairs. He left Reading on the closure there of his classes and in 1960 was appointed senior lecturer at the University of Edinburgh and president of the Institute of Landscape Architects. He was president of the Garden History Society from its inception in 1965 until his death.

Many of the landscape architects working in Britain today were taught by Clark and by that means rather than by practice he achieved his greatest influence. Whilst he was loyal to the professional attention to detail which Cane had so impressed upon him, and deeply conscious that he was training people to enter a profession, the standards of which he was so concerned to establish and

maintain, he was by nature a reluctant spokesman for orthodoxy. He far preferred seminars to lectures, for by that method he could discuss and enquire rather than proclaim. His stated opposition to the tenets of 'Capability' Brown was not particular to the landscape garden; he was, in all things, opposed to stereotype and imposition. His never-failing interest in Alberti, Shenstone and Burle Marx is consistent with that philosophy. Their common denominator, for Clark, resided in their essential humanism.

In his practice, as much as in his teaching, Clark sought for a landscape form which would express his own time, seeking a link between contemporary painting and landscape which would sponsor an effect comparable to the precedents of the eighteenth-century English landscape garden.

Clarke, John (fl. 1761). Arborologist. Although Clarke was a butcher at Barnes, he conceived the idea that he could raise cedars of Lebanon (which tree had been introduced in about 1659) from a fine specimen at Hendon Place. He was so successful in his enterprise that within a comparatively short time he was supplying seedlings to nurserymen and many noblemen. In 1761 he was paid £79 6s for a thousand five-year-old trees that the Duke of Richmond had planted in the spring of that year at Goodwood. Later he successfully raised magnolias and other exotics,

some of which no doubt were added to the famous collection of trees made by the Duke, which still flourish at Goodwood.

Cleeve, (Reverend) Alexander (1747–1805). Cleeve was of Scottish origin and was educated at Eton and Queen's College, Oxford, matriculating from the university at sixteen. Following ordination at Cambridge he was appointed in 1780 as vicar of Wooler, a parish in Northumberland, an incumbency he held until his death, despite the fact that he officiated there for barely a year. In 1781 he let the tithes of the parish to a farmer and moved to Edinburgh, where he stayed for almost twenty years. Then, in his early fifties, he removed to London to become chaplain to the Duke of Portland (later Prime Minister) and lecturer at Trinity Chapel, Knightsbridge. Though he apparently had no outstanding connexion with horticulture, he became associated with the inception of what was then the Horticultural Society of London, later the Royal Horticultural Society, and at the inaugural meeting in 1804 was, somewhat fortuitously, elected the first of the now long line of secretaries. His election seems to have been due to a strong prejudice against the first nominee, James Anderson, voiced by John Wedgwood (qv), founder of the Society. As a result, Anderson's name was not proposed.

Cleeve's tenure of office was,

however, of brief duration. In April 1805 Sir Joseph Banks reported that 'the thanks of the Society be given to the Reverend A. Cleeve for his useful labours as Secretary, that the council be desired to allow him such remuneration as they shall think sufficient; and that he be entitled to attend all the Meetings of the Society in future.'

Clerke, (Captain) Charles (RN) (1741–1779). Navigator. Clerke is included in this DICTIONARY as Captain of the *Discovery*, sister ship to Captain Cook's *Resolution* in the latter's third and last voyage in 1777 to the tropical South Seas and to the Alaskan coast, seeking the possibility of a northern passage between the Pacific and Atlantic. Amongst Clerke's crew was David Nelson (qv), recommended to Sir Joseph Banks (qv) by James Lee (qv) of the Vineyard Nurseries, Hammersmith, as 'a proper person' for the collection of botanical specimens during the voyage.

Clerke took over command of the *Resolution* after Cook was murdered in Hawaii during the tragic and eventful voyaging of the two ships. Nelson had assembled a considerable and valuable collection of plants, known and unknown, from the South Seas to the farthest North. These were lost. Clerke died on board the *Discovery* on August 22nd 1779 during the return voyage.

Clive, Edward (1754–1839). Gardener. He was the son of 'Clive of India' and from him inherited the Irish barony of Clive in 1774, as well as a love of tree-planting. In 1794 he was created Baron Clive of Walcot (in Shropshire, where the house still stands among many fine trees). In 1804 he was made Earl of Powis after ceasing to be Governor of Madras. He was an ardent gardener and tree-planter. At the end of the eighteenth century he is recorded as having planted two thousand seedlings of the Arolla pine, *Pinus cembra*, he had raised at Walcot. Here, too, he also grew the rare exotic *Furcraea*. A visitor recalled seeing the Earl digging in the garden in his shirt sleeves at six o'clock in the morning in his eightieth year.

Coats, Alice (1905–1978). Gardener, horticultural writer and artist. Miss Coats was born in Handsworth, Birmingham. Her parents were Scottish, her father a Baptist minister and later a Worker's Educational Association lecturer in English literature. She was given her first plot of garden at the age of four and, by a series of territorial

*(Opposite) Camellias drawn by Alfred **Chandler** (1804–96) and reproduced in Camellia Britannica (1825), with text by E. B. Buckingham.*

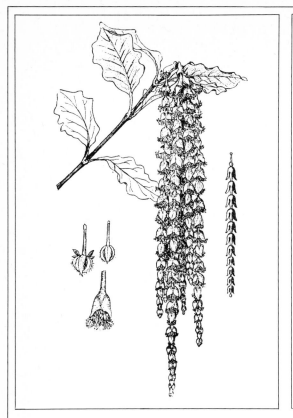

Garrya elliptica *and (right)* Lilac (Syringa vulgaris), *both illustrated in* Garden Shrubs and their histories *by Alice* **Coats.**

encroachments, had taken over her parents' garden by the time she left school. She was educated at the Edgbaston High School for Girls; the Birmingham College of Art; the Slade School, London; and in Paris. As a graphic artist she was at first mainly interested in landscapes, working in various mediums from murals to wood-engraving. She also illustrated children's books, among them *The Story of Horace* (1938), and *The Travels of Maurice* (1939).

During the war she worked in the Women's Land Army, mainly con-

cerned with vegetable and fruit cultivation. After the war, she resumed painting but decided that the interruption of the war had occasioned too sharp a setback to her technical skills. In 1950 she began what became her major interest: a succession of books which reached a wide public. In 1956 she published *Flowers and Their Histories* (new and enlarged edition, 1968) followed by *Garden Shrubs and Their Histories* (1963) and *The Quest for Plants* (1969). All were notable for precise scholarship and wit, particularly the

last. She also contributed articles to *The Gardeners' Chronicle*, *Popular Gardening*, the *Journal of The Royal Horticultural Society*. She was a member of most of the specialist garden societies and though for many years severely handicapped by arthritis, she also successfully cultivated many rare and interesting plants.

Coats, Peter (1910–   ). Garden designer, horticultural writer, photographer, gardening editor of *House & Garden*.

Coats' first garden was a yard-square patch in the grounds of the Scottish castle where he grew up and where his family—founders of the world-famous Paisley cotton firm—lived in Ayrshire. With four elder brothers, there was no place for him in the family business and, after leaving Eton, he decided to go into advertising.

In the 1939–45 war he served in the Middle East and India, being appointed ADC to Lord Wavell, later becoming Comptroller of the Household. Whilst in India, Coats was concerned with the 'Mogul garden' at New Delhi, designed by Sir Edwin Lutyens. There he ploughed up a golf-course to grow vegetables for the hospitals, in which activity he was fancifully described by Harold Nicolson as 'resplendent in a white and gold uniform, directing, with the wave of a trowel, the stupendous creation, stepping gingerly among the cannas and the orioles. Never since the days of Zenophon has a soldier, and an aide-de-camp to boot, been so precise and efficient a gardener.'

Post-war, he began the career on which his present horticultural reputation is founded. This includes the books *Roses* (1962), *Great Gardens of Britain* (1963), *Flowers in History* (1970) and *Garden Decoration* (1970) and his autobiography *Of Generals and Gardens*, and most recently, *The Gardens of Buckingham Palace*(1978) and an *A–Z of Plants* (1979). Authorship, combined with a passion for photographic reportage, has taken him on world-wide travels. He has lectured on his favourite subject on both sides of the Atlantic and in Australia.

During recent years he has

Alice **Coats** *(1905–1978), gardening author and artist.*

Pool pavilion showing light-hearted Indian influences, designed by Peter **Coats** *and Hugh Robson for Mr and Mrs Julian Wellesley at Tidebrook Manor, Kent. (One of the minarets houses the heating-system chimney.)*

*Peter **Coats** photographed with Chinoiserie-motif garden furniture, made to his own designs and (right) his design for a tree seat.*

increasingly specialized in garden design, and his practice now takes him to many large estates throughout Europe. He contends, however, that he derives equal satisfaction from designing small as well as large gardens.

Although he has planned gardens for tycoons and stately homes, he has also designed gardens for many young couples with simple backyards and simpler budgets. He has advised on a garden of scented plants for the blind, and designed garden buildings and furniture, some in the Chinese Chippendale manner.

Cobbett, William (1762–1835). Gardener, propagandist. The celebrated journalist, traveller, sociologist and politician wrote, in his usual lively and well-informed style, on various aspects of horticulture, which he also practised at his home in Hampshire from 1804 until 1817 and later in Surrey. He became early acquainted with the countryside and with gardening generally, for he was born at Farnham in Surrey, the son of a farmer, and worked in the fields as a boy.

William Cobbett then worked for a short time in Kew Gardens before taking up employment in a solicitor's office, afterwards enlisting in the Army serving in Nova Scotia. In 1791, on gaining his discharge from the army, he sought to bring action against his erstwhile officers for fraud and peculation but, on failing to gain the support of necessary witnesses, fled to France. This was the first of several encounters with the legal Establishment. In 1817 Cobbett shipped to the United States where he wrote and farmed, before returning to England in 1819. In 1821 he published *The American Gardener*, based on his experiences in that country, followed in 1829 by *The English Gardener*, although his most widely-read and still-renowned work, *Rural Rides*, dealing with his travels in southern England, had been published in journalistic form between 1820 and 1830 in the *Register*, which he had started himself in 1816.

Among his horticultural enthusiasms was the desirability of planting *Robinia pseudoacacia* (which had been introduced here in the early seventeenth century) on account of its quick growth, allegedly providing valuable timber (which is, in fact, of no great value at all). Cobbett popularized the tree under its American name Locust, then virtually unknown in Britain. Cobbett raised large quantities from seed as well as buying nurserymen's stock and re-labelling them. He sold over a million plants.

William Cobbett wrote of the potato that there appeared to be nothing unwholesome about it and of the horse-radish, 'as a weed I know nothing so pertinacious and pernicious as this', adding that a square rod of it will 'produce enough for a family that eats roast beef every day of their lives.' And, 'for my part, as a thing to keep and not to sell; as a thing, the possession of which is to give me pleasure, I hesitate not a moment to prefer the plant of a fine carnation to a gold watch set with diamonds.'

His *Rural Rides* abound in keen

*William **Cobbett** (1762–1835), gardener, politician and sociologist.*

*William **Cobbett** on his Rural Rides. Decoration by John Nash, RA, for an edition, edited by G. D. H. and M. Cole, published by Peter Davies in 1930.*

71

2

observations, succinctly expressed. For example:

'In coming from Wotton-Basset to Highworth, I left Swindon a few miles away to my left, and came by the village of Blunsdon. All along here I saw great quantities of hops in the hedges, and very fine hops, and I saw at a village called Stratton, I think it was, the first Campanula that I ever saw in my life. The main stalk was more than four feet high, and there were four stalks, none of which was less than three feet high. All through the country, poor, as well as rich, are very neat in their gardens, and very careful to raise a great variety of flowers. At Blunsdon I saw a clump, or, rather a sort of orchard, of as fine walnut-trees as I ever beheld, and loaded with walnuts. Indeed I have seen great crops of walnuts all the way from London.'

Again, when passing through Bollitree in Worcestershire:

'As I came along I saw one of the prettiest sights in the flower way that I ever saw in my life. It was a little orchard; the grass in it had just taken a start, and was beautifully fresh; and, very thickly growing amongst the grass, was the purple flowered *Colchicum*, in full bloom. They say, that the leaves of this plant which come out in the spring and die away in the summer, are poisonous to cattle if they eat much of them in the spring. The flower if standing by itself would be no great beauty; but, contrasted thus, with the fresh grass, which was a little shorter than itself, it was very beautiful.'

Cobbett, one of the most politically percipient, pertinacious and pugnacious men of his time, did much to ameliorate conditions of the labouring classes in the countryside. William Hazlitt said that Cobbett looked like a farmer, and he remained throughout his life essentially a countryman with a passion for the land and the men and women who worked the land.

Cobham, William Brooke, 10th Baron, KG (1527–96). Landowner, courtier, privy councillor. Cobham, a favourite of Queen Elizabeth, entertained her at his seat, Cobham Hall, in Kent, in the first year of her reign. He was frequently employed by the Queen in negotiations abroad, and was appointed warden of the Cinque Ports, Lord Lieutenant of Kent, Lord Chamberlain and a Knight of the Garter.

Despite absence abroad he seems to have administered his estates (of some 1,800 acres) and cultivated his parkland and garden with considerable energy and knowledge. The garden is mentioned by the Rev. William Harrison, in his *Description*

Lord **Cobham** *(1527–1596) and family, from the painting by Hans Eworth, c. 1567.*

Cobham Hall, seat of Lord **Cobham**, *from an engraving in W. H. Ireland's* History of the County of Kent.

of England (1577), William Turner in *Names of Herbes* (1548) and John Gerard in his *Herball* (1597). The garden at Cobham Hall was visited by the famous French botanist, Charles de l'Ecluse, when he stayed in England.

Cobham is reputed to have introduced the Spanish broom, *Spartium junceum*, from Southern Europe though he probably shares this claim. His garden may have been that of which Parkinson in his *Paradisi* of 1629 wrote of having seen at Cobham in Kent, 'a tall or great bodied line (lime) tree bare without boughs for eight foot high, then the branches were spread round about so orderly, as if it were done by art, and brought to compass that middle arbour. And from those boughs the body was bare again for eight or nine foot (wherein might be placed half an hundred men at the least, as there might be likewise in that underneath this) and then another row of branches to encompass a third arbour, with stain made for the purpose to this and that underneath it. Upon the boughs were laid boards to tread upon, which was the goodliest spectacle ever beheld for one tree to carry.'

Codrington, John (1899–). Garden designer. Lieut.-Col. Codrington's interest in botany was aroused (with his mother's encouragement) by reading *Flowers of the Field* by the Rev. Johns when ten years of age. The family lived in Rutland and the young Codrington was given a plot six feet square to cultivate, spending his pocket money on gentians, alpine poppies and the smaller saxifrages and pinks. He made his first essay in garden design when he was sixteen years old, advising Mrs Wentworth Watson, then living at Rockingham Castle, to replace her innumerable small odd-shaped beds by a much simpler layout of two double borders intersecting at a sundial, a plan which has remained much the same for something over half-a-century.

After school, Codrington became a regular soldier (for twenty-six years), followed by work in films and BOAC. After being axed from the latter organization he decided to start professionally as a garden designer at the age of 59. In that capacity he has designed the Herb Garden for Emmanuel College, Cambridge, as well as many smaller gardens in London. He has also been involved with landscape gardening (including tree transplanting) on a far larger scale in Suffolk and Lincolnshire. He has designed gardens in France, Malta, Australia, South Africa, Madagascar, Ethiopia, as well as prepared plans for the future horticultural gardens at Port Moresby in Papua, New Guinea.

One of the strangest of Codrington's commissions was the layout of a courtyard garden in the new resthouse annexe for the tourist bureau in Timbuctu.

Collinson, Peter (1694–1768). Horticulturist and horticultural writer. Collinson came of a Quaker family and was born at Peckham, then in Surrey. As a small boy he visited the gardens of various relations and early developed a love of plants. He described how they were 'remarkable for their fine cut greens and curious flowers', and often went with his family 'to visit the few nursery gardens to buy fruits, flowers, and clipped yews in the shape of birds, dogs, men, ships, etc.'

In this way, Collinson became acquainted with the principal London nurserymen of the day, about whom he later wrote. One was Parkinson of Lambeth, who specialized in the 'cut greens' such as myrtles and oleanders. Wrench of Parsons Green (Fulham) was another, an enthusiast in collecting every kind of variant of the common holly—gold-and-silver-leaved, hedgehog and saw-leaved. He also provided rewards to those spotting such varieties: Wrench's 'Phyllis' and Wrench's 'Variegated' were famed. Derby and Fairchild, nurserymen

Lieutenant-Colonel John **Codrington** *(1899–) in his garden in Pimlico, London.*

with small gardens at Hoxton specializing in tropical plants, and Furber and Gray, nurserymen on a much grander scale, were amongst others encouraged by Collinson, who recorded at the time that 'the taste for gardening was increasing annually'. Collinson's visits to these gardens as a highly observant youth were the foundation of his wide-ranging knowledge of practical horticulture and plants. He also had a profound interest in other branches of natural history.

Although he soon became intimate with many persons eminent in the social and intellectual worlds, Collinson's Quaker modesty never left him. He was always a partner, with his brother James, in the family business of wholesale woollen drapers at the sign of the Red Lion

Peter **Collinson** *(1694–1768), horticulturist and patron of plant-collectors, including John Bartram in north-east America.*

in Gracechurch Street. The firm, having a particular trade with the North American colonies, enabled Collinson to cultivate a correspondence with American naturalists—a number of whom visited him—which was ultimately to prove of great importance.

Although wholly self-taught, Collinson was elected a Fellow of the Royal Society in 1728, and in 1732 served on its council. He was a Fellow of the Society of Antiquaries, and a member of the Royal Societies of Berlin and Sweden. He was particularly associated with the spectacular gardening activities of Lord Petre at Thorndon in Essex and the second and third Dukes of Richmond at Goodwood. He was an intimate friend of Sir Hans Sloane, whose collection of natural history specimens he arranged at Bloomsbury to form the origin of the Natural History Museum. Another close friend was Benjamin Franklin, whose nomination papers for fellowship of the Royal Society he signed.

Collinson made his first garden, in which he grew a number of plants hitherto uncultivated in England, at Peckham, about three miles south of London Bridge. The gardens surrounded a house which he had inherited from a grandmother. Later, he inherited a larger estate from his wife's mother: Ridgeway House, north of London and now the site of Mill Hill School. The removal of his stock of plants from Peckham took him two years.

A great help in his activities as an introducer of new plants into this country was the nearness of his business to the Pool of London and his expertise in the means of swiftly collecting his consignments from incoming ships and getting them to his own garden or to nurserymen.

Collinson undoubtedly annoyed some of his oversea correspondents by his persistent demands for plants or seeds, although he helped others, such as Mark Catesby (qv) in North America, and it is in connexion with the American plants that his work was particularly outstanding. His efforts are also lastingly linked with the work of a pioneer of American botany, John Bartram (1699–1777), member of a Derbyshire Quaker family, who had settled in Pennsylvania and, according to Linnæus, was the greatest natural botanist in the world. Bartram built a stone house with his own hands, read Pope to his children, played the Aeolian harp, farmed beside the Schuylkill river and produced a higher yield of barley than his neighbours. Collinson heard of Bartram indirectly through Franklin and wrote to him. He was not rebuffed as was usual with his American acquaintances who were only anxious to buy his woollen goods and quite uninterested in requests for plants. In 1730, Collinson received his first consignment from Bartram and it has been estimated that of some three hundred new plants introduced from North America, between 1735 and Collinson's death, two-thirds were due to this remarkable partnership. In return, Bartram received English books, useful European plants and equipment from Collinson.

At first, Bartram was financed by Collinson and his friend Lord Petre, receiving five guineas for each box he despatched. In 1740 the Dukes of Richmond, Norfolk and Bedford joined in. This financial help enabled Bartram to widen the range of his collecting expeditions and carry out scientific surveys. In 1765, Collinson and this influential group obtained for Bartram the position of Botanizer Royal for America with a salary of £50 a year and a commission to explore. Bartram, it should be added, also sent many natural history objects such as bird's nests, tortoises, turtles, frogs and crickets.

If Collinson is particularly famed for his receipt and propagation of plants of all kinds from western North America, he was also a recipient (along with Philip Miller of the Chelsea Physic Garden) of seeds sent by Père d'Incarville, the missionary at Nankin, notably the tree of Heaven (*Ailanthus altissima*) in 1751; *Broussonetia papyrifera* from China; a gleditsia from Persia; whilst, in 1727, his friend Sir Charles Wager, first Lord of the Admiralty, gave him a collection of plants that he had brought from 'Gibraltar Hill'. In 1731, Collinson received from Providence Island, in the Bahamas, *Bletia purpurea* which he cultivated and flowered, probably the first tropical orchid to bloom in England. Other correspondents from whom he received plants were Mr Brewer of Nuremburg; Mr Demidoff, proprietor of the Siberian iron mines; and John Custis of Williamsburg.

His only son Michael (1727–1795) was also a botanist.

Colvin, Brenda, CBE (1897–   ). One of the founders of The Institute of Landscape Architects in 1929 (President 1951–53). Also a founder member of the International Federation of Landscape Architects. Her beliefs and practices were set out some twenty-five years ago in *Land and Landscape*. Among her work as consultant are the New Military Town at Aldershot, Bristol Polytechnic, reservoirs on the River Severn, power stations for the Central Electricity Board and several schemes for land reclamation. In making the Trimpley reservoir, on the River Severn, the top soil was reused for modelling banks to form open pasture in contrast with the surrounding woods.

To a wider public she is known

Landscaping by Brenda **Colvin** *of the Trimpley reservoir for the Birmingham Water Board. The river Severn runs through the valley on the left. Water is pumped up into the reservoir to await treatment.*

for her part in the extremely useful and practical *Trees for Town and Country* with drawings by S. R. Badmin, first published in 1947, which has passed through several editions.

Comber, Harold Frederick (1897–1969). Botanist, plant-collector and writer. Comber was born at Nymans, Sussex, where his father James Comber (qv) was the head gardener. At seventeen he went to work at Colesbourne, Gloucestershire, for H. J. Elwes, one of the outstanding and most widely travelled gardeners and naturalists of his time. This was followed by three years at the Edinburgh Botanic Garden where he tried unsuccessfully to join up with one of George Forrest's Chinese plant-hunting expeditions.

In 1925, he was engaged by a syndicate headed by the Hon. H. D. McLaren (later Lord Aberconway) to collect in the Andes of Chile and the Argentine, an area not worked since the days of William Lobb and Richard Pearce in the middle of the previous century. He returned with some notable plants, such as species of *Fabiana* and *Berberis*, and supplies of seeds of others which were scarce in cultivation, such as *Nothofagus*. Between 1929–30 Comber collected for a syndicate headed by Lionel de Rothschild (qv) in Tasmania, aiming to get plants from the higher altitudes which might be hardy in the milder parts of Britain.

Comber next turned to commercial horticulture in England, becoming concerned with the Burnham Lily Company, and later with W. Constable, an eminent producer of lilies. In 1952 he left England and joined Jan de Graff at the Oregon Bulb Farms in the United States, hybridizing and producing lily stocks on a large scale. In 1949 he published *A New Classification of the Genus Lilium*. On retiring from commercial horticulture in 1962 he devoted much time to studying the native plants of Oregon.

Comber, James (c. 1866–1953). Gardener and hybridizer. Comber was trained in private gardens and worked for the then pre-eminent nursery firm of Veitch. In 1894 he became head gardener at Nymans in Sussex, already a fine garden, which was about to be developed and extended by Lt.-Col. Leonard Messel (qv) into what is now the magnificent property belonging to the National Trust. Comber remained at Nymans until his death. His skill

James **Comber** *with Lieutenant-Colonel L. C. R. Messel (right), seen in the gardens at Nymans, Sussex, in 1947.*

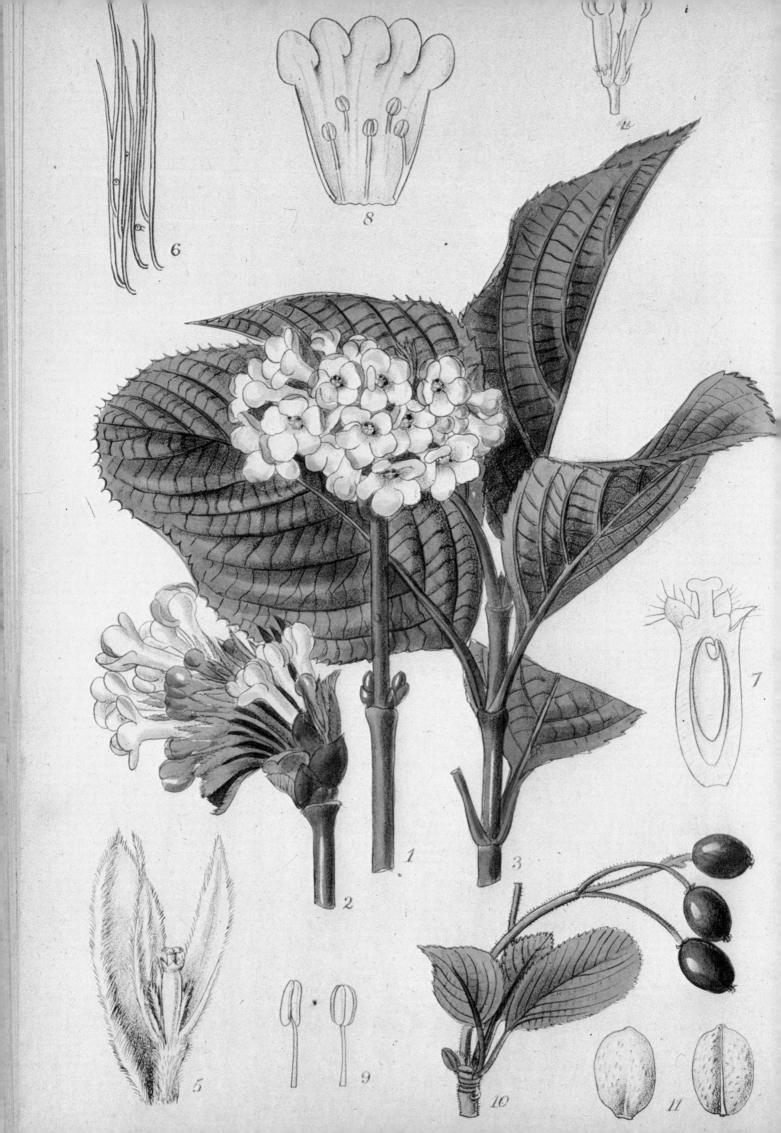

*Bishop **Compton** (1632–1714) and an engraving showing a corner of the garden he established at Fulham Palace.*

*Henry Seymour **Conway** (1721–1795).*

in propagation and cultivation were outstanding, and he did much successful hybridizing, particularly with rhododendrons, although he did not, however, make the cross that produced the *Eucryphia* whose name is associated with Nymans.

Comber was awarded an Associateship of Honour of the Royal Horticultural Society in 1930 and its Victoria Medal of Honour some six years later.

Compton, (Hon. Reverend) Henry (1632–1713). Patron of botanical and horticultural studies; sponsor of plant-collectors. Compton was the son of Spencer Compton, Earl of Northampton, and was born at the family seat, Compton Wynyates in Warwickshire. In his younger days he was a soldier, politician and scholar. He was prominent in church affairs and in 1675 was made Bishop of London, an appointment he retained until his death. As a firm Protestant, however, he was suspended from his episcopal duties when James II ascended the throne in 1685, and was unable to take up his duties again until after William and Mary came to the throne four years later. (Indeed, when Compton was restored to favour on the accession of William and Mary, he officiated at their coronation in place of the Archbishop of Canterbury who had refused to take part.)

During the years of the suspension from his episcopate, Compton was allowed to remain at Fulham Palace. Throughout this time, he made one of the most extensive collections of new and rare plants then known in England. He was aided in these endeavours by his gardener, George London, who was the most renowned and highly skilled practitioner of his day.

---

*(Opposite) Viburnum grandiflorum, collected by Roland **Cooper** during his expedition to Bhutan. It was discovered in forests at a height of over 10,000 feet.*

The extent of Compton's gardening activities is documented in contemporary writings. Thus John Evelyn records in his diary that on October 11th, 1681, he made a visit to the Bishop: 'in whose garden I first saw the *Sedum arborescens* in flower, which was exceedingly beautiful'. Another visitor was Stephen Switzer. In his *Ichnographia Rustica*, published in 1718, he recalled that Compton 'had a thousand species of exotick plants in his

*Eighteenth-century aquatint showing the Mausoleum at Park Place, Oxfordshire, where Henry **Conway** made a notable landscape garden.*

*Engraving showing view from the grotto at Park Place, home of Henry **Conway**.*

stoves and gardens, in which last place he had endizoned a great many that have been formerly thought too tender for this cold climate. There were few days in the year, till towards the latter part of his life, but he was actually in his garden, ordering and directing the Removal and Replacing of his Trees and plants'.

Apart from exotic plants, Compton also introduced many new trees into his garden at Fulham. His friend, John Ray (qv), made a

botanical study of the trees and shrubs, published as *Historia Plantarum*, in 1688.

Compton's particular interest was mainly in North American plants, an interest doubtless encouraged by his position as Head of the Church for the American Colonies. In this capacity he appointed John Banister (qv), the naturalist and botanist, as a missionary in Virginia. Banister was to become the author of the first North American flora.

Compton received seeds and plants from many other collectors, including Samuel Browne in India and Mark Catesby (qv) in North America, and from sources on the Continent. He presumably succeeded in rearing these plants by the use of the stoves referred to by Switzer.

After Compton's death, his successor, Bishop Robinson, did away with many of the trees, and even the greenhouse plants and exotics, in order to enlarge the scope of the kitchen garden, 'to make room for produce for the table.' Two nurserymen, Furber of Kensington and Gray of Fulham, acquired a number of the rare plants to be found only in the neglected Bishop's garden. Fortunately, some of the trees, original or early introductions, remained in the garden and were examined and recorded by Sir William Watson in 1751 for the Royal Society. A paper read in 1757 before the Society, noted nearly forty introductions, including the Virginian flowering maple, the Virginian sumach and the black Virginian walnut tree. Daniel Lysons made comparable reports for his *Environs of London*, and J. C. Loudon surveyed the trees which still remained in the garden in the nineteenth century for his *Arboretum et fruticetum Britannicum* published in 1838.

Conway, (the Hon.) Henry Seymour (1721–1795). Field-Marshal and statesman. Conway was the second son of the first Lord Conway and his

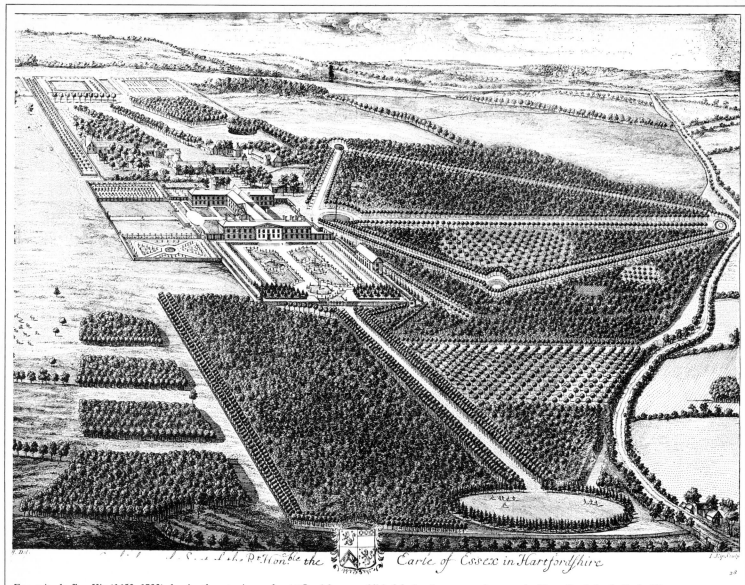

*Engraving by Jan Kip (1652–1722) showing the extensive gardens at Cassiobury, established during the seventeenth century by Moses **Cook** for the Earl of Essex.*

third wife, Charlotte. When he was eighteen he went on the Grand Tour with Horace Walpole and Thomas Gray, the poet, parting company at Geneva. His friendship with Walpole continued and he figures largely in Walpole's correspon-

dence. He had a somewhat stormy career, both militarily and politically, taking the side of John Wilkes and the American colonists. In 1772 he became Governor of Jersey. He retired from political life in 1784 to his estate at Park Place in Oxford-

shire. There he added embellishments to the landscape garden, including a shell grotto, a pyramid tomb, a druids' temple, miniature colosseum and an 'eye-catcher' bridge. He reputedly raised the first Lombardy poplar in England, from

a cutting brought back from Italy by Lord Rochford in his carriage, although it is likely that the 3rd Duke of Argyll (qv) grew this poplar before him.

Cook, James (1728–1779). Explorer. Captain Cook rates a place in this DICTIONARY as the captain of the *Endeavour* which circumnavigated the globe between 1768 and 1771, carrying the great naturalist, Joseph Banks (qv), his assistant, Daniel Carl Solander (1733–82), and Sydney Parkinson (c. 1745–71), botanical draughtsman. After carrying out his specific mission—to observe the transit of the planet Venus—Cook made the first scientific studies of the Australian continent and New Zealand. In 1772–5, Cook's second voyage carried J. R. Forster (1729–98) and his son J. G. Forster (1754–94), botanists and draughtsmen, round Cape Horn, visiting Pacific Islands and skirting the Antarctic ice-fields. His third voyage (1776–9), in which he charted the Pacific coast of North America, ended with his murder in Hawaii.

These voyages were of far-reaching consequence to horticulture, and Cook's personal enthusiasm for bot-

*Captain James **Cook** (1728–1779) and (right) the* Endeavour, *hauled up on the shore of the river named after Captain Cook's ship, for careening and fothering (plugging holes in the ship's hull made by the coral reef).*

any and plant-collecting played a notable part in their success. *Cookii* is a botanical epithet applied to several plants in his honour and a genus *Cookia* was named after him. He also seems to have introduced several plants to British botanists, and he made a personal attempt to succeed (when others had failed) with the Aleppo pine (*P. halepensis*) for one of whose descriptions and synonyms, *P. hispanica*, he was responsible. The plant was not, however, hardy when away from its indigenous habitat and did not survive in Britain.

Cook, Moses (fl.1660s–1715). Gardener. Cook was an outstanding practical gardener. Little is known of his early life. Knowledge of his life and career derives from his remarkable work, *The manner of Raising, Ordering and Improving Forest and Fruit Trees*: also, *How to Plant, Make and Keep Woods, Walks, Avenues, Lawns, Hedges, etc.* first published in 1676, followed by a second edition 'very much corrected' in 1717. The book's title-page declares its author to be 'Moses Cook, Gardiner to that great Encourager of Planting, the Right Honourable, the Earl of Essex.' The work includes much practical horticultural advice:

'. . . having set my Trees streight in their Rows, and trod the Earth close to their Roots, and made my Hills, I then laid round every Tree, upon those Hills, wet Litter taken off from the Dung-hill, a good Barrow-full to every Tree, and covered that with a little Mould, leaving them to take their rest for a time . . .'

Occasionally, the advice which Moses Cook gave was somewhat complicated by rather abstruse mathematical rules for use in laying-out formal gardens.

When Cook first went to work for the Earl of Essex is not known, but John Evelyn in his *Diary* relates that 'No man has been more industrious than his noble Lord in planting about his seate adorn'd with walkes, ponds and other rural elegancies . . . The gardens at Cassiobury are very rare, and cannot be otherwise, having so skilful an artist to govern them as Mr Cook, who is, as to the mechanical part, not ignorant in mathematics, and pretends to astrology'.

Evelyn describes, with evident admiration, Cook's use of the native cherry in avenues and in woodlands, and Cook himself wrote of this unusual practice: 'I know many will say that it is not proper to rank this among forest trees; but if such did see the fine stately trees that we have growing in the woods at Cassiobury they would then conclude it proper . . . Where they like the ground, they make a glorious show in the spring, their white blossoms

THE
Manner of Raising, Ordering;
And Improving
Forest and Fruit-Trees:
ALSO,
How to Plant, Make and Keep
WOODS, WALKS,
AVENUES, LAWNS, HEDGES, &c.
WITH
Several FIGURES in Copper-plates, proper for the same.
ALSO
RULES and TABLES shewing how the Ingenious Planter may measure Superficial Figures, with Rules how to divide Woods or Land, and how to measure Timber and other Solid Bodies, either by Arithmetick or Geometry, shewing the Use of that most Excellent Line, the *Line of Numbers*, by several New Examples; with many other Rules, useful for most Men.

By *Moses Cook*, Gardiner to that great Encourager of Planting, the Right Honourable , the Earl of *Essex*.

Whereunto is now added, that ingenious Treatise of Mr. *Gabriel Plattes, viz.* A Discovery of *Subterranean Treasure*

LONDON:

Printed for *Peter Parker* at the *Leg* and *Star* over against the *Royal Exchange* in *Cornhill*, 1679.

*Title-page of first edition (1679) of a book on trees by Moses **Cook**.*

showing at a distance as though they were clothed with fine white linen; their blossoms are a great relief to the industrious bees at that season.' Certainly a comment indicative of an original, sensitive mind.

Cassiobury, in Hertfordshire, was rebuilt in about 1677 by Hugh May, in the Dutch-Palladian style. An engraving by Kip gives evidence of the scope of the gardens, and there is little doubt that these, originating with the earlier house, were the work of Cook, who mentions a discussion with May, before this date, about pear trees. Further evidence lies in the extreme formality and precision of the garden plan, especially as Moses Cook wrote so exhaustively on the various mathematical and geometrical aspects of the subject.

Cook's ideas and practice were in surprising accordance with those of modern times. His insistence, for example, that seed only from specimens of the best quality should be collected and sown, was quite unusual in his day. He strongly attacked old, unsubstantiated traditions such as that which held sallows and elms to be without seed, quoting the rhyme:

Be gone Tradition, never more appear,
Out of the Kalendar before next year:
Truth with Experience through this Nation
Shall sainted be by a right Observation.
Leave room, Astrologers, for Truth, and see
You write it next year in your Diary.

Cook then added that he had raised successfully elms and sallows from seed.

In 1681 Cook joined the famous partnership of nurserymen, led by George London (qv), on its formation. He retired in 1689 when the firm became London and Wise.

Unfortunately, no published records of gardens or landscapes with which Cook may have been concerned during this period with George London seem to have survived.

He was fortunate in his employer at Cassiobury, of whom he wrote: 'You have not been only a spectator but an actor in most of what is treated in the ensuing lines: for, to your eternal praise be it spoken, there is many a fine tree which you have nursed up from seeds sown by your own hands, and many thou-

sands more which you have commanded me to raise.'

After his involvement in the Rye House plot in 1683 (his captors, according to legend, having 'found him in his garden gathering of nutmeg peaches'), Essex was imprisoned in the Tower, where he died, murdered according to some, but generally considered to have committed suicide.

Cooke, Edward William (1811–1880). Botanical draughtsman. Cooke was born in North London and whilst still at school he made drawings of plants at Loddiges' well-known nurseries at Hackney to illustrate John Loudon's *Encyclopaedia of Plants*. Cooke continued to make drawings and engravings of plants and many were published in Loddiges' own *Botanical Cabinet* (1817). Afterwards he became a marine artist of some standing and travelled extensively throughout Europe, concentrating mainly on coastal and river scenes and shipping. Two of his paintings are in the National Gallery.

Cooper, Roland Edgar (1890–1962). Plant-collector and historian. Cooper had three distinct periods of activity in his life. He was first a plant-collector working in a little-known area in Asia. He then became curator of the Edinburgh Royal Botanic Garden at a period when very many new plants from the north-west China area were being introduced into this country and coming into cultivation. Finally, he published, *inter alia*, several unusual studies on recondite subjects, including a monograph on the anthropological associations of now disregarded plant legends.

Cooper was born at Kingston-on-Thames. His parents died when he was an infant and he was left in the charge of an aunt, the wife of William Wright Smith, long associated with Edinburgh Botanic Garden. In 1907, Smith was appointed Curator of the Herbarium at The Royal Calcutta Botanic Garden and became director of the Botanical Survey of India. Cooper travelled to India with his foster-parents and afterwards studied both botany and horticulture at the Calcutta and Darjeeling Botanic Gardens under George Thomas Lane.

Returning to Scotland in 1910, he became a probationer at the Edinburgh Botanic Garden until he was appointed collector to A. K. Bulley (qv), the rich, eccentric, Fabian cotton-broker. Bulley was a man of imperious character and highly individual humour. (He once requested tablespoonsfuls of seed from one plant of the rare *Meconopsis discigera*.) Although Bulley had failed to get on with two other collectors, Frank Kingdon Ward

*Roland Edgar **Cooper** (1890–1967).*

*Romneya coulteri (The Tree Poppy) named after Thomas **Coulter**.*

(qv), and George Forrest (qv), who had previously worked for him, his relationship with Cooper seems to have been quite amicable, although Cooper's Sikkim expedition in 1913 produced little of value.

During 1914–15, Cooper collected in the difficult terrain of Bhutan. He first found the valuable *Viburnum grandiflorum* and later the tender but important *Rhododendron rhabdotum*. He discovered *Lobelia nubigena* in its sole European or Asiatic locality—a relative of the giant lobelias of the Mountains of the Moon of Africa. From 1916 onwards, he served in the Royal Flying Corps.

After post-war work in Burma, he was appointed assistant curator at Edinburgh in 1930 and, in 1934, curator, from which post he retired in 1950, having served during a period when numerous exotic plants were being established in Britain.

Subsequently, his activities included the esoteric studies previously mentioned, including theses on the effect of Constable's paintings on the early design of the Edinburgh Garden, on anthropology and on the early history of the sycamore.

Coulter, Thomas (1793–1843). Botanist. Coulter was born in Dundalk in Scotland and died in Dublin. He was trained in medicine at Trinity College, Dublin, and later studied botany under Candolle in Geneva. From 1824 he worked as a doctor amongst miners in Mexico, combining this with such extraneous activities as mining speculator and botanical collector. He also travelled to California where he became friendly with David Douglas (qv) during a difficult period for the latter, who was, not very patiently, waiting for a boat to arrive. Douglas—no easy man to please—found Coulter 'a good and congenial companion able to talk of plants, a really good man, and an excellent shot and fisherman'.

Coulter's varied and extensive American exploits and travels, included sending, in 1828, at his own expense, two large collections of living cacti to Europe, one to Trinity College, Dublin, the other to Geneva.

In 1834 he returned to Ireland with a collection of some 50,000 botanical specimens of all kinds. These arrived safely, but his massive and important notes and manuscripts disappeared between London and Dublin. They were never found. The specimens, with himself as curator, went to Trinity College, Dublin, where he spent the rest of his days working on them—a task which he had still not finished at his death in 1843.

Among his many discoveries were two which brought him fame and carry his name. *Pinus coulteri*, which he found in the Santa Lucia mountains of California, has the largest cones of any pine, and in the same State he discovered a new genus in the form of the lovely white-flowered poppy-like *Romneya coulteri*.

Coventry, George William, 6th Earl of (1721–1809). Lord Coventry succeeded to the family title and property at Croome d'Abitot, in Worcestershire in 1738. The estate, eight miles south of the county town, was flat, extremely marshy and subject to floods from the adjoining rivers, Avon and Severn.

In 1751 the earl commissioned the then-virtually-unknown Lancelot ('Capability') Brown to design a new house to replace the old Jacobean house, and to prepare designs for landscaping the estate on which Lord Coventry had already begun a programme of reclamation. For the house, his first notable architectural commission, Brown produced a dignified Palladian design which was followed by a gothic design for the nearby church of St James the Apostle, also commissioned by Lord Coventry.

Following an earlier suggestion by Sanderson Miller (qv), Brown drained the park by means of enormous culverts reaching from the site of the new house to one of his artifi-

(Opposite) Calycanthus praecox *(Japanese All-Spice) cultivated by Lord **Coventry** after receiving a specimen from China in 1766. In 1800, the plant was 16 feet high and 10 feet wide.*

*The Orangery, Croome Court, Worcestershire, commissioned by the Earl of **Coventry** from Robert Adam, c. 1760.*

Croome Court, seat of the Earl of **Coventry**, *seen in an engraving from* Views of the Seats *(1818–1829) by John Neal.*

Recent view of the park at Croome Court, Worcestershire, landscaped for the Earls of **Coventry**.

Early photograph of a garden-house at Croome Court, Worcestershire, built for the Earl of **Coventry**.

cial rivers. With his genius for both the practical and visual sides of his projects, the park was transformed by the imaginative use of water, by introducing what the topographical writer, John Neale termed 'a semblance of hill and dale', and by the usual eye-catching ornamental buildings.

The transformation of the park and the estate was a monumental task, spread over twenty years, yet carried out to the entire satisfaction of Lord Coventry, who wrote of Brown: 'My place at Croome was entirely his creation, and I believe, originally, as hopeless a spot as any in the island.' He endorsed this encomium, recorded by Humphry Repton, with this inscription erected in the grounds of Croome:

To the memory of Lancelot Brown.
Who by the power of his inimitable
genius formed this garden scene
out of a morass.

Nor should the £400,000 which the earl is said to have spent on the improvement be overlooked.

Coventry was not only the earliest large-scale patron of Brown but a planter and horticulturist of unusual discernment. J. C. Loudon, in his *Arboretum et Fruticetum Britannicum* (1838), refers to over ninety trees and shrubs of exceptional quality growing on the estate, and it is generally held that the earl was responsible for the introduction, direct from their native countries, of both *Koelreuteria paniculata* (1763), still surprisingly common in Worcestershire, and the very popular *Chimonanthus praecox* (1766).

A very full account of the garden in its prime by William Dean, 'Botanic Gardener to the Rt. Hon. the Earl of Coventry', was published in 1824 under the title *Croome d'Abitot* 'to which are annexed *Hortus Croomensis* and observations on the propagation of exotics'.

Fittingly, the last visit Brown made to a patron was to Coventry.

In the grounds behind the house, the seventh earl placed an urn, with the following inscription:

TO THE MEMORY OF GEORGE WILLIAM, EARL OF COVENTRY, THE FOLLOWING LINES WERE INSCRIBED BY HIS SUCCESSOR, OCTOBER 25TH 1809.

Sacred to him, the genius of the place,
Who reared these shades, and formed this sweet retreat,
With every incense-breathing shrub adorn'd,
And flow'r of fairest hue! —His cultured taste
And native fancy bade the scene around
Rise perfect; and the muse, whom much he loved,
Still joys to haunt it. Crown'd with length of days
He lived—one wish alone unsated:—much
His loyal heart had cherished a found hope
To hail this day of Jubilee, and close
His earthly course in Britain's hour of joy.

Robert Adam was also commissioned, from 1760 onwards, to design ornamental buildings in the park, including the orangery and conservatory.

Cox, Euan Hillhouse Methven (1893–1977). Plant-collector of Glendoick, Perth. Cox was the last collector to travel with Reginald Farrer (qv) in 1919, when they made their headquarters at Hpimaw near a pass through the mountains into China along the valley in the Salween River. They collected many fine plants which have not done well in cultivation, owing to the very high rainfall in their native habitat. But

*Euan **Cox** (right) (1893–1977) with his son, Peter **Cox** (1934–   ).*

*Juniperus coxii (Chinese Coffin Tree) introduced into Britain by E. H. M. **Cox**.*

Juniperus coxii (the Chinese coffin tree, whose timber is locally of great value) with its blue-green, drooping branches, has proved one of the finest conifers introduced into this country during this century.

In 1920 Cox had to return to Britain, Farrer remaining and dying later that year. Subsequently, though a skilled gardener, Cox became more widely known as an author, particularly of works deriving from his Chinese experiences. Amongst his books are *Farrer's Last Journey* (1926), *The Plant Introductions of Reginald Farrer* (1930), the authoritative *History of Gardening in Scotland* (1938), and *Plant Hunting in China* (1945), which carries the subject to 1939 in which year the great era of European plant-collectors closed.

In 1929 Cox also published the first issue of *New Flora and Silva*, a periodical, which was undoubtedly of too high a quality to be viable in a mass-media era, but which nevertheless continued publication until stopped by the war in 1940.

In conjunction with his son, P. A. Cox (qv), and with illustrations by Margaret Stones, he has published *Modern Rhododendrons* (1956), *Modern Shrubs* (1958), and *Modern Trees* (1961).

Cox, Peter (1934–   ). Horticulturist and writer. Peter Cox, son of the foregoing was trained at Notcutt's Nursery, Suffolk, and passed his Scottish Diploma of Horticulture at Edinburgh College of Agriculture. He was then concerned in plant-collecting expeditions in Turkey and Assam.

After returning to Scotland, Peter Cox started the nursery division of Glendoick Gardens at Perth, specializing in rhododendrons and azaleas. In conjunction with his wife, Patricia, also a trained horticulturist, he started a garden centre at Glendoick. He has co-operated with his father in the writing of several books and is author of *Dwarf Rhododendrons*.

Coys, William (c. 1560–1627). Gardener and plant-collector. Coys was typical of the pioneering amateur gardeners of his period. He is known chiefly through occasional references by contemporaries to his garden at North Ockendon in Essex, and to lists of his garden plants which were compiled in the years 1617 and 1618.

Coys had numerous contacts abroad from whom he received plants. These he plainly cultivated with great skill, for he is believed to have been the first man in 1604 to flower *Yucca gloriosa* in England. (The plant had been introduced from south-east North America in 1550, and was then described as

Modern Rhododendrons

Uniflorum series : R. pemakoense
(two-thirds natural size)

are frosted two years out of three and its value to us is doubtful.

A dwarf form is listed, but we can find no difference between it and the normal one. *R. pemakoense* is very close to *R. uniflorum*, again only differing in the arrangement of the scales, but *R. uniflorum* flowers a week or two later, which is an advantage.

R. pumilum is a dwarf prostrate shrub, growing 2 or 3 inches and then sending out prostrate side branches, and not exceeding 6 inches. The ½-inch leaves are narrower than others in the series. There are occasionally three flowers in the truss ; they are bell-shaped, ½ inch long, rather hairy, and either a clear pink or rose in colour. It is quite hardy and flowers early in May. The true species is uncommon.

146

The Species of Rhododendron in their series

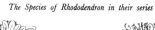

Virgatum series : R. racemosum
(two-thirds natural size)

Virgatum series

This is a small series which all produce axillary flower-buds. *R. oleifolium* is an erect-growing shrub up to 4 or 5 feet with 2-inch leaves lanceolate and narrow, only ½ inch wide. The flowers are almost always single, funnel-shaped about 1 inch long and pubescent on the outside. The colour is usually pink and occasionally almost white. It flowers in April. It is a good plant for the west with its fairly large flowers, but is too tender for cold gardens.

R. racemosum is possibly the best-known species now growing in gardens. It is a variable plant. The well-known dwarf form under Forrest number 19404 remaining about two feet in height, but we have earlier Forrest plants that are more

(1,724)   147   11

Typical pages from Modern Rhododendrons *by Euan and Peter **Cox** (published by Nelson, 1956).*

Yucca gloriosa, *thought to have first been flowered in England by William* **Coys** *(fl. 1604–17).*

Gardens at the Commonwealth Institute, London, designed by Dame Sylvia **Crowe** *CBE (1901   ), seen above.*

Children's amphitheatre and Commonwealth Gardens, Canberra, designed by Dame Sylvia **Crowe**.

coming from 'the Indies' but did not flourish.)

Coys is also known to have grown the American choke-cherry (*Prunus virginiana*); the persimmon (*Diospyros virginiana*); the sweet potato and the common potato. How he obtained these at a time when they were extremely rare seems unknown. Through a certain William Boels he also had connexions with Spain and grew a number of Spanish plants, including the ivy-leaved toadflax (*Cymbalaria muralis*) which was first noted growing in his garden in 1616 and is now naturalized on old walls and similar places over much of the British Isles.

Crowe, (Dame) Sylvia (1901–   ). Landscape architect. Sylvia Crowe's interest in landscape derived from a childhood spent on a Sussex farm. After schooldays she found that no training was available for landscape or garden design, so she took a horticultural course at Swanley in Kent. Later she became a pupil in a landscape architect's office and subsequently worked on the design of gardens until 1939 having, meantime, become a council member of the Institute of Landscape Architects. Thanks to the practical help and encouragement of two of her colleagues, Brenda Colvin (qv) and Geoffrey Jellicoe (qv), she was able, post-war, to start in private practice.

The recommendation, in the Reith Report on New Towns (1946), that landscape architects should be involved in the planning process of these towns resulted in Sylvia Crowe being appointed consultant for Harlow and Basildon New Towns. She has since been involved in master plans for two of the later New Towns: Warrington and Washington. She has enjoyed unusual diversity in her commissions, ranging from the re-designing of Banbury churchyard to the reclamation of sand dunes on the coast of Lincolnshire. She also worked on the landscaping of the Commonwealth Institute in Kensington High Street and various other urban projects.

When the Central Electricity Generating Board sited their controversial Nuclear Power Station in Snowdonia, she was retained to relate the buildings as satisfactorily as possible to the Welsh landscape. She also helped to suggest the least damaging routes for some of the high-voltage power lines for the National Grid.

She was President of the Institute of Landscape Architects for two years, and from 1948 to 1968 was deeply involved in establishing the

(*Opposite*) *Plate from* A Monograph on the Genus Camellia *by Samuel* **Curtis** *(1779–1860), published in 1819. The illustrations for this work were drawn by Clara Maria Pope.*

Single White Camellia   Single Red Camellia

A corner of the gardens at the Teachers' Training College, Oxford, landscaped by Dame Sylvia **Crowe**.

William **Curtis** *(1746–99), founder in 1787 of* The Botanical Magazine: or Flower Garden Displayed, *which continues to the present day.*

International Federation of Landscape Architects, serving as Secretary for ten years and subsequently as vice-president.

During the years from 1950 to 1960 she wrote and edited a number of books on landscape architecture and spent much time lecturing, writing articles and otherwise publicizing the purposes of her profession. In 1964 she was appointed Landscape Consultant to the Forestry Commission, and published a booklet (No. 18, 1966) setting out the principles of forest landscape. The booklet has since been used by the US Forest Service and translated into French for that country's forest service.

She is now deeply concerned with the landscaping of reservoirs, helping both to select sites and subsequently to ensure that they contribute to the beauty, conservation and recreational resources of the countryside.

Sylvia Crowe was made a Commander of the Order of the British Empire in 1967. She is an Honorary Fellow of the Royal Institute of British Architects and an Honorary Member of the Royal Town Planning Institute.

Curtis, Charles H. (1869–1958). Botanist and editor. Curtis was one of the outstanding figures in horticulture during the first half of the nineteenth century. After working in private gardens he spent two years at the nursery of James Veitch, Chelsea. Next came a studentship at the Royal Botanic Gardens, Kew, where he won several prizes and was put in charge of the orchid department. From there he went to the Royal Horticultural Society's Garden, then still at Chiswick, as assistant superintendent. He worked for *The Gardener's Magazine*, the earliest horticultural periodical, founded by J. C. Loudon in 1825, and was its editor until it ceased publication in 1917. The next year he joined *The Gardener's Chronicle*, becoming managing editor in 1919 and remaining in that position until his retirement in 1950.

He judged at the International Horticultural Exhibition of 1912 and at every subsequent Royal Horticultural Society's Show and served on a number of the Society's and other specialist committees. He was an authority on orchids, daffodils, tulips and sweet peas. In 1950 he published *Orchids, Their Distribution and Cultivation*.

He became a member of the Order of the British Empire in 1950 and was awarded the Victoria Medal of Honour in 1933 and the Veitch Memorial Gold Medal for his journalistic work in 1957. He was also

(Left) Charles H. **Curtis** *(1870–1958) and (right) Samuel* **Curtis** *(1799–1860), publisher of* Temple of Flora.

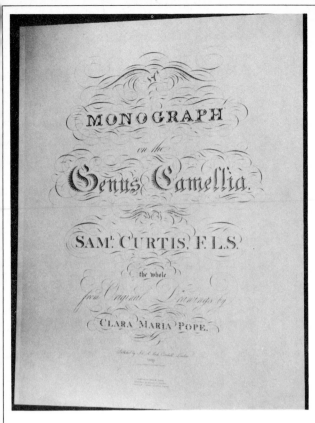

THE

BOTANICAL MAGAZINE;
OR,
Flower-Garden Difplayed:

IN WHICH

The moft Ornamental FOREIGN PLANTS, cultivated in the
Open Ground, the Green-Houfe, and the Stove, are
accurately reprefented in their natural Colours.

TO WHICH ARE ADDED,

Their Names, Clafs, Order, Generic and Specific Charaĉters, according
to the celebrated LINNÆUS; their Places of Growth,
and Times of Flowering:

TOGETHER WITH

THE MOST APPROVED METHODS OF CULTURE.

A WORK

Intended for the Ufe of fuch LADIES, GENTLEMEN, and GARDENERS, as
wifh to become fcientifically acquainted with the Plants they cultivate.

By *WILLIAM CURTIS,*
Author of the FLORA LONDINENSIS.

VOL. I.

" A Garden is the pureft of human Pleafures."
VIRULAM.

LONDON:
PRINTED BY STEPHEN COUCHMAN,
For W. CURTIS, N° 3, *St. George's-Crefcent,* Black-Friars-Road;
And Sold by the principal Bookfellers in Great-Britain and Ireland.
MDCCXCIII.

(Left) Title-page of A Monograph on the Genus Camellia *by Samuel* **Curtis**, *published in 1819; (centre) title-page of the first number of* The Botanical Magazine, *edited by William* **Curtis** *and published in 1787; (right) plate depicting* Iris Persica *from that first number.*

honoured by the French and Belgian authorities.

Curtis, Samuel (1779–1860). Botanist and publisher. Samuel Curtis was a member of an old Quaker family of Walworth, the seventh son of James Curtis, surgeon and apothecary. He was first cousin of William Curtis (qv), founder of the *Botanical Magazine*, who was 'an affectionate father to an only daughter on whom he bestowed a most liberal education'. In 1801 Curtis married this young paragon who bore him a large family. At that time, Curtis had a substantial nursery business at Walworth, but he also had ambitions as a publisher aspiring to rival Robert Thornton's *Temple of Flora* (1799–1807). Between 1806 and 1820 he published *The Beauties of Flora* with life-size colour-plates by Thomas Baxter and Clara Maria Pope (qv) (d. 1838). These plates, with virtually no text, were issued from Walworth.

In 1819 he published *A Monograph on the Genus Camellia*, also with plates by Mrs Pope. The text by Curtis included descriptions, instructions for cultivation and a list of the thirty-one varieties then being grown by James Lee (qv), the Hammersmith nurseryman. The monograph was the first publication issued in England on this then scarcely-known genus.

From 1816 to 1821, Curtis was agent to the Duke of Newcastle at Clumber in Northumberland, and his monograph on camellias was dedicated to the Duchess. At that time he lived at Gamston in Not-

tinghamshire. In 1821 he moved to Glazenwood in Essex, where he established a large nursery, growing a wide range of plants as well as specializing in trees.

In 1852 he retired to La Chaire in Jersey where he built a house and specialized in tender trees and plants in a garden that was carefully sheltered from storms by evergreen oaks.

He was elected a Fellow of the Linnean Society in 1810.

Curtis, William (1746–1799). Botanist, publisher. Curtis was born at Alton, Hampshire. His father, a Quaker, was a prosperous tanner. The boy was apprenticed to his grand-father, a surgeon apothecary. Friendship with a neighbourly ostler

with a passion for plants aroused the enthusiasm of the young apprentice.

When he was about twenty, William was further apprenticed, to two apothecaries in the City of London and lived in the house of the second, William Talwin of Gracechurch Street, for many years. On his death, Talwin left Curtis the

Plates from the Beauties of Flora *published by Samuel* **Curtis** *between 1806 and 1820.*

THE

ENGLISH PHYSICIAN

ENLARGED

With Three Hundred and Sixty-Nine

MEDICINES,

MADE OF

ENGLISH HERBS,

That were not in any IMPRESSION until THIS.

BEING

An *Aftrologo-Phyfical* Difcourfe of the Vulgar Herbs of this Nation; containing a complete Method of Phyfick, whereby a Man may preferve his Body in Health, or cure himfelf, being Sick, for Three-pence Charge, with fuch Things only as grow in England, they being moft fit for *Englifh* Bodies.

Herein is alfo fhewed thefe Seven Things, *viz.* 1. The Way of Making Plaifters, Ointments, Oils, Poultices, Syrups, Decoctions, Juleps, or Waters, of all Sorts of Phyfical Herbs, that you may have them ready for your Ufe at all Times of the Year. 2. What Planet governeth every Herb or Tree (ufed in *Phyfick*) that groweth in *England.* 3. The Time of gathering all Herbs, both Vulgarly and Aftrologically. 4. The Way of drying and keeping the Herbs all the Year. 5. The Way of keeping their Juice ready for Ufe at all Times. 6. The Way of making and keeping all Kinds of ufeful Compounds made of Herbs. 7. The Way of mixing Medicines according to the Caufe and Mixture of the Difeafe and Part of the Body afflicted.

By NICH. CULPEPPER, *Gent.*
STUDENT *in* Phyfick *and* Aftrology.

LONDON:

Printed for E. BALLARD, L. HAWES and Co. W. JOHNSTON, R. BALDWIN, S. CROWDER, B. LAW, and R. WARE, M. RICHARDSON, W. STRAHAN, and W. NICOLL. 1775.

Nicholas **Culpeper** *(sometimes spelt Culpepper), from an engraved portrait from the second edition of* A Physicall Directory *(1650) and (right) the title-page of one of the many posthumous editions of books compiled by Culpeper.*

practice, which he continued, although his main interests were increasingly the studies of entomology and botany.

These interests finally induced him to take a partner to whom he sold the practice in about 1770, although he continued to live at Gracechurch Street. He took over a plot of ground at Grange Road, Bermondsey, where he began to grow British native plants.

In 1773 he became a demonstrator at what is now Chelsea Physic Garden. His success as a teacher encouraged him to begin the publication of his renowned *Flora Londinensis*, an account of the wild plants growing in the London district. He was helped financially by Lord Bute (qv), and his artists included J. Sowerby, F. Sansom, and W. Kilburn. The first part appeared in 1770; yet although the project brought him personal satisfaction and considerable reputation, he suffered from overwork and considerable financial loss.

In 1779 he opened another botanic garden in Lambeth Marsh, which he moved in 1789 to Queens Elm, Brompton.

After the second part of *Flora Londinensis* appeared in 1787, Curtis realized that his losses were now so great that he could no longer afford to continue with the work. The patrons who flocked to his lectures and his garden were not interested in the wild plants which were to be found within ten miles of the metropolis, but in the expensive exotics they imported to grow in their gardens. In 1787, responding to these interests, Curtis published the first issue of *The Botanical Magazine: Or Flower-Garden Displayed*, illustrating and describing *The Most Ornamental Foreign Plants, cultivated in the Open Ground, the Green-House and the Stove*. Information about their culture was added. The illustrations were always drawn from the living plant, and coloured as near to nature 'as the imperfection of colouring will admit'.

The first issue contained three plates. Three thousand copies were sold at one shilling each. The first plant illustrated was *Iris persica*. Most of the early plates were drawn by Sydenham Edwards (qv) (1768–1819) who worked from the second volume onwards. He was brought by Curtis to London from Abergavenny, where he had been discovered by a friend of Curtis.

The Botanical Magazine has continued to this day, surviving many crises and changes, the copyright having been presented to the Royal Horticultural Society in 1921 by a small group of its Fellows after having been refused by the Royal Botanic Gardens, Kew.

Curtis also wrote *Lectures on Botany* with illustrations by Sydenham Edwards, published posthumously in 1805, and also *British Grasses* (1802).

He remained a keen entomologist and is said to have discovered the connexion between honey dew and aphides. On William Curtis' gravestone in Battersea Church was inscribed the following:

While living herbals shall spring profusely wild
Or garden cherish all that's sweet and gay;
So long they works shall praise, dear Nature's Child
So long thy memory suffer no decay.

Culpeper, Nicholas (1616–1654). Herbalist. Culpeper was born in London, the son of a clergyman. He studied at Cambridge and afterwards became an apothecary's apprentice. He was a young man of vigorous personality and wide interests. After fighting in the Civil War on the Cromwellian side and being severely wounded, he established a garden of English medicinal herbs at Red Lion Street in Spitalfields. He was insistent on the indigenous nature of his selected plants, scorning the foreign importations of John Gerard (qv) and John Parkinson (qv), in outspoken terms, as in the introductory or *Epistle to the Reader* in his *Complete Herbal* (1653):

Neither Gerrard nor Parkinson, or any other that ever wrote in the like nature, ever gave one wise reason for what they wrote, and so did nothing else but train up young novices in Physic in the School of tradition, and teach them just as a parrot is taught to speak.

In many ways, Culpeper was a man of his time, caught up in theories coloured by superstition and astrology, relating herbs to the stars and the ills of the body to the movement of the planets. In other ways, however, he was far in advance of his time, as shown in his belief that remedial and thus herbal medicine should be readily and cheaply available to the poor. This outlook and practice upset the College of Physicians with which Culpeper was in continuous conflict from 1640 until his death. Apart from terming the College 'a company of proud, insulting, domineering doctors, whose Wits were born about 500 years before themselves', Culpeper published, in 1649, *A Physicall Directory or a translation of the London Dispensatory Made by the College of Physicians in London . . . with many hundred additions* which rendered the College's latinized pharmacopoeia for doctors into good plain English. The College replied with a broadside directed at 'a farm in Spittlefields where all the knick-knacks of astrology are exposed to open sale'.

Culpeper was undoubtedly a man of great confidence who thrived on contention. Although he lived in straitened circumstances throughout the years, and fathered seven children, he never gave up his struggle to emancipate medicine from the grip of the Collegians. In a message to his 'dear Consort', Mrs Alice Culpeper, writing of his book, *The English Physician*, he claims: 'The works that I have published to the world (though envied by some illiterate physicians) have merited such applause, that thou mayest be confident in proceeding to publish anything I leave thee, especially this master-piece . . .'

After his death, to counter the numerous pirated editions, usually prefaced by a spurious letter to herself, Alice Culpeper wrote her own *Vindication and Testimony* inserted in all genuine editions. Culpeper's *Herbal* has proved one of the most pirated books in history. Over 250 separate editions of the Herbal are recorded by bibliographers.

(Opposite) Over two hundred editions of the Complete Herbal *by Nicholas* **Culpeper** *have been noted by bibliographers. These engravings were prepared for an edition of 1815 with over four hundred illustrations of plants, although Culpeper himself listed only 209. Those reproduced are recorded in the original Culpeper* Complete Herbal.

Nail Wort.

Daisey.

Darnel.

Cud Weed.

Mulberry Tree.

Wheat.

Dock.

Dill.

Doves Foot.

Great Hone Wort.

Dogs Grass.

Narrow Leaved Eyebright.

Common Navelwort.

Night Shade.

Eringo.

Starwort.

Common Mallow.

Wall Flower.

Endive.

Black Willow.

D

Dallimore, William (1871–1959). English arboriculturist. Dallimore was born in Worcestershire. He went to the Royal Botanic Gardens, Kew, as a student gardener in 1891, and was later placed in charge of the arboretum. Subsequently he worked in the museums, building up the Museum of British Forestry, and from 1926 until his retirement in 1936 he was Keeper of the Kew Museums.

In 1923, in collaboration with A. Bruce-Jackson, he produced the first of several editions of *A Handbook of Coniferae* with drawings by Gulielma Lister. This, and a later edition produced by the two authors, plus editions produced by Dallimore alone after Jackson's death, remain invaluable to growers of all species of conifers.

Dallimore's other notable achievement was his share in laying out the National Pinetum at Bedgebury in Kent, an extension of Kew Gardens, in which planting began in 1925. (The pinetum is now in the hands of the Forestry Commission.) Apart from its scientific interest, the pinetum showed Dallimore to be a highly imaginative executant in arboricultural design. He continued his connexion with Bedgebury in an honorary capacity after his official retirement.

He played an important part in the Royal Horticultural Society's Conifer Conference in 1931, and in the same year was awarded the Society's Victoria Medal of Honour. He was appointed a member of the Imperial Service Order in 1935.

Dampier, William (1651–1715). Hydrographer, pirate, navigator, explorer and botanical collector. Dampier was born at East Coker in Somerset, and was orphaned as a child. He was sent to sea at an early age in a ship bound for Newfoundland out of Weymouth. Although of wild and wayward temperament, he was also a young man of ability and application. He began to study hydrography on voyages to Newfoundland and the West Indies, and when ashore—he worked for a while on a Jamaican estate—showed a keen interest in botany, collecting, drying, studying and annotating the specimens he collected. After jumping ship on one of his voyages, he spent two years amongst the logwood-cutters in Yucatan. He moved

on to join a band of buccaneers who ravaged their way across the Isthmus of Darien and into what is now Columbia. Dampier, although a willing member of this gang, must sometimes have appeared a somewhat incongruous figure, ready as

William **Dallimore** *(1871–1959).*

he was to loot and plunder with his confederates whilst always on the alert for new botanical specimens for his collections.

An ability for leadership took him to the head of a band of pirates. Seizing a Dutch vessel at Sierra

William **Dampier** *(1652–1715).*

Leone, they set out on an extraordinary voyage by way of Chile and Cape Horn, across the Pacific to China, thence to Australia. Dampier was thus the first Englishman to touch the Antipodes. Later, abandoned and set ashore in the Nicobar Islands by mutinous subordinates, Dampier crossed the Indian Ocean to Sumatra in a native canoe. Returning to England he completed a book, *New Voyage Round the World* (1697), which enjoyed a resounding *succès d'estime* and the Admiralty, seemingly unaware of his marauding background, gave him the command of the *Roebuck*, especially built for a South Seas expedition of discovery and to report on the prospects of colonizing Western Australia.

Dampier was unfavourably impressed by the aborigines but vastly impressed by his botanical experiences. Amongst his discoveries was the Parrot Glory Pea, named *Clianthus dampieri*. Dampier's expedition came to grief, the *Roebuck* foundering off Ascension Island. Two months later, he and his crew were rescued by East Indiamen,

---

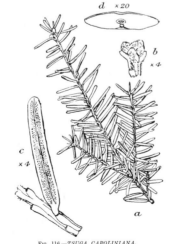

Winter buds ovoid with downy scales. *Leaves* arranged in two opposite ranks, those on the upper side of the shoot, the shortest, ¼–¾ in. long, with a rounded apex, dark shining green and grooved above with two well-defined white bands on the lower surface. *Cones* on the short shoots oblong cylindric, 1–1½ in long, with

d ×20

b ×4

c ×4

a

FIG. 116.—*TSUGA CAROLINIANA.*
a, spray ; *b,* winter bud and pubescent upper side of shoot ; *c,* glabrous under-side of shoot and leaf ; *d,* section of leaf.

oblong, rounded, downy scales which spread widely when the cone is mature. *Seed* with a long wing.

This species closely resembles *T. diversifolia,* but has longer leaves which are scarcely notched at the apex.

As a native tree it has a limited range, being only known from the S. Alleghany Mountains, where it is found at an elevation of

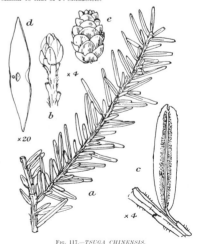

2,500–3,000 ft. It was introduced in 1886, but grows very slowly in this country, and we know of no specimens of any size.

T. caroliniana has similar economic properties to *T. canadensis,* but is not plentiful enough to be of much value. Cultivation similar to that of *T. canadensis.*

d

e

b ×4

a

c ×4

FIG. 117.—*TSUGA CHINENSIS.*
a, branchlet ; *b,* winter bud ; *c,* under-side of leaf and shoot ; *d,* section of leaf, showing single resin canal ; *e,* cone.

Tsuga chinensis, Pritzel. (Fig. 117.)

CHINESE HEMLOCK.

Tsuga yunnanensis, Masters (in part) ; Abies chinensis, Franchet.

A hemlock 100 or more ft. high in China, or occasionally a small, densely pyramidal tree. *Young shoots* with a yellowish tinge, more or less hairy. *Leaves* up to 1 in. long, rounded and minutely notched at the apex in adult trees, with inconspicuous

Typical pages from A Handbook of Coniferae *by William* **Dallimore,** *published by E. Arnold in 1923.*

Wimbledon House, Surrey, the seat of Lord **Danby**, *from an etching by Henry Winstanley (1678). An inscription records that this view is of the house 'as it is seen from the great walk of trees in the principal gardens'. The orangery is seen in the north-east corner of the orange garden. The terrace in front of the house had an elaborate, formal parterre. The steps in the foreground led down from the grass terrace and lime-walk to the main garden.*

homeward bound. Although most of Dampier's botanical specimens were lost in the wreck, a considerable number of dried plants survived. They are now housed in the Oxford Herbarium. Dampier's further adventures included ocean-piloting and privateering. After an extraordinarily varied career, he died in London in 1715.

Although untrained as scientist or botanist, Dampier was a percipient observer and a reporter of rare accuracy.

Danby, Henry Danvers, Earl of (1573–1645). Horticultural patron and innovator. Danvers was page to Sir Philip Sidney and may possibly have been with the soldier-poet at Zutphen where Sidney met his death in the struggles of the Low Countries against the Spanish. In his early twenties Danby travelled widely and adventurously throughout Europe, and for a time, outlawed from England for alleged murder, he lived in France. He was pardoned in 1598, afterwards serving in Ireland and becoming governor of Guernsey. He was made an Earl in 1626.

At that time there was no botanic garden in England, although there were several in Europe, some of which Danby had doubtless visited. We read that 'being minded to become a benefactor to the University of Oxford he determined to begin and finish a place whereby learning, especially the faculty of medicine, might be improved.' Botany was at that time closely concerned with medicine, or more precisely, its physic. Danby leased five acres of meadow which had, until 1290, been the Jews' burying ground. On St James's Day, 1621, with much pomp, ceremony and speech-making, what is now Oxford University Botanic Garden, was opened. A great wall, fourteen feet high, was built around the garden and a heavy weight of dung and

muck brought in to enrich the ground. The operation was so effectively carried out that the garden was raised above the flood level of the Cherwell. The gateway, designed by Inigo Jones and built by Neklaus Stone, was commissioned by Danby and, bearing his statue, is still the entrance to this first botanic garden in Britain.

The cost of establishing the garden took most of the endowment, and is generally given as the reason why the King's gardener, John Tradescant (qv), would not become keeper. Thus it was that a local innkeeper, Jacob Bobart (qv), became the first *Hortus Praefectus*.

In his own gardens at Wimbledon House, Surrey, Lord Danby was equally lavish and extravagant, and a survey in 1649 mentions that the orangery contained forty-two orange trees valued at £10 apiece, also a lemon tree 'bearing great and very large lemons' valued at £20. The garden contained over a thousand fruit trees.

Darby, William (fl. 1670s–1710s). Nurseryman. Although very little is recorded concerning this enterprising early-eighteenth-century nurseryman, he is known to have had his nursery, along with that of the famous Thomas Fairchild (qv), in an alley at the far end of Hoxton in East London. The nursery was small but had stoves and greenhouses in which he grew exotics, specializing in aloes and other succulent plants. He is known jointly with Fairchild to have propagated large numbers of the tulip-tree, *Liriodendron tulipifera*, which was probably introduced from America in 1654. John Loudon (qv), in 1838, suggested that this was probably the source of most of the older specimens then growing in Britain.

Darby was also a noted collector and propagator, by budding, of variegated and other fancy-leaved hollies which were at that time very

popular, and he had some reputation for propagating mistletoe from seed: a large bush he had grown on an apple tree was celebrated. Apparently, other nurserymen used grafting as the means of propagating. He also had a book of pressed specimen leaves to show his customers, and it is said that he did a considerable trade supplying stock for other nurseries.

The identity of his famous plant of *Fritillaria 'Crassa'*, bearing flowers as large as a half-crown, like an embroidered star, seems unknown; although we know that the famous Rev. Dr Uvedale (qv) of Enfield grew it, but could not flower, the plant.

Dartmouth, George Legge, 3rd Earl of (1755–1810). Landowner and horticulturalist. Legge was educated at Eton and Christchurch, Oxford. He succeeded his father in 1801 and, in 1804, was appointed Lord Chamberlain. He had been a member of the Society for Promoting Natural History and was an original Fellow of the Linnean Society. On 11th April, 1804, eight members of the proposed Horticultural Society met to consider its rules. Dartmouth was then present. Later that year he was elected first president of the Society, which became the Royal Horticultural Society in 1861. He continued in the post until his death in 1810, being succeeded in 1811 by Thomas Andrew Knight (qv).

Dartmouth had a fine garden and estate surrounding his home at Sandwell Hall, Staffordshire, on the north-west of Birmingham, traces of which remained well into the present century.

Darwin, Charles Robert (1809–1882). Naturalist. Darwin was born at Shrewsbury, the son of Dr Robert Waring Darwin and Susannah, daughter of Josiah Wedgwood. He was educated at Shrewsbury School, Edinburgh University (where he began but did not finish his medical studies) and Christ's College, Cambridge. From an early age he was a keen botanist and had his own

George Legge, 3rd earl of **Dartmouth**.

Charles **Darwin** *(1809–1882).*

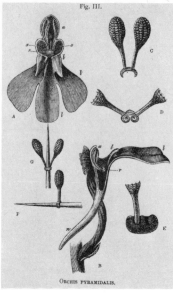

Fig. III.

ORCHIS PYRAMIDALIS.

Although Darwin's fame rests mainly on his theories concerning the evolution of animals, he devoted much time and research to the way in which plant forms were to be found in different areas of the earth, a fact which he considered 'almost the keystone of the laws of creation', basing his belief on the drift of glaciers from the north in the Ice Age, with a consequent struggle for existence between various plant species, with inevitable modification for many and extinction for others. Darwin's discoveries concerning plants and flowers were extensive and widely influential. He conducted a considerable and fruitful correspondence with botanists and growers and his inquiries into the primula were greatly aided by his correspondence with John Scott of the Royal Botanic Garden, Edinburgh (later of the Calcutta Botanic Garden), who examined many plants on Darwin's behalf. Darwin was also an enthusiastic grower of the plants he studied in his own garden at Down House in Kent, his home from 1832 until his death. Darwin's last years were as industriously occupied as his years in the *Beagle*. Between 1875 and his death he wrote several botanical books and papers, viz, 1862, *Fertilisation of Orchids*; 1875, *Insectivorous Plants*; 1876, *The Effects of Cross and Self-Fertilisation in the Vegetable Kingdom*; 1877, *The Different Forms of Flowers on Plants of the Same Species*; 1880, *The Power of Movement in Plants*; 1881, *The Formation of Vegetable Mould, Through the Action of Worms, With Observations on their Habits*.

Darwin, (Dr) Erasmus (1731–1802). Horticulturalist, botanical poet. An early member of the Lunar Society, this remarkable man was also prominent as poet and scientific enquirer. He adumbrated the theory of the origin of species, later developed by his grandson, Charles (qv).

Darwin was born at Elston Hall, Nottinghamshire, son of a studious father, interested in fossils, and an intellectual mother. In his youth, Darwin's interest was in poetry, clocks and electricity. He went to St John's College, Cambridge, in 1750, studying classics, mathematics and medicine, and writing much now-forgotten poetry under conditions of some financial hardship. After Cambridge, he continued his studies, returning to Cambridge for his MB in 1755, before setting up unsuccessfully in practice at Nottingham the following year.

Antuco volcano in the Andes, observed by Charles **Darwin** *during his voyage on the* Beagle *and (right) illustration from Darwin's book on the* Fertilisation of Orchids.

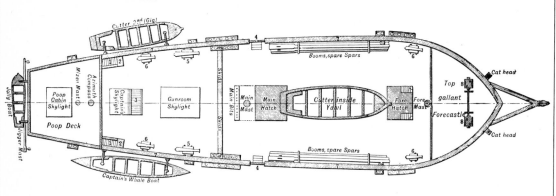

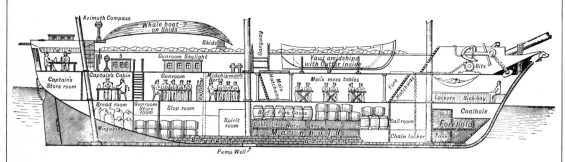

Diagram and section of the Beagle *on which Charles* **Darwin** *sailed round the world with Captain Fitzroy.*

Down House, Kent, where Charles **Darwin** *lived from 1832 until his death.*

corner of the garden. Whilst he was in Edinburgh, his sister wrote: 'It made me feel quite melancholy the other day looking at your old garden and the flowers coming up which you used to be so happy working.' The most decisive event in his life was his recommendation by his Cambridge tutor, John Henslow (qv), in 1831, to Captain Fitzroy, RN, of the *Beagle* as the naturalist for an extended surveying expedition in the South Atlantic. His geological discoveries and researches into animal life during this five-year stint were the basis and preparation for his life's work. In 1859 Darwin published his great work *On the Origin of Species by Means of Natural Selection*, and, nine years later, *The Variation of Animals and Plants Under Domestication*.

(Opposite) Charles **Darwin** *observed that in several parts of Argentina trees were virtually non-existent—except for palms. (These South American palms are illustrated in* Voyage dans l'Amerique Meridionale, *1847.)*

*Two of a series of paintings by William Hannan, c. 1751, showing West Wycombe Park, Buckinghamshire, in the landscape setting planned by Sir Francis **Dashwood** in conjunction with Thomas Cook.*

but he taught the stream to 'wind between shrubby margins. Not only with trees of various growth did he adorn the borders of the fountain, the brook and the lakes, but with various classes of plants, uniting the Linnean sciences with the charm of landscape . . .'

Darwin's two most celebrated and highly original poems were *The Loves of Plants* (1789) and the *Economy of Vegetation* (1792), forming parts of *The Botanic Garden*, a work which displays the original mind of a highly ingenious writer, who, incidentally, claimed that he wrote only for profit. In its time, the poem was very successful.

Adequate footnotes elucidate the more recondite references for readers unaware of the rules of botanical classification and nomenclature. These poems and their footnotes were widely influential in arousing interest in scientific and aesthetic aspects of gardening.

Darwin's first wife died, and in 1781 this lumbering, stuttering, most unusual and understanding of doctors married the young and lively widow of Colonel Chandos Pole, who, however, insisted that he should move to Derby. Within a few years, little remained of his botanic garden at Abnalls, west of Lichfield, and it is now impossible to identify the site.

Dashwood, (Sir) Francis (1709–1782). Landowner and landscape designer. Dashwood, the second baronet, was the son of a wealthy MP and financier, Sir John Dashwood, with considerable mercantile interests in Africa and India. Sir John bought from his brother Samuel, a Lord Mayor of London, the latter's half-share in the family estates at West Wycombe in Buckinghamshire.

Francis Dashwood succeeded his father when he was sixteen. After a series of Grand Tours throughout Europe and Asia Minor, which combined numerous adventurous activities with somewhat fewer academic and artistic pursuits, he returned to England and joined the Prince of Wales' circle and the notorious Hell-Fire Club.

Yet Dashwood had his serious side. Alongside his political career, in which he became a not-so-successful Chancellor of the Exchequer and a more successful joint Postmaster-General, he was pursuing an equally active career as a patron of architecture. He also became a founder member of the Dilettanti Society in 1732. He also proved an imaginative and enterprising landscape gardener on a considerable scale. In the course of his activities he transformed both the house and the park of West Wycombe.

Dashwood began work on these vast schemes sometime after 1735, being aided initially by Morise

*Erasmus **Darwin** (1731–1802).*

*Sir Francis **Dashwood** (1709–1782).*

He moved to Lichfield in 1765 with letters of introduction, including one to Canon Seward whose daughter, Anna, then but nine years old and later famed as the Swan of Lichfield, began her life-long devotion to him, culminating in a biography. The move to Lichfield prompted a spectacular career. He married and bought a house with a derelict garden which he restored, planting roses and other choice plants, and erecting fencing from the road with Chinese-style palings.

About 1777 Darwin purchased what Miss Seward described as 'a little wild, umbrageous valley among the only rocks that neighbour that city so nearly. It was irriguous from various springs'—one of which never froze in the hardest winter. Darwin's plantings are now not known,

One of a series of paintings by Thomas Daniell, showing the island Music Temple designed by Nicholas Revett for Sir Francis **Dashwood** at West Wycombe Park, Buckinghamshire.

Peter Hadland **Davis** (1918–   ), botanical collector.

Lewes Jolivet, designer, draughtsman and 'dutifull servant', and afterwards by Thomas Cook, a onetime pupil of 'Capability' Brown. To Thomas Cook is attributed the scheme for naturalizing the appearance of the park between 1770 and the death of Dashwood, who had, meantime, become Lord Despencer. Nicholas Revett designed various buildings for the park, including the temple of Flora and the Island Temple.

Daubeny, Charles Giles Bridle (1795–1867). Chemist and botanist. Daubeny was born at Stratton, in Gloucestershire, where his father was rector. He was educated at Winchester and Magdalen College, Oxford, where he graduated in 1814. As Daubeny was intended for the medical profession, he had attended lectures on chemistry and these fostered his interest in natural science.

In 1815, he went to Edinburgh to further his medical studies and was introduced to several eminent men of science. He became fascinated by volcanic phenomena and travelled extensively on the Continent to carry out his research.

In 1822, Daubeny was appointed Professor of Chemistry at Oxford. Two years later, he became Professor of Botany and moved to the Oxford Botanic Gardens to continue his work. His approach to botany was very much that of the chemist. Two of his most important publications were *On the Action of Light upon Plants, and of Plants upon the Atmosphere* (1836) and *On the Influence of the Lower Vegetable Organisms in the Production of Epidemic Diseases* (1855). He was a supporter of Charles Darwin's *Origin of Species* and wrote a paper *On the Sexual-*

ity of Plants. His other publications include an *Essay on the Trees and Shrubs of the Ancients* (1865) and *Lectures on Roman Husbandry* (1857).

Davey, John (1846–1923). Tree surgeon. Davey was born in Somerset, the son of the manager of a large farm. He received virtually no formal education but, as a result of his unusual determination and self-discipline, he acquired a vast knowledge of agriculture whilst helping his father on the estate, and himself became an estate foreman at the age of eighteen.

Having first taught himself to read and to write, Davey went to Torquay as an apprentice in 1866, to further his knowledge of horticulture and landscape gardening. In 1872, he emigrated to Ohio, in the United States, where he had a number of contacts. He soon established himself as an authority on agriculture in general and forestry in particular, his advice frequently being sought by estate owners, especially in relation to shade and ornamental trees. In 1902, he published *The Tree Doctor,* in which he outlined the theory and practice of tree surgery. His researches were widely respected and his methods copied throughout the world. This led to the establishment of an institute at Kent, Ohio, to train students in this department of horticulture. His other publications include *A new Era in Tree Growing* (1905) and *Instruction Books on Tree Surgery and Fruit Growing* (1914).

Davis, Peter Hadland (1918–). Plant-collector. Davis was born in Somerset and trained at Ingwersen's Alpine Plant Nursery at Gravetye, Sussex. He then began to collect

botanical specimens in the Cyclades, Crete and Persia with Edward Gathorne-Hardy. Becoming aware of the considerable opportunities for extensive botanical exploration and research in Turkey, he began a life-long interest in the Anatolian flora. During the Second World War, he had opportunities to continue with his interest in the flora of the Middle East, in Greece, the Lebanon, Syria and elsewhere. During this period, he became particularly interested in cliff plants and the manifold problems of identification. After the war, he went to Edinburgh University and took a degree in Botany, followed by a PhD and DSc. His academic studies prompted a shift of interest from horticulture to systematic botany. Between 1949 and 1966 he made a series of expeditions to Turkey, accompanied on some of them by Oleg Polunin and Ian Hedge. These

journeys resulted in many seeds and bulbs of attractive endemics being sent back to Britain. Since 1968 he has collected annually in North Africa, with a growing interest in the floristic connexions between that area and south-west Asia.

Peter Davis is now Reader in Taxonomic Botany at Edinburgh University and deeply involved in preparing an eight-volume *Flora of Turkey,* assisted by a research team financed by the Science Research Council. During his travels, he has collected over 50,000 herbarium gatherings from the Mediterranean and S. W. Asia for the national herbaria, discovered two new genera and described numerous new species. Among plants introduced from the Near East to cultivation in Britain are *Anchusa caespitosa; Aristolochia cretica; Campanula laciniata, C heterophylla, C myrtifolia; Celsia acaulis; Cyclamen mirabile, C pseudi-*

Garden in Pompeii, from Lectures on Roman Husbandry *by Charles* **Daubeny.**

bericum; Fritillaria macrandra (rho-dokanakis), F tuntasii; Helichrysum orientale; Hypericum trichocaulon; Muscari bourgaei, M macrocarpum; Origanum amanum, O laevigatum; Primula davisii; Salvia caespitosa; Sempervivum minus; Sideritis syriaca; Thymus cilicicus; Verbascum dumulosum; Wulfenia orientalis.

De Caus (or de Caux), Isaac (fl. 1625–45). Garden architect and engineer. Although de Caus was born in Dieppe and scarcely anything is known of his early life, he makes his appearance in this DICTIONARY as the man chiefly responsible, with Philip, the 4th Earl of Pembroke, for the 'idyllic' landscape gardens at Wilton House, Wiltshire. He took over from a relative (possibly his father), Soloman de Caus, an itinerant engineer-architect who had gained wide renown as designer of gardens at Heidelberg before coming to England.

In this country he was involved in laying-out gardens, most notably for Robert Cecil, Earl of Salisbury, in 1611 at Hatfield, where he superseded the resident native gardeners and introduced variants of the waterworks for which he was renowned. He also worked for Prince Henry, brother of Charles I, at Richmond, and was author of a book published in 1615, concerned with the mechanical aspects of water-works intended for use in gardens, particularly with grottoes and fountains.

In about 1624, Isaac de Caus designed a grotto for Inigo Jones's Banqueting House and probably another at Woburn a year or so later. He was recommended to the Earl of Pembroke (probably by the King) in connexion with the designing of the proposed gardens at Wilton. There, de Caus was provided with permanent quarters. Despite the upheavals of the Civil War, this vast and elaborate gardening project was begun in 1632–33. In about 1638, de Caus also designed a new front for Wilton, but this was burned down within ten years, and rebuilt by John Webb, Inigo Jones's assistant, with his master's 'advice and approbation'. De Caus described the garden he had planned and supervised in an undated publication, *Hortus Pembrochianus*.

The garden was indeed 'princely', the walled garden alone enclosing over nine acres. The general plan derived from the notions propounded for 'the ideal garden' by

(Left) Anchusa caespitosa and (right) Sideritis syriaca, two plants which were introduced into Britain from the Middle East by Peter Hadland Davis, during his plant-collecting travels in Anatolia.

Painting (detail) by Netscher showing the pineapple grown by the gardener of Sir Matthew Decker, c. 1715.

Francis Bacon (qv) some twenty years before.

Isaac De Caus asserted the supremacy of the French gardening tradition over established Italian influences and his new ideas ended the rigidity and restrictions of the medieval garden. Of the Caroline garden he designed, nothing remains except the carved façade of the grotto, now a garden house. De Caus also designed the stables at Wilton.

Decker, (Sir) Matthew (1679–1749). Landscape gardener. Decker was born in Amsterdam, but emigrated to England and settled in London in his early twenties. He gained renown as an early writer on economics and as a director of the East India Company. He became so thoroughly anglicized that he was elected MP for Bishop's Castle, Shropshire, and held other consequential positions. He was made a baronet in 1702. He had 'a truly Dutch passion for gardening', and his garden at Richmond, Surrey, was celebrated, exemplified by an undated painting by Theodore Netscher, now in the Fitzwilliam Museum, Cambridge. The painting shows a pineapple and the Latin legend to the painting reads: 'To the perpetual memory of Matthew Decker, Baronet, and Theodore Netscher, gentleman. This pineapple, deemed worthy of the Royal table, grew at Richmond at the cost

(Opposite) Mosaics by Mary Delany from the collection of over a thousand now in the British Museum. The mosaics are made of small pieces of coloured paper, cut to the size of individual petals and leaves, then glued to sheets of dark paper. Mrs Delany started this work at seventy-four years of age.

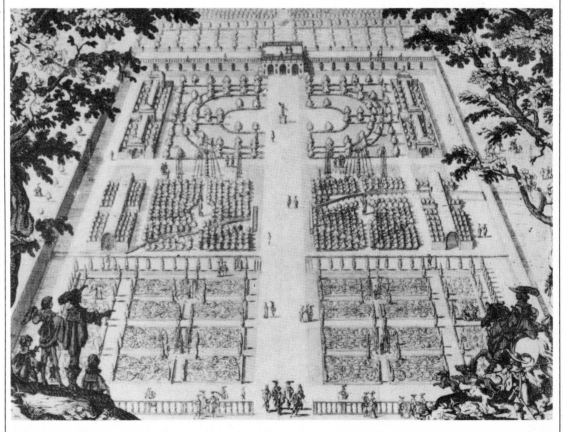

The layout of the earlier garden at Wilton House, Wiltshire, as designed by Isaac de Caus, established c. 1632–33.

of the former, and still seems to grow by the art of the latter. H. Watkins set up this inscription, AD 1720'.

In 1728, Richard Bradley (qv) published an account of the method used by Telende, Decker's gardener, in the cultivation of this pineapple, which is the first description of the construction and management of a tan-bark hot bed, introduced from Holland at about that time. The method was also employed by Philip Miller of the Chelsea Physic Garden, enabling him to germinate the seeds of certain tropical plants which he had hitherto failed to do. The fermenting bark was placed in a brick pit about five feet deep, on top of a foot of hot dung. This was done in February. The frame was covered with glass lights and in about fifteen days the necessary temperature was reached. Seeds or cuttings in pots were then plunged in the tan, which maintained the actual soil in the pots at a steady, unchanging heat.

Decker Paul (fl. 1750s). Architect. Little is known of the career of Paul Decker, apart from the fact that he was one of that army of architectural scribes and draughtsmen who published pattern-books throughout the eighteenth century. His publications were concerned with the fashionable aspects of gothick and Chinoiserie and included *Chinese Architecture, Civil and Ornamental, adapted to this climate (1759)* and *Gothic Architecture Decorated (1759)*. The latter comprised a selection of fanciful temples, hermits' retreats, summer-houses, fences and other ornamental garden structures.

Delany, Mary (1700–1788). Botanical artist. Mary Delany was the daughter of Bernard Granville, brother of Lord Lansdowne. In 1718, against her will, she was married to Alexander Pendarves of Cornwall, a man over forty years her senior. Nine years after his death she married the Reverend Patrick Delany, a Fellow of Trinity College, Dublin, whom she had met on a visit to Ireland some years previously. Unlike her first marriage, this union was extremely happy.

During her life in Dublin, Mary Delany moved in literary circles, but her later fame was founded on what she termed her 'paper mosaicks', which she started a decade after the death of her second husband.

These mosaics were undoubtedly based on her considerable powers of observation and searches for the herbs and flowers of the Wicklow Mountains. Flowers and gardens were her favourite study.

Her skill was described by Dr Erasmus Darwin (qv) in *The Loves of the Plants* in the following footnote to his lines:

Mary **Delany** *(1700–88).*

So now Delany forms her mimic bowers,
Her paper foliage and her silken flowers;
Her virgin train the tender scissors ply,
Vein the green leaf, the purple petal dye:
Round wiry stems the flaxen tendril bends
Moss creeps below, and waxen fruit impends.

'Mrs Delany,' Darwin wrote, 'has finished nine hundred and seventy accurate and elegant representations of different vegetables with the parts of their flowers, fructification etc, according with the classification of Linnaeus, in what she terms paper mosaic. She began this work at the age of 74, when her sight would no longer serve her to paint, in which she much excelled: between the age of 74 and 82, at which time her eyes quite failed her, she executed the curious hortus siccus above mentioned, which I suppose contains a greater number of plants than was ever before drawn from the life by any one person. Her method consisted in placing the leaves of each plant with the petals and all the other parts of the flowers on coloured paper, and cutting them with scissors accurately to the natural size and form, and then pasting them on a dark ground; the effect of which is wonderful, and their accuracy less liable to fallacy than drawings. She is at this time [1788] in her 89th year, with all the powers of a fine understanding unimpaired.'

In 1785, George III gave Mrs Delany a house at Windsor and a pension of £300 a year. Her complete collection of paper mosaics was presented to the British Museum by Lady Llanover in 1897.

Denham, Dixon (1786–1828). Traveller, plant-collector. Denham was educated at Merchant Taylors' School, London, after which he was articled to a solicitor in London. In 1811, he joined the army as a volun-teer and fought in campaigns in Spain, Portugal and France, quickly distinguishing himself for bravery. In 1821, he travelled to Africa, in company with Dr Walter Oudney and Lt Hugh Clapperton, in order to find a route from the north coast to Timbuctoo. The eventful four-year expedition is recorded in his *Narrative of Travels and Discoveries in Northern and Central Africa*. During his journeys, Denham collected plants which are now in the British Museum (Natural History).

View in Africa, from a Narrative of Travels *by Dixon* **Denham**.

Devonshire (Dukes of). The Cavendish family has, through the centuries, been responsible, with notable architects, garden designers and craftsmen, for one of the most magnificent gardens in Britain, Chatsworth in Derbyshire.

Until the making of good roads and the coming of the railway, which was laid through the park in 1847, the situation of Chatsworth was remote. Seventeenth-century engravings show a bleak, steep-sided valley above the River Derwent, almost without trees. Daniel Defoe, although admiring what had been achieved, in his day, wrote '. . . if there is any wonder in Chatsworth, it is, that any man who had a genius suitable to so magnificent a design, who could lay out the plan for such a house, and had a fund to support the charge, would build it in such a place when the mountains insult the clouds, intercept the sun, and would threaten, were earthquakes present here, to bury the very towns, much more the house in their ruins.'

The Elizabethan mansion was one of the many mansions enlarged by that demoniacal builder, 'Bess of Hardwick'. Her descendant, William Cavendish (1640–1707), who succeeded to the earldom of Devonshire in 1684, was created first duke a decade later. He destroyed the remains of the old mansion and built a new and more palatial seat, employing as architects William Talman and Thomas Archer. The new garden was made under the direction of George London, with the assistance of Henry Wise, between 1687 and 1706. It is said that the Duke started rebuilding the place as an excuse for staying away from the court of James II as he was a powerful supporter of William III.

An account of the garden was given by Celia Fiennes when she travelled through Derbyshire shortly before the garden was finished. She wrote: 'The Duke's house lies just at the foot of this steep hill which is like a precipice just at the last, notwithstanding the Duke's house stands on a little rising ground from the River Derwent which runs all along the front of the house and by a little fall made in the water which makes a pretty murmuring noise; before the gate there is a large park and several fine gardens one without another with grand walks and squares of grass with stone statues in them. In the middle of each garden is a large fountain full of images, sea gods and dolphins and sea horses, which are full of pipes which spout out water in the basin, and spouts all about the gardens. There are three gardens just around the house. Out of two of them you ascend by several steps into other gardens, with statues and images in the basins. There is one basin in the middle of one garden that is very large and by sluices several pipes play out the water, about thirty large and small pipes altogether; some flush it up so that it froths like snow . . . So the gardens lie one above another which makes the prospect very fine.

'Above these gardens is an ascent of five or six steps up to a green walk and groves of firs, and a wilderness and close arbours and shady walks. At each end of one walk stand two pyramides full of pipes spouting water that runs down one of them on brass hollow work which looks like rock and hollow stones;

the other is all flats standing one above another like salvers so the water rebounds one from another. About the middle of another green walk by a grove stands a fine willow tree; the leaves, bark and all look very natural, the root is full of rubbish or great stones to appearance, and all of a sudden by turning a sluice it rains from each leaf and from the branches like a shower, it being made of brass and pipes. Beyond this is a basin in which the branches of two artichoke leaves which weep at the end into the basin which is placed at the foot of thirty lead steps, the lowest of which is very deep and between every four steps is a half pace all made of lead and broad on each side; on a little bank stand blue balls, ten on a side, and between each ball are four pipes which by a sluice spout out water across the steps like an arbour or arch; while you are thus amused suddenly there runs down a torrent of water out of two pitchers in the hands of two large nymphs that lie in the upper step, which makes a pleasing prospect. This is designed to be enlarged, and steps made up to the top of the hill, which is a vast ascent, but from the top of it now they are supplied with water for all their pipes so it will be the easier to have such a fall of water even from the top which will add to the curiosity.'

This last project which she mentions was to become Grillet's cascade which flowed from under the cascade house, designed by Thomas Archer. Celia Fiennes does not mention the old orangery of 1696, still standing. The magnificent statuary was the work of the Dutchman, Caius Gabriel Cibber. The replanning of Chatsworth's garden was completed by the time the 1st Duke died.

No significant further aggrandisement took place until the time of the 4th Duke, another Wil-

liam. Between his succession in 1755 and his death in 1764 further changes took place. Perhaps urged on by Horace Walpole's comment on the lack of trees, at Chatsworth, he called in 'Capability' Brown in 1761. Many traces of the ensuing plantings remain.

There is then another quiescent period, until William George Spencer Cavendish (1790–1858), celebrated as 'the Bachelor Duke', ascended to the title as 6th Duke in 1811. His partnership with that remarkable gardener, Joseph Paxton (qv), is one of the legends of British gardening history.

Paxton was only twenty-three and foreman of the arboretum at Kew when, in 1826, on the eve of the Duke's departure for Russia to represent George IV at the coronation of Nicholas, he was appointed head gardener at Chatsworth. Paxton arrived at half-past four on a May morning, found the place locked up and entered his new domain by climbing the wall of the kitchen garden. When the army of gardeners arrived at six, he set them to work.

He next traced the foreman in charge of the waterworks, told him to turn all the cocks on and play them for him. He then found the housekeeper, who gave him breakfast, and by nine o'clock (so it is said) had fallen in love with her daughter—and later married her.

He soon found that owing to the Duke's lack of interest in the gardens, the staff had for some years done the minimum of work. The four pineapple houses were collapsing; the once-famous vineries carried only eight bunches of grapes; there were only eight rhododendrons and no camellias.

The Duke, son of the famous Georgiana, painted by Reynolds and Gainsborough, whose brilliance and gaiety he inherited, also had a serious and even melancholy side to his

Willow Tree fountain at Chatsworth, seat of the Dukes of **Devonshire**.

nature. By degrees he found a response to these qualities in his gardener, in whose schemes of improvement he became more and more interested. Gradually the Duke became one of the most knowledgeable patrons of his day. In the *Gardener's Magazine* for December 1836, J. C. Loudon described the achievements carried, or being carried, out at Chatsworth—with Paxton as executant—and termed the Duke the 'greatest encourager of gardening in England at the present time'.

In 1837, the Duke was elected a member of the council of the Horticultural Society and, in 1838, he became its president, a position he held for twenty years.

The visit of the Queen and Prince Albert in 1843 was an affair of the utmost splendour. The month chosen was—oddly—December. The Queen and her party were met at the station by a coach and six, with eight outriders. Guns thundered out a salute as they entered the park. After dinner, Queen Vic-

toria was led to a window. All was dark. Then, in a moment, the falls, cascades, fountains and statues were gloriously illumined. Coloured flares blazed to be reflected in the water.

Then the party walked into the new conservatory designed by Paxton, where thousands of lamps flickered among the exotic plants, a collection of unique range and splendour. Despite his contribution to such splendid occasions, Paxton remained a master of detail. The next morning when the Duke of Wellington, a member of the party, took a walk round all the paraphernalia, even all the minor litter, inseparable from such a display, had gone: the garden was at its tidiest.

Many other great events and successes were associated with the Duke's era at Chatsworth, such as the cultivation, in a specially-built house, of the giant water lily, *Victoria amazonica*, with leaves that could support a child (Miss Paxton), and which flowered in 1849. The Duke also sent John Gibson in 1835 to collect the very rare Indian tree

(Left) Bust of the 6th Duke of **Devonshire**, *in the grounds of Chatsworth, Derbyshire; (centre) the pavilion and orangery at Chatsworth, seen from the east; (right) the 6th Duke of Devonshire (1790–1858). The engraved views above and at the top of the page are taken from a nineteenth-century guide-book.*

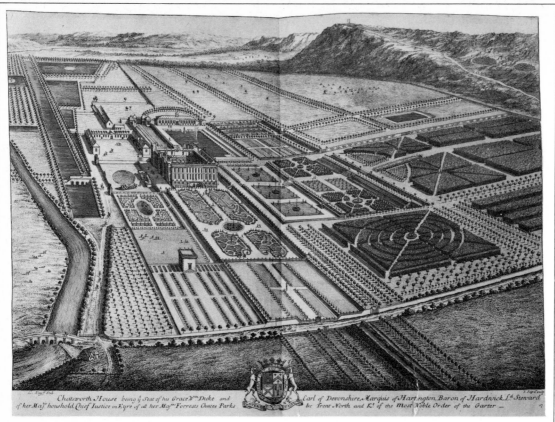

Knyff's Perspective of Chatsworth, engraved in 1699 and taken from Kip's Théatre de la Grande Bretagne, *published in 1716. The engraving shows the house in relation to the formal gardens established by the 1st Duke of* **Devonshire**. *A few of these early features survive, and a new maze has been established within the last few years.*

Amherstia nobilis. This work Gibson successfully carried out, but this astonishing flower opened first on a rival's specimen, belonging to Louisa Laurence (qv). Gibson, however, collected some good orchids and presented the famous Calcutta Botanic Gardens with varieties from Chatsworth. Two other Chatsworth gardeners, Peter Banks and Robert Wallace, went to California to carry on where David Douglas (qv) had left off. They were drowned in a boating tragedy on the Columbia River in 1838.

An important action taken by the Horticultural Society, to which the Duke gave his strong support, was the transfer of the Kew gardens from royal to national ownership.

The Duke died in 1858. Paxton, now knighted, was a man of many interests.

Dickson, James (c1738–1822). Botanist. Dickson was born at Kirke House, Traquair, Peebleshire. Little is recorded of his parentage, but he is known to have worked in the gardens of the Earl of Traquair. The story is that as a boy he heard one of his fellow-workers ask another the name of the buckshorn plantain. The query was answered. The discovery that plants had names so impressed him that he decided to study botany, which he did to such effect that he became an outstanding authority on the subject, particularly on mosses.

Dickson journeyed south while still a youth and worked as an 'improver' in the nursery of Jeffery & Co which was on the site of the famous London and Wise nursery at Brompton Park (now a complex of museums) which had been founded by George London and others in 1681. Dickson held other positions as gardener until, in 1722, he set up as nurseryman and seedsman in a shop in Covent Garden. The business apparently flourished, with wide contacts amongst gar-deners and botanists, until his death.

Dickson was fortunate in two friendships. The first, made whilst working at Brompton Park, was with James Lee (1715–95) (qv) the enterprising nurseryman of Hammersmith. The second was with Sir Joseph Banks (1743–1820) (qv) who was still an undergraduate at Oxford. Through the latter, he later obtained the post of gardener to the British Museum, for which he had supplied Banks with an estimate showing how it could be run more cheaply and efficiently than was then being done.

Between 1785 and 1801, Dickson worked on his study of mosses. He was helped in the work by a Pole, John Zier, who lived in London. Unfortunately, little is known of this unusual aide, although he is believed to have helped several other botanical authors.

Dickson produced other works. He made tours in Scotland, one of which, in 1789, engaged upon the study of Ben Lawers, he was accompanied by Mungo Park (qv). Dickson's friendship with Banks set Park upon his remarkable career. Park married Dickson's sister.

Dickson was one of the seven men who met on Wednesday, 7th March, 1804, at Hatchard's book shop in Piccadilly to form the Horticultural Society, later to become the world-famed Royal Horticultural Society. Dickson proved a very active Fellow, becoming a Vice-president, and was one of the first to stage an exhibit at a meeting—exhibitions at that time not being usual practice—when, in February 1806, he displayed Covent Garden market specimens of a continental variety of rape, *Brassica napus*, about which he read a paper. He was also one of the founders of the Linnean Society in 1788. (The first president of the Society, Sir James Edward Smith [qv], composed the inscription on Dickson's tombstone in All Saints Church, Sanderstead.)

In the 1790s, Dickson moved to Croydon, where possibly he had a nursery. He was an early commentator on American blight and a pioneer cultivator of alpines. Although his name was occasionally mis-spelt Dixon by his friends in their publications, he is remembered correctly and appositely in the genus *Dicksonia*, named in 1788 by the French botanist Charles Louis L'Heritier de Brutelle (1746–1800) who visited England in 1786 with Redouté. These handsome tree ferns with much-divided

The giant water lily, or Victoria amazonica, *at Chatsworth, seat of the Dukes of* **Devonshire**, *with Paxton's daughter, Anne, supported by one of the leaves.*

Detail of a painting of James **Dickson** *(c. 1738–1822).*

(Opposite) The gardens at Chatsworth, Derbyshire, seat of the Dukes of **Devonshire**, *showing (top left) south façade; (top right) lower terrace; (centre) cascade with pavilion by Thomas Archer; (below left) serpentine hedging; (below right) pool in the massive rock garden.*

HORTI ELTHAMENSIS
PLANTARUM
RARIORUM
ICONES ET NOMINA
A
JOH. JAC. DILLENIO, M. D.
DESCRIPTARUM
ELTHAMI IN CANTIO,
IN HORTO
VIRI ORNATISSIMI ATQUE PRAESTANTISSIMI
JACOBI SHERARD,
M. D. SOC. REG. ET COLL. MED.
LOND. SOC.
ADDITIS
DENOMINATIONIBUS LINNÆANIS.
TOMUS PRIMUS

LUGDUNI BATAVORUM.
APUD CORNELIUM HAAK.
MDCCLXXIV.

Sir Kenelm **Digby** *(1603–1665), diplomatist and natural scientist.*

Heathers from The Floral Magazine *edited by Henry* **D'Ombrain**.

Johan Jakob **Dillenius** *(1684–1747) and (right) title-page of his* Horti Elthamensis Plantarum Rariorum *(1732).*

leathery leaves, mostly from Australasia, include one only, *D. antarctica*, which is grown out of doors in the mildest parts of the British Isles.

Digby, (Sir) Kenelm (1603–1665). Diplomatist, essayist, philosopher. Digby, the elder son of Sir Everard Digby, who was executed for his part in the Gunpowder Plot of 1605, was born at Gayhurst Manor in Buckinghamshire. He was brought up in the Roman Catholic faith, but subsequently professed to have become a Protestant and, still later, to have been reconverted to Rome.

In 1618, Digby was admitted as a gentleman commoner to Gloucester Hall (now Worcester College), Oxford, where he studied under the mathematician, Thomas Allen (1542–1632). Two years later, Digby left Oxford without a degree, and travelled on the Continent.

In 1627–8, Digby was in charge of a privateering force to capture French ships anchored off Venice. In the event, he also took a number

of Flemish and Spanish ships, all of which initially pleased James I but led to such vehement protests from the Venetian ambassador that the action was disavowed by the king.

In 1633, Digby's wife died and he retired to Gresham College, where he spent two years in virtual isolation, devoting himself to scientific experiments.

Digby published a number of works, mostly of a philosophical nature. He was a keen student of Natural Science, but his credulity often caused him to draw inaccurate conclusions from his experiments. He is purported to have been the first to observe the importance of oxygen for plant life and published a *Discourse concerning the Vegetation of Plants* (1661).

Dillenius, Johann Jacob (1684–1747). Botanist. Dillenius, a native of Darmstadt, came to England in 1721, where he spent the rest of his life, becoming known as Dr Dill or John Jacob Dillenius. He was closely

connected with William Sherard (qv), who, after a brilliant career at Oxford was British consul at Smyrna 1703–1715. From Anatolia Sherard sent plants to England, where his brother James (1666–1737) had a famous botanical garden, with many rare plants, at Eltham in Kent.

Dillenius wrote and etched the figures for *Hortus Elthamensis* (1732), an accurate account of the new and rare plants in the Eltham garden, and *Historia Muscorum* (1741), a description of plants that were in many cases not mosses. The engravings were of the highest standards of accuracy.

William Sherard returned to Oxford in 1719, on the death of a life-long friend, the younger Bobart (qv), keeper and professor of the city's Botanic Gardens. Sherard took over the Gardens and at his death bequeathed to the University his collection of books, plants, and what was held to be the finest herbarium in Europe. Sherard also bequeathed an endowment for a

Chair of Botany with certain conditions: that the post should be held by Dillenius; that subsequent appointments should be made not by the University but by the Royal College of Physicians, and that the post should never be held by a cleric. Although these restrictive conditions later caused serious problems, their first result was that Dillenius was duly appointed Oxford's first Sherardian Professor in surroundings where his great work in descriptive botany could continue. Dillenius was elected a Fellow of the Royal Society in 1724.

D'Ombrain, (Reverend) Henry H. (1818–1905). Botanist. D'Ombrain was born in Pimlico, London, the son of Admiral Sir James D'Ombrain, Inspector-General of the Coast Guard in Ireland. He came of a Huguenot family which had escaped from France at the time of the St Bartholomew massacre. For some time, the family lived in Ireland, and in 1838 Henry was instru-

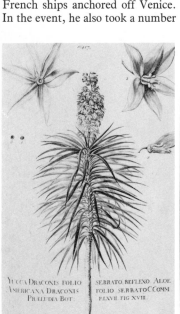

Four plates engraved by Johan **Dillenius** *for his* Horti Elthamensis Plantarum Rariorum, *published in 1732.*

The Reverend Henry Honywood **D'Ombrain** *(1818–1895).*

John **Dominy** *(1816–1891), gardener and orchid hybridist.*

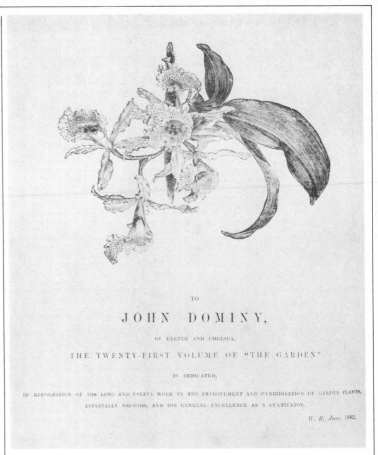

TO

JOHN DOMINY,

OF EXETER AND CHELSEA,

THE TWENTY-FIRST VOLUME OF "THE GARDEN"

IS DEDICATED,

IN RECOGNITION OF HIS LONG AND USEFUL WORK IN THE IMPROVEMENT AND HYBRIDISATION OF GARDEN PLANTS,
ESPECIALLY ORCHIDS, AND HIS GENERAL EXCELLENCE AS A CULTIVATOR.

W. R., June, 1882.

Page from The Garden, *dated 1882, carrying dedication to John* **Dominy**, *'in recognition of his long and useful work in the improvement and hybridization of garden plants, especially orchids, and his general excellence as a cultivator'.*

mental in forming the Natural History Society of Dublin.

He became an authority on flowers and from 1862 to 1873 edited *The Floral Magazine*, which included plates by Walter Fitch (qv), 1817–92, and others, but is best remembered as founder of the National Rose Society in 1876. The Society continues to this day as the largest and most prominent specialist flower society in the British Isles, if not in the world, with its own trial grounds and issuing numerous specialist publications. In 1875, D'Ombrain founded the Horticultural Club. This Society also continues to thrive. D'Ombrain was secretary of both societies for over twenty-five years. In 1897 he received the Royal Horticultural Society's Victoria Medal of Honour. He was also a successful journalist and speaker. For many years he was Vicar of Westwell, which is near Ashford in Kent.

Dominy, John (1816–1891). Orchid hybridist. Dominy was born in Devonshire. After serving an apprenticeship in a private garden, he worked for the firm of Lucombe, Pince and Co of Exeter, before moving to the new and enterprising firm of Veitch of the same city. His unusual skill and intelligence brought him encouragement from his new employers, among whose customers he came to know several outstanding botanists and horticulturists, including a surgeon, John Harris, who showed Dominy how orchids were fertilized. At that time, no hybrid orchids had been produced. On the advice of Harris, Dominy attempted to do so, using the pollen of *Calanthe furcata* on *C. masuca*. A hybrid, *C. dominii*, resulted, which flowered in 1856. The cult of the hybrid orchid, following Dominy's work, has become of great horticultural importance.

Dominy also succeeded with hybrid fuchsias and nepenthes, and initiated another famous Veitch hybridist, John Seden (1840–1921) into the craft. In 1864 he moved to London when Veitch moved to the Royal Exotic Nursery in King's Road, Chelsea.

Don, George (1798–1856). Scottish plant-hunter. Don was the son of George Don, the well-known nurseryman, of Doo Hillock, Forfarshire. After working in his father's nursery gardens, he joined Dickson's nursery in Edinburgh before moving to London to work as a foreman at the Chelsea Physic Garden. When he was twenty-three he was chosen by the Horticultural Society to seek plants on the Gold Coast, the Ivory Coast and in South and North America. He set sail in HMS *Iphigenia*. The voyage, which lasted fifteen months, was extremely hazardous but successful. The list of the plants which he brought back to the Society ranges from orchids

Calanthe Dominii, *the first hybrid orchid, achieved by John* **Dominy**.

Combretum grandiflorum, *a tropical climber found in Sierra Leone, one of the many plants collected by George* **Don** *(1798–1856) during his plant-hunting expeditions for the Royal Horticultural Society.*

Douglas fir trees (Pseudotsuga menziesii) *in the Park Hill enclosure, Park End, Forest of Dean. The Douglas fir was introduced to Britain by the Scottish-born collector, David* **Douglas**, *in 1827.*

David **Douglas** *(1798–1834).*

from Sierra Leone to tropical shrubs and fruits from Brazil, with additions from the island of St Thomas in the Caribbean and New England in the United States. As the official history of the Royal Horticultural Society explains: 'Considerable success attended the germination of many of Don's seeds and the growth of some of the plants he had introduced at the Society's Garden at Chiswick, where the Stove House was enriched by much new material.' Unfortunately, these auspicious beginnings in Don's relations with the Society were bedevilled by later events. Having been given well over a year to prepare his reports, Don was dismissed for publishing accounts of his travels in other journals. Don, undeterred, allowed his *Monograph of the Genus Allium* to be published in 1826 by the Linnean Society which made him a Fellow five years later. His most important work was the four-volume *General System of Gardening and Botany* (1831–1837), founded upon Philip

Engravings from John Ray's Synopsis *to which Samuel* **Doody** *contributed.*

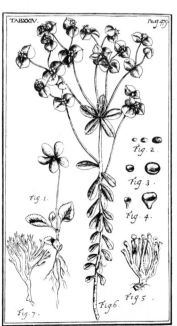

Miller's *Gardener's Dictionary*. He also revised the first supplement to John Loudon's *Encyclopaedia of Plants* and helped Loudon's widow in editing the second edition of the work (1855).

Doody, Samuel (1656–1706). Botanist. Doody was born in Staffordshire, the son of an apothecary, John Doody, who later moved to London. Doody *père* died circa 1696, whereupon Samuel Doody inherited his shop in the Strand. He was an associate of the leading botanists of his time, including Sir Hans Sloane (qv), James Petiver and John Ray (qv).

In 1692, Doody was appointed curator of the Apothecaries Garden in Chelsea (the Chelsea Physic Garden), a post which he held until his death. In the same year, he was elected a fellow of the Royal Society.

Doody's botanical findings were incorporated in the third edition of John Ray's *Synopsis Methodica Stirpium Britannicanum*, issued in 1724.

Douglas, David (1799–1834). Plant collector. Douglas was born at Scone, Perth, the son of a stonemason. As a boy he was an ardent naturalist and spent his pocket-money on food for his pet owlets. At the age of ten or eleven he was apprenticed in Lord Mansfield's garden, but in 1818 went to work for Sir Robert Preston at Valleyfield on the Firth of Forth. Sir Robert, sensing the promise of the young man, gave him the run of his library, while the head gardener encouraged him in his work.

In 1820 Douglas was taken on the staff of the Botanic Garden of Glasgow University, where W. J. Hooker (qv), later Director of Kew Gardens, was Regius Professor. He accompanied Hooker on botanizing trips in the remoter parts of the Highlands and Western Islands which were made in connexion with Hooker's *Flora Scotica*.

In 1823, Douglas was recommended to the Royal Horticultural Society as a collector of herbarium specimens and seeds of trees, shrubs and plants suitable for British gardens, by Hooker and Stewart Murray (c.1789–1858), superintendent of Glasgow Botanic Garden.

At this time, under the aegis of its very enterprising secretary, Joseph Sabine (qv), the Society decided to engage a collector and finance an expedition on a larger scale than had been done in the past. Initially, it was intended to subsidize a plant-hunting expedition to China, whence had come other notable species—the mulberry, for example.

Finally, however, the decision was made to send a plant-collector to the western coast of North America, approaching from the North Pacific Ocean, where Captain George Vancouver had operated in 1792. His

surgeon, Archibald Menzies (1754–1842) (qv) had made observations on the flora of what is now the Californian coast and brought back hitherto-unknown herbarium material growing under climatic conditions not dissimilar from those of the British Isles. The district had also been explored by the transcontinental journey of the Americans, Meriweather Lewis (1774–1809) and William Clark (1770–1838), whose botanical finds had been described by the American, Friedrich Pursh (1774–1820), in 1806. But little else had been done.

In 1823 Douglas made his first journey to the eastern American states, giving particular attention to the study of oak trees, perhaps because of the shortage of British oak timber following the Napoleonic wars, for it was known that several American kinds grew more quickly than British species.

This journey was of little consequence compared with that on which he sailed the following year. To prepare for the expedition, he had studied the accounts that Vancouver had made of his voyage and examined Menzies' specimens and everything possible relating to his venture. The young surgeon on his ship, the *William and Mary*, was John Scouler, MD (qv), as keen a naturalist as Douglas, whose name is commemorated in a botanical epithet Douglas later introduced, one that is quite well known in rock gardens, *Penstemon scouleri*.

The voyage to the mouth of the Columbia River took over eight months. Sailing up river, Douglas saw for the first time the huge conifers and other plants, a few of which he had known only from herbarium specimens and descriptions. Many of the giant conifers he saw, then unknown beyond the American continent, now play an important part in British and other forests and pineta.

Douglas faced great hardships ashore. He wrote of one instance at the appropriately named Cape Foulweather, when, travelling with a few Scots, their porters having been sent home as there was not enough food for them, the wind became a hurricane with sleet and hail. Twice in the night they had to move camp as the tide came in unusually high. They had no protection other than wet blankets and a few pine branches. They were without food. In daylight they walked along the sandy beach for sixteen miles to a small harbour, which they found

deserted. There they remained, feeding on the roots of arrow-head (*Sagittaria*) and a wild lupin. 'From continual exposure,' Douglas wrote, 'I became much reduced.' This particular trip with its tribulations ended in failure. The berries collected for seed had to be eaten, and many specimens they had collected were left behind as they could find no one to carry them.

Many of the native Indians—but by no means all—he described as 'troublesome'. They would come close in a friendly, enquiring manner, then splash water on the white man's gunlocks.

Douglas was one of the first men to describe the exultation that the country could inspire. The country, recorded as the Grand Rapids, is 'grand beyond description; the high mountains in the neighbourhood, which are for the most part covered with pines of several species, some of which grow to an enormous size, are all loaded with snow; the rainbow from the vapour of the agitated waters, which rushes with furious rapidity over shattered rocks and deep caverns, producing an agreeable although at the same time a somewhat melancholy echo through the thick wooded valley; the reflections from the snow on the mountains, together with the vivid green of the gigantic pines, form a contrast of rural grandeur that can scarcely be surpassed.'

On this first journey the tree that most excited Douglas was the sugar pine, *Pinus lambertiana*, which reached 250 feet in its native habitat and had cones eighteen inches in length. He introduced this tree in 1827, but it is rare in the British Isles where it has only reached some eighty feet and produces few cones. The Douglas fir, *Pseudotsuga menziesii*, which he collected on this trip and introduced in 1827, has reached almost two hundred feet in Britain, about twenty feet taller than any other tree grown here, whether indigenous or by introduction.

Until the spring of 1827, Douglas worked only to the west of the Rockies. By April, when he reached the Rockies to cross them on his transcontinental journey, he had travelled seven thousand miles. On this westward crossing, he met several other travellers now famed in the history of American exploration. He carried with him a live eagle caught in the Rockies for the London Zoological Society. He returned to England from Fort York in 1827, a triumphant, exhausted and rather sick man, although he soon recovered, to be lionized by the botanical and horticultural worlds.

In October 1829, he sailed for the Columbia River, with a brief sojourn in the Hawaiian Islands. On this expedition he added the work of a geographer and astronomer to that of botanist and plant-collector.

While in England he had been trained in surveying by Joseph Sabine's brother, Edward, famous for his pioneering work in this and related subjects. Douglas was also helped by the Colonial Office, and it is said that his work as surveyor in North America was outstanding.

But at this time an unfortunate happening gravely upset Douglas. His great supporter and admired friend, Joseph Sabine, left the Horticultural Society. Douglas considered that he had been discharged. What had happened was that Sabine's important activities had so fully occupied him that he had left finance to a junior, who had embezzled the funds. Sabine felt responsible and resigned his secretaryship in 1830. Douglas severed his connexion with the Society in protest, but continued to send it his collections, which were shared with his friend, W. J. Hooker.

On this second expedition Douglas moved south for a time to California. This journey produced many plants, which after attention by subsequent plant-breeders are still amongst the most popular in gardens. Here, too, he saw, but did not introduce, a tree which he described as 'the great beauty of Californian vegetation . . . which gives the mountains a most peculiar, which I was almost going to say awful, appearance, something that plainly tells us we are not in Europe.' This was the coastal redwood, *Sequoia sempervirens*.

On returning from California, Douglas travelled northward. Towards the end of this expedition a daring trip down the Fraser River finished when his canoe was wrecked. His journal, his equip-

ment and a collection of four hundred plants were lost. Fortunately, he was a good correspondent and many of his letters remain.

In the autumn of 1833 he was back in California. On one remote place he pitched his camp where San Francisco now stands. From there he sailed to the Hawaiian Islands. He wrote of his exultation on climbing mountains and volcanoes: 'one day there, is worth one year of common existence.'

On July 12th, 1834, his mangled body was found in a pit dug to trap the savage wild cattle, into which a bullock had already fallen. No one will ever know why Douglas was there; he was believed to be alone.

Some now common plants and shrubs introduced by Douglas, many of which are the species from which numerous garden varieties have been bred, are: *Acer circinatum, Camassia esculenta, Clarkia elegans, Garrya elliptica, Limnanthes douglasii, Mahonia (Berberis) aquifolium, Mimulus moschatus, Ribes sanguineum* and *Symphoricarpos racemosus*.

Amongst the conifer trees commonly grown in the British Isles and elsewhere, and some very extensively used in forestry, are: *Abies grandis, Abies procera, Picea sitchensis, Pinus radiata* and *Pseudotsuga menziesii*.

The trees, shrubs and plants collected and first introduced by David Douglas in his short life have probably had a greater effect on the British landscape and its gardens than those collected by any other single individual. So many of these have now become taken for granted that we are apt not to grasp the magnitude of his activities and achievement.

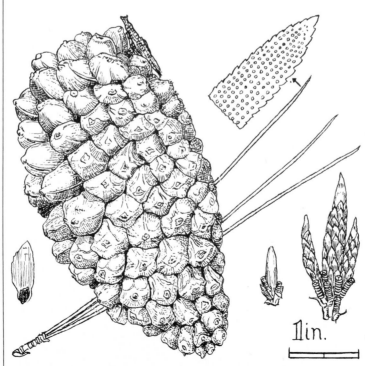

Cone from the Monterey pine (Pinus radiata) *discovered by David* **Douglas** *in 1831 and introduced to Britain in 1833. (Drawing by Miles Hadfield.)*

Dresser, (Dr) Christopher (1834–1904). Botanist, designer. Dresser was born in Glasgow, the son of a Yorkshire excise officer, and was educated at the Government School of Design at Somerset House. Although he is now chiefly known as one of the leaders of the Modern Movement in Design and as author of books on decorative design he showed an early interest in botany and by the age of twenty-one was deemed sufficiently knowledgeable to lecture on botany in English schools. By the time he began to be more widely known as a decorative and industrial designer, he had established a reputation as a reliable botanist.

Drope, Francis (c. 1629–1671). Writer. Author of *Short and Sure Guide in the practice of raising and ordering of fruit trees*, published in 1672, one of the few books of the time which was free from the legends and absurdities of classical eras which were apt to condition and thwart the successful cultivation of fruit

Drummond, James (c 1784–1863). Botanist, plant collector. Drummond, the elder brother of Thomas Drummond (qv), was born in Midlothian, and educated locally. In 1809, he became curator of the Botanic Garden, Cork, a post which he held until 1829 when he travelled to Western Australia, becoming Government Botanist for that area.

Unfortunately, due to lack of funds, his official appointment was withdrawn within a year. By 1835, however, Drummond was well established as a farmer and a dedicated plant-collector. He was a correspondent of William Hooker (qv), sending him reports of his botanizing expeditions as well as collections of dried flowers.

Drummond, Thomas (c 1790–1835). Botanist, plant collector. Drummond took over from George Don (qv) at the Forfar nursery in Scotland. In 1825 he was assistant naturalist with Sir John Franklin's Arctic expedition, and in 1831 botanized in the Western States of North America. In 1828, Drummond became the first curator of the Belfast Botanic Garden, a post which he held for three years before setting off to Mexico and Texas. In 1835 he went to Cuba where he died of fever.

Drummond found a number of new plants but few proved valuable in Britain, apart from the well-known *Phlox drummondii*.

Duff (Sir) Mountstuart Elphinstone Grant (1829–1906). Politician, author. Duff was born in Aberdeenshire and educated in Edinburgh and Balliol College, Oxford. He was called to the Bar at Inner Temple

*Thomas **Drummond** (c. 1790–1835).*

*Sir Mountstuart **Duff** (1829–1906).*

*William **Dykes** (1877–1925), and drawing from his* Handbook of Garden Irises.

in 1854. Three years later Duff became a Liberal MP and, in 1881, was appointed Governor of Madras. He returned to England in 1886 but, disillusioned with politics, devoted himself to research and writing. He was a knowledgeable plantsman and his fourteen-volume *Notes from a Diary* (1897–1905) includes many percipient comments on plants and the botanists of his day.

Dunn, Malcolm (1837–1899). Gardener, pomologist. After serving his apprenticeship in England and Ireland, Dunn returned to Scotland in 1871 to take up an appointment as head gardener to the Duke of Buccleuch at Dalkeith Palace. He was a man of varied talents: a pomologist of the first rank, a grower of grapes in a cold climate, a landscape gardener, a noted arborologist. He was a forceful advocate of the Scottish Arboricultural Society and of the Scheme for establishing a forestry school in Scotland. He was awarded the gold medal of the Royal Horticultural Society in 1897.

Dykes, Percy James (1909–1964). Gardener. Dykes' gardening career was mainly concerned with the development of the Royal Horticultural Society's gardens at Wisley. He joined the garden's staff at the age of twenty and remained for four years. He returned there again in 1946, becoming foreman of the glass-house department and later superintendent, in which position he was responsible for producing large numbers of a wide range of plants for trials, teaching and examinations. The Associateship of Honour of the Society was conferred on him in 1963.

Dykes, William Rickatson (1877–1925). Iris cultivator and hybridist and author. Dykes was educated at the City of London School and afterwards at Wadham College, Oxford, graduating in 1900. He was then for a time at the Sorbonne, before becoming a master at Charterhouse where he remained from 1903 to 1919. He was particularly interested in, and influenced by, the cultivation of little-known species of iris and the hybridization experiments which had been started by Sir Michael Foster (qv) near the end of the nineteenth century. Dykes began to cultivate the species in his own garden at Charterhouse. One consequence was the publication of his *Monograph of the Genus Iris* (1913), which included forty-seven beautiful, life-size colour plates of fine quality drawn by Frank Round (c. 1878–1958), a fellow-master at Charterhouse, who, curiously enough, was quite uninterested in botany.

Dykes had previously published in 1911 a small book for the amateur grower of irises, and in 1924 published a useful and well-illustrated *Handbook of Garden Irises*, with drawings by Elizabeth Kaye.

Dykes grew many difficult varieties and successfully carried out hybridization.

He also wrote for a wide range of periodicals, not only on irises but his other favourites, tulips. The articles on iris, edited by George Dillistone, were later published as *Dykes on Irises*. Dykes also translated, from the French, Louis Lorett's once-famous manual on pruning fruit trees.

Having made himself a considerable authority as a botanically-minded horticulturist, Dykes began what was virtually a new career in 1920 when he took over a key position involving work and responsibilities of which he was entirely without experience. He left Charterhouse and teaching to become secretary of the Royal Horticultural Society. The job was no sinecure, for not only was he entering a new world but he was succeeding the eminent Reverend W. Wilks (qv), who had held the position since 1888 and to 'whose energy, singleness of purpose, and wisdom the Society's transition from poverty to prosperity was largely due', as one obituary notice recorded.

Dykes had all the qualities for success, and soon became involved in the planning of the Society's new

*Victorian view of botanic gardens, Belfast, where Thomas **Drummond** was the first curator.*

I. Polyhymnia, a Regeliocyclus hybrid.

(I. Korolkowi x I. susiana). (Two-thirds size).

A HANDBOOK OF GARDEN IRISES

By W. R. DYKES, M.A., L.-ès-L.

SECRETARY OF THE ROYAL HORTICULTURAL SOCIETY. AUTHOR OF "THE GENUS IRIS," ETC.

LONDON: MARTIN HOPKINSON & COMPANY LTD: 14 HENRIETTA STREET, COVENT GARDEN, W.C. 1924

Frontispiece and title page of A Handbook of Garden Irises *(1924) by William Rickatson* **Dykes**.

hall, on land leased in 1925. Soon after signing the lease on behalf of the Society Dykes died as the result of a motor accident. He had been awarded the Society's Victorian Medal of Honour in 1925, was a founder of the Iris (later British Iris) Society in 1924, and the editor of its first publication, the *Bulletin*.

The obituary in the *Journal* of the Society said of him: 'With all his occupation in the Society's affairs and his interest in his plants he never lost a certain boyish delight in a merry tale, and it was perhaps to this youthfulness in him that his character owed its charm. Like a boy, too, he was almost impetuous in his desire to carry out some new scheme which he had evolved and which he thought would be beneficial to the Society; and by adopting the blunt straightforwardness of the soldier, he has been known to fail to convince his hearers when he might have succeeded had he been prepared to use the tact and skill of the diplomat. After all, this straightforwardness was one of the finest traits in a very attractive character, remarkable for its strength and its sincerity . . .'

The year after Dykes' death one of his yellow irises, which was named 'W. R. Dykes' flowered, and was important in the history of the florist's bearded irises.

His wife, Katherine, was a talented artist and gardener, and worked on their garden at Woking, to which they had moved on leaving Charterhouse. She illustrated in colour and edited her late husband's *Notes on Tulip Species*, published in 1930. An iris she raised, the white-flowered 'Gudrun', played an important part in subsequent iris breeding. She died as the result of a railway accident in 1933, returning from the Chelsea Show.

Dysart family. The Dysarts are represented in this DICTIONARY on account of their long association with Ham House, Petersham, Middlesex, and the gardens of that mansion, now owned by the National Trust and administered by the Victoria & Albert Museum. The house was built in 1610 by Sir Thomas Vavasour, Knight Marshal to James I, but came into the possession of William Murray, first Earl of Dysart in 1637. Ten years later he bequeathed the house to his daughter Elizabeth, who, after the Restoration, obtained the title of Countess of Dysart in her own right, with the power of appointing her successor from among her children.

She, meantime, had married Sir Lyonel Tollemache, 3rd baronet, and three years after his death in 1669, she married the Earl (later the Duke) of Lauderdale.

They were well-matched in ambition and ruthlessness of purpose, and Ham House became a sumptuous background for their extravagant display, necessitating a considerable enlargement of the house between 1673 and 1675. The gardens were also maintained in a manner to match the grandeur of the house. John Evelyn, visiting the house in 1678, recorded the following entry in his diary: 'After dinner I walked to Ham to see the House and Garden of the Duke of Lauderdale,

Elizabeth, daughter of the first Earl of **Dysart**, *made Countess of Dysart in her own right in 1660. She lived at Ham House, Surrey, where she made one of the grandest gardens of her time. She married the Earl of Lauderdale in 1672.*

The Earl (later Duke) of Lauderdale, second husband of the Countess of **Dysart**, *whom he married in 1672. He and his wife were well matched in their ambitious improvements to the house and gardens at Ham House, Surrey.*

(Opposite) Drawing made by Frank Round for The Monograph of the Genus Iris *by William Rickatson* **Dykes** *(Cambridge University Press, 1913).*

which is indeed inferior to few of the best Villas in Italy itself; the house furnished like a great Prince's; the Parterres, Flower Gardens, Orangeries, Groves, Avenues, Courts, Statues, Perspectives, Fountains, Aviaries, and all this at the banks of the Sweetest River in the World, must needs be admired.'

Of these adornments only the orangery, in the singular, survives as a tea-house.

After the death of her husband, the Duchess concentrated her interests on her aviaries in what she termed the 'Volary Room'. A century later, another commentator of note had vastly different impressions of Ham House to record. Horace Walpole, whose niece had married the 5th Earl of Dysart, wrote, in 1770:

'I went yesterday to see my niece in her new principality of Ham. It delighted me and made me peevish. Close to the Thames in the centre of all rich and verdant beauty, it is so blocked up and barricaded with walls, vast trees and gates, that you think yourself an hundred miles off and an hundred years back . . . after journeying all round the house, as you do round an old French fortified town, you are at last admitted through the stable-yard to creep along a dark passage to the housekeeper's room, and so by a back door into the great hall. He seems as much afraid of water as a cat, for though you might enjoy the Thames from every window of three sides of

The South Front of Ham House in about 1680, during the tenure of the house by the Countess of **Dysart**, *shown in a painting by Thomas Rowlandson and now hung in the White Closet at Ham House.*

the house, you may tumble into it before you would guess it was there.'

Yet these impressions are difficult to relate to those recorded by Thomas Rowlandson in his painting of Ham House made during the same ownership.

After remaining in the possession of the descendants of the Countess of Dysart for over three centuries, Ham House was presented to the National Trust in 1948.

Much of the present garden at Ham House is a relatively modern reconstruction.

Charlotte Walpole, 5th Countess of **Dysart**, *after Sir Joshua Reynolds.*

Bird's-eye view of Ham House and formal-style garden at Petersham, Surrey, during the time of the 4th Earl of **Dysart**, *described by Horace Walpole as 'close-fisted' and 'a strange brute'.*

E

Earle, Maria Theresa (née Villiers) (1836–1925). Gardener, writer. Maria Villiers became early interested in gardening and, after her marriage to Captain Charles Earle of the Rifle Brigade, became a keen gardener at her home at Woodlands, at Cobham in Surrey. She was a prolific writer on popular gardening, although her observations often tended to be more social than horticultural. Her books include: *Potpourri from a Surrey Garden*; *More Pot-pourri*; *A Third Pot-pourri*, 1903; *Letters to Young and Old*, 1906; *Memoirs and Memories*, 1911; *Gardening for the Ignorant*, 1912.

Eckford, Henry (1823–1905). Gardener. Eckford was born at Stenhouse, Midlothian, Scotland, and his early training was in the gardens of Beaufort Castle, the seat of Lord Lovat. Subsequently he was employed by James Hogg of Newliston; at Penicuik by Sir Peter Murray; and at Oxenford Castle by the Earl of Stair.

In 1847, on the recommendation of James McNab, who was to become Curator of the Edinburgh Botanic Garden, he moved south to work for Sir Hugh Low, the famous orchid-grower of Clapton, then a village on the outskirts of London. After working for some time for Low he moved to a Colonel Baker of Salisbury, in Wiltshire, a famous dahlia expert, and then, after a spell at Trentham Park in Staffordshire, he moved, in 1854, to become head gardener to Lord Radnor at Coleshill, Berkshire, where he made a reputation as a hybridizer, raising verbenas, pelargoniums, dahlias.

In 1870 he left to work for a Dr Sankey of Sandwell, Gloucester, a raiser of florists' flowers. Here Eckford began his serious work on developing the Sweet Pea by cross fertilization of the very few kinds then in cultivation. This was a notoriously difficult undertaking, for the flowers are self-fertile. In 1882 he introduced the first modern kind, 'Bronze Prince', through the nurseryman Bull of Chelsea. Six years later Eckford left Sankey and set up his own small nursery at Wem in Shropshire.

Of the 264 species exhibited at a Bi-Centenary Sweet Pea Exhibition, held in 1900 to celebrate the raising of the first plants of *Lathyrus odoratus* by Dr Uvedale from seed sent to

*Maria Theresa **Earle** (1836–1925), author of books on popular gardening.*

him in 1699, by the Sicilian monk Cupani, over one hundred were raised by Eckford. Curiously, the apotheosis of Eckford's achievement was not directly from his own hand, but from one, Silas Cole, gardener to Earl Spencer at Althorp, who, among seedlings from Eckford's plants, found one with a shell-pink flower, whose standard and wings had wavy edges.

Edwards, John (fl. 1742–1795) Botanical artist. Little is known of this

*Modern Sweet Pea, derived from cross-fertilization work by Henry **Eckford**.*

*Carnation, 'Franklin's Tartar', drawn by Sydenham **Edwards** (1788).*

artist, although his work ranks with the best of the eighteenth-century flower artists. He published a *British Herbal* in 1770, but his chief work is *A Collection of Flowers Drawn After Nature & Disposed in an Ornamental & Picturesque Manner*, which was published between 1783–1795 and contained 79 coloured plates, including roses, rhododendrons, hyacinths, jasmine and several bouquets. The colouring of the plates in reproduction is particularly fine, due to the use of a pale

printer's ink which gives an unusually accurate rendering of the true tones of the flowers.

Edwards, Sydenham Teast (1768–1819). Botanical artist. Edwards was the son of a schoolmaster at Abergavenny, Monmouthshire, Wales, and showed precocious talent as an artist. Copies he had made from figures in William Curtis's *Flora Londinensis* were shown to Curtis, who was so impressed that he summoned the youth to London for further training. The two became close friends, Edwards joining Curtis in many botanical expeditions.

Edwards' first drawing for Curtis's *Botanical Magazine* was, unusually, of a florist's bizarre carnation, 'Franklin's Tartar', in 1788. He was responsible for over 1,400 drawings. In 1815 he disagreed with Curtis's successors and founded *The Botanical Register* (1815–47), continuing his interest until his death. His contributions consisted of coloured figures of exotic plants cultivated in British gardens. He illustrated *The Complete Dictionary of Practical Gardening* (1805–7) which was edited by R. W. Dickson (under the pseudonym Alexander McDonald). The *Complete Dictionary* was subsequently republished under various other titles.

Edwards was elected a Fellow of the Linnean Society in 1804, and is commemorated in the important genus *Edwardsia* which has, however, now been incorporated within the *Sophora* family.

*Coleshill House, Berkshire, the seat of Lord Radnor where Henry **Eckford** became head gardener and where he made his reputation as a hybridizer.*

Ehret, Georg Dionysius (1708–1770). Botanical artist. Although born in Heidelberg, Georg Ehret worked largely in England where his work was enthusiastically acclaimed. He was the son of a smallholder who trained his son both as gardener and artist. After the death of his father, his mother married a gardener to the Elector of Heidelberg. The young Ehret was given charge of part of the gardens and spent most of his spare time drawing the plants he tended. His work was noticed by the Margrave of Baden. The rest of the garden staff decided that the young man was being given preferential treatment and the Margrave was driven to part with his young *protégé*. Ehret then made his way to Vienna, shortly moving on to Regensberg, where he worked on the plates of Weinmann's *Phytanthoza Iconographia*. After being deceived over payment he was employed by a banker at Regensberg named Leskenkoht. Here he began to find more time for his original work, producing figures for over five hundred plants growing around Regensberg. They were seen by Dr C. J. Trew, a Nuremberg physician, who was also an ardent botanist and was the first to realize that Ehret, as well as being a gardener, was an artist of quite exceptional talent.

In about 1733 Ehret set out on a solitary journey, visiting Basle, Montpellier and Paris. During his journey he met the celebrated French botanist Bernard de Jussieu who advised him to visit London. This he did, armed with several important letters of introduction. In London he met Sir Hans Sloane (qv), Philip Miller (qv), author of the *Gardener's Dictionary*, and other outstanding botanists and gardeners, including Peter Collinson (qv). He sent two hundred of the drawings he made in England back to Dr Trew.

After a year in London he journeyed in Holland, meeting the young Linnaeus (qv), from whom he heard of the new system of classification. Ehret made some explanatory drawings, which Linnaeus later republished in his *Species Plantarum* without acknowledgement.

Linnaeus was at this time staying with a wealthy banker and enthusiastic gardener, George Clifford, who lived near Haarlem. The latter appreciated the merit of Ehret's work and paid him generously for drawings, later engaging him to illustrate the descriptions of his plants that Carl Linnaeus had made. The drawings were later engraved and published in *Hortus Cliffortianus* of 1737.

(Opposite) One of the 79 plates by John Edwards made for A Collection of Flowers Drawn After Nature published between 1793–1795.

(Left) Laurus foliis integris trilobisque *drawn by Georg* **Ehret** *for Dr. C. J. Trew's* Plantae Selectae *(1750–1753) and (right) an engraved portrait of Georg Ehret (1708–1770).*

In 1736, when Georg Ehret returned to England, the patronage of botany, horticulture and botanic gardening was at its height. Here he lived for the rest of his life, marrying Philip Miller's sister-in-law, Susannah Kennet.

His friends and patrons included Dr Richard Mead, who was physician to George II, and the Duchess of Portland who purchased large numbers of his drawings. He also held drawing classes which attracted girls from aristocratic families. He spent part of the summer visiting the houses of the nobility, making drawings of rare plants. In 1750 he began to work in the Oxford Botanic Gardens, but left because of petty quarrels among the staff. In 1757 he was elected a Fellow of the Royal Society.

His principal published drawings include those in *Plantae et Papiliones Rariores* (1748–59), *Plantae Selectae* (1750–73) and *Hortus Amoenissimorum Florum* (1750–86). He also contributed drawings to travel books.

He occasionally engraved his own work for publication, but it is his paintings, usually in body colour on vellum, superbly designed, of which many still exist, that show his work at its best.

Eley, Charles (1872–1960). Rhododendron specialist and author. Eley was a successful industrialist with two hobbies which became major interests in his life. The first of these was typography; the second, Hima-

Charles **Eley** *(1872–1960).*

layan plants. The first interest was sparked off by dissatisfaction with the standards of commercial printing of the post-First-War era. As a leading light in the printing revival of the 'twenties, sponsored by Stanley Morison, Eley founded, within his own company, the Kynoch Press, later absorbed into ICI. His other interest was in gardening in its widest aspects. One consequence was the development of his own garden at East Bergholt Place, near Colchester in Essex, where he was particularly successful in growing rhododendrons and other Hima-

layan plants, not normally a feature of the East Anglian scene. He was one of the founders of the Rhododendron Society in 1915 and its secretary for sixteen years. For his work in this connexion he was awarded the Royal Horticultural Society's Victoria Medal of Honour in 1945.

Eley is best remembered for his book, *Gardening for the Twentieth Century* (1923), which was written with considerable practical knowledge and imagination and pointed the way to what might be called a permanent informal type of garden integrated with a careful selection from the immense number of trees and shrubs now available. The book was published at an apposite moment when the difficulties, following the First World War, were recognized as likely to prove a long-term rather than temporary condition. Eley advocated the abolishing of the formality which had for so long attended the design of small gardens, divided into a series of component parts, and, in its place, proposed an irregular unity, taking advantage of the increased variety of plant shape, colour and form. Eley's proposals have been called an organic form of garden design and were, in essence, a latterday restatement of the principles laid down by William Robinson (qv) and Gertrude Jekyll (qv).

Ellacombe, (Reverend) Henry Nicholson (1822–1916). Gardener, author. Ellacombe spent most of his

The Reverend Henry Nicholson **Ellacombe** *(1822–1916).*

An Elizabethan garden in summer, from Hortus Floridus *(1614), reproduced from* Plant Lore and Garden Craft of Shakespeare *by the Reverend Henry Nicholson* **Ellacombe** *(1896).*

life at Bitton in Gloucestershire, of which parish he became Rector in 1850, having graduated at Oxford in 1844. His garden at Bitton, in an old-established property enjoying a mild climate, was of great interest and he wrote learnedly and lightly about that particular garden and gardening in general. He was, in fact, a typical 'curious gardener', bringing into fashion a large number of delightful plants both new and too-long-neglected.

His first publication was *Plant Lore and Garden Craft of Shakespeare* (1878), a refreshing contrast to so many critical literary studies of the great playwright. He published *In A Gloucestershire Garden* (1895) and *In My Vicarage Garden and Elsewhere* (1902). He wrote a number of articles on the plants in the works of Spencer, Gower, Chaucer and comparable subjects. He also encouraged E. A. Bowles (qv) in his early enthusiasm for gardening. When awarded the Royal Horticultural Society's Victoria Medal of Honour in 1897, Ellacombe was described as 'one of the great gardeners of his day'.

Elliott, Clarence (1881–1969). Horticulturist, plant-hunter, nurseryman. Elliott was a figure of consequence in the history of British gardening following the social revolution after the First World War. Gardens became much smaller with a consequent emphasis on showing natural wild species rather than florists' plants. The patrons of this cult were mainly professional men—doctors, lawyers and so on—who frequently happened also to be mountaineers.

Elliott was the son of the founder of the well-known firm of photographers, Elliott and Fry, and was later concerned in the manufacture of photographic plates and papers. Both these businesses prospered, though Elliott's father was neither photographer nor chemist. The family lived in a pleasant country house with a large garden, then only twelve miles north of London, at Hadley Green, Hertfordshire. The large family gardened from earliest childhood.

Clarence **Elliott** *(1881–1969), a founder member of the Alpine Garden Society.*

After attending Giggleswick School in Yorkshire, where his main occupations seem to have been long walks and climbs in the Yorkshire dales, searching for wild plants, Elliott decided not to join either of the family businesses. As he was devoted to wild flowers and fishing he spent a year's pupillage with the old and famous fruit nursery firm of Rivers at Sawbridgeworth in Hertfordshire. Whilst still a student, he went to Backhouse of York, pre-eminent among British nurserymen

as propagators and suppliers of alpine plants, and remained with them until he was twenty-one. He then went back to fruit-growing, this time to the Cape in South Africa where he lived for three years. On his return he proposed to take up fruit-farming in Essex, but instead founded, in 1907, his Six Hills Nursery (so-called because it was adjacent to six ancient burial mounds) at Stevenage in Hertfordshire.

His interest was in mountain plants and he began to undertake collecting expeditions. In 1908 he went to Corsica, bringing back a number of plants which are now found in many gardens. In 1909 he went to the Falkland Islands ('I found that they were a little further away than I imagined, away down in the south-west corner of the Atlantic, but it was a pleasant month's voyage . . .') and in 1910 he visited the European Alps with Reginald Farrer. (This expedition was the source of the latter's *Among the Hills*, published in 1911.)

In 1927 Elliott went to South America with William Balfour-Gourlay, who was collecting for the botanic gardens of Kew and Edinburgh. He also made other, less esoteric plant-collecting journeys, including excursions to old and sadly derelict gardens in the English countryside, from which he brought back many older and, by that time, virtually forgotten plants. These plants he was instrumental in bringing back into cultivation through his nursery and through the medium of his lively, light-hearted propaganda on behalf of his nursery.

Elliott's gardening activities were numerous and frequently ingenious. He was the pioneer of the now fashionable trough gardens; of the development of the use of tufa for alpine plants; of alpine lawns and much else. He was a founder member of the Alpine Garden Society in 1929. He was awarded the Victoria Medal of Honour of the Royal Horticultural Society in 1951—a little late, some thought.

His nursery catalogues were accurate, informative and well-written. The 1926 edition was illustrated by John Nash (qv), gardener, Royal Academician and an old friend. Elliott also wrote *Rock Garden Plants* (1935) but a second book, *Manavlins From My Garden*, was never completed.

In 1946, with the approach of Stevenage New Town, the nursery was taken over by Frank Barker, a colleague for many years, whilst Elliott moved to Broadwell in the Cotswolds, close to the nursery of his son, Joe.

Elliott's later activities included much journalism, most notably almost five hundred weekly articles which he contributed to *The Illustrated London News* between 1949 and 1959.

Elwes, Henry John (1846–1922). Soldier, big-game hunter, traveller, ornithologist, lepidopterist, botanist, gardener, arboriculturist, forester and writer. The protean Elwes was born at Colesborne in Gloucestershire, the son of wealthy parents. He was educated at Eton and joined the Scots Guards as an ensign in 1865. He served for only four years before resigning his commission as he found 'that there was little or no prospect of any real soldiering'. A more compelling reason, perhaps, was that he had already discovered the pleasures of travel and natural history, especially ornithology. His travels in the Scandinavian countries and the Near East had been lengthy and extensive.

His release from the army set him on a lifelong course of almost Renaissance versatility, of which only his horticultural interests find a place in this DICTIONARY. Although his interests in agriculture and forestry were aroused by his acting as a tenant farmer on his father's estate, he did not become interested in gardening until after his marriage in 1871.

In the intervals between his continuing travels, Elwes had begun to take an interest in growing lilies. Between 1877 and 1880, he published his *Monograph of the Genus Lilium* with plates by Walter Fitch (qv). This was a considerable work for one untrained as a botanist, a pioneering project to which various supplements have since been added.

At the Daffodil Conference of 1884, Elwes proposed a resolution, which was carried, urging that garden hybrids and varieties should be

Colesborne, Gloucestershire, where Henry **Elwes** *lived and carried out his remarkable tree-planting experiments.*

subject to a system of nomenclature quite distinct from that used by botanists. This seems to have been the first practical step by the Royal Horticultural Society towards the development of such international rules, finally accepted and ratified in 1935.

Among Elwes' other activities was his Presidency of the Royal Forestry Society (now of England, Wales and Northern Ireland) in 1907–8, a difficult period, during which he was particularly concerned with the launching of the Society's *Quarterly Journal of Forestry* (which concerns ornamental aspects of the subject as well as strictly arborological considerations). The *Journal of Forestry* soon became internation-

ally famous and respected.

Yet Elwes' wide renown rests chiefly on his studies and writing on trees. Here again he was concerned with both utilitarian and ornamental factors. With the assistance of Augustine Henry (qv), a pioneer of botanical studies in Western China, and, later, Professor of Forestry at Dublin, he embarked on *The Trees of Great Britain and Ireland*. The work bore a dedication from the authors 'by special' permission 'to His Majesty King Edward VII'.

The first volume of this seminal study was published in 1906, the seventh and final volume in 1913. Its object was 'to give a complete account of all the trees which grow naturally or are cultivated in Great

Britain.' The work did not include shrubs, and its most notable feature is epitomized in one sentence: 'We have the special qualification that we have seen both with our own eyes and studied on the spot, both at home and abroad, most of the trees which will be included in the book.' Henry was the trained scientist, Elwes the acute and widely-travelled observer. Circumstance and fashion (which can colour such subjects as botany) are apt to change the worth of many weighty publications, but this great book, dealing so closely with observable fundamentals, and written always in a lucid prose which few scientific writers of today could emulate, has rightly justified the recent republication of the work. Elwes visited some 600 places to make careful notes and take superb photographs of many of his subjects. In addition to multitudinous train journeys, Elwes claimed to have worn out two motor cars in the preparation of the work. He also wrote an engaging and interesting autobiography, *Memoirs of Travel, Sport and Natural History* (1930).

Despite these manifold home-based interests, Elwes' passion for foreign travel never abated. In 1870 he extended his range to India (with W. S. Blanford of the Geological Survey, originally based on Darjeeling). This expedition was mainly ornithological and geological in purpose, but Elwes also made a collection of ferns. In addition he acquired a share in an estate which later proved a valuable asset as a tea plantation.

In 1874 he visited Anatolia on his first true plant-collecting expedition. He visited Smyrna early in March, but the season was still too early, so he went by way of Samos and Cos southwards to the port of Macri which was his base for two journeys through places well-known to archaeologists but little travelled

Henry John **Elwes** *(1846–1922) and a corner of the arboretum he established at Colesborne in Gloucestershire.*

by botanists. He had no camping equipment, the villages were somewhat less than hygienic, and he had to live on bad bread, onions and sour milk. But he found and collected a number of good hardy plants, including the charming snowdrop *Galanthus elwesii*. Missing his steamer back, he returned overland to Smyrna, where he met a Greek who later sent him a large number of bulbs, including the snowdrop, a fortunate gesture as most of what Henry Elwes himself had collected was stolen on the journey home.

In 1876 he visited the tea plantation in India in which he had a share and also made a successful plant-collecting foray into Western Sikkim. A second visit in 1879 was less successful as a source of plants but provided more birds and insects. In 1886 Elwes was appointed naturalist to a proposed official mission to Lhasa but the project was finally abandoned, although he made two short plant-collecting journeys, based on Darjeeling. In 1914 he made his final visit to India at the invitation of the Maharajah of Nepal, taking a pedigree Aberdeen Angus bull along with him as a present to his host.

Elwes also played a notable part, with Lionel de Rothschild and R. Cory in 1920, to acquire the copyright of *The Botanical Magazine*, which was to have ceased publication. They offered the magazine to the Royal Botanic Gardens at Kew whose management refused the gift. Fortunately, the Royal Horticultural Society took it over.

Elwes became a Fellow of the Royal Society in 1897 and of the Linnean Society in 1874. He received the RHS Victoria Medal of Honour in 1897.

Engleheart, (Reverend) George Herbert (c. 1851–1936). Gardener and poet. Engleheart was a native of the Channel Islands, was educated at Elizabeth College, Jersey, and Exeter College, Oxford. He gained an eclectic renown as a translator from the Greek, Latin and French and from the distinguished English, French and German poets of his own day, frequently rendering them into Latin and Greek. He was also a master of Greek calligraphy.

Having become friendly with the Quaker family of William Evans, of Worcestershire, Engleheart married, in 1878, the deeply religious daughter, who had moved from Quakerism towards the Roman Catholic faith. Engleheart was a

Title-page of A Monograph of the Genus Lilium *(1880) by Henry* **Elwes**.

member of the established church and the religious difficulties which resulted between the couple had a profound emotional effect on him. These problems undoubtedly influenced his growing interest in horticulture. In these pursuits—notably in plant breeding—he had a remarkable aptitude, near to genius.

Engleheart's first curacy was in a poor district of Leicester. There was little in the way of a garden; nevertheless he sought to develop what there was. In 1880 he accepted the living of Chute Forest, north of Andover. The vicarage at Apple-shaw, two miles from his church (in which he made a reputation as a preacher) had a large garden. His most serious attention was directed to the genus *Narcissus*, in the study of which one of his ancestors had claimed to have made a new kind of daffodil, crossing the wild pheasant's eye (*N. poeticus*) with the ordinary trumpet kind. The botanists of the time had denied that he had done this, saying that it was not possible. George Engleheart tried and succeeded, waiting seven years for his seedlings to flower. In 1934 E. A. Bowles (qv) wrote in his

Handbook of Narcissus: 'Engleheart has enriched gardens with many lovely flowers with charming names. His "Horace" was one of the first, and I have heard him say that he would not have believed a prophet who told him that the small bed of his of this variety, which at one time contained the whole stock, could in so short a time have provided the Old and New Worlds with millions of this popular flower.'

In 1902, Engleheart moved to Little Clarendon, Dinton, near Salisbury, a pre-Reformation manor-house which he and his wife restored. He ceased parish work, becoming interested in archaeology, discovering a Roman villa (with a pewter dinner service) near his own house.

He continued his search for little-known species of daffodil and in the eighteen-eighties and 'nineties obtained, from old gardens in Ireland, white forms, quite forgotten or unknown in England. He corresponded with other breeders, the Brodie of Brodie, Guy Wilson and J. C. Williams (qv).

His greatest popular triumph was undoubtedly at the Birmingham Daffodil Show of 1898, when he exhibited six bulbs of his 'Will Scarlett' with a striking orange cup. John Pope, nurseryman of King's Norton, paid £100 for three of them; Engleheart kept the others for his own breeding. No comparable price for a daffodil had ever been paid before and the event led to a good deal of speculative breeding. Happily, Engleheart is better remembered for his great white daffodil, one of the first of its kind, which he named 'Beersheba', one of the first 'whites' to have a sturdy constitution. As a contrast to his daffodil breeding, Engleheart was a contributor to the horticultural press on vegetable growing.

In 1938 the Royal Horticultural Society instituted the Engleheart Cup in his memory. The Cup is awarded for the best exhibit of twelve cultivars raised by the exhibitor. The Society awarded Engleheart its Victoria Medal of Honour in 1900.

Evelyn, John (1620–1706). Gardener and writer. Evelyn was a complex character with many interests, much of his writing remaining unpublished or is in course of publication. One of his foremost interests was gardening. After attaching himself to the cause of Charles I, he wisely left England in 1641 to travel on the Continent, meeting many fellow *virtuosi* of the arts and sciences and visiting many places of interest. Accounts of these activities are given in his diaries. He returned in 1653 to live quietly under the Lord Protector and made his garden at Sayes Court, Kent.

In 1662 Evelyn was appointed one

(Opposite) Lilium elegans, *a plate by Walter Hood Fitch, published in* A Monograph of the Genus Lilium *(1877–1880) by Henry John* **Elwes**. *This was a pioneering project to which various supplements have since been added.*

Daffodil Beersheba, the most successful of the introductions made by the Reverend George Herbert **Engleheart** *(1851–1936).*

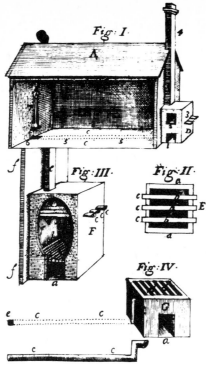

(Left) Frontispiece of Kalendarium Hortense *(1664) by John* **Evelyn**; *(centre) Evelyn's plan of a stove for a greenhouse and (right) portrait of Evelyn.*

of the original members of the first Council of the newly-founded Royal Society, an appointement no doubt due to his first-hand knowledge of European development in the arts and sciences.

At that time the shortage of timber for building the British ships had become acutely serious. Throughout the period of the Commonwealth no steps had been taken to conserve the nation's dwindling supplies. The great heritage of British oak had been squandered. This matter was put before the Royal Society in the year of its foundation by Sir Robert Moray who submitted a list of the problems involved. This was referred to a small committee which included Evelyn, who on October 15th, 1662, delivered his conclusions in a paper he read to the Society. The consequence was the publication in 1664 of his great *Sylva or a Discourse on Forest-Trees.* His knowledge was so cyclopaedic in scope that the book went far beyond its original brief and covered every aspect of forestry and arboriculture, including the use of trees in gardens and garden design.

Later editions of this great work (the first had as an introduction, Abraham Cowley's poem *The Garden,* written from Chertsea, August 16th, 1666) included also *An Historical Account of the Sacredness and use of Standing Graves, Terra* (a discourse of Earth), *Pomona* (on fruit trees as relating to cider making), *Actaria* (on salads) and *Kalendarium Hortense.*

The book is not only thoroughly practical in its instruction, but pleasantly digressive, including quotations only remotely connected

Juliana Horatia **Ewing** *(1841–1885).*

with the utilitarian uses of timber. After references to Macrobius and other classical authors in his account of the holly he writes:

'But to say no more of these superstitious Fopperies, which are many other about this Tree, we still dress up both our churches and houses, on Christmas and other festival days, with its cheerful green and rutilant berries.

Is there under Heaven a more glorious and refreshing object of this kind, an impregnable hedge of about four hundred foot in length, nine foot high, and five in diameter; which I can show in my own now ruined garden at Say's Court (thanks to the Czar of Muscovy) at any time of the year, glittering with its armed and varnished leaves? The tallest standards at orderly distance, blushing with their natural coral: it mocks at the rudest assaults of the weather, beasts or hedge breakers.'

(Peter the Great had proved a somewhat rumbustious tenant of Evelyn's house during his study of English shipbuilding techniques at Deptford.)

Another of Evelyn's publications, *Kalendarium Hortense: or the Gard'ner's Almanac,* is wholly practical. One typical example is for January:

Set up your traps for vermine; especially in your nurseries of kernels and stones, and amongst your bulbous roots; which will now be in danger. A paste made of coarse honey, wherein is mingled green-glass beaten, with copperas, may be laid near their haunts. About the middle of this month, plant now your anemone roots, and ranunculus's, which you will be secure of, with covering, or farther trouble: preserve them from too great and continuing rains (if they happen), snow and frost, our choicest anemonies and ranunculus's sowed in September or October for earlier flowers: also your carnations, and such seeds as are in peril of being washed out, or over-chill'd and frozen; covering them under shelter, and striking off the snow when it lies too weighty; for it certainly rots and bursts your early-set anemonies and ranunculus's, unless planted now in the hot-beds; for now is the season, and they will flower even in London. Towards the end, earth-up, with fresh and light mould, the roots of those auricula's which the frosts may have uncover'd; filling up the chinks about the sides of the pots where your choicest are set, but they need not be hous'd; it is a hardy plant.'

Evelyn lists fruits in season which now have a somewhat legendary flavour, such as the apples 'Marigold', 'Pomewater' and 'Golden Doucet'; 'Winter Norwich' (bakes

well) and the 'Great Survein' pears.

Elsewhere in this practical volume, we have the plan of a garden, which shows the typical outlines of a Carolean estate. The *Kalendarium* concludes with Evelyn's remarkably advanced design for a heated conservatory, or greenhouse, for raising tender plants.

Evelyn died at Wotton House, Surrey, where, it is said, trees that he planted still survive. He also designed the terrace at Albury, Guildford, for the Duke of Norfolk. His interests in subjects other than horticultural and arboricultural were numerous and influential.

Ewing, Juliana Horatia (1841–1885). Gardener and author. Juliana Gatty married Major Alexander Ewing in 1867 and became a prolific writer of stories for the young, many of which were first published in *Aunt Judy's Magazine* founded by her mother. *Mary's Meadow* which first appeared in the *Magazine* in 1883–1884 was concerned with a family, its library and a garden which the children created. A copy of Philip Miller's *Dictionary,* especially its pictures, was the supposed inspiration for their horticultural endeavours. The book is practical and refreshingly unsentimental. Bound with the book is *Letters from a Little Garden.* Mrs Ewing's attitude towards gardening was well in advance of her time and must have prepared many youngsters for the views of William Robinson and Gertrude Jekyll.

Juliana Ewing's own garden, which she made after a life of frequent moving from place to place as a soldier's wife, was at Taunton in Somerset.

F

Fairchild, Thomas (1667–1729). Botanist, nurseryman, writer. Virtually nothing is known of Fairchild's early life, but he must have been a young man of outstanding energy and ambition. By his mid-twenties, he had established on a sound footing a nursery business in Shoreditch, which he called The City Gardens. There he developed a large concern and made a name for himself as a cultivator of vines. A contemporary authority, Richard Bradley, writes of Fairchild's 'curious garden . . . where I find the greatest collection of fruits that I have yet seen . . . no one in Europe excels him in the choice of curiosities, such as a universal correspondence can procure.'

Fairchild combined practical knowledge with a profound interest in scientific research. He corresponded with Linnaeus, and helped in establishing the gender of plant life and was the first botanist to produce an artificial hybrid, the *Dianthus caryophyllus barbatus*, a cross between a sweet william and carnation pink.

In 1722 he published *The City Gardener*, which dealt with plants and trees which would grow in urban conditions and gave interesting details of plants and fruit which then flourished in London—vines in Leicester Fields, pear trees in the Barbican and so on. He also read papers before the Royal Society on the motion of sap in plants and trees, the raising of grass seeds and other horticultural subjects. In 1725 he was a founder member of a Society of Gardeners which was established in London. He also contributed to *A Catalogue of Trees and Shrubs both Exotic and Domestic which are propagated for Sale in the Gardens near London.*

Falconer, Hugh (1808–1865). Botanist. Falconer was born at Forres, Morayshire, Scotland, and was educated locally and at the Universities of Aberdeen and Edinburgh, where he studied geology and medicine. After graduation he joined the East India Company as a surgeon and went to India. In 1832 he was appointed superintendent of the Saharanpur botanic gardens in the Himalayan foothills. He was involved in the production of the first Indian tea. After two years in this appointment he returned to

*Thomas **Fairchild** (c. 1667–1729), botanist and nurseryman.*

*Sir John Bretland **Farmer** (1865–1944), botanist and writer.*

*Reginald John **Farrer** (1880–1920), plant-collector and author.*

England, joined the British Museum where he supervised the arrangement and display of Indian fossils. He returned to India in 1848 to succeed Nathaniel Wallich (qv), as superintendent of the Calcutta Botanic Garden, and also became Professor of Botany at the Calcutta Medical College. He returned to England in 1855, his health seriously undermined. From that time until his death he was occupied in research into prehistoric man.

Farmer, (Sir) John Bretland (1865–1944). Botanist. Farmer was born at Atherstone in Warwickshire, the son of well-to-do parents, and was educated at the grammar school in that town and at Magdalen College, Oxford, where he studied natural science. He was appointed university demonstrator in botany in 1887 and five years later assistant professor of botany in the Royal College of Science (later Imperial College) at South Kensington. In 1895 he became Professor, retaining the title until his retirement in 1929. In the first year of his appointment to South Kensington he visited India and Ceylon, and his experiences there, especially in the rubber plantations, moved him to recast contemporary botanical teaching so that students could apply their knowledge to practical purposes. By the time he retired many of his onetime students were working throughout the world.

Farmer was a prolific writer. Apart from his *Practical Introduction to the Study of Botany* (1899) and *Plant Life* (1913) he published over sixty papers on botanical matters, particularly on plant cytology. He was a theorist of unusual percipience and opened up several areas of botanical research to further inquiry. He also edited the *Gardener's Chronicle* between 1904 and 1907. As Farmer was a highly efficient administrator and a man of balanced judgement, he was inevitably co-opted on to many advisory committees. He was knighted in 1926.

Farrer, Reginald John (1880–1920). Botanist, traveller, flower-painter, author. Farrer was born of well-to-do parents at Clapham, a village lying below Ingleborough in Yorkshire. Owing to a malformed jaw and the physical suffering caused by

Ingleborough Fell in Yorkshire, where the plant-collector and author Reginald John **Farrer** *(1880–1920) grew up.*

this disability he was educated at home, later proceeding to Balliol College, Oxford. This somewhat solitary boyhood sponsored an early interest in botany and at fourteen he had already rebuilt a rock-garden in his parents' Yorkshire garden, and in the same year published a note in *The Journal of Botany*, concerning the occurrence of *Arenaria gothica* on Ingleborough Fell. At Oxford he was responsible, with the Reverend H. J. Bidder (qv), for the construction of the now-famous rockery at St John's College.

After leaving Oxford, Farrer visited Japan which resulted in his adoption of the Buddhist faith and the publication of his first book *The Garden of Asia: Impressions from Japan*. This was followed five years later by *Alpines and Bog Plants* (1908), *My Rock Garden* and *In A Yorkshire Garden* (1909) and *Among the Hills* (1911).

In 1911 he stood unsuccessfully for Parliament as a Liberal for Ashford in Kent, but, typically, spent the £1,000 his father gave him to aid his expenses on buying cypripediums.

His books were unlike those of any of his contemporaries or, for that matter, his successors. His prose style was sharp and percipient. At a time when William Robinson was eulogizing the wild garden, Reginald Farrer forthrightly expressed his own somewhat contrary views thus:

'The ordinary wild garden is the very worst and most extravagant of frauds, requiring a supervision no less incessant and close than any parterre or border . . . I hate the sight of respectable elderly persons doddering whole days through the "wild garden" and picking up a weed an hour, so that ultimately the whole place has an air of spick and spanness.'

Or:

'. . . the very first thing one sees is a large fat clump of the common primrose. It contains at its heart Miss Massey, which is the scent of its presence. Miss Massey, if I am right about the name . . . is a single scarlet primrose, of intense and violent scarletness, or rather blood-crimson. Not only that, but she is also a hose-in-hose—each flower, as it were, clad in breeches of another flower, a bold suffragette is Miss Massey, with which, for my own part, I would gladly dispense. However, here is Miss Massey, wedged among her common kin, and I am always meaning to segregate them and honour Miss Massey with a lovely place all to herself. But one cannot do this while she is in flower, and I always forget to mark her as I go by . . . This year, though, I must really buckle to, and rise to the enormous effort of poking in a piece of stick to identify Miss Massey.'

Farrer also wrote novels and plays, some of an experimental nature. These are now forgotten although they seem to have been of an entertaining character.

These literary endeavours were a prelude to more remarkable achievements. In 1912, Farrer had begun work on a massive encyclopaedia, *The English Rock Garden*, but due to the First World War, the work was not published until 1919. His researches had persuaded Farrer that great possibilities for collecting new rock plants existed in North West Kansu in China. William Purdom (qv) was in this district, collecting for the Arnold Arboretum of the USA and the famous nursery firm of Veitch & Co (who had sponsored the first plant-collecting expedition to Western China by E. H. Wilson in 1899). Farrer joined Purdom in 1914. They introduced, among a number of lilies and primulas, such plants as *Viburnum farreri*, *Buddleja alternifolia*, *Gentiana farreri*, and *Rosa farreri*. Farrer wrote two accounts of the expedition: *The Eaves of the World* (1917) and *The Rainbow Bridge* (1921).

In 1919, in company with Euan Cox (qv), Farrer set out again, this time to Upper Burma. The most considerable result of this expedition was the introduction of the delightful *Juniperus coxii*. Cox had to return, leaving Farrer to travel on into even more remote regions in wet and sunless conditions. Farrer died at Nyitadi on the Northern Frontier in October 1920 and was buried at Konglu.

Farrer's herbarium specimens survived, but the seeds he had collected did not. An account of this expedition was written by E. M. Cox, *Farrer's Last Journey* (1926) which includes a vivid picture of Farrer in the hills:

'. . . his stocky figure clad in khaki shorts and shirt, tieless and collarless, a faded topee on his head, old boots, and stockings that gradually slipped down and clung about his ankles as the day wore on . . . his enjoyment of our evening tot of rum, a necessity in the rains; and, above all, his indomitable energy that never spared a frame which was hardly built for long days of searching and climbing.'

A neat brass memorial tablet was erected in a remote but beautiful spot in northern Burma and reads: 'In loving memory of Reginald John Farrer . . . of Ingleborough, Yorkshire . . . he died for love and duty in search of rare plants.'

Robert **Fenn** *(1817–1912).*

Fenn, Robert (1817–1912). Gardener, horticulturist. Fenn was born at Rushbrooke, Suffolk, the son of a London–Bury St Edmunds coachman. He broke his apprenticeship to a London watchmaker in order to adopt an open-air life. Foiled in an attempt to go to sea he became a gardener at Stanton Lacy in Shropshire, becoming steward to his employer, the Rev. G. St John, a member of the Bolingbroke family. He remained with the family for over fifty years, the last thirty-six at Woodstock Rectory in Oxfordshire. After his patron's death, he retired to a smallholding at Sulhampstead, Berkshire, where he experimented in the cross-breeding of plants and potatoes.

Robert Fenn was also a notable authority on bees and was awarded a certificate by the RHS in 1867 for bee products and his improvements of bee skeps. He was a frequent contributor to the *Journal of Horticulture*.

Field, Ernest (c. 1878–1970). Gardener. Field was one of that vast army of gardeners, from apprentices to head men, who, throughout the Victorian era, worked on the estates of the plutocrats—patricians and *nouveaux riches* alike—maintaining the image of their worth and wealth, mainly by the length of their bedding-plant lists. Outside the legend of Joseph Paxton (qv) little is known about the working lives of such gardeners, for few wrote accounts of their work. Field was one of the few who was able to put down some record of such a life, from apprentice to head gardener.

He served his apprenticeship at the Duke of Beaufort's seat at Badminton, in Gloucestershire, followed by a stint as second journeyman at Yeaton-Perry in 1900, and as first-journeyman-propagator at Halton House, Tring, in Hertfordshire, then belonging to Alfred de Rothschild (qv). Rothschild was a somewhat larger-than-life character used to getting his own way and convinced that money could achieve anything. The gardens at Halton exemplified these convictions and late-Victorian lavishness in the most ostentatious manner. At the owner's whim, anything could be changed overnight. Legend asserts that only unexpected rain prevented the lawn, burned brown after a long drought, being painted green!

Field was paid sixteen shillings a week with keep and was housed in

(Opposite) Watercolours painted by Reginald **Farrer** *during his plant-hunting expeditions in Kansu and Upper Burma. (Above left)* Primula agleniana; *(above right)* Lilium hyacinthinium; *(below left)* Primula sonchifolia; *(below right)* Nomocharis basilissa. *From* The Plant Introductions of R. Farrer *(1930).*

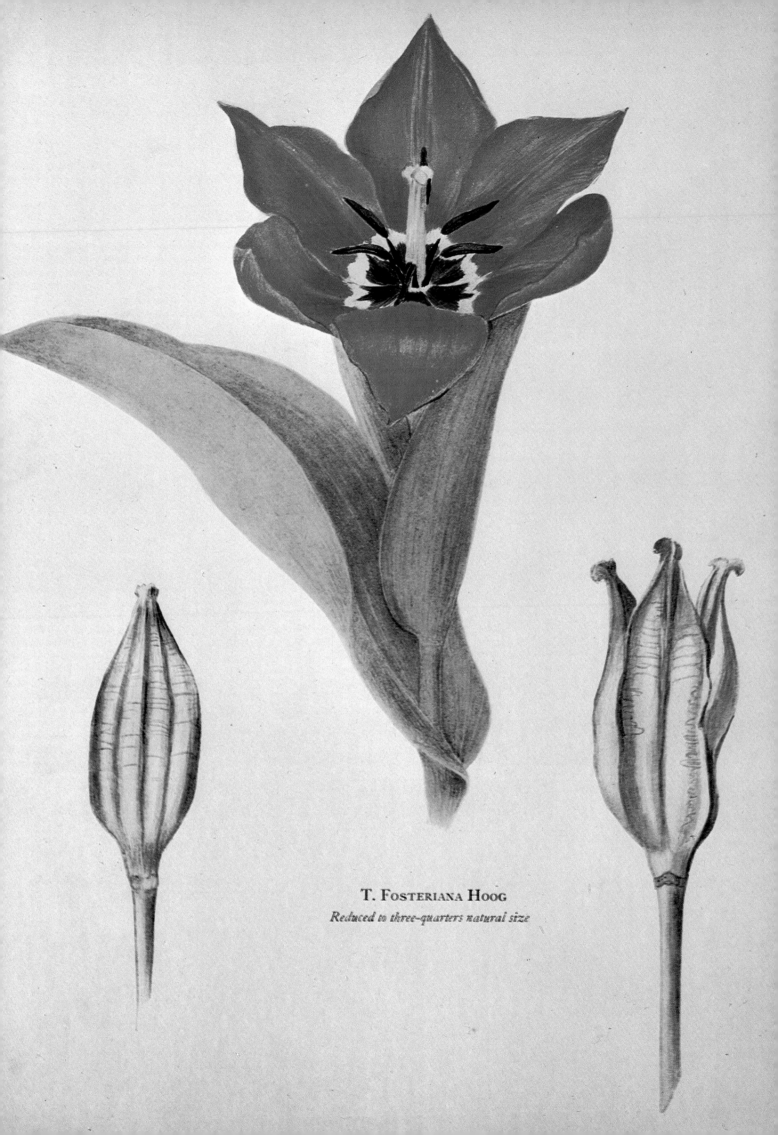

T. Fosteriana Hoog

Reduced to three-quarters natural size

Tea Garden at Shanghai, illustrated in Wanderings in China *by Robert* **Fortune** *(John Murray, 1847).*

were granted easier access to the interior and defined rights at the ports with possession of the island of Hong Kong. In 1827, John Lindley (qv) became assistant secretary of the Horticultural Society. His early ambition had been to become a plant collector. Although he never achieved his wish he did become a considerable authority on the subject. The signing of the Treaty suggested opportunities to collect, visit and study the Chinese flora. At the suggestion of the Society, Lindley approached the Government, asking for permission and aid. Following prolonged official delays, Lindley and his friends among the Society decided to go ahead on their own. One of the Fellows, John Reeves (qv), had earlier spent twenty years in China, and had continued to send plants and drawings of plants by Chinese artists to the Society's Chiswick garden, obtained via his friends among the captains of the East Indiamen. Reeves became the foremost member of the Society's committee which decided to act without official co-operation.

Fortune, who had never been overseas, was chosen to make the journey. He was loaded with instructions, advice, equipment, a heavy stick and, reluctantly, a gun. His botanical instructions were complex and multifarious. He was requested, *inter alia*, to collect peaches weighing two pounds apiece that reputedly grew in the Emperor's garden; two sorts of double yellow roses; peonies with blue flowers; lilies of Fokien (again reputedly) eaten like chestnuts when boiled; the azalea from Loufou-shan; the cocoons of a moth called Tseemtsam and camellias

with yellow flowers. And so on.

Fortune reached Hong-Kong in July 1843. He disliked the Chinese from the outset, affirming that all, from mandarins to the meanest beggar, were filled with the most con-

ceited notions of their own importance and the wonders of their land, with which no other country could be compared.

He almost died of fever, but recovering, set out on his travels,

Dr John **Fothergill** *(1712–1780), gardener, botanist and patron.*

gaining the confidence of nurserymen and others. He found gardens filled with plants that he had neither seen or heard of previously. He was the first collector to carry Wardian cases, invented by Nathaniel Bagshaw Ward, which revolutionized the means of transportation of living plants over long distances. Despite the fact that he was sometimes attacked by gangs employed by nurserymen who suspected him of stealing plants, Fortune quietly and unobtrusively continued to collect plants he believed the British public would appreciate. Proceeding to Chusan he was delighted by the flowery landscape: 'Few can form any idea of the gorgeous and striking beauty of these azalea-clad mountains, when, on every side, as far as our vision extends, the eye rests on masses of flowers of dazzling brightness and surpassing beauty. Nor is it the azalea alone which claims our admiration; clematises, and a hundred others, mingle their flowers with them, and make us confess that China is indeed the "central flowery land".'

Fortune undoubtedly changed the character of English gardens by the plants he sent home, and, almost as a footnote, provided the first accounts of the cultivation of tea in China, of the artificial incubation of ducks, irrigation systems, and—of considerable horticultural importance—the cultivation of chrysanthemums. He was also the first collector to describe the dwarfing and fanciful shaping of conifers.

Despite alarming experiences, including a gang's murderous attack, the quiet but quick-witted Scotsman proved a tough and resourceful plant-collector during the three years he remained in China. He returned to London in May 1846. In that year he saw the *Anemone japonica* that he had collected flowering in the Society's Chiswick garden 'as beautiful and luxuriant as it ever grew on the graves of the Chinese near the ramparts of Changhai'.

Following his return he was appointed Curator of the Chelsea Physic Garden, but two years later he set out on another journey to China. As he had seen something of the tea industry, he was engaged by the East India Company to collect the Chinese tea plant and learn still more of its management, then a closely guarded secret. After a second journey, in 1853, and using his Wardian cases, he was successful. Fortune's knowledge of the country and its people was so considerable that he was able to pass himself off as a Chinese native, a highly dangerous undertaking.

Between 1860 and 1862 he made a third journey to the Far East, collecting principally in Japan. This journey he apparently financed himself, although he seems to have had

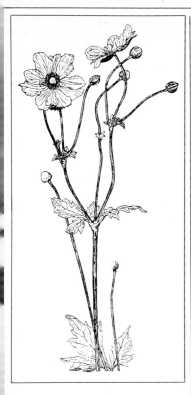

Anemones, collected by Robert Fortune.

some arrangement with the enterprising nurseryman, John Standish, to market plants he sent back. This Japanese journey coincided with that of J. G. Veitch, representing the well-known Exeter nursery. In some instances it is doubtful whether Fortune or Veitch (qv) first introduced a particular plant.

Fortune certainly introduced numerous specimens, which, with their offspring and hybrids, are still among our most important plants. Such are *Anemone japonica*, the winter jasmine, weigela, dicentra, *Prunus triloba*, *Primula japonica*, *Cryptomeria japonica*, numerous rhododendrons, azaleas, tree peonies, pom-pom chrysanthemums, the double deutzia and Japanese chrysanthemums.

Fortune spent the last years of his life living comfortably in Kensington, writing his books, *Visits to the Capitals of Japan and China* (1847) and *Residence Among the Chinese* (1857), and writing occasionally for the gardening press and for the Horticultural Society.

Foster, (Sir) Michael (1836–1907). Iris specialist. Foster was born in Huntingdon and became one of the most eminent physiologists of his day. He was appointed Professor of Physiology at Cambridge in 1883, having been elected a Fellow of the Royal Society in 1882. He was knighted in 1899.

He became absorbed in studying, raising and breeding the genus *Iris* and, despite the comparatively difficult circumstances of a small garden in Shelford, near Cambridge, and the unsatisfactory soil, he grew and flowered about two hundred species obtained from many parts of the world, a total not previously seen in this country. His notebooks record his studies and experiments between 1878 and 1902 and are illustrated by his drawings. Some of these species, of which he published descriptions, were hitherto unknown in this country but are now frequently grown. In addition to forming his collection of species, between 1878 and 1901, he made many crosses, again recording the results with great care. Those crosses in which he made use of the species *Iris cypriana*, *I. trojana*, *I. amas* and *I. kashmiriana* were among those which supplied the fundamental features from which the modern bearded iris has been evolved.

Foster made his material and notes available to several friends, notably William Dykes (qv) and George Yeld (qv), the latter introducing a number of famous crosses during the fifty-two years that he was a master at St Peter's School, York.

Fothergill, (Dr) John (1712–1780). Gardener, botanist, alpine plant grower. Fothergill was born in Wensleydale, Yorkshire. After studying medicine at Edinburgh University and gaining his doctorate in 1736, he continued his studies in Flanders before settling in London where he quickly established a lucrative practice in Lombard Street.

In 1762 he began to form a botanic garden at Upton House, West Ham, then a village on the outskirts of London, which gradually became internationally famous. He received plants from correspondents throughout the world. The most spectacular feature of the garden was a greenhouse, 260 feet long, entered direct from his house, built at vast expense and said to have been the largest in the world. Fothergill also created a 'wilderness' in which he naturalized exotic plants that were likely to survive in the English climate. He was probably the first botanist to study alpine plants scientifically and to grow them in Britain. He and Dr Pitcairn (1711–91) were the first patrons of plant-collecting to commission a botanist to visit the Alps. The collector was Thomas Blaikie (qv) who set out for Switzerland in April 1775, and sent back about four hundred and forty packages. Fothergill and Pitcairn took all the credit for the introduction of these plants, never mentioning Thomas Blaikie.

Fothergill probably shared with Peter Collinson the achievement of being the first to flower an exotic orchid in England, when, in 1778, *Phaius grandifolius*, imported from China, opened its blooms.

Fothergill had another celebrated garden, Lea Hall, his summer residence in Cheshire, which he began in 1765.

*Robert **Fortune** (1812–1880).*

*Sir Michael **Foster** (1836–1907).*

Fraser, John (1750–1811). Nurseryman, plant-collector. Fraser was born in Inverness and in his late teens journeyed to London, soon establishing himself as a hosier and linen-draper in Chelsea. There he met William Forsyth (qv), a fellow-Scot and Director of the Chelsea Physic Garden. Thanks to the combined offices of Forsyth and Admiral Campbell, then in command of the Newfoundland station, Fraser was persuaded to travel to Newfoundland in 1780 for reasons of health. (Tuberculosis had been suspected.) Fraser stayed in Newfoundland for four years, becoming a knowledgeable botanist and plant-hunter.

On his return to London, Forsyth was greatly impressed by the specimens which Fraser had brought back and encouraged him to set up as a professional plant-hunter. Fraser made some half-dozen further trips to North America, working from a base in Charleston. On his later journeys he was accompanied by his son. In about 1795, after earlier disappointments and a costly lawsuit, he decided to establish a nursery near Sloane Square for the reception, propagation and sale of his American plants. His expeditions were frequently complicated by financial troubles, conflicts with other plant-hunters, delayed shipments, stolen horses and other misadventures. In Charleston, Fraser became friendly with Thomas Walter, another botanist who was compiling a flora of Carolina. Between them they discovered over a thousand species. On Walter's death, Fraser took over responsibility for preparing *Flora Caroliniana* for the press. Fraser was outstandingly successful as a collector and introducer of hardy plants, but he was no businessman, and was frequently unlucky in his financial affairs. In 1796 he made his first visit to Russia and was immediately successful, Catherine the Great purchasing all the specimens he had taken with him. Two years later he was appointed botanical collector to the Emperor Paul of Russia. On returning from a subsequent expedition—during which he had been shipwrecked off Cuba and lost all he possessed—he found that his patron had been murdered, and that his successor, Czar Alexander, had repudiated the agreement. Fraser died after a fall from a horse.

*John **Fraser** (1750–1811), who introduced* Rhododendron catawbiense *(right).*

JOHN GERARD
ÆTATIS SVÆ 51

A. D.
1586

Gerard (or Gerarde), John (1545–1612). Herbalist. Gerard was born at Nantwich, Cheshire. He came to London and qualified as a member of that oddly mixed profession, the barber-surgeon, completing his long apprenticeship in 1569. To acquire this rank, he had inevitably studied several authors who wrote in Greek and Latin and touched on herbs, medicines and 'simples'. He would also have been acquainted with that pioneering English study, *Names of Herbes*, compiled by William Turner (qv) and published in 1548. Above all, Gerard was a clever and practical gardener and one of the earliest, if not indeed the first, to keep records of the plants he grew.

He was in charge of the gardens of Lord Burghley, Queen Elizabeth I's treasurer, both in the Strand and at Theobalds in Hertfordshire, a position which introduced him to an unusually intellectual circle. Gerard also had his own nursery garden, known to have been sited close to what is now Furnival Street in Holborn. In 1596, he published his *Catalogue*, a list of the plants that he grew in this nursery garden. (The date of publication accounts for the fact that 1596 is cited for the introduction of a number of plants, although some may well have been introduced into England some years previously. Gerard's book, however, is the first known reference to their presence.)

Gerard travelled in Europe, and corresponded with such eminent botanists as Jean Robin in France, Camerarius in Nuremberg, as well as with London merchants occupied in overseas trade and with numerous British botanists and physicians. (At least fifty are mentioned in his published writings.) He was also involved in an investment in 'an adventure into Virginia'.

Despite the authority and renown of the *Catalogue*, Gerard's most famous work is undoubtedly that commonly known as the *Herball*, first issued in 1597. A printer, John Norton, commissioned a Dr Robert Priest (c. 1560–1596) to translate into English *Pemptades*, a book published in 1583, written by Rembert

(Opposite) Portrait (oils on wood) of John **Gerard** *in Elizabethan dress, c. 1586. Artist unknown.*

Creeping Milkwort

Birch

The Yellow Rose

Wood Sorrell

The white dwarfe Cistus of Germanie

Five engravings from the Herball *by John* **Gerard** *(1545–1607), reproduced in an edition published by Gerald Howe in 1921, the illustrations after the original engravings.*

Dodoen (1518–1585), an eminent Flemish pioneer of botany. Due to Priest's death, Gerard was commissioned to complete the translation, and saw this as an opportunity—which succeeded—of establishing his own reputation. He changed the system of botanical arrangement from that followed by Dodoen to that devised by the French botanist, Matthias de Lobel (1538–1616), and duly claimed the work as his own, directing its appeal towards gentlewomen readers. To this end, Mrs Gerard gave her husband a hand in adding finishing touches. The decorative appeal of the publication derived from a number of new wood engravings, mostly from Frankfurt-am-Main, several of which were attached to the wrong subjects.

Lobel made an attempt to put things right, but Gerard replied that what Lobel thought were mistakes were indeed nothing of the sort. The unfortunate Frenchman, he implied, had forgotten his former knowledge of the English language.

The *Herball* proved an immediate success and has maintained its popular appeal for almost four hundred years. The book undoubtedly increased the study of botany, particularly among women who seemed to have found such passages as the following irresistible:

'But what our eies have seen, and hands touched, we shall declare. There is a small island in Lancashire called the Pile of Foulders, wherein are found the broken pieces of old and brused ships, some whereof have been cast thither by shipwrecks, and also trunks or bodies with the branches of old and rotten trees, cast up there likewise; whereon is found a certain spume or froth, that in time breedeth unto certaine shells, in shape like those of the muskle, but sharper pointed, and of a whitish colour; one ende whereof is fastned unto the inside of the shell, even as the fish of oisters and muskles are; the other end is made fast unto the belly of a rude masse or lumpe, which in time cometh to the shape and forme of a bird . . . (which) in short space after it cometh to maturitie, and falleth into the sea, where it gathereth feathers, groweth to a fowl, bigger than a mallard, and lesser than a goos.'

On the more utilitarian level, and certainly more tactful in a man-run world, was his comment on what we

Title page of the first edition of The Herball *or* Generall Historie of Plantes *'gathered' by John* **Gerard**.

The Derwent Reservoir, Durham, landscaped by Sir Frederick **Gibberd**.

Sir Frederick **Gibberd** *(1908–   ).*

now call *Polygonatum multiflorum*:

'The roote of Salomans Seale stamped while it is fresh and greene, taketh away in one night or two at the most, any bruse, black or blew spots gotten by fals or womens wilfulnes in stumbling upon their hastie husbands fists or the like.'

Gibberd, (Sir) Frederick (1908–   ). Architect, landscape architect, town planner. Gibberd was born in Coventry in 1908, and educated at King Henry VIII School in that city, and at the Birmingham School of Architecture. He set up in private practice in London in 1930.

Gibberd's best-known buildings include London Airport Terminal Buildings; Liverpool Catholic Cathedral; the London Mosque and Inter-Continental Hotel, Hyde Park Corner. He also qualified as a town planner, his work in that field being recognized by the award of the Gold Medal of the Royal Town Planning Institute in 1978.

He has specialized in large-scale design of twentieth-century industrial sites encompassing buildings and landscape. Amongst these Harlow is his most important work. This New Town, first designed in 1946, was a break with both the functional and 'garden city' tradition. Based on the belief that the configuration of the land should determine the character of the design, the town is contained by surrounding high ground, visually separating it from the countryside. Internally, the existing valleys are extended to form a broad overall landscape design which separates the built-up areas from each other and unifies the town.

In 1959 Gibberd designed Llyn Celwyn Reservoir in North Wales, which was followed by Derwent Reservoir, Durham (both of which received design awards). The Kielder Reservoir, a lake some six miles long, sited in a forest and designed to be a recreation centre for the North East, is planned for completion in 1981. His interest in the relationship of architecture to large-scale landscapes is exemplified by his design for Didcot Power Station and Cleveland Potash Mine. Visual surveys from the surrounding hills determined the places of the cooling towers of Didcot; similar surveys resulted in the mine having a background of hills instead of being silhouetted against the sky. His other large-scale designs include the Hinkley Point Nuclear Power Station and Dinorwic pump storage scheme in Snowdonia. Public garden projects include Queen's Gardens, Hull, Harlow's Civic Water Gardens and the Garden Court of Coutts Bank, the Strand.

He lives near the town he designed. For some twenty-five years he has been making a large modern garden with landscape vistas on the side of a small river valley, a series of interrelated compartments, or 'rooms', formed against the house to become completely natural in the valley bottom.

Gibson, John (1815–1875). Plant-collector and landscape gardener. Gibson was born at Astbury in Cheshire, the son of a gardener at Eaton Hall in Cheshire. At the age of sixteen he was apprenticed to Joseph Paxton (qv), head gardener to the Duke of Devonshire (qv) at Chatsworth in Derbyshire. Paxton formed a high opinion of Gibson's intelligence and character, and two years later sent him to study orchid cultivation under the renowned grower, Joseph Cooper, at Wentworth Woodhouse in Yorkshire, the seat of Earl Fitzwilliam. Soon after his twentieth birthday, Gibson was sent by the Duke of Devonshire, at Paxton's suggestion, to India to collect rare plants, most notably the *Amherstia nobilis*, which already had a legendary renown in England, thanks to its published description by Dr Nathaniel Wallich, the Danish superintendent of the East India Company's botanical garden at Calcutta and a leading authority on Asiatic plants. After numerous delays and setbacks which would have daunted a less determined young man, Gibson sailed in the HMS *Jupiter*, as a member of the staff of the recently-appointed Governor-General of India, Lord Haytesbury. He took with him seeds and plants from the Royal Horticultural Society for Dr Nathaniel Wallich.

By way of Madeira and the Cape of Good Hope, where leisurely stays enabled him to collect various plants, for both Chatsworth and Calcutta, Gibson arrived in India in the following March, after a voyage which had taken five months.

Despite the problems of communication, Gibson kept Paxton

*Architectural fragments and a canal in the garden designed by Sir Frederick **Gibberd** for his own home at Harlow, Essex.*

*John **Gibson** (1815–1875).*

well informed concerning his collecting ventures, making many practical suggestions relating to the two-way exchange of seeds and plants between Derbyshire and Calcutta. Following an itinerary planned by Dr Wallich, Gibson set out on his plant-collection expedition into East Bengal, Assam and the Khasi Hills. Despite innumerable problems in transport, occasioned by the rainy season, Gibson dried out and packed a vast and remarkable collection of orchids, ferns and rare plants for despatch to Chatsworth, aided throughout by the resourceful Dr Wallich, who supervised the despatch of Gibson's collections to England by Royal Navy ships.

Gibson left India in March 1837 in HMS *Zenobia* and arrived in Plymouth nearly five months later, including amongst his charges the *Amherstia nobilis*, 'unequalled in the flora of the East Indies and perhaps not surpassed in magnificence and elegance in any part of the world'.

In the same year Gibson was appointed foreman of the Exotic Plant House at Chatsworth, where he remained for the next twelve years.

In 1849 Gibson was appointed Superintendent of Victoria Park, London, and thus was able to help Paxton during his considerable labours in connexion with the Great Exhibition of 1851. In the same year, he was appointed Superintendent of Greenwich Park, where he remodelled the Park, draining the whole site and laying new drives and pathways. In 1858, he designed the layout and planting of Battersea Park, including the sub-tropical garden.

In 1871 Gibson took charge of Hyde Park, Green Park, St James's Park and Kensington Gardens. In this capacity he was also responsible for the redesigning of the Leicester Square garden. In 1874, due to ill-

*The East India Company's Botanic Gardens at Calcutta, used as a base for the plant-collecting expeditions of John **Gibson**.*

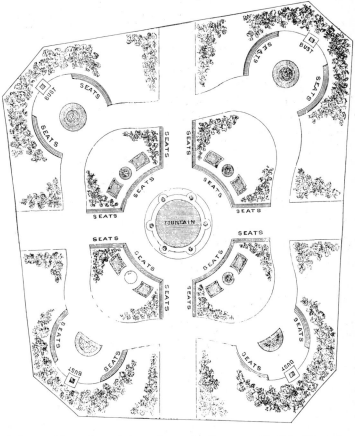

*The layout of the gardens at Leicester Square, London, proposed by John **Gibson** in 1874 and, in the main, carried out.*

health, John Gibson resigned from these appointments, and died the following year at Argyll Lodge, Kensington.

Gilbert-Carter, Humphrey. (1884–1969). Botanist. Humphrey Gilbert-Carter was the second son of Sir Thomas Gilbert-Carter, KCMG, and was educated at Tonbridge School, and Edinburgh, Marburg and Cambridge Universities. In 1913 he was appointed as economic botanist to the Botanical Survey of India, and was recalled in 1921 to take over the newly-created post of Director of the Cambridge University Botanic Garden, a post which he held, in conjunction with the curatorship of the Herbarium and later with a university lectureship, until his retirement in 1950. In 1922 he published *A Guide to the University Botanic Garden* and in 1924 *Descriptive Labels for Botanic Gardens*. According to a contemporary he was essentially the scholar-director and his successor to the Herbarium, Dr S. M. Walters, said that Gilbert-Carter 'practised naturally and without strain that fundamental technique of the gifted teacher'. He was a learned philologist and translator from several languages, including Raunkiaer's *Plant Life Forms* (1937). He also published *British Trees and Shrubs* (1936) and a *Glossary of British Flora* (1950).

Gilmour John Scott Lennox (1906–). Botanist, author. Gilmour became keen on wild flowers as a boy at Downs School, near Malvern. At Uppingham he was again fortunate in a housemaster who was also a keen botanist and gardener: Charles Mountfort, later editor of the Alpine Garden Society's *Bulletin*. At Clare College, Cambridge, he forsook medicine for botany.

After Cambridge, Gilmour was appointed Curator of the Herbarium and Botanical Museum in the Cambridge University Botany School in 1929, a post he held until being appointed, at the age of twenty-five, Assistant-Director of Kew Gardens in 1931.

In 1946, he was appointed Director of the Royal Horticultural Society's Garden at Wisley at a difficult time when not only was the garden understaffed and run-down following the war, but very large numbers of ex-service men were being rushed through a one-year course. In 1951, he returned to Cambridge as Director of the

(Opposite) Three views of the garden designed by Sir Frederick **Gibberd** *for his own home at Harlow, Essex. (Top) Architectural fragments, including Victorian columns from the remodelled Coutts building in the Strand; (below left) avenue of soaring lime trees; (below right) paving and raising beds near the house.*

Two of the plants brought back by John **Gibson** *(1815–1875) from his expedition to Assam. (Left) Amherstia nobilis, and (right) Rhododendron gibsonii, both illustrated in Curtis's Botanical Magazine.*

One of Humphrey **Gilbert-Carter's** *favourite views of the Botanic Garden at Cambridge where he was Director: Pinus gerardiana.*

Humphrey **Gilbert-Carter** *(1884–1969).*

John Scott Lennox **Gilmour** *(1906–).*

(Above) Two drawings by William Sawrey **Gilpin** *(1762–1843) from* Practical Hints for Landscape Gardening *(1832), showing examples of his recommendations for the use of the Lombardy poplar.*

'Before' and 'after' drawings by William Sawrey **Gilpin,** *illustrating the benefits of a terrace wall (1832).*

University Botanic Garden, succeeding his teacher and friend Humphrey Gilbert-Carter. Under his directorship, the gardens were greatly enlarged and diversified. Today, the limestone rock garden, having matured, constitutes a major attraction, and the new area, including the Winter Garden, has become established, with such features as a Chronological Border, Scented Garden and the three-acre 'research area'. He retired in 1973 after twenty-two years as Director.

Gilmour's main purpose has consistently been to seek to bridge the gap between botany and horticulture. His chief contribution has been in the controversial sphere of nomenclature. He was one of the original architects of the 1953 *International Code of Nomenclature of Cultivated Plants*, and Chairman of the International Commission responsible for the Code. When Chairman of the Royal Horticultural Society Orchid Committee and of its Orchid Registration Advisory Committee, he was specially concerned with what is probably the most complex area in botanical nomenclature—the naming of orchid hybrids—and he took a significant part in the production of the recent *Handbook on Orchid Nomenclature and Registration*.

Gilmour's other main botanical interest has been in the history and bibliography of the British Flora. He published *British Botanists* in the *Britain in Pictures Series*, and, in 1972, edited for the Hunt Botanical Library, Pittsburg, a facsimile and translation of the two first accounts of botanical journeys in Britain: Thomas Johnson's *Iter* (1629) and *Descriptio* (1632). He has served on the Advisory Committee of the Hunt Library since its foundation in 1960. He also maintained his early interest in British wild flowers and wrote, with Dr Max Walters, *Wild Flowers* in the Collins New Naturalist Series, of which he was an editor from 1943 until the mid 'seventies.

Honours include the Victoria Medal of Honour, in 1956, and a Veitch Gold Medal, in 1966, by the Royal Horticultural Society, and the Award of Honour from the Australian Orchid Council.

Gilpin, William Sawrey (1762–1843). Landscape designer. Gilpin was the son of Sawrey Gilpin, the celebrated animal painter, and also had considerable talent as an artist, but decided not to follow this career. Instead, he followed Sir Uvedale Price (qv) in the 'requisite necessary to form a just taste in landscape . . . having been bred to the study of landscape painting in the first instance', and applied the 'principles of painting to the improvement of real scenery'.

Gilpin had no training as a practical gardener or garden designer, but was immensely successful. He was much more imaginative, particularly in the employment of a greater variety of trees, than his predecessors: Brown, Repton and their schools. Much of his work, still in sound condition, has been identified in recent years. Clumber in Nottinghamshire; part of Nuneham Courtney, Oxfordshire; Hawarden, Flintshire; Bicton, Shropshire; Sudbury, Derbyshire; Oakley Park, Gloucestershire; Hadzor, Worcestershire. Gilpin's work was also appreciated in Scotland and Ireland. In addition, he made suggestions for siting the new house at Scotney Castle in Kent and for the gardens at Westonbirt in Gloucestershire.

Amongst the basic principles which Gilpin expounded was that trees existing in the foreground of ground to be landscaped should not be removed until their effect has been carefully observed both in winter and summer. He also suggested that variety in a group of trees should be occasioned more by the general form of the trees themselves than by a variety of species.

In Gilpin's view, round-headed trees were usually more picturesque than columnar varieties, although the latter could be important when used in connexion with buildings. He was adamant that belts should never be planted, a contention in direct opposition to the general practice of Lancelot Brown. Generally, in aborological theory and practice, he showed an eclectic and indigenous approach.

Gilpin illustrated his book on *Practical Hints for Landscape Gardening* (1832) with fine crayon drawings, reproduced by lithograph.

Glenny, George (c. 1793–1874). Grower, exhibitor, editor. Glenny began his successful career when, as a youth, he acquired a collection of auriculas and hyacinths. His later reputation was chiefly due to his success as an exhibitor, particularly of florist's flowers bred to, and judged by, precise standards. His exhibits included carnations, auriculas, tulips, hyacinths and polyan-

*Brick and stone pergola at Kidbroke Park, Sussex, designed by Walter **Godfrey** and E. Wratten (1925).*

*The Jerusalem artichoke tuber, Helianthus tuberosus, raised by John **Goodyer** and distributed to friends in 1617.*

thus. By 1863, Glenny was of the opinion that these standards were beginning to decline. He was so consistently successful that it is said that on one occasion, he entertained fifty-seven guests and set before each a silver cup which he had won as an amateur exhibitor.

He was editor of *The Gardener's Gazette* and the *Horticultural Journal* and a prolific writer. The best known book was *The Properties of Flowers and Plants* (1869).

He is today chiefly remembered for his series of *Golden Rules*, some of which were considered worthy of reprinting in *The Journal of the Royal Horticultural Society* in 1944. They include such practical dicta as the following:

Never grow a bad variety of anything, if you can help it. It takes the same room, and wants the same attention as a good one.

Never look out for cheap seedshops. It is only by getting good prices that a seedsman can supply articles to be depended upon . . .

In removing trees and shrubs, never lose a fibre by violence. You can remove what you please with a knife; but if broken off you lose the best.

Buy nothing in 'collections of named varieties'. You get forty-nine useless for one useful. Find out which are best and purchase them only . . .

The most humble practical gardener can often teach you more than the most popular authors. Listen always with patience to any account of their doings.

Glenny lived at Norwood where he died.

Godfrey, Walter (1881–1961). Architect. Godfrey was born in London and educated at Whitgift grammar school. After a course at the Central School of Arts and Crafts, he was articled to James Williams. In 1905, he set up in practice with Edmund Wratten. Although Godfrey specialized in the restoration of old build-ings, he designed a number of country houses and their gardens.

Goodyer, John (1592–1664). Naturalist, botanist and gardener. A collection of Goodyer's letters reposed unexamined in the library of Magdalen College, Oxford, for almost three centuries. These letters seemed at first sight to be about business matters, but sometime after the First World War, the librarian at Magdalen, R. T. Gunther, a student of the history of botany, examined the letters and found that, on the reverse sides, Goodyer had written various botanical and horticultural notes. These were published under Gunther's editorship in 1922. There were references to well-known contemporaries including Gerard (qv), Parkinson (qv) and the Tradescants (qv), plus minor enthusiasts. Other notes included comments on the books in Goodyer's library.

Goodyer was born at Alton in Hampshire. Later, he lived at Droxford and Petersfield, the same countryside that was to bring fame to Gilbert White of Selbourne. Goodyer probably went to Alton Grammar School, where he learned Greek which he later put to useful purpose. He became what we should now call 'agent' to Sir Thomas Bilson, a large landowner, on whose behalf he travelled widely. Probably on Bilson's behalf he went to London, where he came to know Ralph Tuggy who had 'the best place for clove gillyflowers, pinks and the like' at Westminster; John Parkinson (qv) of Long Acre from whom he obtained seeds; Mr Pemble of 'Marrybone'; Mr Wilmot at Bow and John Millen of Old Street who 'grew the choisest fruits this kingdom yeelds'. In London, too, he bought books which are now at Magdalen.

A particular friend was William Coys (qv), of Stubbers, near Dagenham, in Essex, who was known also to Gerard. Goodyer also had American connexions through whom, presumably, he obtained the first yucca to flower in England—in 1604. Goodyer made lists of the plants grown by Coys, which gives us a very full account of a gentleman's garden of this period.

In 1617 Goodyer distributed the Jerusalem artichoke tuber (*Helianthus tuberosus*) to friends, having 'received two small roots thereof from Master Franqueville of London no bigger than hen's eggs, the one I planted, the other I gave to a friend. Mine brought me a peck of roots, wherewith I stored Hampshire.' (There were two de Franquevilles, both John, the elder being a French refugee from Cambrai, who died in 1608. Both were merchants, apparently living in Coleman Street; the son was presumably Goodyer's friend.)

As a botanist, Goodyer was the first to study the elm scientifically and probably the first to show that yews carry their berries on different trees from those that produce the pollen.

His final work (begun, he notes, at 11 am on 10th March 1655) was the translation from the Greek of *Materia Medica* of Dioscorides into English. The manuscript fills 4,540 pages.

Gordon, James (c. 1708–1780). Little is known of Gordon's early life, apart from the fact that he was born in Scotland. He travelled south at an early age and worked in the gardens of Dr James Sherard (qv) at Eltham in Surrey and Lord Petre at Thorndon Hall, Essex, until 1742. A few years after the death of Lord Petre, Gordon opened a nursery at Mile End, then in the countryside to the east of London, but kept in close touch with metropolitan clients with a seed shop in Fenchurch Street. He acquired a wide renown for his skills in raising plants from imported seed, and Peter Collinson (qv), the authority on plants from North America and prodigious writer of letters concerning the gardens and gardeners of his day, recorded that he had never 'heard of any man [except Gordon] that could raise the dusty seeds of the Kalmia's, Rhododendrons or

Philip **Gosse** *and an engraving from his book,* A Canadian Naturalist.

Robert **Graham** *(1786–1845).*

Leslie **Greenwood** *(1907–).*

Azalea's,' and that 'he furnishes to every curious garden; all the nurserymen and gardeners come to him for them; and this year, after more than twenty years' trial, he shewed me the Loblolly Bay of Carolina coming up from seed in a way not to be expected'. The plant was later named *Gordonia* in his memory. Another contemporary, John Ellis, writing to Linnaeus in 1758, asserted that Gordon had 'more knowledge in vegetation than all the gardeners and writers on gardening in England put together, but he is too modest to publish anything'. Gordon also raised imported seeds from China, and in 1754 he was the first gardener to grow the Chinese maidenhair tree, as well as popularizing the camellia and gardenia.

Gosse, Philip Henry (1810–1888). Naturalist. Gosse was born at Worcester, the son of an eminent late-Georgian miniature painter but unsuccessful literary figure. The family moved to Poole in Dorset, and the young Gosse was educated first in the town and later at Blandford Grammar School. He had literary ambitions, but in 1827 was sent to work in a whaling office in Newfoundland where he remained for

eight years. Between his far-from-arduous duties, he studied to become a naturalist. After a disastrous attempt at farming in Canada, he travelled in the United States, and for some months was a schoolmaster in Dallas. During the voyage home to Liverpool he wrote his first book, *Canadian Naturalist*, published in 1840. In England he opened a small school on the outskirts of London and in 1843 published his *Introduction to Zoology*, which brought him to the notice of the scientific world. The following year he was appointed by the British Museum to travel to Jamaica to collect hitherto undescribed tropical birds and insects. He stayed in Jamaica for almost two years and, as a result, published *Birds of Jamaica* in 1847, followed in 1851 by *A Naturalist's Sojourn in Jamaica*.

The remainder of his life was mainly devoted to the study of marine zoophytes. He published *The Aquarium* in 1854. He had earlier experimented with the construction of an aquarium, a subject documented and elaborated upon in his two-volume *Manual of Marine Zoology* (1855–56). He published other volumes on marine zoology. He finds a place in this DICTIONARY as

a knowledgeable, enthusiastic and skilful cultivator of orchids at his home in St. Marychurch in South Devonshire.

A remarkable biographical study of Philip Gosse is to be found in the book *Father and Son* by his son, Edmund Gosse (1907).

Grafton, Charles Fitzroy, 2nd Duke of (1683–1756). He inherited Euston Hall in Suffolk when he was only seven years of age. Forty or so years later, he became interested in the fashionable gardening notions of William Kent (qv) and commissioned Kent to prepare plans for rebuilding Euston and to make proposals concerning the landscaping of the park. Kent's proposals entailed symmetrical plantations in clumps. He also designed, in 1746, a banqueting house, now known as the Temple. The plans for planting did not meet with universal approval. Horace Walpole (qv) thought the older woods 'much grander than Mr Kent's passion—clumps—that is, sticking a dozen trees here and there until a lawn looks like the ten of spades. Clumps have their beauty, but in a great extent of country, how trifling to scatter arbours, where you should spread forests.'

Graham, Robert (1786–1845). Botanist. Graham was born at Stirling, the son of a doctor, and was educated in that city before being apprenticed to an Edinburgh surgeon, becoming a licentiate of the College of Surgeons and graduating from Edinburgh University in 1808. He afterwards studied at St Bartholomew's in London, later setting up in practice in Glasgow. In 1812 he was appointed physician to Edinburgh Infirmary. By this time he had become seriously interested in botanical studies and in 1818 was appointed to the first Chair of Botany. He was also energetically involved in the formation of the Royal Botanic Institution of Glasgow. In 1820, on the death of Daniel Rutherford, he was appointed Professor of Medicine and Botany at Edinburgh University, Keeper of the Royal Botanic Garden and King's Botanist, and was largely responsible for the transfer of the city's Botanic Garden to a new site.

Greenwood, Leslie (1907–). Horticultural artist. Greenwood was born in London, the son of an artist and architect. He studied etching and lithography, but only became interested in the study of flowers and plants whilst serving with the army in the Middle East. He began by painting exotics, and extended his travels to the Far East, travelling amongst the Himalayan foothills, and painting specimens well above 10,000 feet.

Greenwood's work has been bought for collections throughout the world. He has received many awards, including two gold medals, from the Royal Horticultural Society. For Frances Perry's *Flowers of the World* he drew 800 illustrations, which took six years to

Temple designed by William Kent in 1746 for the park at Euston Hall, Suffolk, the seat of the Duke of **Grafton**.

(Opposite) Summer Flowers (1) *by* Leslie **Greenwood**, *produced in a signed, limited edition of prints, by the Medici Society in London.*

Sir Alfred Daniel **Hall** (1864–1942), scientist and agriculturist.

Painshill, Surrey, in the eighteenth century, showing the lake made by the Hon. Charles **Hamilton** *as part of the landscaping of his estate, now seen as one of the most influential of all landscape gardens.*

described the mystique and rites of such bodies when comparing and judging the weights of this fruit. It is recorded that he raised one seedling of which he thought so poorly that he discarded it to a friend. The friend's cultural skill, however, produced fruit of such excellence that, years later, Sir Daniel included the gooseberry, now widely known as 'Dan's Mistake', in the Wisley Fruit Trials. His greatest contribution to horticulture was his scientific study of commercial apple-growing. He firmly believed—and proved—that many apple orchards were the equivalent of human slums. He was insistent that some of the old kinds, such as Cox's Orange Pippin, Ribstone Pippin, Blenheim and James Grieve, when properly grown in England, were superior to all imported kinds. This was one of the subjects he covered as Principal of the South Eastern Agricultural College at Wye, 1894–1902, later as Development Commissioner, from 1909–17, and then as Chief Scientific Adviser to the Ministry of Agriculture and, finally, as Principal of the John Innes Horticultural Institute. He published, jointly with W. B. Crane, *The Apple* (1933), dealing with its every aspect, from its history down to such commercial considerations as picking and storing. For these services he was made a Knight Commander of the Bath and Fellow of the Royal Society. During the war of 1939–45, he helped the Royal Horticultural Society in many ways. His activities had already gained him the Society's Victoria Medal of Honour in 1935, particularly as editor (with assistance) of its publications.

As a gardener, he was devoted to

(Opposite) Four views of the extensive gardens of Tyningham in East Lothian, Scotland, home of the Earls of **Haddington**. *The 6th Earl was a pioneer forester in the Lowlands, planting over 800 acres of his estate with more than fifty species.*

tulips. In 1929, he published *The Tulip*, and in 1940 the exhaustive *Genus Tulipa*, illustrated with plates by Osterstock.

Hamilton, (the Hon.) Charles (1704–1786). Landscape gardener. Hamilton was the fourteenth child, ninth and youngest son of James, 6th Earl of Abercorn. After studying at Christ Church, Oxford, he travelled in Europe and was in Rome between 1725 and 1732, where undoubtedly he spent much time in seeing the then fashionable sights and works of art. Following these travels, Hamilton was for a time on the staff of Frederick, Prince of Wales, who, although appearing in history books as a somewhat useless creature, was of some consequence in the arts, particularly of landscape gardening.

Hamilton's contribution to the history of the English landscape garden was profoundly influential, for he was amongst the originators of the *ferme ornée*. He first acquired the lease of land at Painshill, adjoining the River Mole, in Surrey, in 1738. During his sojourn in Italy, he had studied the paintings of Poussin and the other Italian masters, with a view to reproducing their qualities in real gardens. At Painshill, he was the originator of the Picturesque, combined with real gardening. Thus he translated the poor soil of much of the undulating land at Painshill into such fertile areas that he was able to establish his own vineyard. He enlarged the river as it passed through his property and designed a pump to raise the water level so that it irrigated his garden. He built appropriately 'ruined' and classic buildings, comparable with, if not of such high quality as, those at Stourhead in Wiltshire. He

designed and built a hermitage, gothic abbey, temple of Bacchus, a Turkish tent and offered a display of fossils and other ingenuities to visitors. Above all, he was an innovator in planting. Probably through his friend, Peter Collinson (qv), he assembled a collection of American trees, newly introduced. The walks were carefully designed to lead the visitor from scene to scene, with a number of seats so that the views from above the small valleys could be enjoyed.

Unfortunately, Hamilton spent too much of his extremely modest fortune on this imaginative undertaking, so different from the parks of Brown and Repton. In 1773, Hamilton moved to Bath, where he built a house in The Crescent and continued his gardening activities, on a substantially diminished scale, until well into his eighties.

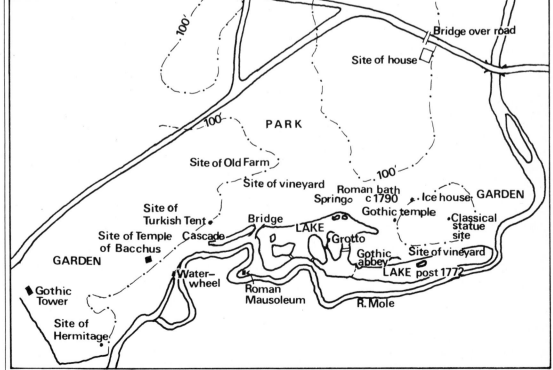

Layout of the gardens at Painshill as planned by Charles **Hamilton**, *based on a 1973 reconstruction by Peter Hodges.*

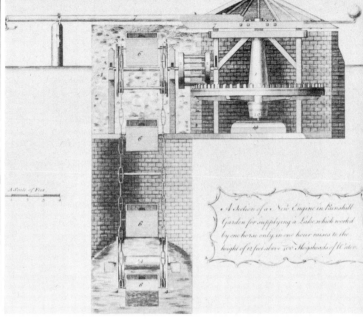

A section of the pump designed by the Hon. Charles **Hamilton** *at Painshill, Surrey, for raising the water level for irrigating his garden. Worked by one horse only, the pump raised water by twelve feet in one hour.*

The Hon. Charles **Hamilton** *(1704–1786), by Antonio David (1732).*

Under its subsequent owners, Painshill sadly deteriorated as a garden, although J. C. Loudon, visiting the garden in 1838, reported that there still remained some remarkably fine silver cedars, pines, American oaks, cork trees and ilexes, tulip trees, deciduous cypresses, Lombardy and other poplars, a tupelo tree, and the first North American species of rhododendrons and azaleas introduced in England. Hamilton was married three times, his last wife surviving him.

Hampton, Frank Anthony, MC (1888–1967). Essayist and natural historian. Hampton was born in Surrey and educated at Charterhouse and New College, Oxford, then proceeding to Guy's Hospital for medical training. At the outbreak of the First World War in 1914 he was commissioned as a medical officer. He had an adventurous war and was awarded the Military Cross for conspicuous bravery under fire. He later joined the Royal Flying Corps. Between the wars he practised as a psychiatrist. His major hobby was horticultural research of a light-hearted yet esoteric order. He would serve guests with edible fungi collected in the neighbourhood of his home in Buckinghamshire. Amongst his books (written under the pseudonym of Jason Hill) were *The Curious Gardener* (1932) and *The Contemplative Gardener* (1940), erudite and entertaining essays decorated by John Nash (qv). He also wrote *Wild Foods of Britain* (1939) and with X. M. Boulestin, the eminent French author and restaurateur, wrote *Herbs, Salads and Seasonings* (1930).

A friend, Dr W. T. Stearn, wrote of Hampton's books that 'they possess an unusual quality, perhaps best described as psychological, derived from Hampton's interest in the sensory exploration of the garden and in man's aesthetic and other reactions to the form, texture, scent and taste of plants as well as their colour.'

Hanbury, (Sir) Thomas (1832–1907). Gardener and horticultural patron. Hanbury was born at Clapham in South London of Quaker parentage. After schooling at Croydon and Epping, largely under the aegis of the Society of Friends, he joined a firm of Mincing Lane tea-brokers in 1849. When he was twenty-one he helped to set up a business in Shanghai and during the next twenty years built up a wide-ranging business, established an enviable reputation for acumen and integrity and amassed a considerable fortune.

In 1867, on one of the two holidays he took in Europe during those two decades, he became extremely attracted to the beauties of the area around the promontory of La Mortola, near Ventimiglia in Liguria in northern Italy, close to the French border. There he bought the derelict Palazzo Marengo and over two hundred acres of the surrounding olive groves with the

Gothick pavilion and (right) Temple of Bacchus (in early 1960s) at Painshill, landscaped by the Hon. Charles **Hamilton**.

*Sir Thomas **Hanbury** (1832–1907), who created an exotic garden for his house, La Mortola, in Italy.*

*View from the gardens at La Mortola, in Italy, showing the approach to the house, restored by Sir Thomas **Hanbury**.*

object of making his home there after retirement. With the aid of his brother, Daniel, a noted botanist and pharmacologist, he immediately set about a vigorous if long-distance programme of planting trees and shrubs, including acacias, eucalyptus, magnolias, yuccas, and other species.

After his retirement from his business in China he settled at La Mortola, rebuilt the house and continued, at an ever-increasing rate, his planting and sowing programme, importing seeds from several countries on the advice of his brother. In 1878 he was elected a Fellow of the Linnean Society.

Hanbury also devoted much time and money to the local Ligurian community, building schools and libraries, as well as establishing and presenting to the University of Genoa in 1892, a Botanical Institute.

In the previous year he had been knighted and in 1903 was awarded the Victoria Medal of Honour. In the same year he made one of the most munificent gifts ever made to British horticulture, buying the sixty-acre estate at Wisley in Surrey and presenting it to the Royal Horticultural Society, which moved there from Chiswick. The Society later erected a memorial stone to Hanbury in the grounds.

After his death in 1907 the gardens at La Mortola became sadly neglected, but after his son, Cecil, took over the gardens in 1920 the gardens were once again brought back to their erstwhile glories. In 1959, after the death of Sir Cecil, his widow, who remarried and became Mrs Dodo Hanbury Forbes, finding the maintenance of the gardens too arduous a task after forty years of continuous care and management,

handed over La Mortola to the Italian State. The gardens are opened to the public and form a memorable halt for all travellers on the Riviera road.

As Fred Whitsey, editor of *Popular Gardening* has written: 'Few gardener's gardens have survived so long and few have such a future. For the present, anyone who loves plants and travels on the Riviera road should make plans for a stop there. A long one, for it really is the stuff of dreams.'

Hance, Henry Fletcher (1827–1886). Botanist and plant-collector. Hance, one of the most eminent of that small group of plant-collectors who introduced flora from south-western China into Britain, was in the true tradition of English eccentrics. He was educated partly in London and partly on the Continent and early on showed a remarkable aptitude for foreign languages, becoming fluent in French and German as well as a notable Latinist. Yet, with the invincible obstinacy of the congenital eccentric, he refused to learn either Mandarin or Canton Chinese, despite his profound understanding of and affection for the people of China and over forty years' residence in the country as a consular official. This obduracy

*Henry **Hance** (1827–1886), vice consul at Whampoa in China.*

prevented his promotion. Nevertheless, despite his relatively junior positions (which probably allowed him a good deal of leisure and freedom from responsibility), first, as assistant to the consul at Canton and, later, as vice-consul at Whampoa, he established a singular renown and influence as a plant-collector and contributed material which was incorporated in *Flora Hongkongensis*, J. G. Bentham's vast compilation. His considerable knowledge was of incalculable help to a steady stream of plant-collectors through the years, and he was assiduous in seeking plant specimens from other missionaries and other travellers, especially after the Anglo-French conflict with the Chinese in 1860, after which far greater freedom within the interior of China was allowed. In this manner he assembled an impressive herbarium (which is now housed in the Natural History section of the British Museum, a memorial to his knowledge and energy).

Hanger, Francis (1900–1961). Horticulturist. In 1927, Hanger joined Lionel de Rothschild's gardening staff at Exbury in Hampshire, becoming head gardener in 1934, and six years later agent of the estate. He made a considerable reputation as a cultivator of plants and grew many hybrids, especially of rhododendrons and azaleas, which were exhibited at the RHS shows. In 1946 he was appointed curator at the Society's gardens at Wisley. His expertise and enthusiasm brought speedy results, notably in the development of Battleston Hill, which he had planted with magnolias, rhododendrons, azaleas, camellias and a wide range of trees and shrubs. In the Chelsea Show of 1957, his exhibit of a mossy glade of primulas, poppies, lilies and rhododendrons from Wisley was one of the finest ever staged in the history of the show. He also contributed outstanding exhibits to overseas shows: a woodland garden at the quinquennial shows at Ghent in 1955 and 1960, the Floralies Internationales in Paris in 1959 and to the International Horticultural Show at Hamburg, 1963, which he sadly did not live to see.

Hanmer, (Sir) Thomas (1612–1678). Horticulturist and writer. Hanmer was born into an ancient family that lived at Bettisfield on the Welsh borders. At an early age he was made page and, later, cup-bearer at the Court of Charles I. In his mid-twenties he set out on what was to prove a three-year tour of the Continent. He returned to England in 1641. He made many acquaintances amongst his peers, but also amongst those who were later to prove useful to him in his horticultural pursuits. Amongst these acquaintances was

*Sir Thomas **Hanmer** (1612–1678). Detail from portrait by Van Dyck, c. 1638.*

*Francis **Hanger** (1901–1962).*

*Sir Christopher **Hatton** (1530–1591).*

John Rose (qv), later gardener to Charles II.

During the Civil War, Hanmer, despite his early Royalist allegiance, took neither side, but retired to his home at Bettisfield in Flintshire, cultivating his garden and following precepts established by French and Dutch gardeners whose handiwork he had seen during his travels. By 1659 Hanmer had put much of his gardening philosophy into a manuscript *Garden Book*, which was not, curiously enough, published until almost three centuries later, edited by I. Elstob under the title of *The Garden Book of Sir Thomas Hanmer* (1933). The book contained descriptive and cultural notes concerning the cultivation of plants, trees and fruit that are still cogent. Amongst flowers he favoured tulips

above all, followed by anemones, primroses, cowslips, all of which he cultivated in Flintshire. Amongst trees favoured by Hanmer, pride of place is given to the Cedar of Lebanon, then comparatively little known or grown in England, and to which Hanmer not only made the first English reference but for which he prophesied a notable future, a prophecy nobly realized. He also, less accurately, made reference to the virtues of the evergreen oak, or ilex, which he surprisingly confused with the far less stately Kermes Oak. Hanmer also grew a good deal of fruit in Flintshire, including pears and vines, about which he also left copious notes.

Hanmer was in the vanguard of those who sought to escape from the constriction and formalism of earlier garden design and wished to open up wider vistas for themselves. All that is 'now commonly near the house', he wrote, 'is laid open and exposed to the sight of the rooms and chambers.' He was also concerned with the popularization of the winter-house or winter-room, an early form of the conservatory utilized for the unseasonal cultivation of more tender plants and what were then generally known, thanks to a still somewhat hazy knowledge of geography, as 'Indians', a term loosely applied to plants from both the West Indies and the Far East.

Hanmer was one of the most significant, influential, accurate and patient of the gardeners of the Cromwellian and Restoration eras. From his records we can gain a rare yet clear picture of a gentleman's garden of the time; yet few gentlemen in those troubled times were prepared to give so much time and care to so pacific a pastime.

Hatton family:

The Hattons are chiefly concerned with the ownership of Kirby Hall in Northamptonshire, the great Elizabethan house which has been described as 'perhaps the most noble building of its time,' and the gradual development of the gardens under successive generations of the Hatton family. Kirby was first acquired by SIR CHRISTOPHER HATTON (1530–1591), courtier and statesman. Whilst still in his twenties, he became one of Queen Elizabeth's favourites and was the recipient of several estates and sinecures from the Queen. He also built a vast new house on his family estate at Holdenby in Northamptonshire, and bought Kirby Hall, also in Northamptonshire, from Sir Humphrey

*(Opposite) Views of the house and gardens at La Mortola, in Liguria, Italy, designed by Thomas **Hanbury** and maintained by his family until handed over to the Italian State in 1959.*

West garden, at Kirby Hall, now replanted to the formal layout established circa 1685 by Christopher **Hatton** *IV.*

Michael **Haworth-Booth** *(1896–   ).*

Stafford who died in 1575. Hatton completed building the house.

After Sir Christopher's death, Kirby passed to his nephew, SIR WILLIAM NEWPORT, who took the name of Hatton. On his death, in 1581, the estate passed to a cousin of Sir Christopher. This CHRISTOPHER HATTON II entertained lavishly at Kirby, but his son, CHRISTOPHER III, who inherited Kirby in 1619, was responsible for making the gardens in the seventeenth century.

CHRISTOPHER IV (1632–1706) inherited the estate in 1670 and under his care Kirby enjoyed its golden age. Unlike his forebears he could scarcely be induced to leave the estate, which included one of the finest gardens in England. He was created Viscount Hatton of Gretton in 1683.

Yet it was a Hatton, non-resident at Kirby, who is best known to garden history. CHARLES HATTON (1635–1705), younger brother of

Christopher IV, was a copious letter-writer on all horticultural matters to his brother at Kirby and to a wide circle of friends, including John Evelyn, Pepys and Sir Hans Sloane. That his interest in flowers, trees and the produce of the kitchen garden was highly regarded by serious students is clear from the dedication to Hatton of John Ray's seminal *Historia Plantarum* in 1686.

The book is chiefly significant for his work on plant transpiration. His

second volume, *Haemostaticks*, was published in 1733.

Haworth-Booth, Michael (1896–   ). Plantsman and garden designer. Haworth-Booth was born at Cottingham in Yorkshire and whilst barely out of school became a lieutenant in an artillery regiment serving in the Middle East throughout the First World War. After demobilization he studied ecological conditions in the Middle East, India

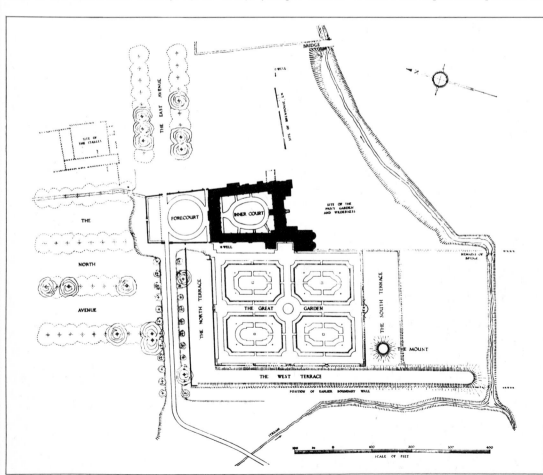

Gardens at Kirby Hall, Northamptonshire, originally laid out in 1685–86 by Christopher **Hatton,** *now replanted by the DoE.*

Dr Augustine **Henry** *(1857–1930).*

'*Close Boskage*' *by* M. **Haworth-Booth**.

Magnolia grandiflora from Hardy Trees *by William* **Hemsley** *and (right) portrait of the author.*

and the United States. On his return to England he set up as a garden designer and, applying the Close Boskage system of no-maintenance—working with, not against, nature—designed over seven hundred gardens. In 1946 he set up the Farall Nurseries, some 500 feet above sea level on the east face of Black Down Hill, near Haslemere in Surrey, where Close Boskage theories have been applied to provide a foreground of vivid colour harmonizing with a panoramic view of the English countryside.

Haworth-Booth's books include *The Flowering Shrub Garden* published in 1938 and *Hydrangeas* (1974) now in its fourth edition. He has also written a manual on the French game of boules, which is also one of his hobbies. His awards include the RHS Lindley Bronze Medal 1946 and the RHS Banksian Silver Medal 1947.

Hemsley, William Botting (1843–1924). Botanist. Hemsley was born at East Hoathly in Sussex, the son of a gardener. At an early age he entered Kew as an apprentice-gardener, having been recommended to the notice of the Director, Sir William Hooker. Although without formal education Hemsley learned to read and speak French and German fluently and became proficient in Latin. In 1865, after experience in the Kew Herbarium, he was made Herbarium clerk, but a breakdown in health caused him to resign after two years in the post. He spent his time in preparing several papers on Sussex flora and his *Handbook of Hardy Trees, Shrubs and Herbaceous Plants*, which was published in 1877. Between 1874 and 1890, when he became a civil servant, being appointed Principal Assistant in the Kew Herbarium, he established a notable reputation as a systematic

botanist, publishing the five-volume *Biologia Centrali-americana* between 1879–1888 and the *Report on the Scientific Results of the Voyage of HMS Challenger Expedition* in 1885–86. In 1899 William Hemsley was appointed Keeper to the Kew Herbarium.

Henry, Augustine (1857–1930). Plant collector and botanist. Henry was born in County Antrim, Ireland, and studied medicine at Queen's University of Ireland, graduating in 1878. Two years later he was appointed officer in the Imperial Maritime Customs Service of the Chinese Government. After a year in Shanghai he was transferred to Ichang where he was stationed for seven years. His work and fluency in the language enabled him to visit many areas of China unknown to Europeans. Thus he began serious study of the flora of the country, sending his first consignment to Kew in 1886, augmenting this with further consignments from Hupeh. Whilst on leave in 1889 he studied for the Bar and became a member of the Middle Temple. After returning to China he was stationed in Formosa. There he made a collection of two thousand plants and published an account of the island flora. He was transferred to Southern Yunnan for several years, where he continued his botanical studies. It is estimated that he sent Kew over 150,000 specimens. On his return to England, in 1900, he took up the study of forestry, travelled extensively and, from 1903, collaborated with H. J. Elwes (qv) on *The Trees of Great Britain and Ireland*. He also wrote *Forests, Woods and Trees in relation to Hygiene* (1919). In 1907 he was appointed to a readership in Forestry at Cambridge and from 1913 to 1926 was Professor of Forestry in the Dublin College of

Science, later incorporated in the National University of Ireland. He retired in 1926 and died in Dublin four years later.

Henslow, (Reverend) John Stevens (1796–1861). Cleric and botanist. Henslow was educated at Cambridge, where he took Holy Orders. Following a brilliant academic career, in which he gained high mathematical honours and became widely known as a theologian, he was appointed Professor of Botany at Cambridge in 1825. Amongst his pupils was Charles Darwin, whom he recommended as naturalist to the *Beagle* expedition. Following the closure of the old Botanic Garden in Cambridge, in 1831, Henslow was also mainly responsible for the forming of the existing Cambridge Botanic Garden on forty acres of land to the south of the city. This was formally opened in 1846.

Following his deep religious beliefs, Henslow left the academic life of Cambridge in 1837 to become rector of Hitcham in west Suffolk,

one of the most notoriously backward and irreligious parishes in East Anglia. Here, Henslow founded a school; taught botany to the children; encouraged villagers to cultivate the half-acre allotments he gouged out of a resistant farming community; started flower shows; organized excursions and made Hitcham into one of the most enlightened parishes in rural England. Although he returned to Cambridge University each year to give a series of lectures, the professor always thought of himself primarily as a parish priest.

Henslow's son, the Reverend George Henslow (1835–1925), became headmaster of Hampton Lucy School, Warwickshire, and was a popular lecturer and writer on gardening and honorary professor of botany to the Royal Horticultural Society.

Herbert, (the Hon. and Rev.) William (1778–1847). Botanist. Herbert was the son of the 1st Lord Carnarvon. He was educated at Eton (where he

John Stevens **Henslow** *(1796–1861).*

The Hon. William **Herbert** *(1778–1847).*

showed talent as a poet) and Exeter and Merton Colleges, Oxford. After graduating he was first interested in politics and was elected MP for Hampshire in 1806, but retired from Parliament in 1812 in order to enter the Church. He was ordained in 1814 and for almost a quarter-of-a-century remained rector of Spofforth in Yorkshire until he was appointed Dean of Manchester in 1840. During his years at Spofforth he became interested in the experimental hybridization of plants. His most important work was *The Amaryllidaceae*, published in 1837.

Hibberd, James Shirley (1825–1890). Horticulturist, writer. Hibberd was born into a maritime family living in Stepney, then a village outside London. After working in a bookselling and binding business he turned to journalism and, on marrying, began to study the problems of urban and suburban horticulture. Moving to Stoke Newington and, later, Muswell Hill, he built up a considerable collection of pot-grown hollies and ivies. His manifold interests were finally fused into a career as editor. In 1858 he became editor of a new and highly successful periodical, *The Floral World*, which he continued to edit until 1872, combining this with the editorship of *The Gardener's Magazine*. He also wrote several lighthearted books for small urban gardeners, including *Profitable Gardening*, *The Amateur's Rose Book* and *The Amateur's Greenhouse*. He also wrote books on garden decoration, foliage plants, ferns and ivies. Of these *Rustic Adornment* (1856), *The Fern Garden* (1869) and *The Ivy* (1872) were phenomenally successful.

Higgins, Vera (1892–1968). Botanist and botanical artist. Vera Higgins (née Cockburn) grew up in Croydon and was educated at Newnham College, Cambridge, where she studied botany, an interest greatly aided by her aptitude for drawing. After graduating she worked as a scientific officer for the National Physical Laboratory where she met her husband, William Higgins, a brilliant scientist, who shared her interest and kept her records with great care until his death in 1963, working closely with his wife on temperature measurements.

During the Second World War she edited the *Journal* of the Royal Horticultural Society and in 1946 was awarded the Victoria Medal of Hon-

Typically decorative pages from Rustic Adornments (1856) *by J. Shirley* **Hibberd** *(1825–1890).*

our. She was also President of the National Cactus Society and wrote, edited and translated various books on cacti, succulents, rock gardens, water-plants and indoor plants. Among her own books were *The Study of Cacti, Succulent Plants* and *Crassulas in Cultivation*.

Hiley, Wilfred (1886–1961). Forester, editor. After a brilliant academic career at Oxford with a 'double first' in mathematics and botany, Hiley lectured in forest economics at the Oxford School of Forestry and wrote a book on the subject. In 1931, at a time of considerable economic pressure, he took over two thousand acres owned by the Dartington Hall Trust and began the mammoth task of reafforestation. Despite the arduous duties and problems of this new job, he also undertook the editing of the monthly *Journal* of the Royal Forestry Society.

In an obituary in *The Times*, Leonard Elmhirst of Dartington wrote of Hiley: 'Since the British Forestry Commission was tied by the Treasury to a policy of afforestation on poor soils, Hiley set to work to convince various governments and the Treasury that only by a reasonable kind of partnership between state and forest owner, municipal, college, trust, or private, could the rehabilitation of the most fertile forest areas of Britain, devastated by the raids of two world wars, be most cheaply and efficiently undertaken, once the idea of "dedi-cating" such areas to sound forest practice was accepted.

'In 1956, Hiley's services as the doyen of British forest scientists and practical managers were finally recognized when he was made CBE. His many colleagues in the field will miss not just his expert comment and advice but the warmth and friendliness with which he made his contribution . . . Foresters are accustomed to take a long view. They will realize that for Hiley one of the moving moments of his career was when the gold medal of the Royal Forestry Society—of which he had been elected president in 1950—was handed to him in 1960 for outstanding and meritorious service in company with two former presidents, Lord Bolton and Charles Ackers'

Hill, Oliver (1888–1968). Architect. From an early age, Hill was deeply interested in architecture and resolved to make this his career, taking the advice of Sir Edwin Lutyens (qv) to gain practical knowledge in a well-established firm of builders. This experience proved invaluable in his later architectural work, which is distinguished by an unusual understanding and sensitive handling of building materials. He was a larger-than-life, somewhat theatrical character, and his designs often reflected this.

In 1937, he designed the British Pavilion at the Paris International Exhibition, but he is best remembered for the many country houses he designed. In each case, he took

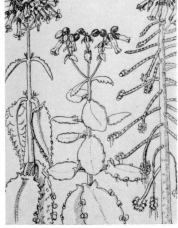

Vera **Higgins** *and (right) drawing from her* Succulent Plants Illustrated *(1949).*

*House and courtyard, with formal paving and pool, at Maryland, Hurtwood, Surrey, designed by Oliver **Hill** (1922).*

*Thomas **Hill** (fl. 1577), author of* The Profittable Arte of Gardening.

*Harold **Hillier** (1905–   ), nurseryman at Jermyns House, Hants.*

particular care to relate the garden to the house, often by the use of courtyards and terraces.

Hill (or **Hyll**), Thomas (fl. 1540s– 1570s). Probably the author of the first book on gardening to be published in England, printed almost entirely in black letter and published in 1563. The somewhat lengthy title ran thus:

Briefe and pleasaunt treatyse, teachynge howe to dress, sowe and set a Garden, and what propertyes also these few herbes heare spoken of, haue to our comodytie: with the remedyes that may be used against such beasts, wormes, flies and such lyke, that commonly noy gardes, gathered out of the principallest Authors in this art by Thomas Hyll Londyner

The significance of the book resided perhaps less in its contents than in the fact that there had grown up in the Elizabethan era a public prepared to buy gardening books.

The later editions of the book were issued under a fresh title, *The Profittable Arte of Gardening*, which was followed in 1577 by *The Gardeners Labyrinth*, issued under the name of Didymus Mountain, almost certainly a pseudonym for Hill. The book includes wood-cuts depicting Tudor gardens and contains much practical advice, both original and

borrowed, or to quote his own acknowledgements: 'parte purchased by friendshippe and earnest suite, of the skilfull observers and wittie searchers in our tyme of laudable secrets in Garden matters, serving as well for the use and singular comforts of mannes life, as to a proper gayne and delight of the mind.'

Hillier family:

Nurserymen, horticulturists. The remarkable Winchester firm was started by EDWIN HILLIER (1840– 1929) who bought the small Farthing Nursery in the city in 1864.

Within a decade his venture had so prospered that he was able to start the now-famous West Hill nursery. The business was continued by his two sons, EDWIN (1865–1944) and ARTHUR RICHARD (1877–1963) to become what is undoubtedly the largest hardy tree and shrub nursery in the world. The nurseries are now under the direction of HAROLD HILLIER (1905–   ), son of the former Edwin, and Harold's sons, JOHN GIFFORD HILLIER (1935–   ) and ROBERT TRANT HILLIER (1943–   ), both of whom gained wide experience in the United States and Europe before joining the firm. Harold Hillier was awarded the RHS Victoria Medal of Honour in 1957 and the Veitch Memorial Medal in 1962. He was made CBE in 1971.

The firm cultivates some 14,000 kinds of plants, which have been incorporated in the 85-acre Jermyns gardens and arboretum at Ampfield near Romsey in Hampshire, thus forming the largest and foremost privately-owned and commercially-run botanical gardens in Britain.

Apart from the development of the nurseries, Hilliers published, in 1971, a compendious *Manual of Trees and Shrubs*, which contains practical and botanical expertise relating to 8,000 trees, shrubs, climbers, conifers and bamboos hardy in the northern hemisphere. The manual has gone through many editions and has been republished in book form by David & Charles.

The firm also specializes in the growing and transplanting of large trees and supplied over sixty specimen trees for the precincts of the Royal Festival Hall before its opening in 1951.

Although Hilliers continue with their policy of growing rare plants (some of which are so specialized that they sell only one in two or three years) they also grow trees and shrubs by the thousand for wholesale distribution and to public

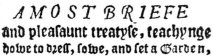

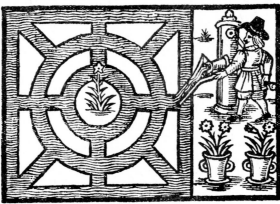

(Left) Title-page of A Most Briefe and Pleasant Treatyse *(1563), the first book on gardening to be published in England, and (right) woodcuts of garden scenes from* The Gardeners Labyrinth *(1592), both by Thomas **Hill**.*

*Henry **Hoare** (1705–1785), landscapist at Stourhead in Wiltshire.*

*(Top) Eighteenth-century engraving and (below) a recent photograph showing the lake, ornamental buildings and surrounding plantings at Stourhead in Wiltshire, laid out by Henry **Hoare**.*

authorities. The nursery exports to over thirty different countries.

Hoare, Henry (1705–1785). Landscape gardener. Hoare's fame is based upon his planning and supervision of the vast landscaping project which he carried out at Stourhead, the Wiltshire estate which he inherited. In this enterprise he gave full expression to the quest for the arcadian garden, although an alternative plan for a scheme along more traditional and formal lines still exists in the library at Stourhead.

In 1714, Lord Stourton sold his family estates in Wiltshire, which extended to a thousand acres or more, to the trustees of Richard Hoare, son of Sir Richard Hoare, goldsmith, founder of the bank which still carries his name. He died six years later, and his younger brother, Henry, took over the estate from the trustees and set about building a new house in the Palladian manner to the designs of Colen Campbell. He died in 1725, when the new house was reaching completion, leaving the estate to his widow for her lifetime and then, on her death, to his elder son, also Henry.

Mrs Hoare died in 1741 and Henry II, then aged thirty-six, and in Italy buying works of art, returned to Stourhead to take over the estate and to begin the landscaping which was to turn Stourhead into what Horace Walpole termed, in 1762, 'one of the most picturesque scenes in the world'. Walpole also reported that Hoare had made the fine woods, the water and the ornamental buildings, thus confirming that Hoare was his own landscape designer, despite the fact that he was also, like his forebears, an enterprising and successful London banker. For the structural adornments, however, Hoare consulted Henry Flitcroft (1697–1769) who was employed in the Office of Works, of which he later became Comptroller.

Stourhead is basically a lake-landscape, its many features established between 1741 and 1750, a decade or more before 'Capability' Brown had made his name. Garden historian Georgina Masson has suggested that Hoare may have gained his inspiration for Stourhead from Pliny's description of the source of the Clitumnus between Rome and Perugia, which he may well have seen during his Italian travels.

Certainly, one of Hoare's earliest projects was to enlarge the headwaters of the River Stour, fishponds and other waters which lay in the valleys below steep hillsides. He thus formed an informal, twenty-acre lake encompassed by picturesque slopes, which were copiously planted with beech and fir trees.

By the 1760s the great garden was already sufficiently impressive to be an attraction to visitors from far and wide and an inn had to be built to accommodate sightseers. Coincidental with the vast planting schemes, on which fifty gardeners were continuously employed, Hoare was embellishing Stourhead with numerous (some claimed 'innumerable') objects and buildings, many of which remain and some of which have disappeared. Still others were planned but not built.

Amongst the buildings which have helped to give Stourhead its widespread renown are the Grotto (probably deriving from Alexander Pope's highly celebrated folly at Twickenham); the Rustic Cottage, with its gothic porch and bay window; the Pantheon designed by Flitcroft as a miniature version of the original Roman building; the Temple of the Sun (also designed by Flitcroft, with its domed rotunda deriving from the Temple of Venus at Baalbec) and the Convent in the Woods, another gothic folly. One of the finest views is to be gained from Alfred's Tower, some three miles from the house, designed by Flitcroft in 1772.

Hoare continued with his plans and plantings until the last years of his long life. In 1783 he made over the estate to his grandson, Richard Colt Hoare, a notable antiquary, who kept the gardens more or less as his grandfather had planned them, although he made alterations 'to render the design of these gardens as chaste and correct as possible, and give them the character of an Italian villa.' He was responsible for laying the gravel lakeside paths and considerably enriched the planting at Stourhead. He was an authority on geraniums.

In 1947, Stourhead was given to the National Trust by the designer's descendant, Sir Henry Hoare, the 6th baronet.

Hodgkin, Eliot (1905–1973). Plant collector with special interest in small bulbs and alpines. Hodgkin was educated at Eton and Christ Church, Oxford. He joined Imperial Chemicals Industries in 1928 where, with the exception of the war years when he served in the RAF, he remained throughout his business life, becoming General Manager Overseas until his retirement in 1968. His numerous journeys abroad enabled him to collect many rare plants for his Berkshire garden, mainly specimens of the genus *Helleborus*. In 1972, he was awarded the Victoria Medal of Honour of the Royal Horticultural Society, of which he was a council member for some years. He was also president of the Alpine Garden Society, 1971–1973.

Hogg, (Dr) Robert (1818–1897). Pomologist, botanist, writer. Hogg was born at Duns in Berwickshire, the son of a leading nurseryman of the nearby town of Coldstream. He was originally intended for the medical profession, but an early interest in natural science caused him to turn to botanical studies at Edinburgh University. After leaving the university, he furthered his practical knowledge of horticulture, first in one of the city's leading nurseries and later with Dr Hugh Ronalds, the noted pomologist, at Brentford. He completed his botanical studies in Rouen and in Paris at the *Jardin des Plantes*.

In 1845, Hogg bought a partnership in the Brompton Park Nursery, but his hopes of a successful business career were unfulfilled and he retired to continue research for a work entitled *British Pomology* in which he listed 940 varieties. Only one part of the projected series was published, however, as no backers or patrons were forthcoming. Undaunted, Hogg took a leading part in the formation of the British Pomological Society in 1854, with Sir Joseph Paxton (qv) as its first president. The society was merged in the Fruit Committee of the Horticultural Society in 1858, of which Hogg became secretary, also taking an active share in the management of the society's garden at Chiswick and paying particular attention to the selection of varieties for the fruit garden. In 1860 he published his *Fruit Manual*, the most important of

(Opposite) Views of Stourhead, Wiltshire, landscaped by Henry **Hoare**. *(Above) Lake with Bridge and Temple of Apollo and (below) The Pantheon and Gothic Cottage, both painted in watercolour by Francis Nicholson (1753–1844).*

The Convent in the Woods, a folly at Stourhead, landscaped by Henry **Hoare**.

his independent publications, which passed through five editions during the next twenty years. In association with G. W. Johnson, he edited for several years the *Journal* *of Horticulture* and also collaborated with his colleague on the *Wild Flowers of Great Britain*, an illustrated work comprising some eleven volumes in all, which was published

Eliot **Hodgkin** *(1905–1973).*

Robert **Hogg** *(1818–1897).*

between 1863 and 1880.

Hogg was elected a Fellow of the Linnean Society in 1861 and, in 1875, he was elected secretary of the Royal Horticultural Society.

1 Seat
2 Temple of Flora
3 Paradise Well
4 Boathouse
5 Grotto
6 Gothic cottage
7 Pantheon
8 Iron bridge
9 Dam
10 Cascade
11 Rock bridge
12 Hermitage (site)
13 Temple of Apollo
14 Grotto underpass
15 Stone bridge
16 Bristol Cross
17 Church
18 Obelisk
19 St Peter's Pump
20 Convent
21 Alfred's Tower

Recent plan showing the disposition of existing ornamental buildings at Stourhead, landscaped by Henry **Hoare**.

Drawing from The Wild Flowers of Great Britain *by Robert* **Hogg**.

Samuel Reynolds **Hole** *(1819–1904), rosarian and writer.*

Robert **Holford** *(1808–1892), plantsman at Westonbirt, Gloucestershire.*

Captain Sir Everard **Home** *Bt (1798–1853).*

Amongst Hogg's other books were *The Vegetable Kingdom and Its Products* (1857–58); *A New Classification of Apples* (1876) and *The Herefordshire Pomona* with Henry Graves Bull (1876–85).

Hole, (Dean) Samuel Reynolds (1819–1904). Rosarian, writer, organizer. Hole was born at Caunton Manor at Ardwick in Manchester, the son of a prosperous Manchester cotton merchant. He was educated at Newark Grammar School and Brasenose College, Oxford. In 1844, he became curate at Caunton, and later vicar of the same parish, a post he held for over forty years.

During his curacy he became interested in rose-growing, his first interest aroused by rose d'Aguesseau (*gallica*) which remained one of his favourites. This new interest soon ousted his earlier passions for fox-hunting and archery. He became one of the most involved of rosar-

ians, and was frequently invited to act as judge at flower shows.

His experiences persuaded him that the rose did not hold the eminent position it should have: on the show-bench it was merely one shrub or flower amongst many. Having decided to raise the rose from this mundane status, he wrote to *The Florist* in 1856, suggesting that a Grand National Rose Show should be held. The response was poor, but Hole, a man of considerable energy, called a meeting of the country's chief rosarians at Webbs Hotel, Piccadilly, and the project for a national rose show was planned. This was held at St James' Hall, London, in 1858, proving an immediate success. Two years later, the show was transferred to the Crystal Palace at Sydenham, when 16,000 visitors attended.

The National Rose Show continued to be staged annually, but, in 1861, the year of his marriage, Hole found that he could no longer afford

the time demanded by the exhibition and he handed over its supervision to the Royal Horticultural Society. Yet his interest in rose-growing and rose-showing in no way abated (in 1868 he won fourteen first prizes including that for amateurs at the RHS show) and, in 1869, he published *A Book About Roses* which became an immediate best-seller and went into over twenty editions. In 1876, a year after he had been appointed Canon of Lincoln, he chaired the meeting at which the National Rose Society was founded. The new society also took over the annual show. In the following year, he was elected President of the Society.

In 1887, Hole was appointed Dean of Rochester. Two years later he presided at the Rose Conference of the Royal Horticultural Society and again in 1902.

Amongst Hole's other books are: *A Little Tour of Ireland* (1858); *The Memories of Dean Hole* (1892); *Our Gardens* (1899); *A Book About the Garden* (1904).

Holford, Robert Stayner (1808–1892). Plantsman. Holford succeeded to the estate at Westonbirt in Gloucestershire in 1839. He inherited a considerable fortune, derived mainly from a large interest in the New River Co, and immediately set about building a new, grander house to display his collection of paintings. He also began a considerable programme of laying out the gardens at Westonbirt, the progress of which was carefully recorded by Holford's head gardener, Jonah Neale. Holford is chiefly known as the founder of the arboretum at Westonbirt, which he started in 1829, some ten years before his succession, and developed over the next sixty years. The arboretum was formed on an area of over 150 acres of open, agricultural land in typical Cotswold country of low relief. The first plantings were of yew, laurel, Holm oak and other trees on the boundary for shelter; these were followed by

the north-west American conifers which had been introduced by David Douglas (qv). In about 1875, Holford was joined in the work on the arboretum by his son, George Holford, who was responsible for further plantings, especially those of Silk Wood, begun in 1876. (Sir) George Holford (1860–1926) added extensive plantings for autumn colour and was a renowned orchidist. On his death in 1926, he was succeeded at Westonbirt by his nephew, the 4th Earl of Morley who, with the continued help of W. J. Mitchell as curator, added further plantings on a considerable scale. He died in 1951.

Home, (Captain) (Sir) Everard (Bt) (1798–1853). Home was the elder son of the first baronet of the same name, Sergeant-Surgeon to George III. Although Home spent most of his life in the Navy he deserves recognition in this DICTIONARY by reason of his correspondence with, and collections on behalf of, Sir William Hooker (qv). He entered the Navy when he was eleven years of age. After serving on various foreign stations and seeing action in South America and China, he was appointed senior naval officer in New Zealand. His letters to Hooker from New Zealand recorded observations on the condition of the Norfolk Island pines, extracts from which were published in the proceedings of the Linnean Society for 1874.

He underlined his interest in extra-nautical affairs by suggesting that naval officers should be encouraged and technically instructed to make collections of plants. He was elected a Fellow of the Royal Society in 1825.

Hooker, (Sir) Joseph Dalton (1817–1911). Botanist, artist, administrator, plant collector. Hooker was born at Halesworth in Suffolk, the second son of William Jackson Hooker (qv). He was educated at Glasgow High School and Glasgow University, where he studied medicine. On graduation he was gazetted assistant surgeon and botanist to the *Erebus*, which, *en route* to Antarctic exploration, was to visit New Zealand, Australia, Tierra del Fuego and the Falkland Islands, where plant-collecting expeditions were to be made. Hooker assembled a vast amount of botanical specimens during his forays ashore, and the results of his researches were later published in three two-volume works: *Flora Antarctica*, *Flora Novae Zelandiae* and *Flora Tasmaniae*. Hooker made another notable expedition to the Himalayas, where he spent some time exploring Sikkim. His adventures there were later recounted in *Himalayan Journals*, as much an adventure story as a narration of botanical inquiry. His more

Mixed planting at Westonbirt Arboretum, founded by Robert **Holford**, *in 1829.*

Sir William Jackson **Hooker**
(1785–1865), director of Kew.

erudite botanical studies, with Dr Thomas Thomson (qv), were published in *Flora Indica.*

In 1855, Hooker was appointed assistant director at Kew under his father, but was given leave of absence to visit Syria and Palestine in 1860 to study the Lebanon cedar groves.

In conjunction with George Bentham, Hooker began preparation of the *Genera Plantarum*, the first part of which was issued in 1862. Three years later, on his father's death, he was appointed Director of Kew, and although administrative tasks became an increasingly demanding element in his life, he continued with his botanical researches, publishing numerous books as well as editing the *Botanical Magazine* for several years and completing the *Flora of British India*. He also continued his travels with a botanical expedition to Morocco and the Atlas Mountains in 1871, and, six years later, to Colorado, Utah and the Sierra Nevada in the United States. Throughout this arduous working life, Hooker maintained a warm friendship and remarkable correspondence with Charles Darwin and

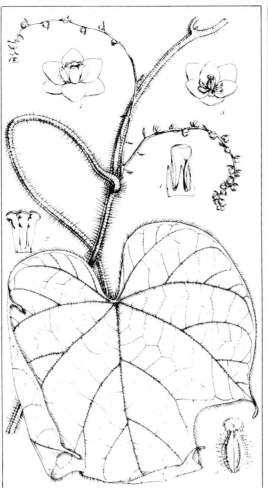

Two drawings from Niger Flora, *edited by Sir William Jackson* **Hooker**, *published in 1849.*

was closely associated with Darwin's great work on the origin of species.

He gained many honours and awards from British universities. He was president of the Royal Society for five years and received the Society's Royal Medal in 1854. He was knighted in 1897. He continued to work until an advanced age and died in his ninety-fifth year.

Hooker, (Sir) William Jackson (1785–1865). Botanist, plant-col-

lector, artist, administrator. Hooker was born in Norwich, the son of a cloth merchants' clerk who was also a collector of succulents and exotics. He was educated at Norwich Grammar School. In the early years of the nineteenth century, having come into a sizable property in Kent, he was sent to learn the rudiments of estate management at Starton Hall in Norfolk. His discovery of a specimen of the moss, *Buxbaumia aphylla*, brought him to the notice of Dawson Turner, an eminent banker

of Yarmouth who was also a keen topographer and botanist, specializing in mosses, ferns and other cryptograms. On attaining his majority, Hooker took nominal possession of his Kentish property, and was induced by Turner to take a financial interest in a Suffolk brewery, but persisted in his botanical studies, which led to an introduction to Sir Joseph Banks (qv), President of the Royal Society. From that meeting on, Hooker became a dedicated botanist. He had also shown himself

Bridge crossed by Sir Joseph **Hooker** *during one of his plant-hunting expeditions and reproduced in his* Himalayan Journals; *(right) the author (1817–1911).*

Kew Museum of Economic Botany in 1855, founded by Sir William **Hooker**.

John **Hope** *(left) (1725–1786).*

to be a draughtsman of uncommon talent, having made many drawings for Turner. In 1808, however, he published his own first paper on Nepalese mosses, which was followed in 1812 by the first part of his history of the *British Jungermanniae*, again illustrated with his own drawings. During these years he was also beginning to assemble what was to become his renowned herbarium. After two modest botanical excursions to Scotland, Hooker was invited by Banks to engage in a plant-collecting expedition to Iceland. This, the first of Hooker's oversea journeys, ended in disaster as far as his plants were concerned, for his ship, *The Margaret and Anne*, was destroyed by fire on the return journey. The ship's company and Hooker were rescued by a Danish man o' war.

In 1812 Hooker married Maria, one of Turner's three daughters, and their honeymoon was spent in leisurely botanical excursions in the Lake District and Ireland. They then settled in Halesworth, Suffolk, but, thanks to the beneficent directive of Banks, Hooker was enabled to quit his somewhat shaky brewery interests for the Professorship of Botany at Glasgow University, to which he was appointed in 1820. An added inducement in the project was the university's botanical garden which was to be under the professor's direction.

Hooker's twenty-one-year tenure of the professorship brought considerable fame to the botanic garden and himself, and it was almost inevitable that he should be offered, in due course, the direction of Kew.

This appointment was made in 1841. One of Hooker's early innovations at the Kew gardens was to open the gardens to the public. In the first year 9,000 people visited the gardens. (In 1865, the last year of his life and directorship, there were 73,000 visitors.)

In co-operation with the Admiralty he also organized numerous plant-hunting expeditions to remote regions, from the Zambesi to British Columbia, from the Fiji Islands to California. These expeditions resulted in the formation of the vast herbarium which was to become one of the glories of Kew. He also formed a large collection of hardy herbaceous plants and commissioned the Palm House from Decimus Burton (qv). He sponsored the building of the tropical aquarium for the giant Amazonian water-lily.

Hooker was a man of outstanding character and talent, an imaginative administrator of the highest order, a skilled botanical artist and, above all, one of the most practical and authoritative botanists of his time. Unlike many men of action and initiative, he seems also to have been a politician of unusual patience and persuasiveness, gradually winning the support of those initially opposed to some of his more far-sighted projects whilst gaining the enthusiastic support of others. Amongst his most lively supporters was the Duke of Bedford, who had paved the way for Hooker's revival of the authority of Kew. Other valuable allies included Queen Victoria and the Prince Consort, who were personally responsible for saving fine trees in the park, not then part of the Kew terrain. Hooker was succeeded at Kew by his younger son, Joseph Dalton Hooker (qv).

Hope, John (1725–1786). Botanist. Hope, the son of a surgeon, was born in Edinburgh and was educated at Dalkeith School. He studied medicine at Edinburgh University and at various medical schools on the continent. He graduated from Glasgow University and joined the College of Physicians at Edinburgh, devoting himself to the study of botanical science. In 1761 he was appointed Professor of Botany at Edinburgh University and was also made King's Botanist for Scotland and Superintendent of the royal garden in the city. In 1768 he was appointed regius professor of medicine and botany which he combined with his election as physician to the Edinburgh Royal Infirmary. Finding the medical botanical

(Opposite) Snow beds at 13,000 feet in the Th'lonok Valley, with rhododendrons in blossom, Kinchin-junga in the distance. Drawn by Joseph Dalton **Hooker** *and used as the frontispiece of the second volume of his* Himalayan Journals, *published in 1854.*

West Park, Sir William Jackson **Hooker's** *house at Kew, where he established his herbarium.*

*Sir Arthur Fenton **Hort** (1864–1935), who edited* inter alia Enquiry into Plants *(1916), seen in his garden in Hampshire.*

garden there based on poor, swampy ground he was instrumental in exchanging it for a more suitable and congenial site where all plants were arranged on the Linnean system. He not only edited Linnaeus's *Genera Animalium* (1771) but raised a statue to his Swedish mentor in the Edinburgh Botanical Gardens. Hope's efforts as botanist and gardener duly received the approbation of the Danish master who named the genus *Hopea* after him. Hope was elected a Fellow of the Royal Society and at his death was President of the Edinburgh College of Physicians.

Hort, (Sir) Arthur Fenton (1864–1935). Botanist. Hort was born at Hurstbourne Tarrant, Hampshire, the son of the 5th baronet. He was educated at Harrow and Cambridge and had a long connexion with Harrow School, extending over thirty years. He was a master from 1888 until 1922. He was particularly interested in irises and much influenced by Sir Michael Foster (1836–1907) (qv), the pioneer in breeding the modern bearded iris.

Hort edited several works, including Theophrastus's *Enquiry into Plants* (1916). He also translated Linnaeus's *Critica Botanica* (1938). In 1928, he 'perpetrated' (his own word) *The Unconventional Garden*, a small book written to 'suggest to the owners of small flower-gardens some ways in which their efforts might come to possess a greater variety of interest'. He based this book and a successor entitled *Garden Variety* (1935) on his personal experiences with a chalk-soil garden. Unlike many botanists he wrote mostly about plants that he had grown and his books are written in a personal, rather chatty manner, full of anecdotes and interesting references to those who had given him useful advice.

Hulme, Frederick Edward (1841–1909). Botanist. Hulme was the only son of Frederick Hulme, landscape artist, and was born at Hanley in Staffordshire. He studied art at South Kensington and was appointed art master at Marlborough College in 1870, and professor of geometrical drawing at King's College, London, in 1885. From boyhood he drew plants, and in 1868, he published a *Series of Sketches from Nature of Plant Form*, followed by other volumes. In 1878, he issued the first of his most notable volumes on *Familiar Wild Flowers* illustrated with his own drawings. He published eight volumes in the series. Hulme also illustrated books by other writers, notably *Familiar Garden Flowers* by Shirley Hibberd (qv). Hulme's graphic range was extremely wide, including thirty-five coloured plates for *Butterflies and Moths of the Countryside* and *Familiar Swiss Flowers* (100 coloured plates). He became a Fellow of the Linnean Society in 1869.

Hussey, Christopher CBE, FSA, Hon. ARIBA (1899–1970). Archi-tectural and landscape historian. Hussey was born at Scotney Castle in Kent, which had been designed for his grandfather by Anthony Salvin in 1830, and which Hussey later inherited. He was educated at Eton and Christ Church, Oxford. Whilst still a schoolboy he became interested in historic houses which he visited by bicycle. He began to contribute articles to *Country Life* whilst still an undergraduate. When he was twenty-eight, he published *The Picturesque*, 'an essay on a way of seeing', which was the first of his major contributions to the history of the landscape movement culminating in his *English Gardens and Landscapes, 1700–1750*, published forty years later. Alongside these interests he was writing regular articles in *Country Life* on country houses, which were collected in his scholarly and comprehensive trilogy on *Georgian Country Houses*, published between 1955 and 1958. He was architectural adviser to *Country Life* from 1930 until 1964 and edited the magazine between 1933 and 1940.

An obituary in that magazine said that it would be wrong to think of Hussey exclusively as a scholar: 'he lived a full and rounded life, quite as absorbed in walks round his own woodlands as in choosing a Sussex bull or wrestling with the more recondite aspects of the Rococo in his study. Hussey combined his writing and research with a great deal of committee work for the National Trust and the Historic Buildings Council, and numerous other amenity societies, both in London and in Kent.' To these comments should be added the tribute by Dr Mordaunt Crooke: 'Hussey put his inherited advantages to excellent use, delighting in the appreciation of architecture by a wider and wider audience. His whole life was really a triumphant vindication of the English amateur tradition. During his lifetime, architectural history was transformed from a species of *belles lettres* into a serious academic discipline.

*Two engravings by Edward **Hulme** (1841–1909) from* Familiar Garden Flowers *by J. Shirley Hibberd.*

*Christopher **Hussey** (1899–1970).*

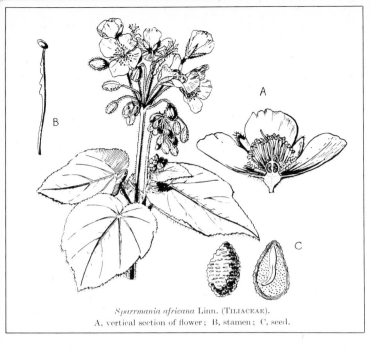

Sparrmania africana Linn. (TILIACEAE).
A, vertical section of flower; B, stamen; C, seed.

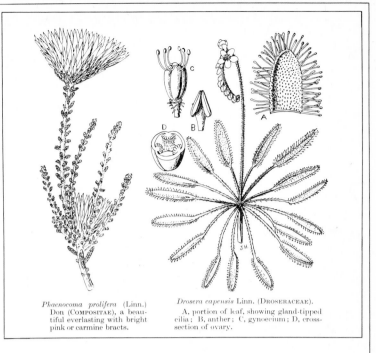

Phaenocoma prolifera (Linn.) Don (COMPOSITAE), a beautiful everlasting with bright pink or carmine bracts.

Drosera capensis Linn. (DROSERACEAE).
A, portion of leaf, showing gland-tipped cilia; B, anther; C, gynoecium; D, cross-section of ovary.

Two engravings reproduced from A Botanist in Southern Africa *(1946) by John* **Hutchinson** *(1884–1972), a specialist in African flora.*

Almost accidentally, Hussey played a crucial part in this process. Rather more consciously, he helped to turn preservation from a minority cult into a major national concern.'

As well as being a scholar of unusual dedication and range, Christopher Hussey was a talented watercolour artist and documented his visits to country houses and gardens with his own paintings.

Hutchinson, John (1884–1972). Horticulturist. Hutchinson was born in Wark-on-Tyne, Northumberland. In 1904 he went to Kew as a student gardener and in the following year was transferred to the Herbarium as assistant. From 1936–48 he was keeper of Kew Museums. He was a specialist in plant taxonomy. As a result of handling thousands of plants from all over the world during his years at Kew, he began to evolve his own theory of classification. His botanical studies were furthered by two botanizing expeditions to South Africa in 1928 and 1930.

Hutchinson was a prolific writer. His first publication was the two-volume *Families of Flowering Plants*, first issued in 1926. He was an artist of considerable talent and illustrated several of his own books. These included several volumes on wild flowers, including *Common Wild Flowers* (1945); *More Common Wild Flowers* (1948); and *Uncommon Wild Flowers* (1950). He also wrote two volumes deriving from his experiences during his botanizing expeditions: *A Botanist in South Africa* (1946) and *The Flora of West Tropical Africa*, compiled with J. M. Dalziel and issued between 1927 and 1936. He also contributed to a number of horticultural journals.

Hutchinson's reputation as a specialist in African flora was inter-

national. The study and cultivation of rhododendrons (in particular in the elepidote) were his other main interests. In 1930 he helped to compile *The Species of Rhododendron* which has been termed 'a lasting monument to the Rhododendron Society'.

Even after his retirement, in 1948, he visited the Herbarium at Kew almost daily, and continued to work on the third volume of his *Genera of Flowering Plants* (two volumes of which had already been published) until within a short time of his death. He had also completed the index to the third edition of *Families of Flowering Plants*.

Hutchinson was awarded the OBE in 1972. His plants, drawings and an autobiography in manuscript are at Kew.

Huxley, Thomas Henry (1825–1895). Scientist. Huxley was born at Ealing, the son of a schoolmaster. In later years, he claimed that his formal education had been negligible.

He early showed a profound interest in biological subjects, and when he was seventeen began medical studies at Charing Cross Hospital, graduating in 1845, publishing his first scientific paper in the same year. He was appointed surgeon to HMS *Rattlesnake* for surveying work in Torres Strait and sent back numerous communications to the Linnean Society. Most of his scientific inquiries and discoveries are outside the scope of this DICTIONARY but his genius was so protean and all-pervasive that he influenced botanical research as he did those of a score of other specialized interests.

Hyams, Edward (1910–1975). Gardener and gardening historian. Hyams was born in London and was educated at University College School, Hampstead, and the University of Lausanne, although he contended that his real education only began after leaving school. He spent some years in France, an experience which made him a life-

long Francophile with a profound interest in French satire. His literary career began with the publication of several novels but he gradually turned to gardening and gardening history. He early specialized in the history of the vine and published *The Grape Vine in England* in 1949 and *Vineyards in England* in 1953, culminating in *Dionysus* in 1966. Meantime, he had become an enthusiastic and knowledgeable gardener, and published an account of his experiences in making his Suffolk garden in *An Englishman's Garden* in 1965. His larger works comprise the three-volume *Ornamental Shrubs for Temperate Zone Gardens* (1965–66); *A History of Gardens and Gardening* 1971. He also published (with Edwin Smith's photographs) *English Cottage Gardens* (1970) and studies of Brown and Repton in the following year. He was a prolific journalist, contributing weekly garden features to the *Illustrated London News* and *The New Statesman*.

John **Hutchinson** *(1884–1972).*

Thomas Henry **Huxley** *(1825–1895).*

Edward **Hyams** *(1910–1975).*

I - J

Ingwersen, Walter Edward Theodore (1883–1960). Nurseryman. Ingwersen was of Danish origin, although born in Hamburg. At an early age he travelled widely throughout Europe, eventually settling in England, where he opened a nursery in Croydon. The First World War forced the closure of this venture and he spent the war years in charge of the rock garden department at Wisley.

After the war he spent a period in partnership with the late Clarence Elliott in the famous Six Hills Nursery at Stevenage, later moving on to partnership with the late Gavin Jones at Letchworth. In 1925 he founded another nursery of his own, this time near East Grinstead in Sussex, where he remained until he died in 1960.

He was a founder member of the Alpine Garden Society, and was deeply involved in all its activities, travelling widely to study the plants in which he specialized in their native habitats. He was recognized as one of the foremost plantsmen of his time. In 1944, he was awarded the Victoria Medal of Honour by the Royal Horticultural Society and the Gold Veitch Medal in 1950.

Irvine, (Major) Walter (1890–1963). Landscape gardener. Irvine was born in Birkenhead and was educated at Birkenhead School. He served with the Cheshire Regiment in the First World War, in which he was wounded and lamed for the rest of his life, but remained remarkably active. Irvine became a senior official in a Liverpool oil company, but in his mid-forties, retired from his business interests to take up landscape gardening, becoming a member of the Institute of Landscape Architects. He was responsible for many landscaping projects in the North of England, including the memorial garden to the Cheshire Regiment in the precinct of Chester Cathedral, as well as hundreds of

(Opposite) Paintings by George Elgood depicting typical garden layouts designed by Gertrude Jekyll. (Above) Stone Hall, Easton, showing border of lavender, Japanese anemones, golden Rudbeckias. (Below) A corner of Gertrude Jekyll's own garden at Munstead Wood, Surrey, as it was in 1901, showing a border of Michaelmas daisies.

*Walter Edward **Ingwersen** (1882–1960).*

*Major Walter **Irvine** (1890–1963).*

private gardens. For several years, he was also a regular contributor on gardening matters to *The Liverpool Post.*

Jackman family:

This family, which was eminent as nurserymen at Woking in Surrey for well over one hundred and fifty years, was founded by WILLIAM JACKMAN, who was born in 1763, on a site of over fifty acres at St John's, Woking, and remained there until 1885 when the nursery was removed to a larger site between Woking and Mayford. The most renowned of all the plants raised at the earlier site was the *Clematis jackmanii*, which received the First Class Certificate from the Royal Horticultural Society in 1863. Some doubt exists

Title-page of The Theory and Practice of Gardening *translated by John **James**.*

concerning the true nature of the cross, which is generally considered to have been *C. lanuginosa x C. hendersonii* or *C. viticella*. The nursery continued under the direction of successive members of the family: GEORGE JACKMAN (1801–1869); his son of the same name, who died in 1887; ARTHUR GEORGE JACKMAN (1866–1926), and, finally, GEORGE ROWLAND JACKMAN (1902–1977) who, due to the growth of the town of Woking, was responsible for removing the nursery for the second time, in 1960, to a seventy-acre site at Havering Farm, about two miles from the earlier site.

The nursery was sold in 1967.

James, John (1672–1746). Architect, translator. Although James's reputation rests almost entirely

*George **Jackman** (1837–1887).*

upon his works as an architect and as Clerk of the Works at Greenwich under Wren, Vanbrugh (qv) and Hawksmoor, his translation of the highly influential book, *The Theory and Practice of Gardening*, by A. J. Dezallier d'Argenville (1690–1765), the French *savant* and naturalist, gives him a significant place in the history of British gardening. The book was published in London in 1712, with the admission that the translator did not know the name of the author, but sufficiently admired its precepts and instructions to propound them to English land-owners and gardening enthusiasts.

James, the son of the Reverend John James, master of the Holy Ghost School at Basingstoke in Hampshire, seems to have received a somewhat more liberal education than was gained by most contemporary architects. He later wrote that 'no person pretending to Architecture among us, Sir Chr. Wren excepted, has had the advantage of a better education in the Latin, Italian and French tongues'.

These accomplishments undoubtedly aided his translation, which is accurate and fluent, and carefully annotated for the benefit of English readers. The confidence he enjoyed amongst the *cognoscenti* of the time is well shown by the list of over two hundred subscribers, which included many of those whose landscape gardens were to become renowned.

The book was dedicated to the Hon. James Johnston, for whom James had designed Orleans House at Twickenham (and to which James Gibbs later added the celebrated Octagon Room).

A second edition of the book, published in 1728, included a new

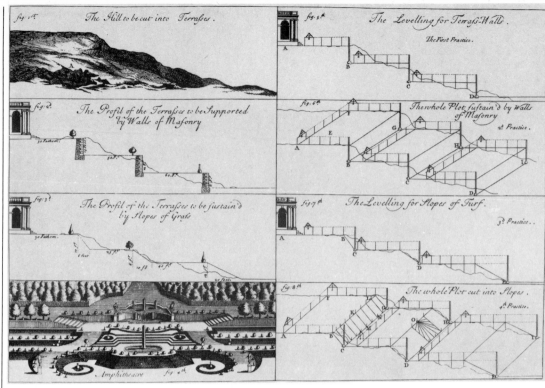

Diagram from The Theory and Practice of Gardening, *translated by John* **James**, *showing how to construct terraces.*

treatise on flowers and orange trees. Many of the precepts in the book were certainly adopted and widely practised by English gardeners. They summarized the rules which obtained during that phase of garden design when geometric art was combined with horticultural skill to a degree never since surpassed.

The garden which was probably most influenced by the publication was that at Canons, in Middlesex, owned by James Brydges (qv), later Duke of Chandos, one of the subscribers to the translation, who employed James to remodel the

house after William Talman had been dismissed in 1714.

Among James's other architectural works are St George's Church, Hanover Square, London (1712–1725) and St Laurence's Church, Whitchurch, Middlesex (1714–1716). He also designed, for his retirement, the handsome Warbrook House at its garden at Eversley, Hampshire.

Jekyll, Gertrude (1843–1932). Garden designer, artist, writer. Gertrude Jekyll, the fifth child and younger of two daughters of a

retired Grenadier Guards officer and a mother with banking connexions, was born in London. The family was typical of those well-established upper-middle-class Victorian families which have produced generations of lawyers, clergymen, naval and army officers. One of her forebears was Sir Joseph Jekyll (1662–1738), Master of the Rolls.

When Gertrude Jekyll was five, the family moved to Bramley House near Guildford. Here she enjoyed a tomboyish childhood, encouraged by her father to take part in outdoor games and indoor hobbies. During

West front and canal at Warbrook House, Eversley, Hampshire, where both house and garden were designed by John **James** *for his retirement.*

Detail from the painting of the garden-designer and writer, Gertrude **Jekyll** *(1843–1932), by Sir William Nicholson.*

the absence of her brothers at school, she began to take a keen interest in the garden, a childish pastime which was to form the basis of her extensive and ever-increasing knowledge of wild flowers. These interests were continued after the family moved to another house in the Thames Valley, and extended as her skills as an artist developed, both at home and at the South Kensington School of Art. After much travelling in Europe and the East, and some early success as artist and designer—she designed furnishings for the Duke of Westminster at Eaton Hall—she met William Robinson (qv), author of *The Wild Garden* (1870) and an indefatigible gardening publisher, editor and writer. His influence upon her career as a gardener and garden-designer was to be profound and enduring.

After her father's death she returned with her mother to Surrey where she supervised the building of the house and layout of the garden which was to provide her with the scope she needed for her development as a garden designer. The house was at Munstead, then a remote spot amidst Surrey heathland. Her talent as a practical and imaginative gardener was early demonstrated at Munstead House. A wide acquaintance with artists and musicians and their delight in visiting the house and making known its excellences caused her advice and plans to be sought after by other house-owners, notably G. F. Wilson (qv), who was then laying out his estate at Wisley, later to become the garden of the Royal Horticultural Society. Also at this time she met Edwin Lutyens (qv), son of a neighbouring family, then starting on his career in architecture. She began to advise him on the gardening aspects of the houses he was designing and thus began a life-long friendship.

At this period, however, these advisory activities were little more than an interesting side-line to her main interests as artist and embroiderer but, in 1891, she was warned that her eyesight was failing and that to continue with her painting might result in blindness. Undaunted, she put aside her palette-board and paints and began in earnest her long and fruitful professional partnership with Lutyens. The partnership was further strengthened after her mother's death when she began to build her own house, Munstead Wood, for which Lutyens was inevitably the architect. The house and its garden became the focal-point of her life. Here she was to practise the precepts she had adopted from Robinson and later adapted to her own strong personal predilections.

Robinson had called for the simply-outlined border, using hardy and more or less permanent plants,

Illustration from Colour Schemes for the Flower Garden *by Gertrude* **Jekyll**, *showing 'grey' borders.*

but Gertrude Jekyll, thanks to her profound knowledge of flowers and her training as an artist, vastly enlarged Robinson's themes, adding both colour and subtlety in form to her suggestions for greater use of flower and foliage. She also took full advantage of the wide range of hardy trees, shrubs and plants then being introduced into general gardening.

Munstead Wood thus became one of the most influential gardens in history. Whereas Kent at Rousham and Stowe and, later, Brown, throughout England, had planned for landscape effects on the scale suitable for parks and estates, the schemes suggested and developed by Robinson and Miss Jekyll were applicable to the tens of thousands of gardens that were then being provided and cultivated in the great expansion of house-building for the rising middle classes in Britain. Gertrude Jekyll's views on the use of colour, water and stone in the garden found enthusiastic and widespread acceptance.

Her own record of her gardening life at Munstead Wood can be read in her book *Home and Garden*. She designed over three hundred gardens, many as memorials to men killed in the 1914–1918 war, yet the most memorable were those she designed for houses of moderate size similar to her own, possessed of an acre or so of garden. With Robinson, she sponsored one of the most lasting of twentieth-century social and aesthetic revolutions.

Jellicoe, Geoffrey Alan (1900–). Architect, landscape architect, town-planner. Jellicoe was educated at Cheltenham College and at the Architectural Association School. In 1925, following extended

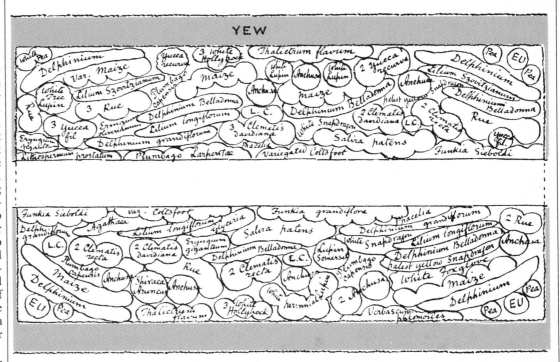

Schemes for a 'blue' garden from Colour Schemes for the Flower Garden *by Gertrude* **Jekyll**, *showing her controlled use of colour and the natural growth effects of planting in what she called 'drifts'.*

*Water-garden for a private house in the West Country and (right) water-gardens at Hemel Hempstead New Town, both designed by Geoffrey **Jellicoe**.*

study in Italy, he published jointly with J. C. Shepherd *Italian Gardens of the Renaissance*, and in 1929 became a founder member of the Institute of Landscape Architects.

In 1935 he was commissioned by Ronald Tree to design what was probably the last great classical garden in England at Ditchley Park in Oxfordshire, a house designed by James Gibbs between 1720 and 1723, and now the home of the Ditchley Foundation, an Anglo-American study centre. This commission was followed by others for the gardens at the Royal Lodge at Windsor and for Sandringham.

Since that time, Jellicoe's practice has included commissions for such considerable landscaping projects as Hemel Hempstead New Town and the Plymouth Civic Centre, as well as more classical gardens for the Prime Minister's house at Chequers in Buckinghamshire and Chevening in Kent, the erstwhile estate of the Stanhopes, now a residence of Prince Charles. His practice has also included memorial landscapes such as that for President Kennedy at Runnymede; the Via Sacra at Gloucester; the projected gardens around Armagh Cathedral and the Close and Processional Way at Exeter. A project of somewhat different order was that for the twin hills of Harwell Research Station.

Although he had written a dozen books on more specialized aspects of landscape design, Jellicoe had long meditated on a book that would, in his own words, 'comprehend the world's landscape and give landscape design equality with the other arts of mankind.' To achieve his objective, Jellicoe and his wife, Susan, visited, studied and photographed hundreds of landscapes. The result of this joint study, *The Landscape of Man*, was published later in 1975.

Joad, George Curling (1837–1881). Alpine plant-collector and cultivator. Joad was born at Walmer, Kent, and educated privately. In pursuit of his hobby as an entomologist, he travelled widely in Egypt, South Africa and the West Indies, usually with his wife, Laura, collecting butterflies and moths. He then began to concentrate on the alpine flora of Switzerland. In his gardens at Wimbledon he had two

*Geoffrey Alan **Jellicoe** (1900–   ).*

*Part of Ditchley Park, Oxfordshire, laid out in 1935, on the site of the Victorian garden, under the direction of Geoffrey **Jellicoe**.*

*George Curling **Joad** (1837–1881).*

*Hafod house and garden, as developed by Thomas **Johnes**, shown in an aquatint by Warwick Smith.*

rock gardens constructed and was one of the first English gardeners to collect and cultivate alpines on a large scale. On his death, his collection was left to the Royal Botanic Gardens, Kew, and was described in the Kew Report for 1881 as 'a very splendid and munificent gift', the specimens being of 'great beauty and in the best possible state of preservation.'

To accommodate the legacy, the Kew rock garden had to be entirely rebuilt. One plant from the collection, a beautiful cactus from Uruguay, flowered five years after Joad's death and Sir Joseph Hooker, the Kew director, decided that this was a new species of *Echinocactus*, recording the species in the *Botanical Magazine* as *E. joadii*. Joad was on the Scientific Committee of the RHS and a Fellow of the Linnean Society.

Johnes, Thomas (1748–1816). Land-owner and landscape designer. Johnes, usually known as Thomas Johnes of Hafod to distinguish him from his namesake father of Croft Castle, was the most ambitious and enterprising of all Welsh landscape gardeners. He transformed a vast area of west Wales into an idealized landscape, almost bankrupting himself in the process. Johnes grew up at Croft Castle on the borders of Herefordshire and Wales and was educated at Shrewsbury, Eton and Edinburgh University. He then travelled widely in Europe and on his return was elected MP for Cardigan. After his marriage to a rich heiress he became enamoured of the area around Hafod in Cardiganshire, although

he had previously acquired considerable properties in Monmouthshire. After his wife's death, within three years of the marriage, he fleetingly thought of a diplomatic career, but after a second marriage to his cousin, Jane, began to devote all his energies to the redevelopment of Hafod.

In 1786 he began to build a gothick mansion at Hafod, designed by Thomas Baldwin, city architect of Bath, set within a landscape of mountains, rivers and waterfalls. Much of this landscape Johnes transformed into a vast and idyllic

*Thomas **Johnes** of Hafod, Cardiganshire (1748–1816).*

garden, one of the most extravagant ventures in the Picturesque in Britain. Additions were made to the gothick house to designs by John Nash, then practising in Carmarthen, and embellishments were continuously added to the landscaped gardens as well as ornamental walks. A flock of peacocks and another of the much-prized merino sheep were also introduced into this Welsh Virgilian scene.

The establishment of so idyllic a landscape cost Johnes dear: his endeavours ended in fire, financial failure and the death of his beloved

daughter, Maria, who was a talented botanist and gardener, greatly admired by Sir James Smith (qv) founder of the Linnean Society.

Johnes died virtually penniless, leaving a young son and an impoverished estate. His widow lived a retired life in Devonshire until her death in 1833. The previous year, Hafod with its contents was bought for £70,000 by the Duke of Newcastle at the London Auction Mart under an order of the Court of Chancery. The house and estate later passed into the hands of speculators and thus gradually fell into decay and desolation. The full story of Thomas Johnes and Hafod is recounted in *Peacocks in Paradise* by Elizabeth Beazley.

Jones, Inigo (1573–1652). Architect and innovator. Jones was born in Smithfield in London, one of eight children of a cloth-maker of Welsh descent. Although considerably more renowned as one of the most influential of all English architects, Jones also has a significant place in the history of garden and landscape design. Little is known of Jones's early years, but that he was out of England for long periods seems fairly certain, for in 1605 he was termed 'a great traveller'. Although much remains conjecture, he may well have been attached to the entourages of the Rutland family in Italy, France and Denmark. Certainly, Jones learned to speak Italian fluently. On his return to England in 1604, he was involved in preparing sets and costumes for the court *Masque of Blackness*. By 1616 his renown as an architect was well-established. Apart from being the first architect

Title page of Scots Gardiners Director, *1754, by John* **Justice**.

Inigo **Jones**, *architect and garden innovator, c. 1640.*

Design by Inigo **Jones** *for a royal masque,* The Spider's Paradise, *showing architectural elements in a garden setting.*

to introduce classical architecture into England, he also introduced numerous gardening ideas from abroad into the scenery which he designed for the royal masques for which he was responsible following his appointments as surveyor of the King's works in 1615. Several of these scenes, for which drawings still exist, show gardens adorned with classical temples and other buildings. One from Sir William Davenant's *Temple of Love* (1635)

showed what was reputedly an Indian landscape; another showed the supposed place 'where the souls of ancient poets are feigned to rest'; and there is a prophetic touch of Chinoiserie in a pavilion and timbered knoll in the *Shepherd's Paradise* (1633). Another garden pavilion, this time in the style of a temple, terminates an *alleé* in *Florimene* (1635). These scenes, with their emphatic Italian *ambiente*, undoubtedly influenced the court

circle, especially those beginning to be involved in a sizable way with the embellishing of their country estates. The passion for evergreens may well have been stimulated by the depiction of cypresses in Jones's sets, particularly the Mediterranean cypress, *Cupressus sempervirens*, a species which was to prove so enlivening to the English winter scene.

In the same manner that Jones's earlier years are shrouded in mystery, so, too, are his last years. He

was seventy at the outbreak of the Civil War in 1642, captured by Cromwell's men in 1645, and his estate sequestered but later restored. He died in Somerset House in 1652, a wealthy man.

Few men in history have exercised so substantial an influence on the architecture and art of posterity, yet left so insubstantial a record of their achievements. Both in architecture and garden design, Jones's influence was widespread, although few traces of his work remain, apart from gateways, such as at Wilton and the Botanic Gardens at Oxford.

Justice, James (1698–1763). Horticulturalist and author. Justice was born in Midlothian, the son of a merchant whose connexions in the Low Countries led to his importing, amongst other things, bulbs from Holland. This interest seems to have given Justice, then Principal Clerk to the Court Sessions, so great an interest in cultivating these imports that it was, in the phrase of a contemporary, an 'uncontrollable passion'. Justice certainly seems to have been a gardener of some consequence, to judge from his reports on his own horticultural achievements in his garden near Dalkeith, published in his book, *Scots Gardeners Director* (1754).

In common with other gardeners of extreme single-mindedness, he lavished so much care and money upon his property that, after thirty years of painstaking endeavour, he was obliged to sell the place. His book includes much valuable comment on the bulbs he had obtained from Holland, which he twice visited to study Dutch methods. He has a singular claim to fame, having been the first gardener to introduce the pineapple to Scotland.

Design of a garden and a princely villa by Inigo **Jones** *(1573–1652) for a royal masque.*

166

K

*William **Kent** (c. 1685–1748).*

*Casino and serpentine river at Chiswick House, designed by William **Kent**, seen in an engraving of 1779.*

Kent, William (c. 1685–1748). Architect, painter and landscape designer. Kent was born at Bridlington in Yorkshire, the son of poor parents. Doubts exist concerning the exact date of his birth, for, at his death, he was deemed by some contemporaries to be three or four years older than his attributed sixty-three.

At an early age he was apprenticed to a coach-painter in Hull, quitting before finishing his time in order to go to London. There, thanks to the generosity of three patrons – Burrell Massingberd, Sir William Wentworth and Sir John Chester – who were impressed by his precocious artistic promise, he was enabled to travel to Rome in 1710 in order to further his studies, make copies from the Italian masters and buy works of art for his patrons' country houses. That Kent, although still in his twenties, was possessed of both talent and charm seems clear, both on account of the nature of his commissions and his early and enduring friendship with his patrons, particularly with Lord Burlington, with whom he became acquainted during his first year in Rome. There he studied under Benedetto Luti, winning the Pope's medal for drawing in 1713, an unusual honour for an English artist.

Kent sent back to England a considerable number of architectural works, copies of paintings in the

*View across the Great Bason to the entrance between twin Ionic pavilions, designed by William **Kent**, at Stowe, Buckinghamshire.*

Baroque manner and numbers of the inevitable *bustos*, apart from more mundane household stores requested by Massingberd's wife. These commissions entailed journeys to Florence, Venice, Bologna and other Italian cities, so that Kent acquired an unrivalled knowledge of the Italian scene. He stayed in Italy for nine years, returning as an intimate of Lord Burlington.

In London, Burlington at once began to promote Kent's interests on all possible occasions, commissioning him to complete ceilings started by Sebastiano Ricci in his own Burlington House and causing Sir James Thornhill, the Serjeant Painter, to be ousted from a royal commission to decorate the Cupola Room at Kensington Palace, in favour of Kent. This unusually close friendship between patrician and artist aroused much surprise, comment and envy in London society, yet Kent seems to have been wholly imperturbed. Despite his supplanting of Thornhill in the royal favour, which made him several enemies, including the relentless William Hogarth, William Kent's social and artistic progress continued unabated. He became Master Mason in 1735 and Deputy Surveyor General in 1737.

The emergence of Kent and his patron, Lord Burlington, as architects of wide influence in the English Palladian movement has no place in this DICTIONARY, but their impact was equally significant upon English landscape garden design. Kent's

A view across the lake to the Temple of Venus and Hermitage, at Stowe, Buckinghamshire, designed by William **Kent**.

pictorial skills, allied with his knowledge of the arts, antiquities and gardens of Italy, made him an innovator of considerable and lasting influence. To his contemporaries, his schemes soon seemed to add a third dimension to the landscapes of Claud Lorrain. He also gained adherents to his theories by the skill with which he exploited the ha-ha, or sunk fence, a French innovation. Such a device fused the more distant parkland with the garden. The gar-

den was also made more 'natural' so that the fusion was even more smoothly facilitated. As Alexander Pope (qv), a friend of Kent, opined: 'All gardening is landscape painting; you may distance things by darkening them, and by narrowing towards the end, in the same manner as they do in painting'. Kent was a master of such effects.

Needless to say, such schemes, demanded too quickly by land-owners wishful to transform their

estates into these idyllic landscapes, necessitated immense manual labour. Armies of labourers were employed to transform Stowe, Claremont, Rousham and Chiswick, four of Kent's most considerable achievements in landscaping.

Chiswick House, designed by Lord Burlington for his own pleasure on a flat site, needed terraces and the semblance of knolls as well as water in order to match up to these new notions. These were duly car-

ried out to achieve what remains a delightful and characteristic Kent garden. Sir Thomas Robinson summed up what he regarded as Kent's notion of gardening: 'to lay them out and work without level or line. By this means I really think the twelve acres the Prince's Garden (at Carlton House) consists of, is more diversified and of greater variety than anything of that compass I ever saw, and this method of gardening is the more agreeable, as, when finished, it has the appearance of beautiful nature . . .' (1732).

At Stowe, the river was 'serpentized', the lake reshaped to a greater carefreedom of outline, and the walks diversified. In addition, many (according to Horace Walpole, far too many) pavilions, temples, statues, urns, fountains and so on were added. Yet it was at Rousham in Oxfordshire between 1738 and 1741 that the essential style of Kent's gardening revolution was (and still is) to be seen. Walpole wholeheartedly approved of this project carried out for General Dormer: 'the most engaging' of Kent's works he declared. At Rousham what had been a rectangular enclosure was transformed into a natural-seeming landscape, incorporating the distant River Cherwell. Formal terraces were made into a slope, a series of modest despressions became a capacious vale, all was made natural and the scene studded with buildings: a temple, a sham ruin, a bridge, a gigantic statue.

Inevitably, such schemes cost vast sums of money, yet Kent never seemed to lack clients. Landscape designing came to occupy more of his time than architecture, although his most impressive work, the great house at Holkham in Norfolk for Lord Leicester, was still building at his death, and his most charming design, the Horse Guards, was built after his death.

Kent died in 1748 at Burlington House after a brief illness brought on by, 'high feeding and life and much inaction' as Vertue recorded in his *Notebooks*. He was buried in the Burlington family vault at Chiswick House.

Kerr, William (d. 1814). Plant collector. Kerr was born at Hawick, Roxburghshire, Scotland, and in 1803, whilst still a young man, was appointed by Sir Joseph Banks, at a salary of £100 a year, to travel to China as the first botanical explorer and collector to spend more than a few weeks in that vast country. He was enjoined, in a briefing by both Banks and William T. Aiton (qv), to note indigenous methods of cultivation and to continue in regular communication with Kew. High amongst the objects of the exploration, apart from the acquisition of plants and flowers, was Banks' wish to obtain oranges, peaches and other

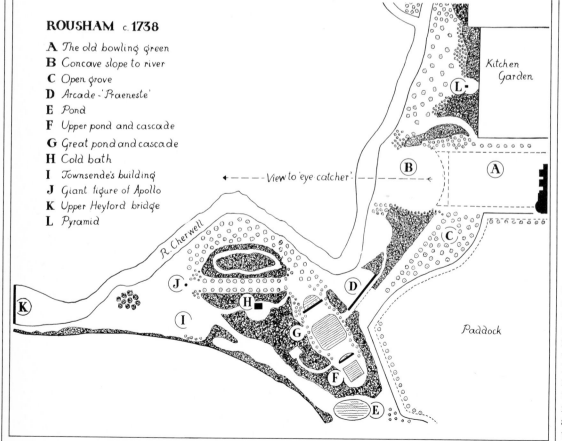

ROUSHAM c. 1738

A *The old bowling green*
B *Concave slope to river*
C *Open grove*
D *Arcade - 'Praeneste'*
E *Pond*
F *Upper pond and cascade*
G *Great pond and cascade*
H *Cold bath*
I *Townsende's building*
J *Giant figure of Apollo*
K *Upper Heyford bridge*
L *Pyramid*

Kitchen Garden

← - - - View to 'eye catcher' - - - →

R. Cherwell

Paddock

Plan (redrawn) by William **Kent**, *c. 1738, for establishing the landscape garden at Rousham, Oxfordshire, for General Dormer.*

George **King** *(1840–1909).*

Frank **Kingdon Ward** *(1885–1958).*

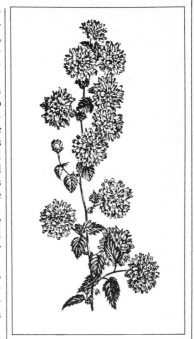

Kerria japonica, introduced by W. **Kerr.**

Medical College in 1871, and Superintendent of the Royal Botanic Garden. In 1891 he was appointed, additionally, to the newly-established post of Director of the Botanical Survey of India.

As the Calcutta garden had been made virtually derelict by two cyclones in the 1860s, King's manifold tasks were arduous in the extreme. He remodelled the gardens and vastly enlarged the practical scope of the botanical-medicinal side. King was also an assiduous writer and in 1887 he founded the *Annals of the Royal Botanic Garden, Calcutta* and also published a study of the Malaysian flora. He retired from service in India in 1898, after over thirty years' employment.

King was not only a writer, administrator and botanist of outstanding skill but a resolute plant-hunter in India, the Andaman Islands, Burma and the Philippines.

He was awarded the Victoria Medal of Honour by the Royal Horticultural Society in 1901 and knighted in 1905.

fruits so that, in his own words, 'both England and her colonies will derive solid and substantial benefit.'

Kerr based himself at Canton near the renowned Fa-tee gardens of that great seaport. By March in the following year, he had already despatched by an East Indiaman various species of peony 'in grand growing state', and he continued to send further specimens in the plant cabins of various warships and merchantmen. Not all the tranship-ments arrived in good heart, a fact which Dr John Livingstone, Chief Surgeon of the East India Company and resident in Canton since 1892, also a plant-collector and friend to Kerr, put down to want of sufficient encouragement and to the meagre-ness of the latter's salary: 'too small for his necessary wants'. To these facts, Livingstone attributed a loss of respect and consideration in the eyes of even the Chinese assistants whom he was obliged to employ. Judging by the high cost of plants in China, Livingstone's strictures

upon Kew's attitude were amply justified.

However, Kerr persevered, and amongst the plants he despatched to Kew was the double-flowered form of the plant which bears his name, *Kerria japonica.*

Kerr made plant-collecting forays to Java and the Philippines. In 1812 he was appointed superintendent of the colonial Botanic Gardens at Colombo in Ceylon, a post he held until his death two years later.

King, (Sir) George (1840–1909). Botanist. Born at Peterhead in Aberdeenshire, in Scotland, King was educated at the Grammar School and University in that city, graduating in medicine in 1865. He joined the Indian Medical Service in the same year and was posted to the Bengal Presidency.

In India he spent much of his leisure in botanical studies, which had been a major interest of his school-days, and was appointed to the Chair of Botany at the Calcutta

Kingdon Ward, Francis (1885–1958). Plant collector, geographer, author. Kingdon Ward was the son of H. M. Ward, FRS, Professor of Botany at Cambridge. He was educated at St Paul's School and Christ's College, Cambridge.

After a brief spell as a schoolmaster in Shanghai, Kingdon Ward made a journey into the interior of China, the first of many expeditions extending over the next half-century in which his skill and flair for selecting unusual flowers for English gardeners was clearly demonstrated. Rhododendrons, primulas, lilies, gentians and poppies were his special interest and the abundance of species of these plants now seen in Britain is to a large extent due to Kingdon Ward's travels and care in documentation and transhipment. His most outstanding introduction was probably the blue poppy, *Meconopsis betonicifolia*, which he collected in south-east Tibet and has

now become a cherished variety in British gardens.

In all, Kingdon Ward engaged in about twenty-five large-scale expeditions, mostly to the border lands of south-west China and India, living frugally off the country. In his fiftieth year, whilst exploring the Assam-Himalaya, he lived chiefly on milk, as he had done in his twenties.

He worked much on his own, eschewing subordinate collectors, making his own selections and notes, which clearly show his remarkable powers of observation and accurate botanical knowledge. He was also a geographer of determined and original ideas, with highly personal views on the full extent of the Himalayan range. In addition, Kingdon Ward was a knowledgeable geologist, an outstanding photographer and a vivid narrator, his books being considered classics of their kind.

During the Second World War his skills were directed to the

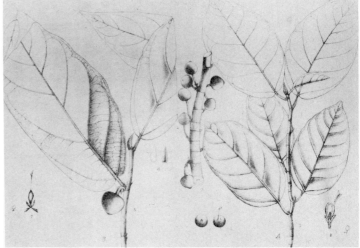

Two engravings from the first volume (1887) of the Annals of the Royal Botanic Garden, Calcutta, *founded by George* **King** *(1840–1909).*

organization of a jungle-survival school, teaching soldiers how to recognize plants which could be safely used for food. After the war he continued his expeditions in company with his wife, Jean. On one trip they were close to the epicentre of one of the biggest earthquakes ever recorded in the area. He was also commissioned to track down wrecked aircraft on the Burma-Assam-Tibet border. Kingdon Ward was the author of ten books and the recipient of many honours and awards for his services to geography and horticulture. His publications included, *In Farthest Burma* (1921); *Romance of Plant Hunting* (1924); *Plant Hunting in the Wilds* (1931); *Pilgrimage for Plants* (1960).

Kirk, (Sir) John (1832–1922). Botanist. Kirk was the son of the Rev. John Kirk and studied medicine at Edinburgh University. In 1854, the year of his graduation, the Crimean War broke out and Kirk served on the medical staff in Turkey, finding time, between duties, to continue the botanical studies he had begun in Edinburgh. On his return to Britain he accepted the post of surgeon-naturalist on Dr Livingstone's expedition to Central Africa and became the explorer's 'tried and valued associate'. Kirk also sent back many plant specimens to Kew. Over a hundred commemorate his name. In addition, he sent copious zoological notes and specimens to the Natural History Museum at South Kensington.

Kirk returned home in 1863 after a severe attack of dysentery and settled in London. The papers he contributed to learned journals include those on *The Palms of East Africa; A new African Musa* and *A new Zambesian Dye-Wood.* He also helped in the compilation of Livingstone's *Narrative* (1865).

Two years after his return Kirk once again set out for Africa, having been apointed surgeon to the political agent at Zanzibar, afterwards taking over the agency himself. In this capacity he was largely responsible for suppressing the slave trade in East Africa. He remained in Zanzibar for over twenty years and set up and maintained a notable experimental garden there. The genus of African plants *Kirkia* commemorates his name. John Kirk was knighted in 1881.

Knight, Joseph (c. 1777–1855). Gardener and botanist. Knight was born at Walton-le-Dale in Lancashire. At an early age he began to work as a gardener for a well-to-do botanist and sponsor of plant-collecting in Jamaica, George Hibbert, then living in Clapham. Impressed by his young gardener's knowledge and character, Hibbert set him up the Exotic Nursery in Chelsea, providing him with the nucleus of a sound stock from his own garden. On George Hibbert's death in 1837, Knight acquired the Hibbert collection of plants *en bloc.*

Knight not only gained a high reputation as a knowledgeable and reliable nurseryman, but an additional renown as a landscape gardener, designing the parkland at St Edmund's College, Oxford. Yet his reputation rests chiefly on the extraordinary range of the plants he cultivated and marketed, and his enterprise. Indeed, with the sale of garden tools, his was one of the first garden centres in the modern sense. He imported plants from collectors throughout the world, and annually visited European seedsmen. He also aided Richard Salisbury (qv), one of the founder members of the Horticultural Society, in establishing his six-acre botanical garden where Cadogan Place gardens now stand. He published some highly informative catalogues, one of which, *A Synopsis of Coniferous Plants* (1850), listed over 140 varieties.

Knight, Richard Payne (1750–1824). Land-owner. Knight was the eldest son of a clergyman who had inherited large estates on the borders of Shropshire and Herefordshire, and whose considerable wealth derived from the iron industry established at Madeley in Shropshire. Due to a delicate childhood, Knight's education was conducted at home, a fact which helped to sponsor his prodigiously wide reading. Soon after he came of age, he began to spend part of his immense fortune in building the mock-medieval Downton Castle in Herefordshire, decorating and furnishing the house in opulent manner. He also acquired a house in Soho Square, London, as an appropriate background for his collection of early Egyptian and Etrurian bronzes.

Knight was a man of keen, if dogmatic, intellect, with an intense and practical interest in nature and landscape, a passion he shared with a wealthy neighbour, Uvedale Price (qv). Together they began a sharp vendetta against the theories and practices of 'Capability' Brown (qv) and Humphry Repton (qv), deriding the clumps of the former and Repton's

'*prim gravel walks, through which we winding go, in endless serpentines that nothing show.*'

These denunciations were given

Frank **Kingdon Ward** *plant-hunting on the Burma-Assam border.*

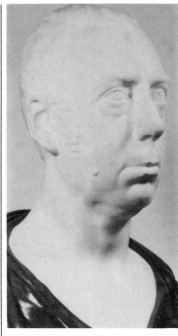

Downton Castle, Herefordshire, designed by Richard Payne **Knight**, *c. 1772.*

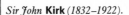

Sir John **Kirk** *(1832–1922).*

Richard Payne **Knight** *(1750–1824).*

Two drawings showing different treatments of the same landscape in The Landscape, *a poem by Richard Payne* **Knight**. *Knight preferred the Picturesque setting at left.*

full flow and venom in a long, somewhat didactic poem, entitled *The Landscape*, which praised the virtues of the romantic, picturesque, beautiful and natural, and denigrated the well-groomed parks of Brown. In place of the latter, Knight called for:

'*The bright acacia, and the vivid plane,*
The rich laburnum with its golden chain;
And all the variegated flow'ring race,
That deck the garden, and the shrubb'ry grace,
Should near to buildings, or to water grow,
When bright reflections beam with equal glow,
And blending vivid tints with vivid light,
The whole in brilliant harmony unite . . .'

The principles adumbrated in the poem did much to shape the post-Repton landscape gardens of England.

After handing over the running of the Downton Castle estates to his younger brother, Thomas Andrew Knight (qv), he spent most of his time in London, where, although he entertained the foremost artists and intellectuals of his time, he grew progressively more despondent and depressed. He died, reputedly of apoplexy, but Samuel Roger, a relative, contended that Richard Payne Knight's death was self-administered—by prussic acid.

Knight, Thomas Andrew (1759–1838). Botanist. Knight, the younger brother of the foregoing, was educated locally at Ludlow and Balliol college, Oxford, where he spent most of his time in the surrounding countryside with dog and gun. During his university vacations, and for some years afterwards, he fre-

quently stayed with his brother, in Herefordshire and London, doubtless as an agreeable escape from his own Herefordshire menage, which he shared with his mother.

Thanks to his wealth, he was enabled to spend his days in continuous and serious nature study and in horticultural and agricultural experiments which were to continue for half a century.

In 1795, at his brother's London house, he met Sir Joseph Banks, who, impressed by Knight's account of his experiments, suggested that the latter should keep accurate

Thomas Andrew **Knight** *(1759–1838).*

records of them. These were later published in papers presented to the Royal Society and to the newly-formed Horticultural Society, of which Knight was a founding member. These papers included accounts of his experiments in plant-breeding; the incidence of sap in trees; the movements of tendrils in plants; methods of cultivating fruits and vegetables; the construction of greenhouses.

Knight's lifetime work was at first mainly concerned with fruit trees. By trial and error he accumulated a vast amount of valuable material and caused others to experiment. In 1791, on his marriage, he went to live at Elton Hall, which gave its name to the variety of cherries he grew. Some years later, when his brother chose the life of intellectual London, having spent too much of his fortune on Downton Castle, Thomas Andrew Knight took over the management of the estate that went with the sham castle and its collection of antiques (later to become part of the British Museum).

Knight managed the big estate without interrupting his experiments. He was an enlightened landlord, bettered the condition of his tenants, worked on the improvement of his stock, and raised a very hardy breed of sheep.

His energies were also devoted to many activities in Herefordshire, particularly towards raising the general standard of farming. He was elected a Fellow of the Royal Society. He was President of the Horticultural Society from 1811 until 1838. He seldom moved far from his native habitat between the Wye and the Teme.

As the years passed, he made only an annual visit to London in order

to give his presidential address to the Horticultural Society, the institution with which he had closer ties than any other. In 1838 he travelled to London for the annual meeting. The long coach journey was too much for him and he became ill, dying a few days later.

Thomas Andrew Knight was a pioneer of the practical adaptation of scientific methods to horticulture and made a particular study of the extremely important work of plant-breeding.

Knowlton, Thomas (1692–1781). Gardener and botanist. Knowlton was born at Chislehurst in Kent and at an early age entered the service of James Sherard (qv) to work in his renowned botanic garden at Eltham in Kent. He remained in the doctor's service until he was in his mid-thirties when he moved to Yorkshire to work in the gardens of Richard Boyle, 3rd Earl of Burlington. There he remained for the rest of his life, becoming known as an assiduous botanist, corresponding with Mark Catesby (qv) and other plant-hunters and gaining the approval of Sir Hans Sloane (qv) for botanical experiments and discoveries, which included the discovery of the *Aegagropila*, or moor-ball, a species of freshwater algae. Knowlton was also something of an amateur archaeologist, locating the site of the ancient settlement of Delgoricia in Yorkshire.

John Knowlton, who was a gardener to Earl Fitzwilliam, was probably his brother, and the Rev. Charles Knowlton, who studied at St John's College, Cambridge, and was subsequently presented by Lord Burlington with the living of Keighley in Yorkshire, was probably Thomas Knowlton's son.

L

Lambert, (General) John (1619 – 1683). Horticulturist and botanist. Lambert was born at Calton in Yorkshire, the son of a wealthy father who owned considerable estates in the West Riding deriving from acquisitions made by a forebear at the time of the dissolution of the monasteries. Little is known of his early years, but he was probably educated at Kirkby Malham Grammar School, Trinity College, Cambridge, and one of the Inns of Court in London. When he was twenty he married Frances, daughter of Sir William Lister, and related to Sir Thomas Fairfax, the Parliamentary General, in whose regiment he first served on the outbreak of the Civil War in 1642. As the war developed, Lambert's military skills were quickly recognized and in his second year of service he was given command of a cavalry regiment operating mainly in the northern counties, although he was made Governor of Oxford after its surrender to the Parliamentary forces.

After the trial and execution of Charles I, Lambert was active in the north of England and in Scotland with Cromwell, and between 1652 and 1657 he became one of the most important men in the kingdom, being appointed Cromwell's Vice Regent in 1654.

In 1652 he purchased for £7,000 the splendid mansion of Wimbledon House, which had formerly been a royal residence. Here, he occupied his time in painting, for he was an artist of considerable skill, and in cultivating his garden, which was noted for its plants, many obtained from abroad. He reputedly 'had the finest tulips and gilly-flowers that could be had for love or money.'

At the Restoration, Lambert, along with other Cromwellian leaders, was confined to the Tower of London. Whilst awaiting trial he was deported to Guernsey. His house at Wimbledon was appropriated and he was in dire financial straits. He was later exiled to Guernsey, under the charge of Lord Hatton (qv), an enthusiastic botanist. In return for past favours, Hatton, when abroad, obtained for Lambert irises, anemones, tulips and other plants unobtainable in England. Previously, Lambert had supplied him with rare plants of his own cultivation not to be found in even the most famous gardens of France.

General John **Lambert** *(1619–1684), a seventeenth-century horticulturist and botanist, and (right) a satirist's view of General Lambert illustrated on a seventeenth-century playing card as* Knight of the Golden Tulip.

Lambert remained in Guernsey until 1670 when he was removed, reason unknown, to St Nicholas Island in Plymouth Sound, where he continued with his favourite pursuits of gardening, painting and study. His wife, who had been his courageous companion throughout his trials, died in 1676. According to a contemporary account, Lambert 'always loved gardening, and took a delight during his confinement to work in a little one he had there. One day as he was at work some gentlemen came in a boat to see the island, and the Major-General went in to change his night-gown that he might wait on the company in a more decent dress, and catched a cold that brought him to his grave.' The Earl of Clarendon, in *History of the Rebellion*, wrote of Lambert: 'he was a man of extraordinary wit, a great understanding, which pierced into and discerned the purpose of other men with wonderful sagacity.'

Lambourne, Lord (1847–1928). Horticulturist and administrator. After Eton, Mark Lockwood, as he then was, served in the Coldstream Guards from 1866 until 1883. He was then elected MP for Epping, which he represented for twenty-five years. He was raised to the peerage in 1917 and two years later succeeded Lord Grenfell (qv) as the President of the Royal Horticultural Society. The history of the Society records that 'although in later years he cultivated some rhododendrons and magnolias, it was dahlias, hippeastrums, carnations and other richly-coloured garden plants which appealed most to him'. He proved to be a highly popular and successful leader of the Society.

Lancaster, Roy (1937–). Botanist and plant-collector. Lancaster was born in Bolton in Lancashire. On leaving school, he joined Bolton Parks Department and began work on a projected *Flora of Bolton*. After National Service in Malaya (where he collected over a thousand specimens of plants for museums and botanic gardens) he returned to Bolton, but, after two years further service, joined the University Botanic Garden at Cambridge as a student gardener. There he became increasingly interested in the botanical aspects of plants. In 1962 he joined

Lord Lambourne (1847–1928).

173

*Batty **Langley** (1696–1751), from a mezzotint by J. Carwithian.*

*Garden temple designed by Batty **Langley** (from his* Gothic Architecture, *1747).*

Hillier & Sons of Winchester as horticultural botanist, his responsibilities ranging from the preparation of the famous catalogues to the 'sexing' of plants. In 1964 he moved to the Hillier Arboretum at Ampfield, Near Romsey, and, six years later, became first curator of the gardens. In 1971 he was a member of the University College, Bangor, Expedition to East Nepal where he spent three months studying and collecting seeds and plants in the Himalayas. In 1972 he was awarded the RHS Veitch Gold Memorial Medal for services to horticulture and was elected a Fellow of the Linnean Society. He has since travelled widely in India, Persia and Greece on plant-collecting journeys. In 1974 he published *Trees for Your Garden* and has since written many other articles and books.

Langley, Batty (1696–1751). Horticulturist, artist, writer. Langley, son of a Twickenham gardener, seems to have begun his somewhat eclectic career, or careers, as a practical gardener. Within a comparatively short time, however, he was exploiting his considerable talent and flair as a draughtsman. He sought architectural commissions and in 1735 submitted designs for the projected new Mansion House in London. He was also employed by the Duke of Kent at Wrest Park in Bedfordshire, although whether as an architect or garden consultant is not known. In 1740 he established an academy for instruction in architectural drawing and design. In this project he was aided by his brother, Thomas, who was his partner in more than one engraving and publishing enterprise. His first book (on Newgate Prison) appeared in 1724, and he published *Practical Geometry*, a book for builders, surveyors, gardeners, two years later. Batty was certainly no man to hide his talents and in 1728 he wrote what was to become one of the most influential of books in publicizing the new 'irregular style of gardening': *New Principles of Gardening, Or The Laying out and Planting Parterres, Groves, Wildernesses, Labyrinths,*

*An invitation card designed and engraved by Batty **Langley** in 1741 for the* Friendly Society of Gardners and Florists.

*(Opposite) Roy **Lancaster** (top) seen against the Himalayan skyline during a plant-hunting expedition on the Nepal-Tibet border. (Below left) Rhododendron* arboreum *above Basanteur, East Nepal; (centre right) fruits and seeds drying in the sun, collected at Topke Gola, Nepal; (below right) Roy Lancaster with Sherpas and porters at Thudam, Nepal.*

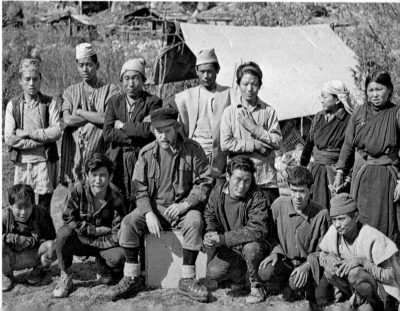

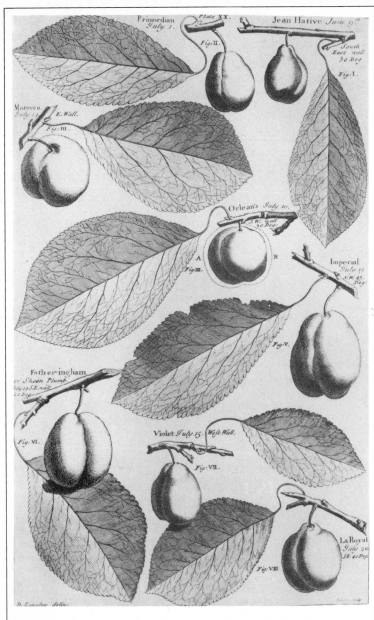

Typical page from Pomona, or the Fruit Garden Illustrated *by Batty* **Langley**.

Avenues, Parks &c., After a more Grand and Rural Manner, than has been done before. In this work Langley made clear the wide range of services he offered.

His activities were indeed comprehensive: 'Buildings in general are Surveyed, Valued and Measured, as also Timber growing or felled. Grottos, Baths, Cascades, Fountains &c. made, and Engines for raising Waters to any height required for the service of Towns, private Families, Canals, Fish Ponds, &c. Cities, Lordships, Estates, Farms, &c., Survey'd, Measur'd, and Mapp'd, and Sun Dials of all kinds made for any Latitude. Gardens in general Made, Planted and Furnish'd with Fruit and Forest Trees, Ever-Greens, Flowering-Shrubs, &c. of the best Kinds . . . , at very reasonable rates.'

The book enjoyed considerable success and was still popular in the late 1750s. He adumbrated a series of rules for garden design, deprecating topiary work and the precise parterres of the formal French fashion, then in decline. In the fashion of the time, following the practice of William Kent, he encouraged the making of serpentine and meandering paths, and he contended that the designer of 'a beautiful rural garden' should seek to enhance his property with a selection from a list which included avenues, groves, wildernesses, 'green openings like meadows', moats, terraces, basins, canals, fountains, cascades, aviaries, menageries, cabinets, statues, obelisks, kitchen gardens, bowling greens, dials and amphitheatres. Little wonder that Lady Luxborough

Sir J. J. Trevor **Lawrence** *(1813–1913).*

(qv), the noted garden designer, wrote that 'I wish his ideas had been more confined or his territories less so.'

Langley further proposed that 'The Pleasure of a Garden depends on the variety of its Parts', requiring 'a continued Series of Harmonious Objects, that will present new and delightful Scenes to our View at every Step we take, which regular Gardens are incapable of doing. Nor is there anything more shocking than a stiff regular Garden', he states, giving graphic point to his argument by providing twenty-eight designs in his new style. These new gardens are avowedly irregular, sometimes perversely so, but many exhibit a formal framework with only an infilling of irregular detail: of serpentine paths in wildernesses, of labyrinths improved after Versailles, of formal 'Amphitheatres' or 'Double Mounts' set beside gently serpentining canals, and of irregular parterres formally disposed on either side of an axial walk.

Much of *New Principles* is concerned with practical information on the raising and culture of fruit trees, herbs and the like, but one of its most interesting elements is the series of plates devoted to 'Views of Ruins, after the old Roman manner, for the termination of Walks, Avenues, &c.'—the forerunners of many a ruined folly in the later parks of the century. A year later, Langley followed up his *New Principles of Gardening* with a handsome volume, *Pomona, or the Fruit Garden Illustrated*, in which his skill as a draughtsman is ably shown.

His notions for embellishing gardens did not stop at literary injunction. In his *Gothic Architecture*, published in 1742, he provided numerous elevations and plans for garden pavilions, temples, or 'umbrellos' as he termed them, which have considerable ingenuity and charm. They certainly provided prototypes for the innumerable small buildings which were then being added to the gardens of those

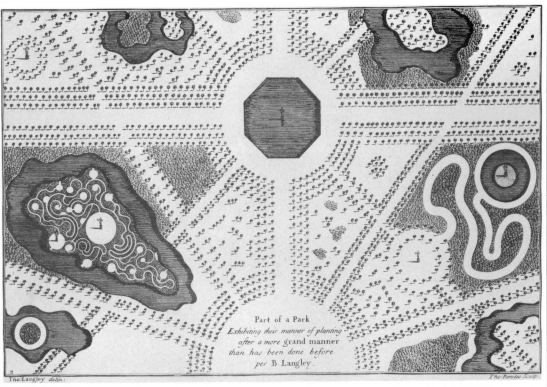

Formal and informal elements in a garden design by Batty **Langley** *in his book*, New Principles of Gardening, *1728.*

Louisa **Lawrence** *(c. 1803–1855).*

Three specimens of Cupressus Lawsoniana, *introduced via Charles* **Lawson**.

Charles **Lawson** *(1794–1873).*

who were caught into the fashion for redesigning their gardens in the 'natural' manner. Such temples added focal-points for serpentine walks and avenues. Their design also gave Langley ample scope for promoting his own interpretation of the principles of gothick, a subject which became something of an obsession with him. Yet, despite manifold quirks and oddities, his bombast and assertiveness, Langley was responsible for a considerable body of work in his pattern-books which was readily taken up by provincial builders anxious for models and guidance.

Although his contemporaries, especially Horace Walpole, affected a genial contempt for Langley (an attitude also taken by Kenneth Clark in his *Gothic Revival*, 1928) he had a wide and beneficial influence on English garden design. He died in Soho in 1751.

Laurence, (Reverend) John (1668–1732). Gardening writer. Laurence was born in Northamptonshire, and after graduating from Cambridge entered the Church, becoming chaplain to the Bishop of Salisbury, and afterwards rector, first of

Yelvertoft in Northamptonshire, and then of Bishop's Wearmouth, where he remained until his death. Apart from sermons and other liturgical writings, Laurence was author of *The Clergyman's Recreation, showing the Pleasure and Profit of the Art of Gardening* (1714), which was reprinted three times, and *A New System of Agriculture, being a Complete Body of Husbandry and Gardening* (1726), which covered such esoteric addenda as the making of fish-ponds and bricks, as well as more basic horticultural activities.

Lawrence, James John Trevor, Bt (1831–1913). Gardener and horticulturist. Lawrence was educated at Winchester and then studied medicine at St Bartholomew's Hospital before joining the Indian Medical Service in 1854, serving in the Himalaya area. In 1867 he succeeded his father as baronet and in 1875 was elected an MP, remaining a member until 1892, when he became Treasurer of St Bartholomew's.

He had inherited Ealing Park from his father, and like his mother, Louisa Lawrence (qv), became one of the foremost orchid growers of his time, having what was generally

thought to be the best private collection in Britain. An orchid from the Andes was named *Trevoria chloris* in his honour.

He was president of the Royal Horticultural Society from 1885 until 1913. Under his aegis the society prospered: membership rose; the hall in Vincent Square was built and finances were appreciably improved. He was awarded the Victoria Medal of Honour in 1900 and the Veitch Memorial Gold Medal in 1913. The Society founded the Lawrence Medal in his honour.

Lawrence, Louisa Trevor (c. 1803–1855). Gardener and botanist. This notable gardener was born at Broughton House, Aylesbury, Buckinghamshire. In her mid-twenties she married William Lawrence, one of the foremost surgeons of the day and President of the Royal College of Surgeons. The Lawrences lived first at Drayton Green, Middlesex, where Louisa Lawrence's passion for garden design and cultivation was soon demonstrated. In 1840 her husband bought Ealing Park, Middlesex, an estate possessed of extensive gardens which gave Mrs Lawrence full scope

for her horticultural interests and energies. One of her earliest triumphs was to bring the night-flowering cactus to blossom, an event marked by a visit from Queen Victoria and the Prince Consort. She was also a highly successful grower of orchids. In 1849, soon after the introduction of the beautiful *Amherstia nobilis* from India, she was the first gardener in England to bring the plant to flower, this being well ahead of the Duke of Devonshire and Paxton at Chatsworth. In 1854 she gave the plant to Kew where it took pride of place in one of the larger glasshouses and flowered profusely, but died on removal to the giant Palm House.

Mrs Lawrence was also a figure of some importance in the Victorian social scene and her garden parties were attended by Queen Victoria and leading members of the government and the aristocracy.

Her widowed husband was created a baronet in 1857 and died in 1867, the baronetcy passing to his son, James Lawrence (qv).

Lawson, Charles (1794–1873). Botanist and writer. Lawson was born in Edinburgh, son of the Peter

(Left) The span-roofed greenhouse and (right) the French parterre in the garden at Ealing Park, designed by Mrs Louisa **Lawrence**.

177

*Looking across the Great Parterre at Blickling Hall, Norfolk, a formal design by Norah **Lindsay** for Lord Lothian in the nineteen-thirties.*

amateur-professional garden designers who did much to uphold the renown of English gardens during the years immediately preceding and succeeding the First World War. Her own garden at Sutton Courtenay became famous and was the source of the legend that Lady Oxford—the famous Margot—was so entranced by one of the earliest specimens of the blue poppy, *Meconopsis bailey* (now *M. betonicifolia*), that she uprooted the specimen and removed it to her own nearby garden!

Norah Lindsay held firm views on the subject of flowers and garden design, which were expressed in colourful, occasionally even purple, prose as, for example, 'Bignonia is heavy with bud—in dry bilious bunches—like the desiccated beaks of birds.' Amongst the gardens which Norah Lindsay designed were the great Parterre for Lord Lothian at Blickling Hall in Norfolk, Fort Belvedere for the then Prince of Wales (later the Duke of Windsor) and the magnificent gardens overlooking the Venetian lagoon for the Eden family.

Lindsay, Robert (1846–1913). Botanist and horticulturist. Lindsay was

(Opposite) Plates from Ladies' Botany: or a Familiar Introduction to the Study of the Natural System of Botany, *by* John **Lindley***. They are: (top left) Naked-stalked Poppy; (top right) Stemless Gentian; (centre left) Heartsease and (centre right) large-flowered Calandrinia; (below left) Dwarf Convolvulus and (below right) the Larger Mallow.*

born in South Leith, Edinburgh, and entered the Edinburgh Royal Botanic Garden as a boy. He passed through all the grades of his apprenticeship, becoming general foreman, and in 1883 was appointed curator, retaining the position until his retirement in 1896. In the course of his career he made a special study of rock and alpine plants and after his retirement devoted most of his attention to the further study and cultivation of these plants, adding to these interests the intensive study of the shrubby *Hebe*, raising the particularly beautiful pink-flowered *Hebe lindsayi*. In 1889, he was elected to the Presidency of the Botanical Society of Edinburgh. In 1896, Lindsay was awarded the Neill Prize.

Lindsay, William Lauder (1829–1880). Lichenologist. Lindsay was born in Edinburgh and studied medicine at Edinburgh University, graduating in 1852. In common with many other medical men he had a profound interest in botany and specialized in lichens. In 1856 he published *A Popular History of British Lichens*, for which he also made the drawings.

Linnaeus, Carolus (or Carl von Linné) (1707–1783). Botanist. Although Carl Linnaeus was Swedish, he exercised so remarkable and wide-ranging an influence upon European botanists and horticulturists, especially the British, that he figures in this compilation. More particularly, perhaps, because the Linnaeus books and collections were acquired after the great botanist's death by Sir James Smith (qv),

*Norah **Lindsay** (1866–1948).*

*Robert **Lindsay** (1846–1913).*

Linnaeus *discussing the natural history collection at the Royal Palace, Sweden. An illustration from a later English translation of his* Calendarium Florae.

*Portrait medallion of **Linnaeus**.*

CALENDAR of FLORA.

I. REVIVING WINTER MONTH.
From the winter folftice to the vernal æquinox.

Dec. XII.
   xxii. *Butter fbrinks and feparates from the fides of the tub.*
   xxiii. *Afp flower buds begin to open.*
Jan. I. i. *Ice on lakes begins to crack.*
   ii. *Wooden walls fnap in the night.*
     Cold frequently extreme at this time, the greateft obferved was 55.7.
   iv. **Horfe dung fpirts.*
   viii. *Epiphany rains.*
   xxvi. *St. Paul's rains.*
Feb. II.
   xxii. *Very cold nights often between Feb. 20 and 28, called* STEEL NIGHTS.

---

* Note. This was explained to me by Mr. Solander, an ingenious and learned difciple of Linnæus, now in England, who fays, that horfe dung, in very fevere frofts, throws out particles near a foot high, and that no other dung does the like.

Page from an English translation of Calendarium Florae, *or* Calendar of Flora, *first published by **Linnaeus** in 1756.*

*Woodcut showing Carl von Linné, known as Carolus **Linnaeus**, on one of his weekend botanical forays with friends and students in Sweden.*

*Christopher **Lloyd** (1921–   ).*

then a twenty-four-year-old naturalist who, urged on by Sir Joseph Banks (qv), bought the collection from Fra Linnaea despite the interest of many other European libraries and private collectors. The collection comprised almost 20,000 sheets of pressed plants, over 3,000 insects, 1,500 shells as well as mineral specimens, 2,500 books and all Linnaeus's correspondence and many manuscripts. Four years after this immense acquisition, the Linnean Society was formed in London, under the presidency of Smith who was knighted in 1814. The declared object of the society was 'the cultivation of the Science of Natural History in all its branches and more especially of the Natural History of Great Britain and Ireland,' an ironical touch, perhaps, as its origins were essentially Swedish. After Smith's death in 1828, the collection was purchased for 3,000 guineas from Smith's widow.

Linnaeus was born in the village of Stenbrohult in Smaland, a southern province of Sweden, the son of a Lutheran curate, who was also a keen horticulturist and botanist. He was educated at the Vaxjo Gymnasium and Lund University where he concentrated his studies on botany, geology and zoology, as the basis for a medical career, although his parents had wished him to be ordained. When he was twenty-one Linnaeus transferred to Uppsala University, forty miles north of Stockholm. Here he was befriended by the Dean, Olaf Celsius, and helped in the latter's preparation for publication of a two-volume work, *Hierobotanicon*, dealing with plants mentioned in the bible, published in 1745 and 1747. A paper on the sexuality of plants written by Linnaeus brought him to the notice of the University authorities, who made him an assistant to Professor Olaf Rudbeck.

After his studies, Linnaeus journeyed to Lapland, covering over 3,000 miles, the first of many exploratory journeys he was to make. In 1741 he was appointed a Professor of Botany at Uppsala, with supervision of the Botanic Garden amongst his responsibilities. Under his direction (and that of the Intendant or head gardener, Dietrich Nietcel) the Uppsala Garden became renowned, although decline set in after Nietcel's death in 1756. Linnaeus's lectures became famous far and wide; so, too, were his practical weekly botanical forays into the Swedish countryside. In 1758, now a family man, with five children, Linnaeus bought a country estate at Hammerby, near Uppsala, where he spent the rest of his life when not at the University. Linnaeus's writings were prodigious, ranging from works on pharmacology to dissertations on animal life. For botanists, however, his most important works were *Philosophia Botanica* published in 1751, a complete exposition of the Linnean classification, and *Species Plantarum* (1753) in which he dealt with nearly 6,000 species known to him, arranged according to the sexual system.

Lloyd, Christopher (1921–   ). Gardener, writer. Christopher Lloyd, the son of Nathaniel Lloyd, the author of *The History of the English House* (1931), was born at Great Dixter in Sussex, a renowned fifteenth-century house with an even more renowned garden, which was first opened to the public in 1929 and is now open regularly throughout the summer months. This background gave him an early interest in gardening, which was enthusiastically fostered by both parents. He was educated at Rugby and at Wye College, Kent, attached to London University, taking a B.Sc. degree in horticulture in 1950. He returned to the College as an assistant lecturer, remaining there until 1954 when he went back to Great Dixter to start a nursery of unusual plants. The house and its gardens have been his base for over twenty years. He divides his year between supervising the gardens during the summer months and writing books during the winter, although he contributes a weekly commentary, *In My Garden*, throughout the year to *Country Life*. His best-known books are *The Well-Tempered Garden*, published in 1970, and *Clematis*, first published in 1965.

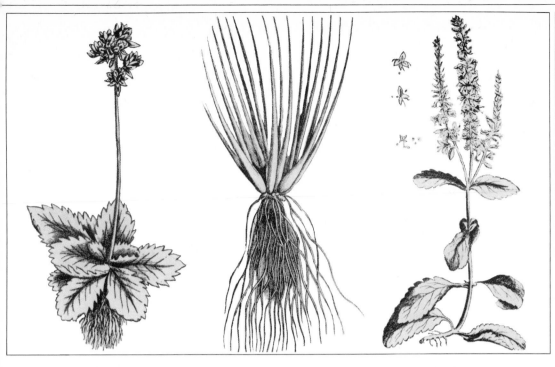

Three plants recorded by Edward **Lloyd** *(or Lhuyd) and reproduced in* Synopsis *by John Ray (1690).*

Edward **Lloyd** *(1660–1709).*

Lloyd (or **Lhuyd**), Edward (1660–1709). Botanist, geologist, naturalist. Lloyd was born at Llanfihangel in Carmarthenshire, the son of Edward Lloyd. He was educated at Oswestry Grammar School and Jesus College, Oxford, where he augmented a scanty allowance by acting as assistant at the recently-founded Ashmolean Museum. Whilst still an undergraduate he began those intensive botanical studies which were to remain a lifelong interest, despite his later passion for fossils, Celtic antiquities and linguistic research. He spent his summers in Snowdonia studying the flora of the hills, especially ferns, and made the first recorded find in Britain of the rock cinquefoil and spiked speedwell. A list of the plants of Snowdonia which he compiled came into the possession of the eminent botanist, John Ray (qv), and started a lifelong correspondence, although they were never to meet. Lloyd sent Ray many packages of specimens of Welsh plants and Lloyd's Welsh listing was included in Ray's *Synopsis*, first published in 1690. One plant, Snowdon lily, sent by Lloyd puzzled both botanists and was only named *Lloydia serotina* posthumously. This plant is known only in Snowdonia in Britain and the mountainous areas of Europe, the Middle East and the Himalayas.

Lloyd remained at the Ashmolean for the rest of his life, becoming Keeper in 1690. His botanical interests were gradually superseded by the study of fossils, and he became one of the earliest paleontological authorities in Britain. This interest was, in turn, ousted by the study of antiquities, and then by a profound passion for Celtic Britain. He proposed to compile a cyclopaedia covering every aspect of the subject and to this end spent four years in intensive research throughout England, Scotland and Ireland. Unfortunately, despite several years of study (combined with his keepership of the Ashmolean) he published only the first of the projected eight-volume work. This study of the Celtic language brought him considerable renown before his early death. A result of his interest in Celtic matters was that he changed his name to Lhuyd. After his death his reputation languished, but he is now recognized as one of the earliest of systematic botanists.

Lobb brothers:

William and Thomas Lobb were two of the most resolute, knowledgeable and successful of the Victorian plant-collectors and responsible for some remarkable introductions to English gardening.

THOMAS LOBB (1820–1894). The younger of the brothers, Thomas became the chief Veitch collector in the East Indies and one of the foremost authorities on orchids, although he sent back other exotics including a collection of tender rhododendrons. He was an extremely taciturn man, reputedly willing only to discuss the subject of orchid collection and cultivation. Like his brother, he was a dedicated plant-hunter, losing a leg in an orchid expedition to the Philippines, but unlike his brother he spent his last years in the countryside of his youth, retiring to the village of Devoran in Cornwall. In the village church a memorial commemorates *Two collectors of plants from foreign countries, who rendered distinguished service to British horticulture,* whilst specimens of their

A towering Wellingtonia, one of the species of trees introduced by William **Lobb**, *seen by a lake in Hampshire.*

Gerald **Loder** (1861–1936).

Wakehurst Place, Sussex, the home of Gerald **Loder**, President of the Royal Horticultural Society, 1928–31.

Rhododendron loderi, *first raised in 1901 by Sir Edmund* **Loder** *at Leonardslee, Sussex. The gardens at Wakehurst and Leonardslee are open to the public.*

introductions still flower regularly each summer in the churchyard.

WILLIAM LOBB (1809–1863). The elder of the brothers, William was born at Perran-ar-Worthal in Cornwall, and was first employed as a gardener by a John Williams of Scorrier House, also in Cornwall. In 1837, William and his younger brother joined Veitch and Company, the well-known Exeter firm of nurserymen. Both brothers were despatched on plant-collecting expeditions, the elder Lobb being sent to South America. Lobb arrived in Rio de Janeiro in 1840 and

spent the next four years in extended wanderings and dedicated seed and plant-collecting, becoming also something of an explorer over the years. His travels ranged through the Argentine pampas, over the Andes and through the Chilean forests. In Chile, he virtually discovered the *Araucaria araucana*, better-known as the Monkey Puzzle tree. This tree had been introduced to English botanists by Archibald Menzies (1754–1842) (qv), the Scots surgeon on Captain Vancouver's voyages of 1790–95, but the introduction had been on an extremely limited scale, rather as a botanical oddity than a tree likely to appeal to enthusiastic gardeners. Lobb, who was primarily a gardener, sensed its possibilities for popularization and sent quantities of the pine kernels back to Veitch, also to his erstwhile employer at Scorrier House.

Lobb's instincts, both as botanist and gardener, were amply justified and the tree quickly became an exotic favourite in large Victorian gardens and parklands. On the one hand, botanists were intrigued by this singular conifer, the only one from south of the Equator to grow to any size in Western Europe; on the other, the tree enjoyed widespread popularity amongst amateur gardeners.

On his return to Exeter, Lobb was persuaded to undertake a further expedition to Chile and Patagonia. On this journey he found the *Lapageria*, an evergreen climber with clusters of rose-coloured trumpet flowers, which became an immediate favourite in Victorian conservatories. Amongst Lobb's other innovations were the scarlet

Holly, *Desfontainea spinosa; Berberis darwinii*, resistant to coastal seaspray; and the Fire Bush, *Embothrium coccineum*, of which W. J. Bean (qv), in his book on *Trees and Shrubs Hardy in the British Isles*, says, 'Perhaps no tree cultivated in the open air in the British Isles gives so striking and brilliant a display as this.' Lobb also discovered the Flame Nasturtium, a perennial with a propensity for moist, peaty conditions. Lobb continued his plant-hunting in the Sierra Nevada area of the United States. Amongst the trees deriving from the last of his forays were *Thuja plicata*, *Abies grandis* and *Abies concolor* as well as the *Sequoiadendron*, introduced to Britain in 1853. Lobb severed his connexion with the Veitch nursery in 1857 and settled in California, dying of paralysis in San Francisco.

Loder, Gerald Walter Erskine (1861–1936). Gardener and administrator. Loder (later the 1st Lord Wakehurst) was the fourth son of Sir Robert Loder Bt, MP for New Shoreham and owner of the famous Sussex garden of Leonardslee. He was educated at Eton and Trinity College, Cambridge, and was called to the Bar in 1888.

Gerald Loder then held several important civil service posts before becoming Member of Parliament for Brighton, a seat he held from 1889–1905. In 1926 he became President of the Royal Arboricultural Society and three years later was elected President of the Royal Horticultural Society.

In 1903 Gerald Loder bought Wakehurst Place, in Sussex, not very far from Leonardslee, which

had been inherited, on the death of Sir Robert, by his elder brother Sir Edmund Loder (1849–1920), who raised many species of rhododendrons there.

Wakehurst had been restored by Sir William and Lady Boord in the Edwardian era, and the gardens had become famous for the Boords' plantings, but that renown was enhanced under the new owner, particularly for his cultivation of rhododendrons and plants indigenous to New Zealand and Chile, for which the climate and terrain at Wakehurst were well-suited. By the mid-nineteen-thirties the garden was recognized as one of the great gardens of Britain.

After Lord Wakehurst's death, the estate was bought by Sir Henry Price, but on his death the house and garden, thanks to the National Trust, came under the direction of the Royal Botanic Gardens of Kew. The acid soil of Wakehurst is ideal for the cultivation of many plants which cannot be grown successfully at Kew.

The gardens at Leonardslee are now owned by Sir Giles Loder, BT (born 1914), another renowned twentieth-century gardener.

Logan, James (1674–1751). Naturalist, scientist. Logan was born at Lurgan, Co Armagh, Ireland, but afterwards moved, with his parents, first to Edinburgh, then to Bristol,

(Opposite) Four views of the renowned gardens at Great Dixter, in Sussex, arranged as a series of outdoor 'compartments' and cultivated by the garden writer Christopher **Lloyd**.

186

1 Oxylobium retusum   2 Brachysema latifolium   3 Euchilus obcordatus.
4 Dillwynia parvifolia   5 Eutaxia pungens   6 Hovea pungens.

1 Oxytropis Lamberti 2 Hedysarum roseum 3 Galega Persica 4 Coronilla Iberica
5 Astragalus procumbens 6 Dalea mutabilis

1 Gladiolus Neriginenus 2 Gladiolus Natalensis 3 Gladiolus trichonemifolius
4 Gladiolus Alpenus 5 Gladiolus Colvilei 6 Gladiolus Watsonius

1 Aconitum heterophyllum 2 Aconitum barbatum 3 Aconitum ochroleucum 4 Aconitum Australe
5 Aconitum paniculatum 6 Aconitum Cammbe 7 Aconitum napellus 8 Aconitum variegatum

Numbers 3 and 5 Porchester Terrace, Bayswater, London, semi-detached villas designed by John **Loudon** *after his marriage to Jane Webb, and seen in a drawing by E. B. Lamb (1838).*

Loudons' many other activities continued.)

The *Arboretum* appeared in 1838. The introduction shows once again Loudon's preferences:

Trees are not only, in appearance, the most striking and grand objects of the vegetable creation; but, in reality, they are those which contribute the most to human comfort and improvement. . . . Man may live and be clothed in a savage, and even in a pastoral, state by herbaceous plants alone; but he cannot advance further; he cannot till the ground, or build houses or ships, he cannot become an agriculturalist or a merchant, without the use of trees.

Loudon's daily timetable while engaged on this undertaking was formidable in the extreme. He breakfasted at seven o'clock in the morning, and after that spent the daylight hours supervising his draughtsmen. (Many of the drawings were made close to London, particularly of the Duke of Northumberland's trees at Syon and at Conrad Loddiges' nursery at Hackney, though sometimes he travelled far afield.) At eight o'clock in the evening he returned home and dined. Then, after a brief rest, he set about his writing (much of it dictated to Jane) until two or three in the morning. Sadly, no fortune

resulted from these long hours.

The *Arboretum* sold well at first, but in 1841 the book trade suffered a severe depression, and Loudon's indebtedness, mainly to his publishers, Longmans, remained until his death. On the unsold copies of the eight-volume work alone, he owed £2,600, and it has been reckoned that his total debts exceeded £10,000. His creditors pursued him; and he was only able to fend them off by selling the work outright. Unfortunately, the long-anticipated profit never materialized.

Despite failing health and the rise of rival publications, Loudon continued his writing, seeking to stave off creditors. In December, 1843, whilst dictating to Jane at midnight, he stumbled, collapsed and died.

After her husband's death, Jane Loudon continued, with the help of her daughter, Agnes, to write gardening books and some enjoyed notable success, chiefly *Gardening for Ladies*, the four-volume *Ladies' Flower Garden*, with several beautifully-drawn colour plates, and *The Lady's Country Companion*. She undoubtedly enjoyed her busy life,

Plan of the gardens at Porchester Terrace, Bayswater, as designed for his own use by John **Loudon** *and reproduced in his Villa Gardener.*

Decorative title-page from Gardening for Ladies, *one of the many practical gardening books written by Jane* **Loudon**, *wife of John Loudon.*

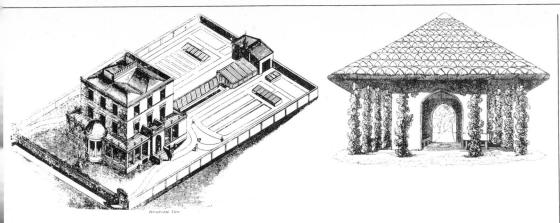

(Left) The villa and gardens in Porchester Terrace, Bayswater, designed by John **Loudon** (1783–1843), reproduced in his book, the Villa Gardener, and (right) an engraving from Jane Loudon's book entitled Ladies' Companion to the Flower Garden.

Frank **Ludlow** (1885–1972), plant-collector in the East.

continuing to work from the house in Bayswater. She died in July 1858.

Ludlow, Frank (1885–1972). Plant-collector. Ludlow was born in London and was educated at Cambridge University where he studied natural science, paying particular attention to botany. After graduating he was appointed vice-Principal of Sind College at Karachi, an appointment which also incorporated a professorship in biology and a lectureship in English. During the First War he was an officer in the Indian Infantry, and, post-war, entered the Indian Education Service as an Inspector of European Schools, a position he relinquished in order to become headmaster of a new school in Tibet, to be based on Western lines. This three-year appointment endeared him to the Tibetan scene and spurred his determination to explore the eastern Himalayas. In 1927 Ludlow moved to Srinagar in Kashmir but a journey to Kashgar at

the invitation of the Consul General introduced him to George Sherriff (qv) with whom, during the succeeding twenty years, he was to make a series of seven immensely productive plant-collecting expeditions in the eastern Himalayas and south-eastern Tibet, resulting in thousands of plants, including many species new to botanical science, being sent to Britain. During the Second War Ludlow was appointed British Resident in Lhasa. The story of this unique partnership, based on their diaries, is told in A Quest for Flowers, by Harold R. Fletcher (qv), published in 1976 (Edinburgh University Press).

Lutyens, (Sir) Edwin (1869–1944). Although Lutyens' renown chiefly derives from his architectural designs, he was also a notable designer of gardens for town and country houses, particularly for those he had designed himself.

His interest in gardens was

aroused by his early friendship with Gertrude Jekyll (qv), whom he met in 1891 whilst only in his twenties. Although she was some thirty years older than Lutyens, they both realized that each complemented the other's talents. Thus began a remarkable partnership. Their garden designs owed a good deal to the naturalism espoused by William Robinson (qv), but added a quality of formalism which Robinson eschewed. Miss Jekyll's own garden at Munstead Wood in Surrey was their first collaboration, completed some five years after their first meeting. The stir occasioned by this essay in what might be termed sub-urban Picturesque, inevitably led to other commissions, which arose equally from Miss Jekyll's extensive contacts with the cognoscenti and to Lutyens' growing practice as a domestic architect. Yet despite his success, both architecturally and socially, the collaboration continued for almost thirty years.

The main theme of Lutyens' garden designs was that the essential design of the house should exercise a significant effect upon the garden, extending the lines of the house, unifying building and garden. The theory was well summed up in his own dictum: 'Every garden scheme should have a back-bone, a central idea beautifully phrased. Every wall, path, stone and flower should have its relationship to the central idea.' Certainly, all the gardens designed by the partnership demonstrated these convictions. Amongst the gardens designed by Lutyens and Gertrude Jekyll were: Munstead Wood, Godalming, in Surrey (1896); Orchards, Goldalming (1896); Deanery Garden, Sonning, Berkshire (1899); Marsh Court, Hampshire (1901); Hestercombe, Somerset (1905); and Gledstone Hall, Yorkshire (1923). But Lutyens' greatest achievement as a landscape garden architect was undoubtedly seen at Tyringham, in Buckinghamshire, a

Bois des Moutiers, at Varengeville in northern France, an early design by Sir Edwin **Lutyens**. The garden, with its grass paths between informal shrub borders, provides an appropriate setting.

Sir Edwin **Lutyens** (1869–1944), from the drawing by Sir William Rothenstein.

Loggia with statues, designed by Sir Edwin **Lutyens** *at Tyringham, Buckinghamshire.*

One of the glass-houses at the Cambridge Botanic Garden where Richard Irwin **Lynch** *amassed a vast collection of plants.*

Tree-transplanting exercise: Richard **Lynch** *(at far left with his son) and staff at the Cambridge Botanic Garden, from a photograph of 1896.*

Lady **Luxborough** *(1699–1756).*

Richard Irwin **Lynch** *(1850–1924).*

house which had been designed by Sir John Soane in 1793, and which provided an ideal architectural background for Lutyens' increasing preoccupation with and reinterpretation of the theories of classical garden design.

Lutyens' most unusual and esoteric landscape design was reserved for India where he was responsible for the planting of the King's Way and the approaches to the Vice Regal buildings in Delhi.

Luxborough, Lady (1699–1756). Landscapist. Few people have engaged upon landscape gardening after so uncompromising a beginning as Lady Luxborough's, for she was banished by her husband to his derelict estate, Barrels, near Henley-in-Arden in Warwickshire, as punishment for alleged infidelities. Instead of sinking into despair and obscurity, she took up with the local aristocracy and literary figures, including the Plymouths, Hertfords, and, most important for her future pleasure, William Shenstone (qv), poet-gardener, owner of the Leasowes, some sixteen miles distant from Barrels, with whom she regularly corresponded.

Enthused by these neighbours, Lady Luxborough set about the formidable task of improving her house and garden.

'The prospect is a very near one', she wrote, 'being surrounded by hills, but is diversified and pretty enough, and I have made a garden which I am filling with all the flowering shrubs I can get. I have also made an aviary, and filled it with a variety of singing birds, and am now making a fountain in the middle of it, and a grotto to sit and hear them sing in, contiguous to it.'

She was almost fifty before she began in earnest upon her gardening ventures, but her energy and enterprise were prodigious.

'I am now busy in planting the lane that joins the coppice, and have chosen trees according to my years.

The abele is what I plant; which in four years time will produce a multitude of setts, and grow to be a good shade.'

Spurred on by Shenstone and aided by a Scottish gardener and occasionally by Shenstone's man, trusty Tom, she built a hermitage (to Shenstone's design), made her gravel paths wider, formed a bowling green, planned *inter alia* a serpentine walk, read Batty Langley (qv) and Isaac Ware. She wrote of days spent in the woods, 'or to be less poetical, I have stood from eleven to five each day, in the lower part of my long walk, planting and displanting, opening views, etc.' Her practicality was evident in another letter to Shenstone:

'My brother Bolingbroke . . . has sent me the most exquisite sorts of melon seeds, and lettuce. Mr. Hall has got me seeds of the greatest curiosity of a flower which the world produces, if I can but raise it. The merchant showed him one pod only, which is as big as a pineapple, and perfumes a room even now it is not in flower. He has also got a water-engine made of lignum vitae, which will water my garden with much ease. . . . The snowdrop, to which Mr. Whistler pays so genteel a compliment, I have had also given me, as double as a yellow rose. My gardener designs to raise some Spanish broom from seed; and you may command what you please of it.'

She suffered from failing health during the last five years of her life, but spent much time in her garden.

Lynch, Richard Irwin (1850–1924). Gardener, botanist, curator, author. Lynch was born at St Germans, Cornwall, where his father was head gardener to the Earl of St Germans. After an early apprenticeship under his father's direction, Lynch

(Opposite) View towards one of the pair of canal-side pavilions designed in 1924 by Sir Edwin **Lutyens** *for the gardens at Tyringham, Buckinghamshire.*

planning the gardens and conservatories. For the last six years of his life he practised as a landscape gardener and garden architect. From his mid-thirties, he was a prolific writer on gardening matters. Amongst his most important publications were *The Practical Gardener and Modern Horticulturist* (2 vols, 1828–29); *Flora and Pomona, or the British Fruit and Flower Garden* (1829); *The Greenhouse, Hothouse and Stove* (1838); *The Orchard* (1839).

McNab, William (1780–1848). Botanist. McNab was born at Dailly, in Ayrshire, one of the twelve children of James McNab, a farmer. When he was sixteen he was apprenticed in a garden at Dalynharran, in Carrick, and after three years moved to the garden of the Earl of Haddington (qv), at Tyninghame, in East Lothian, but after little more than a year, moved south to take up work at the Botanic Gardens, Kew.

There he impressed William Aiton (qv), for in 1803 he was made a foreman, a position he held until 1810 when he returned to Scotland to take up the position of Curator and Principal Gardener to the Edinburgh Botanic Garden. Thanks to McNab's energy and enterprise, the gardens, which had fallen into a neglected state, were swiftly revived, and through the wide acquaintances he had established at Kew and with gardeners in the South, he was able to introduce into the Edinburgh Garden many new and rare species of stove and greenhouse plants, which had never previously been cultivated in the garden.

The official history of the garden records that, in the two years following his appointment, William McNab vastly increased the garden's collection of plants. 'For the first time, the Egyptian Paper Reed, or the Papyrus of the ancients, *Cyperus papyrus*, was grown. So, too, were five species of the Australian *Banksia*, the Javanese *Magnolia coco*, the close ally of the *Pancratium—Eurycles sylvestris* from Amboina, a relative of the barberry—the monotypic *Nandina domestica* of China, and the plant which commemorates the name of Capt. Bligh (qv), *Blighia sapinda*, the Akee tree of Guinea. The cultivation of tender aquatics had scarcely been known in Scotland until McNab arrived. By 1812 the flowers of several water lilies were to be seen for the first time in Scotland, including the white—or

(Opposite) Frontispiece to Charles **M'Intosh's** *book on* The Greenhouse, Hothouse and Stove. *The illustration shows* Epiphyllum splendidum, Opuntia monocantha *and* Aechina septiflora, Mamillaria turbinatus.

William **McNab** *(1780–1848).*

rose-tinted—Egyptian Lotus *Nymphaea lotus*, the deep red *N. rubra* of Bengal, and pale blue *N. stellata* of S. Asia. From the Eastern United States the yellow-flowered *Nuphar microphylla* was introduced, as were the East Indian Lotus, *Nelumbo nucifera*, and the annual plant with leaves which are second only in size to *Victoria*, *Euryale ferox*.'

McNab also acquired a considerable knowledge of Scottish flora, required for the instruction of students at the garden. Not only was McNab a vigorous gardener, but was able to record his experiences and experiments. In 1830 he published a *Hints on the Planting and General Treatment of Hardy Evergreens in the Climate of Scotland*. His paper on the *Propagation, Cultivation and General Treatment of Cape Heaths* followed two years later.

John **Martyn** *(1699–1768).*

On the death of William McNab, his son, James, was appointed Curator of the Edinburgh Botanic Garden, an appointment which proved highly successful and resulted in considerable improvements.

Maries, Charles (1850–1902). Planthunter. Maries was born at Stratford-on-Avon in Warwickshire and educated at the grammar school in the town, where he came under the influence of George Henslow, a notable botanist and teacher. After leaving Stratford, Maries joined James Veitch, the famous Exeter firm of nurserymen, and within a short time was deemed sufficiently trained and experienced to travel to the Far East to collect plants for the firm. He travelled first to Japan, whence he sent back conifers and maples, then to Formosa before

travelling on to his main destination, the interior of China. Unfortunately, Maries had no great understanding of the Chinese and received little cooperation from those who would otherwise have been ready and willing to help him as they had his predecessors. However, although his results were not comparable with those planthunters of greater determination and expertise, some of the plants he sent back were widely marketed by Veitch. Amongst these are *Platycodon grandiflorum mariesii*, with balloon-like buds and expansive campanula-like blossoms, and the flowering shrub, *Viburnum tomentosum mariesii*, which remain as a modest memorial to Maries' expedition. In 1882, Maries returned to the East to become botanical advisor to an Indian prince. He died at Gwalior in India.

Martyn, John (1699–1768). Botanist, author. Martyn was born in London, the son of a merchant. At sixteen he started work in his father's counting-house but he was already very knowledgeable in the botanical studies which, with the subject of plant terminology, were to prove a lifelong interest. He began his plant-collecting career as a rambler in the Home Counties, which was furthered by his membership of a botanical society, under the presidency of German-born Johann Dillenius (qv).

In 1722 he was elected to the Royal Society and in the following year gave a series of lectures on botany. Two years later, on the recommendation of Sir Hans Sloane, he lectured at Cambridge, and commissioned, for his pupils' use, a *Methodus Plantarum circa Cantabri-*

Recent view of part of the rock garden at Edinburgh Botanic Garden, where William **McNab** *was Curator.*

Engraving showing the Flower Garden at Nuneham Courtenay, Oxfordshire, designed in 1772 by William Mason for the 2nd Earl Harcourt, and a demonstration of the cleric-poet's passion for informal planting.

Francis Masson (1741–1806), the first plant-collector sent out by Kew.

giam Nascentium. (Martyn also practised as an apothecary.) In 1728 he published the first issue of *Historia Plantarum Rariorum*, with mezzotint plates by Kirkall, which was a magnificently produced folio, intended as a series, but lack of support limited the publication to five issues.

When he was thirty he entered Emmanuel College, Cambridge, as a mature student, and in 1732 was elected Professor of Botany in the University. Martyn engaged in a wide correspondence with other botanists, including Linnaeus, Sherard, Sloane and Patrick Blair. On the succession of his son, Thomas (1735–1825), to the Professorship, Martyn presented the University with his botanical library specimens and drawings.

Mason, Maurice (1912–). Horticulturist. Although Mason is one of the foremost sugar-beet farmers in East Anglia, he is also widely acknowledged as a collector and cultivator of exotic plants.

With his wife, Margaret, he travels extensively throughout the world in search of plants to enrich his considerable collections, which include some 400 species of begonia alone, as well as a vast number of species of pineapple and a varied miscellany of cacti. His collections are housed in a series of greenhouses, ranging from traditional timber-framed structures to modern, lightweight aluminium-frame buildings.

Mason, (Reverend) William (1725–1797). Writer, artist, garden designer. William Mason was born in Hull, the son of the Vicar of the Holy Trinity Parish Church. He was educated at Hull Grammar School, St John's College, Cambridge, and Pembroke Hall, Cambridge, where he enjoyed a highly successful career, both academically and socially.

It was during his time at Cambridge that Mason met William Gray, Richard Hurd, Horace Walpole (qv), Lord Holdernesse, David Garrick, and many others who were to have considerable influence on his later life.

After the death of his father, and consequential loss of paternal allowance, William Mason entered the church in 1754 and was given the living of Aston, near Sheffield, by Lord Holdernesse.

By 1775, Mason had established a pleasant way of life, although his lack of progress in the Church may have caused him to appear somewhat embittered. His poetry and musical skills, however, were highly esteemed and he was able to divide his time between the charming rectory at Aston, quarterly residences at York, an extended winter visit to London plus a summer tour of the countryside, including Nuneham, near Oxford, home of the 2nd Earl Harcourt, with whom Mason remained friends throughout his life. It was at Nuneham that Mason's abilities as a garden designer were first put into practice. Viscount Harcourt succeeded to the title in 1777, but two years before he had 'begged an acre' from his father, in which to display his, and Mason's, ideas. It was an informal flower garden, full of sentiment and charm, with '*Bowers, statues, inscription, busts, temples*'.

William Mason had a marked influence on the garden design of his time, not only by example, as at Nuneham (the only surviving evidence of his work), but by way of his didactic poem, *The English Garden*, published in four books between 1772 and 1781.

The idea of Nuneham was described in the fourth book of Mason's poem, in such lines as:

. . . Where frequent tufts of sweetbriar, box, or thor,
Steal on the green sward, but admit fair space
For many a mossy maze to wind between.
So here did Art arrange her flow'ry groups
Irregular, yet both in patches quaint
But interspos'd between the wand'ring lines
Of shaven turf which twisted to the path,

As well as the gardens of Nuneham and Aston, William Mason was associated with the gardens of Richard Hurd at Thurscaston; Prior Park; Papplewick and Newby Hall. Many other landowners sought to imitate his ideas, including Thomas Johnes (qv) of Hafod.

In many ways, Mason's passion for, and preoccupation with, the more informal if somewhat high-flown aspects of the floral garden presaged the wild gardens of William Robinson (qv) and Gertrude Jekyll (qv).

Masson, Francis (1741–1805). Plant-collector. Masson was born in Aberdeen, and as a young man was apprenticed to Kew. At the age of thirty he was selected to become the first plant-collector sent out by Kew, under the aegis of Sir Joseph Banks

Maurice Mason.

William Mason (1725–1797).

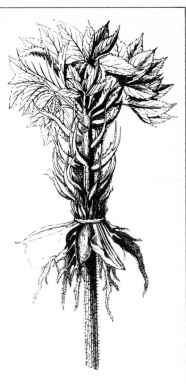

Contemporary engraving showing the rugged terrain of the Cape hinterland through which Francis **Masson** *travelled on his extended plant-hunting expeditions.*

Maxwell Tylden **Masters** *(1833–1907) and (right) a drawing from his book on* Vegetable Teratology *(1869), showing a malformed rose.*

(qv). His first expedition was in 1772 to the Cape of Good Hope where, travelling by ox-drawn trek wagon on difficult and frequently virtually impassable tracks, he set about the task of collecting and sending back plants to Kew which were new to Britain. He explored a considerable area of the Cape, and 'collected seed of so many beautiful species . . . which have succeeded so well in the Royal Gardens at Kew', as he wrote later. After an initial 400-mile reconnaissance, he prepared for more extensive Southern African travels, and in company with a noted Swedish botanist, Carl Per Thunberg, a former pupil of Linnaeus, he set out on a second journey in 1773, during which the two men collected ixias, gladioli, gazanias, romuleas, chincherinchees, irises and discovered the famous Cape succulents, the stapelias. Later they found the Cape Jasmine, *Gardenia stellata,* and the coral tree *Erythrina corallodendron.* Their journey was hazardous in the extreme: rocky, mountainous terrain, the continuous threat of attack by hyenas, leopards and lions, shortage of stores and water and the gradual disintegration of their trek wagon and the oxen attacked by disease. Fortunately, they received hospitable treatment at the Dutch settlements and farms where they rested *en route,* and the Hottentot natives were invariably friendly and helpful. Following this second 500-mile expedition, Masson arranged, catalogued, mounted and despatched plants to form the major contribution of Cape plants to the vast and ever-increasing herbarium of Sir Joseph Banks. Masson added over 400 species to the Kew collections alone.

Francis Masson returned to England in 1775. Three years later, he undertook another expedition to take in Madeira, the Canaries and the Azores, Tenerife and the West Indies. He sent back many seeds and plants to Banks and added much to the collections then being made by the younger Linnaeus, with whom he continued to correspond as he had done with the great Linnaeus *père.* This expedition also proved adventurous in an entirely unbotanical manner, for, whilst in the West Indies, Masson was captured in the French attack upon Grenada in 1779 and lost all his specimens during a hurricane in St Lucia a year later. Although Masson professed himself disappointed with the results of his two-year expedition, a major treasure was the *Senecia cruenta,* or *Cineraria cruenta* as it was captioned in the illustration in William Curtis's *Botanical Magazine,* the progenitor of popular indoor pot-plants of the present day.

In 1783 Masson made a further collecting trip to Portugal and Tangier, returning in 1785, but sailed for another expedition to the Cape soon after his return. Despite restrictions placed upon his travels by the Dutch, then at war with Britain, and despite a limit of forty miles from Cape Town imposed by Banks, Francis Masson was able to send back over one hundred fresh species to Banks and extended his travels far inland. He returned in 1795 and sought to settle in England, working on the collections at Kew and preparing his book *Stapeliae novae* (with forty-one colour plates) for its publication in 1796. But Masson

was unable to settle down. Banks submitted to the King, on Masson's behalf, a request for the collector to undertake an expedition to North America. The request was granted and Masson sailed for New York in 1797. He journeyed to Niagara, thence to Ontario and Montreal, sending home seeds and specimens to Banks, but the cold of North America was too much for a man, already sixty-five, who had spent so much of his life in the burning sun of Southern Africa and he died in Montreal. So died the first of the great Kew collectors, who had introduced to Britain so many exotic plants from the Cape and the Canaries.

Masters, Maxwell Tylden (1833–1907). Botanist. Masters was born at Canterbury in Kent, the son of a nurseryman. He was educated at King's College, London, and at St Andrews University, where he took his MD. Following his university career he was appointed sub-curator of the Fielding Herbarium at Oxford and began to specialize in botanical teratology, the study of abnormal and/or monstrous growths in plant life. From 1855 to 1868 he was Lecturer in Botany at St George's Hospital in London and was also examiner in botany to London University and the Society of Apothecaries. He was elected to the Linnean Society in 1860. His definitive study of *Vegetable Teratology* was published in 1869, four years after he had undertaken to share the responsibilities of editing the *Gardener's Chronicle* with Thomas Moore (qv). This unusual co-editorship lasted until Moore's death in 1887. From that time on, until a short

time before his own death, Masters was solely responsible for the editorial direction of the journal, maintaining the high scientific renown. He was elected to the Royal Society in 1870 and for many years served on the Scientific Committee of the Royal Horticultural Society. His name is commemorated in the plant genera *Maxwellia* and *Mastersia.* Two years after his death the Royal Horticultural Society instituted a fund in order to establish the annual Masters Memorial Lectures.

Mawson, Thomas (1861–1933). Landscape architect. Mawson was born at Scorton, a village between Preston and Lancaster in Lancashire, one of five children of somewhat genteel but impoverished parents. Whilst he was still young the family moved to the West Riding of Yorkshire, where he began to study at the local Church school, but left when he was twelve years of age, to start work in Lancaster as an office boy for an uncle, a builder. In this job, despite his extreme youthfulness, he was responsible for making tracings and working drawings for the building craftsmen. Thanks to his uncle's gardening enthusiasm he acquired the rudiments of a sound horticultural expertise while developing his talent as a draughtsman by studies at the Lancaster Mechanics' Institute.

When he was fourteen he worked briefly in the designing department of Gillows, the famous Lancaster cabinet-making firm, but left to help his father start a nursery and market garden, which seems to have been doomed from the start, the soil being heavy clay and his father no business man. The worries of the

Pergola and pool at The Hill, Hampstead, designed for Lord Leverhulme by Thomas **Mawson**.

business plainly hastened his father's death, but the mother, a woman of outstanding character and resolution, decided to remove the family to London, and Mawson was despatched, in advance, with his fare and twenty shillings. He was taken on by John Wills, a Kensington landscape gardener, and his two brothers followed to take up similar jobs in a nursery in Roehampton. Whilst still in his early twenties Mawson joined the Hale Farm Nurseries at Tottenham, leaving, on his marriage, to take up a promised partnership with a smaller firm. This came to nothing, whereupon Mawson, with his two brothers, started their own firm, the Lakeland Nurseries at Windermere. After early struggles the firm began to prosper, not only in supplying plants but also, on Mawson's initiative, in

designing gardens for the local nobility and gentry. He extended the scope of this aspect of the nursery's work, gaining contracts for the design of public parks at Hanley and Burslem in the potteries and at Newport in Monmouthshire. These commissions, coinciding with the success of his first book, *The Art and Craft of Garden Making*, led him to set up as a landscape architect rather than landscape gardener. Despite various vicissitudes, his drive and ambition so enlarged his practice that he opened additional offices in London and Lancaster as well as retaining an interest in the Windermere nurseries. His interest in the wider aspects of landscape design inevitably led him into town-planning projects and he was involved in many major projects in Britain (Bolton, Northampton,

Exeter, Southport, Weston-super-Mare) and overseas (Athens, Vancouver BC, Banff, Calgary).

He was elected President of the Town Planning Institute. Amongst his other publications were *Civic Art*, various studies on town planning projects and his autobiography, *The Life and Work of an English Landscape Architect*.

Menzies, Archibald (1754–1842). Gardener, naval surgeon, plant-collector. Menzies was born in Aberfeldy, Perthshire, Scotland, and was educated at the local church school before entering the Royal Botanic Garden in Edinburgh as a student, whilst also attending Edinburgh University Botanic classes under Dr John Hope (qv), with the intention of entering the medical profession.

In 1778 he made a botanical tour

through the Highlands and the Hebrides before becoming assistant to a surgeon at Caernarvon in Wales. In 1782 he joined the Royal Navy as an assistant surgeon in the *Nonsuch* and took part in the war against the French, later serving on the Halifax station, but continuing his botanical studies, which led Dr Hope to introduce Menzies to Sir Joseph Banks. Menzies then began to correspond with Banks direct, sending him seeds for the Kew Collection, which in turn led to Menzies' appointment first as a naturalist and, later, after the illness of the ship's surgeon at the Cape, as surgeon-botanist to Captain George Vancouver's projected voyage round the world in *The Discovery*. Vancouver later wrote that not one man died from ill-health between that date (1790) and the expedition's return in 1795.

Although relations between Vancouver and Menzies were sometimes strained and at one point Menzies was placed under arrest for protesting at the loss of plants, he brought back a number of seeds and plants to Britain. The most important of these was the *Araucaria araucana*, more popularly known as the Monkey Puzzle tree, from Chile. Legend claims that whilst dining with the Spanish viceroy at St Jago, Menzies noticed some nuts unknown to him, pocketed some, and planted them in a glazed frame on the ship's quarter-deck and that by the time *The Discovery* returned to Britain

Garden house at Bidston, designed by Thomas **Mawson** *for Joseph Bibby.*

Archibald **Menzies** *(1754–1842).*

(Opposite) Two designs by Thomas **Mawson** *from* The Art and Craft of Garden Making. *(Above) A garden with steps and arched stone wall, designed for W. W. Galloway of Preston. (Below) Paths bounded by trellis screen and rose-covered arches, proposed for H.M. Queen Alexandra's garden at Hvidore.*

(Left) Araucaria araucana *(Monkey Puzzle tree) introduced to Britain by Archibald* **Menzies** *and (right) a scene from Vancouver's* Voyages.

View near the Monterrey River, Canada, scene of Archibald **Menzies'** *travels.*

Philip **Miller** *(1691–1771).*

five of the seeds had taken root, one of which was at Kew for almost a century.

Menzies was elected a member of the Linnean Society in 1790, becoming President in the year of his death. On his retirement from the Navy, Menzies lived in Notting Hill, London, bequeathing his herbarium of grasses, sedges and cryptogams to the Edinburgh Botanical Garden.

Messel, Leonard (1873–1953). Son of Ludwig Messel (qv). Colonel Messel, 'the plantsman', and his wife, Maud, were both plant-lovers, and saved many old roses from extinction. He subscribed to many of the plant-collecting expeditions of the 1920s to China and the Himalayas. Harold Comber, whose father, James, was head gardener at the

Messels' garden at Nymans in Sussex, travelled to the Andes and Tasmania to collect plants for Nymans. Some distinguished plants bear the Messel name or Nymans name, such as Camellia Leonard Messel, a cross between *Camellia reticulata,* Captain Rawes and Williamsii Mary Christian and, most famous of all *Eucryphia Nymansay,* a cross raised at Nymans about 1915 between *Eucryphia cordifolia* and *glutinosa,* and combining the good qualities of both. Colonel Messel was the father of Anne, Countess of Rosse, the present owner—with the National Trust—of Nymans.

Messel, Ludwig (1847–1915). Messel was the owner and founding architect of the celebrated garden at Nymans in Sussex. He was operative there from 1890 until his

death. He came to Nymans at a time of great gardening activity, when many new plants were coming in from China and Japan, for which the soil of Nymans was ideally suited. Ludwig Messel determined the plan of the Nymans garden as the thousands of visitors to Nymans see it today. All his gardening life, his mentor was James Comber, one of the great head gardeners of the time, who worked at Nymans for over sixty years.

Miller, Philip (1691–1771). Horticulturist and author. Miller seems to have been born at either Deptford or Greenwich. Little is known of his early life, apart from the fact that after leaving school he worked for a time in his father's market garden before setting up on his own as a florist in St George's Fields in Pim-

lico, a favourite venue for nurserymen and gardeners. That he made some wider reputation as a gardener and horticulturist is certain, for on the advice of Sir Hans Sloane, physician to George I, chatelain of the Manor House in Chelsea, and whose collections later formed the nucleus of the British Museum collections, Miller was appointed curator of the Apothecaries' Garden in Chelsea, where he remained in charge until his death.

Under his direction the physic garden gained an international renown, enhanced by the authority of Miller's several publications, the most important and influential of which was *The Gardener's Dictionary,* first published in 1731 (and dedicated to Sloane). This went through many editions, remaining a definitive work for over a century

*The view in 1799 from the River Thames to the Physick Garden at Chelsea, where Philip **Miller** was curator.*

*Sanderson **Miller** (1716–1780).*

and highly praised by Linnaeus, although when the latter visited the Garden in 1736, the two men's views on the nomenclature of plants caused sharp controversy between them. Yet Miller's activities were not only literary: he was amongst the most practical and experimental of horticulturists and during his tenure at the garden he designed and had constructed two hothouses and a greenhouse. He was also the first gardener in Britain to sponsor the germination of seeds from tropical and remote areas by subjection to the heat of a tan pit, and the first to describe a system of flowering bulbous plants in water-filled bottles. In 1751 his experiments in the fertilization of plants and the influence of insects in pollination brought him further acclaim. He was also responsible for providing seed for the increasing area of the cotton plantations in Georgia in North America, then an English possession. Although Miller and Linnaeus had disagreed over the correct naming of plants at their earlier meeting, Miller incorporated the great Swedish botanist's system of plant classification in the last edition of his *Dictionary* (1768) for which he was responsible. Amongst Miller's other publications were *A Catalogue of Trees Near London* (1730) and *A Gardener's Kalendar* (1732). A monument to Miller was erected in Chelsea Old Church in 1815 by the Linnean and Horticultural Societies.

Miller, Sanderson (1716–1780). Landscape architect. Although Miller's reputation in his own day was that of 'a gentleman architect' his later renown rests mainly on his

THE

GARDENERS DICTIONARY:

Containing the METHODS of

CULTIVATING *and* IMPROVING

THE

Kitchen, Fruit *and* Flower Garden.

AS ALSO, THE

Physick Garden, Wilderness, Conservatory,

AND

VINEYARD,

According to the PRACTICE of the

Most *Experienc'd Gardeners* of the *Present Age.*

Interspers'd with

The History of the PLANTS, the Characters of each GENUS, and the Names of all the particular SPECIES, in *Latin* and *English*; and an Explanation of all the Terms used in BOTANY and GARDENING.

Together with

Accounts of the Nature and Use of *Barometers, Thermometers,* and *Hygrometers* proper for GARDENERS; And of the Origin, Causes, and Nature of METEORS, and the particular Influences of *Air, Earth, Fire* and *Water* upon *Vegetation,* according to the best NATURAL PHILOSOPHERS.

Adorn'd with COPPER PLATES.

By *PHILIP MILLER,* Gardener to the BOTANICK GARDEN at *Chelsea,* and F. R. S.

----------*Digna manet divini gloria ruris.*   VIRG. GEO.

Printed by S. POWELL,

For RICHARD GUNNE in *Caple-street,* GEORGE RISK, GEORGE EWING, and WILLIAM SMITH, in *Dame's-street,* and JOHN SMITH and WILLIAM BRUCE on the *Blind-Key,* Booksellers. MDCCXXXII.

Frontispiece and title-page of The Gardener's Dictionary *by Philip **Miller**, first published in 1731.*

seminal role in the development of the Gothic Revival and its impact on the Picturesque. Miller was the son of a wealthy wool merchant at Banbury, and was born at Radway Grange, Warwickshire, which his father, High Sheriff of the County, had bought some five years previously. Although he was entered as

an under-graduate at Oxford, he seems not to have completed his studies and took no degree. When he was twenty, his father died. Miller inherited Radway and a comfortable fortune, so was well able to afford the indulgence of his interests in literature, architecture and in romantic landscaping. The latter

interest was given practical shape in a small thatched cottage which he designed in 1744 and built in the village of Edgehill. In the following year, becoming bolder in his gothicism, he gave his own Tudor manor house a pronounced latterday gothic appearance with canted bays, pointed arches, angle turrets and the

The mock-ruined castle at Wimpole Hall, Cambridgeshire, designed for Lord Hardwicke by Sanderson **Miller** *in 1760 and seen in a contemporary engraving.*

Recent view of the tower which formed part of the castle 'ruin' (seen in the engraving above) at Wimpole Hall, designed by Sanderson **Miller** *in 1760.*

Sham castle at the top of Claverton Down, designed by Sanderson **Miller**, *c. 1755, for Ralph Allen, as an 'eye-catcher' to be seen from the latter's town house in Bath.*

rest. The hills and valleys of the Radway estate included the Edgehill site of the Civil War battle, and this fact doubtless inspired Miller to his next venture, a sham ruined castle with an octagonal tower, nearby the cottage he had already built. This immediately became both a notable eye-catcher and vantage point for viewing the surrounding country-side, an area of outstanding beauty.

(Opposite) Two views of the gardens at Honington Hall, Warwickshire, where Sanderson **Miller** *designed various garden features, including a cascade and grotto, for Joseph Townsend. The paintings, by Thomas Robins, were commissioned in 1759, soon after the garden had been laid out.*

The completion of this handsome if unconvincing complex gave Miller a reputation amongst the wealthy dilettantes of the time, then preoc-cupied with all the engaging prob-lems of the Picturesque. Within a comparatively short time Miller, aided by various architects, masons, stuccoists and other craftsmen, was involved in the gothicizing of the estates belonging to friends and neighbours. The most renowned of these structures was the sham castle he designed for Sir George Lyttelton (qv), at Hagley Hall in Worcester-shire. The ruin, over seventy feet long, with towers at each end and incorporating lesser buildings, was an enormous success. The local gen-try picnicked beside the sham ruins and even the hard-to-please Horace

Walpole was moved to enthusiasm, asserting that the building would get Miller 'the freedom even of Straw-berry. It has the true rust of the Barons' wars'. Within a short time Miller's practice as a specialist in what was essentially anachronistic architecture was firmly established. His work ranged from a second gothic castle for Lord Hardwicke at Wimpole in Cambridgeshire to a gothic summerhouse for Lord Stamford at Enville in Stafford-shire, from the Shire Hall at War-wick to a cascade and grotto for Joseph Townsend at Honington Hall in Warwickshire. Although Miller had a competent knowledge of classical architecture, his inclina-tion was towards a scholarly but light-hearted gothick. Yet it is less

as an architect that he is now remembered, but rather as one of the more vigorous and engaging innovators of the Picturesque, with all its decorative oddities and extravagant fancies. In exploiting these innovations, Miller was an inventive practitioner who left his mark, even if he did not acquire the 'everlasting fame' which Lord Dacre, another amateur architect, foretold for him as a result of the castle at Hagley Hall. Certainly, Miller gave to the English landscape garden more than a touch of histor-ical romance, and, although he had numerous detractors, chiefly led by William Shenstone (qv) who was attempting the same kind of indulg-ence, his buildings exercised an impressive and enlivening influence

Lord **Milton** *(1786–1857),*
commemorated by Miltona spectabilis.

David **Moore** *(1807–1879), author of a*
Synopsis of the Mosses of Ireland.

Sir Frederick **Moore** *(1857–1950),*
curator at Glasnevin, Dublin.

of the Picturesque. His rich friends might build castles but gardening enthusiasts with more constricted purses could at least build their gothick summerhouses and gazebos in flattering if miniature imitation of Edgehill and Hagley.

Milton, Lord (1786–1857). Horticulturist. Charles Wentworth Fitzwilliam, son of the 2nd Earl Fitzwilliam, was educated at Cambridge, and as Viscount Milton represented Yorkshire in the House of Commons from 1807 until the death of his father in 1833. On his

consequent move to the Upper House, Lord Milton was an ardent supporter of the Free Trade policy. He was a keen and successful gardener at the family seat at Wentworth Woodhouse in Yorkshire and several of the rare plants cultivated there were depicted in the *Botanical Magazine.* In 1837, John Lindley (qv) gave the name *Miltonia spectabilis* to an orchid representing a new genus, and termed the grower 'one of the oldest and steadiest friends of Natural Science in this country'. He was the first President of the British Association.

Moore (or Muir) David (1807–1879). Horticulturist. Moore was born Muir but changed his name from the Scottish variant to the Irish on moving from Scotland to Ireland. He was born at Dundee and at an early age started work in the gardens of the seat of the Earl of Camperdown, later becoming foreman. He then moved to the Cunningham Nurseries in Edinburgh. When he was twenty-one he became assistant to James Mackay, Director of the Dublin University Botanic Garden. Six years later he was appointed to the Ordnance Survey of Ireland,

and to the Irish Volume of the survey's *Memoirs* Moore contributed a paper on the flora of Antrim and Londonderry. These activities brought him to the notice of the Royal Dublin Society and he was elected to take charge in 1838 of the Society's Botanic Garden at Glasnevin, where he remained for the rest of his life. Moore's skill and energy as an administrator and abilities as a botanist raised the standing of the garden from that of a little-known and virtually private garden to a centre of international renown. He was one of the first growers to raise orchids from seeds and a pioneer in the production of hybrids in *Sarracenia.* He was the first British gardener to cultivate such introductions as the pampas grass (*Moorea argentea,* now *Cortaderia,* was named after him in 1855), *Lilium giganteum* and *L. wallichianum* in addition to several species of *Nymphaea* and *Passiflora.* He had kept in touch with his mentor, Mackay of the University Botanic Garden, and assisted him in his compilation of Irish plants. With A. G. More he edited *Contributions towards a Cybele Hibernica,* an account of the geographical distribution of plants in Ireland, published in 1866. He was also deeply interested in cryptograms, and published a *Synopsis of the Mosses of Ireland,* 1873, and a *Report on Irish Hepaticae,* 1876. He became a Fellow of the Linnean Society in 1861.

Moore, (Sir) Frederick William (1857–1950). Botanist. Moore, the son of David Moore (qv), was educated in Dublin and Germany and

Rock-garden and mixed conifers at the Glasnevin Botanic Gardens, Dublin, where David **Moore** *was curator, 1838–1879.*

Recent view of the Glasnevin Botanic Gardens, Dublin, showing part of the range of glasshouses established by Sir Frederick **Moore***, who was successor to his father, David Moore, as curator of the Gardens.*

Thomas **Moore** *(1821–1887), author of* British Wild Flowers, *1867.*

was trained in horticultural studies at Leiden University. When he was twenty he returned to Dublin and was appointed curator of Trinity College Botanic Gardens, and, on the death of his father in 1879, succeeded to the curatorship of the Glasnevin Gardens, where many improvements and innovations were made under his direction, including the erection of new glasshouses and the planting of an arboretum. He was a specialist in orchid cultivation and established a remarkable collection at Glasnevin. He was knighted in 1911. He also advised on the planning and planting of a number of renowned Irish gardens.

Moore, Thomas (1821–1887). Botanist. Moore was born at Stoke, near Guildford in Surrey, and from his earliest years was trained as a gardener. He was first employed at Fraser's Lee Bridge Nurseries and later worked on the laying out of Regent's Park gardens. In 1848, thanks to the patronage of Dr John Lindley (qv), he was appointed curator of the Apothecaries' Company garden at Chelsea, following Robert Fortune (qv).

Moore was a resourceful and energetic editor of various gardening magazines and a prolific writer on horticultural matters. He edited the *Gardeners' Magazine* for two years and co-edited the *Gardeners' Chronicle* from 1866–1882. Amongst his publications were *British Ferns*, 1851; *Treasury of Botany* (with John Lindley), 1866, and *British Wild Flowers*, 1867.

He made a special study of ferns and after his death his collection, formed over many years, was purchased by the Kew Herbarium. He was secretary to the Floral Committee and Floral Director of the Royal Horticultural Society.

Pampas grass, Cortaderia argentea, *which was first cultivated in Britain by David* **Moore***, curator of the Glasnevin Botanic Garden from 1838 to 1879.*

Illustrations from British Wild Flowers *by Thomas* **Moore** *(1867). From left:* Crocus vernus, Galanthus nivalis, Scilla verna, Hyacinthus nonscriptus.

N

Nash, John Northcote, CBE, RA (1893–1977). Artist, gardener. Nash was the younger son of W. H. Nash, Recorder of Abingdon in Oxfordshire. His elder brother was the more renowned Paul Nash. He was educated at Wellington College, and after having shown artistic talent at school was encouraged by his brother to devote himself to painting. The two brothers staged a modest exhibition of their work in a Kensington gallery in 1913, and John Nash was invited to join the London Group. In the First War he joined the Artists' Rifles, served as an infantryman, but was appointed an official war artist in 1918. After the war he began to paint the Chilterns countryside and many of his paintings of that time are now in public galleries, notably *The Corn-field*, in the Tate Gallery. His flower paintings also attracted much attention for their beauty and accuracy, for Nash was not only a meticulous draughtsman and sound colourist but a passionate gardener. He was also an accomplished wood-engraver and his engravings for *Poisonous Plants*, published in 1927, gained him considerable renown. In his introduction to these engravings Nash showed something of his unusual botanical interests and his fresh and poetic use of language. He wrote of his lively engravings as forming 'a community of elegant malefactors' and continued:

> 'At one end of the scale of interest are the two Umbelliferous plants, both inhabitants of damp meadows and stream banks, and members of a generally dowdy family. At the other end is the strange Thorn Apple, with its twirling white funnels and prickly fruit, cousin to tropical plants even more exotic and terrifying. The Bear's Foot, or Stinking Hellebore, is a peculiarly handsome plant in leaf and flower, and is, with the Spurge Laurel, the earliest to bloom: these two, and our common Foxglove and Herb Paris, form the woodland group. The Yellow Horned Poppy lights up the sea shingles; Taxus stands gloomily in burial grounds; the Pasque Flower is Spring's forerunner on the chalk Downs; while the Deadly Nightshade, pre-eminently in appearance the King of Poisoners, is found in copses and on waste ground.'

In the Second World War he was again appointed an official war art-ist, but after a few months opted out to take a more active part as a Major of Royal Marines concerned with port defences.

After the war he settled at an old farmhouse at Wormingford in Essex, above the Stour Valley, and continued with his painting. He was elected RA in 1951.

Nelson, David (–1789). Plant-collector. Nelson, a young under-gardener at Kew, was recommended to Sir Joseph Banks (qv) by James Lee (qv) of the Vineyard Nurseries at Hammersmith as a 'proper person . . . exactly suited for the purpose of a collector' to sail as a botanist with Captain Cook on his third and fateful voyage in 1776. 'He knows the general run of our collections and plants about London, understands something of botany, but does not pretend to have much knowledge in it,' Lee added.

Lee's shrewd judgement of character was amply confirmed by Nelson early on in the voyage when he discovered, in Tasmania, *Acacia verticillata,* known later as Nelson's Mimosa, which remains a popular greenhouse favourite.

In New Zealand and the Tonga and Society Islands, Nelson made further botanical discoveries, apart from being consulted on more everyday matters. 'By the assistance of Mr Nelson, whose business . . . was to collect the vegetables and other curious productions through which we passed, we were enabled to stock ourselves with a large proportion of culinary plants which was of infinite service to us in our more northerly progress,' wrote the chronicler of the voyage in reference to the passage of the *Discovery* towards the chilly Aleutian Islands (still associated with his name in *Ranunculus nelsonii,* one of the islands' common buttercups) and the Alaskan coast. The *Discovery* and companion ship, the *Resolution,* after failing in their attempt to discover a North-West passage, returned to Hawaii were Captain Cook was killed. Following further adventures and hazards, they

John **Nash** *(1893–1977).*

(Opposite) Fuchsia fulgens, *depicted in pencil and watercolour, by John* **Nash** *(1930), who was a keen gardener as well as a meticulous draughtsman and accurate colourist.*

Fuchsia fulgens.

Abbotsbury 1930.

Inside of leaves in
light ribs.
rich brunswick gn
flowers pale apple ysr

John Nash

returned to England in 1780 after voyages which had taken well over four years. Nelson brought back over two hundred packets of seeds for Banks, which were shared between Kew and Göttingen Botanical Gardens in Germany, dear to the Hanoverian George III.

Nelson also introduced to England numerous species, many of the dried seeds of which are still to be seen in the herbarium of the British Museum. His voyages in the tropics are remembered in *Nelsonia campestris*, a charming violet flower.

After remaining as a gardener at Kew for some years, his adventures and misadventures in the oceans of the world seemingly forgotten, Nelson was again recruited by Banks as botanist and gardener-in-chief on a projected voyage for the collection of bread-fruit on the island of Tahiti for transhipment to Jamaica, where, it was hoped, the plant could be cultivated and prove a cheap and suitable food for the slaves. The ship was the *Bounty*, under Captain Bligh (qv), the former sailing-master in the *Resolution* and thus well-known to Nelson. After a stay in Tahiti of nearly six months, almost eight hundred potted breadfruit trees were loaded in the *Bounty* in addition to seven hundred other plants for Kew.

None of these hard-won plants, however, was ever to reach the West Indies or Kew, for, on the supposed passage to the West Indies the famous or infamous mutiny, led by Fletcher Christian, broke out and Bligh and eighteen others, including Nelson, were put into a long-boat and cast off. The breadfruit, the sole purpose of the journey, was thrown overboard. The story of the epic voyage of this craft has been the sub-

Captain Bligh of the Bounty *and eighteen of the ship's complement, including David* **Nelson**, *were cast off in a ship's boat in the famous mutiny.*

ject of several books and films. After a voyage of over 3,500 miles, through unknown seas and coral reefs, countering the effects of storms, mountainous seas, and blood-thirsty savages, Bligh finally brought his fragile boat to Campang, a Dutch settlement in Timor. There, as a result of the hardships he had endured, Nelson caught fever, and died within a few days, being interred in the burying grounds of the settlement.

There is scant record of the plants that Nelson introduced to Kew, for they were incorporated in Banks' publication *Hortus Kewensis*, yet he was certainly responsible for the introduction of species from South Africa, Australasia and even from the bleak Aleutians, and the botanical results of Cook's last voyage are all based on Nelson's specimens which are now in the British Museum Herbarium.

Nesfield, William Andrews (1793–1881). Garden designer. Nesfield, the son of the rector of Brancefreth in Durham, was one of the most successful of the Victorian garden designers, although his early training was as an engineer destined for the army. He joined the 95th Regiment and as a twenty-year-old lieutenant fought, under Moore and Wellington, at San Sebastian and in the battles of the Pyrenees in the Peninsula War. He also served in Canada at the siege of Fort Erie and in the defence of Chippawa.

At the early age of twenty-three he retired on half-pay, married and took over one of a pair of villas in Muswell Hill, North London, designed by his brother-in-law, Anthony Salvin (1779–1881). Nesfield undertook the design of his own garden and of the adjoining villa, an area of well over two acres. The gardens were designed in a

manner sympathetic to the Italianate character of the houses. At the same time Nesfield began to devote himself to painting, specializing in seascapes and landscapes (with the emphasis on waterfalls) both on the continent and in northern England and Wales. His paintings received the approbation of Ruskin, who, in his *Modern Painters* enjoined readers to reflect upon Nesfield's *Fall of Schaffhausen*, and the artist's skilful 'management of the changeful veil of spray or mist'.

An illustrated account in the *Gardeners Magazine* of Nesfield's garden designs, allied with his reputation as a landscape artist, brought him to the notice of Sir William Hooker (qv), Director of Kew, who commissioned Nesfield to prepare plans for the projected arboretum at Kew. From 1845 Nesfield developed his plan, opening up the great Syon vista in 1851 and designing both the Broad Walk and the Pagoda vista, schemes which remain basically unaltered today. In the late 1850s Nesfield was commissioned to design the Royal Horticultural Society's gardens at Kensington, on a site of over twenty acres near the present Albert Hall, on land which had probably been part of London and Wise's Brompton Park Nursery. The new RHS gardens were opened by the Prince Consort in 1861.

Nesfield also designed gardens at Drayton in Northamptonshire and at Stoke Edith in Herefordshire. At Grimston, near Tadcaster in Yorkshire, he designed, for Lord Londesborough, an Italianate Emperors' Walk flanked by busts of the Caesars. His grandest garden designs in the Italian manner, however, were for the 1st Earl of

The villa at Muswell Hill, in North London, where William Andrews **Nesfield** *began to practise his skills as a garden designer. Illustrated in the* Villa Gardener *by J. C. Loudon.*

The Pagoda vista at Kew, laid out by William Andrews **Nesfield**.

(Left) The Emperors' Walk, flanked by busts of the Caesars and terminating in a classical temple, and (right) the Western Garden at Grimston in Yorkshire, designed for Lord Londesborough by William **Nesfield,** *showing his preference for the formal, Italianate style which became popular in the mid nineteenth century.*

Dudley, at Witley Court in Worcestershire, where over a quarter of a million pounds was spent in embellishing the 700-acre estate. Nesfield also worked, with Sir Charles Barry (qv), at Trentham in Staffordshire, and at Alnwick in Northumberland.

Of the great gardens designed by Nesfield virtually nothing now remains. Only at Kew and at Broughton Hall in Yorkshire can his work still be seen, although gardens on a lesser scale probably remain but are undocumented.

Nesfield died at his house in York Terrace in Regents Park. His practice was continued by his son, Markham, who was killed in an accident soon after his father's death.

Nevill, (Lady) Dorothy Fanny (1826–1913). Orchidist. Lady Dorothy Walpole was the daughter of the 3rd Earl of Oxford, and spent most of her early life in Norfolk, with many journeys abroad, particularly to Rome and Munich. After her marriage to Reginald Nevill, a cousin, she became one of London's leading social-political hostesses and also a successful grower of orchids and tropical plants at her country home near Midhurst in Sussex. By the 'seventies her collection of rare plants was considered one of the finest in Britain until dispersed on the sale of the estate in 1879. Although so deeply involved in the cultivation of rare plants, her favourite flower was the primrose and she was a leading figure in the promotion of Primrose Day in honour of Disraeli, one of her closest political friends. During her later years she published her *Reminiscences* in three volumes.

Nicholson, George (1847–1908). Botanist and writer. Nicholson, the son of a nurseryman, was born at Ripon in Yorkshire, and after attending Ripon Grammar School, began to work for his father, gaining further experience in nurseries in France. In 1873 he joined Kew as clerk to the curator and within a short time was involved in the preparation of a paper on the *Wild Flora of Kew Gardens and Pleasure Grounds*, published in the *Journal of Botany* in 1875. In 1886 he was appointed curator. He had already started to publish his great work, *The Illustrated Dictionary of Gardening* (1884–1888), which was followed by a *Supplement* in 1900–1901. During a sojourn of some months in the United States in 1893 he was involved in the study of the indigenous trees of North America which resulted in his *Handlist of Trees and Shrubs in the Kew Arboretum* (1894–96). He visited the United States again in 1902. He was the recipient of many honours and awards, including the RHS Veitchian Medal.

The palm, *Neonicholsonia georgei*, and the moss, *Fissidens nicholsonii*, were named in George Nicholson's honour. He was also an outstanding collector of fungi. His remarkable herbarium was left to Aberdeen University.

North, Marianne (1830–1890). Botanical artist. Marianne North was the daughter of a wealthy Liberal MP for Hastings with scientific and artistic interests. When she was twenty-five her mother died and she began a series of Middle Eastern journeys with her father, which prompted her to engage upon a copious graphic documentation of her travels, particularly as far as botanical subjects were concerned, which was to prove a lifetime's vocation. On the death of her father in 1869, she set about the fulfilment of what

Lady Dorothy Fanny **Nevill** *(1826–1913), orchidist.*

An illustration from The Illustrated Dictionary of Gardening *(1884–1888) compiled by George* **Nicholson** *and published in four volumes.*

George **Nicholson** *(1847–1908), author of* Handlist of Trees and Shrubs.

had already become her major ambition, if not obsession: a determination to record 'tropical vegetation in all its natural abundant luxuriance.' In this endeavour she was spectacularly successful. Two years after her father's death she started on the first of what was to prove an unusual series of adventurous journeys to distant places typical of those travel sagas engaged upon by so many Victorian spinsters of middle-age and private means. She travelled widely in North and South America, the Caribbean and later in Australasia, and one hitherto unknown plant which she painted in the Seychelles Islands in the Indian Ocean was named in her honour *Northea seychelliana*. The famous nurseryman, Harry Veitch, also named a rare plant from Borneo in her honour: *Nepenthes northiana*. In 1882 Marianne North provided the funds whereby the collection of some hundreds of her paintings could be housed in the North Gallery in the Greek temple in Kew Gardens.

*Marianne **North** (1830–1890).*

Nuttall, Thomas (1786–1859). Botanist. Nuttall was born at Long Preston, near Settle in Yorkshire. His father died when he was twelve. He left school at fourteen and was apprenticed to his uncle, Jonas Nuttall, a Liverpool printer. Thanks to the companionship of a friend, John Windsor Nuttall, he became early interested in botanical studies through his rambles in the Pennines. Whilst still an apprentice he decided to emigrate to the United States, a decision which caused a break with his uncle. After a year of extreme privation in London, Nuttall sailed from Liverpool in 1808 for Philadelphia. There he was befriended by Benjamin Smith Barton (1768–1815), professor of botany at the University, and William Bartram (1739–1823) the then-aging plant collector, son of the famous John Bartram (1699-1777) (qv), the doyen of American plant collectors. After early difficulties, Nuttall obtained work as a printer, but a year later was enabled to set out on his first plant-collecting trip sponsored by Professor Barton. These early excursions were fruitful and pleased Barton, who, two years later, sent Nuttall off on a plant-collecting expedition to the Far West. In company with John Bradbury (1768–1823) he ascended the Missouri, 1,600 miles above its mouth.

In 1812 Nuttall returned to his family in England, began to publish results of his collecting in William

*Thomas **Nuttall** (1786–1859), plant-collector and botanist.*

*The Western Dogwood depicted with the band-tailed pigeon by Audubon, for whom Thomas **Nuttall** supplied the specimens.*

Curtis's *Botanical Magazine* and attended meetings of the Linnean Society. In 1815 he returned to America and after further plant collecting published in 1818 his *Genera of North American Plants*, which gained him international recognition as a botanist. In 1822, Nuttall was appointed curator to the Harvard College Botanic Garden and lecturer in botany, retaining these positions until 1834, although his duties did not limit his plant-collecting expeditions. He made various trips throughout the United States and Canada, crossing the Rocky Mountains and exploring the Oregon and Upper California.

In 1835 Nuttall took passage to the Sandwich Islands to study and to collect Pacific flora. In 1842, he had to return to England to take over his uncle's estate, Nutgrove, near Wigan, Lancashire, an inheritance which smoothed his material life but caused him considerable unhappiness as his career had been dedicated to the natural history of North America. He paid one last visit to America in 1847. From then until his death, he resided at Nutgrove, corresponding with European and North American botanists and raising plants, especially rhododendrons, in his own greenhouses.

Nuttall was a careful yet prolific writer on botany and ornithology. Apart from the *Genera of North American Plants*, his publications include a journal of *Travels into Arkansas Territory* (1821); *An Introduction to Systematic and Physiological Botany* (1827); *North American Sylva* (1842).

(Opposite) The passion flower, Passiflora, one of the eight hundred paintings by Marianne **North** now housed in the Marianne North Gallery at the Royal Botanic Gardens, Kew, which is devoted to her pictures of exotic flora.

*Topographical drawing reproduced from the journal of Thomas **Nuttall**.*

Daniel **Oliver** *(1830–1916), editor of* The Flora of Tropical Africa.

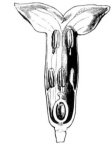

OBSERVE the tenacious liber-layer of the bark, characteristic of the Family : the highly-coloured perianth of some garden and greenhouse genera.

FIG. 120. Vertical section of flower of Spurge Daphne.

Fig. 121. Vertical section of fruit of same, showing a solitary suspended seed.

The berries of Mezereon (*D. Mezereum*) are poisonous, and those of Spurge Daphne are also

said to be poisonous to all animals excepting birds. From the liber of *D. papyracea* of the Himalaya a coarse, but very tough, paper is made. *Lagetta lintearia* is the Jamaica Lacebark tree, the liber of which may be separated into many thin layers resembling lace, by maceration. It is made up into various ornamental articles.

55. *Natural Order* — Euphorbiaceæ. The Spurge Family.

DISTRIBUTION.—A very large Natural Order, widely dispersed in both hemispheres ; most numerous in tropical and subtropical regions.— British genera 3, species 15.

Herbs, usually with milky juice, or an evergreen shrub. Ovary 3-celled (2-celled in Mercury).

FIG. 122. Staminate flower of Perennial Mercury.

FIG. 123. Pistillate flower of same, with two imperfect stamens.

Q 2

Typical pages, illustrated with line engravings, from Lessons in Elementary Botany *by Daniel* **Oliver** *(1830–1916), first published in 1864, three years after his appointment as Professor of Botany at University College, London.*

Oliver, Daniel (1830–1916). Botanist and writer. Oliver was born in Newcastle-on-Tyne and educated at the Friends' School at Wigton in Cumberland. When a child he showed keen interest in botanical studies and as a youthful member of the Tyneside Naturalists' Field Club contributed papers to the *Phytologist.* Oliver was yet another of those young men recruited for Kew by the redoubtable Sir William Hooker; in 1858 he joined the Kew Herbarium and helped Hooker in cataloguing the Australasian, Antarctic and Indian collections, also helping in the editorial work on the *Botanical Magazine* and the *Icones Plantarum.* In 1861 he was appointed Professor of Botany at University College, London, combining these academic duties with his work at Kew, mainly by lecturing at 8am in the summer term. Three years later he also added the curatorship of the Herbarium to his manifold tasks, still finding time for his scientific and editorial work, including the official guides to the Kew Museums and Gardens. His *Lessons in Elementary Botany* (1864) went into many edi-

tions and he edited, and wrote much of, *The Flora of Tropical Africa.* As if these tasks were not sufficient he instituted a course of free lectures— from 1859 to 1874—for the gardeners at Kew.

He disliked personal honours, but accepted a Fellowship of the Royal Society (1863), the Society's gold medal (1884) and the Linnean gold medal (1893). He is commemorated in the plant genera *Oliverella* and *Oliverodoxa.*

Page, Russell (1906–). Landscape and garden designer. Page was educated at Charterhouse and the Slade School of Fine Art, University of London, and afterwards began to study painting in Paris, but soon decided that he would do better to garden than to paint. As he had been a gardener from his earliest youth, and, at the age of seventeen, had been given part of the family garden to develop his love of planting and cultivations, his decision was perhaps inevitable. From then on, he learned his gardening, as he says, 'by doing it'. He found that by making rock gardens for friends he

could experiment with the principles of landscape design in miniature scale, and compose with plants instead of paint.

In 1928 he set up in partnership with Geoffrey Jellicoe (qv), one of the founders of the Institute of Landscape Architects. They were soon involved in many large garden projects, including Royal Lodge, Windsor; Holme House, Regent's Park and several gardens in France. Another of their early commissions was to design the nearby buildings for the Cheddar Gorge caves so that they were in sympathy with the majestic cave structure. This was followed by the commission to landscape the grounds of Charterhouse School at Haslemere in Surrey. The partnership continued until 1939. After the war, he settled in France, making numerous gardens there as well as in Belgium, Switzerland, Italy and Spain. His work has also taken him to Egypt, Persia, Australia, Venezuela and the United States. In England Page was responsible for the designing and planting of the Festival Gardens in Battersea Park, London, for the Festival of

Russell **Page** *(1906–), one of the founder-members of the Institute of Landscape Architects.*

*(Left) A terraced garden in the Italian style and (right) lawn and yew hedges at Lake Geneva, both designed by Russell **Page** (1906–   ).*

*Two examples of the many garden designs by Russell **Page**. (Left) One of the* allées *at Longleat in Wiltshire and (right) a water-garden in the French classical manner.*

Britain in 1952.

In 1962 he published *The Education of a Gardener*, which describes his theories on garden design and planting. This international career, collaborating with architects, decorators, painters and sculptors, and his study of plants, guided by eminent plantsmen in many different parts of the world, has given him an exceptional status amongst landscape architects.

He is currently working on projects in Paris, New York, Caracas.

Palmer, Edward (1831–1911). Botanist, plant-collector. Palmer was born at Hockwold cum Wilton in Norfolk. Little is known of Palmer's early life. He had scant formal education and at the age of eighteen emigrated to the United States. He served as a hospital steward on a naval expedition to Paraguay between 1853 and 1855 and acquired a basic knowledge of medicine, further extended by lectures at the Homeopathic College at Cleveland, Ohio. From 1857 he practised as an army physician and surgeon in Colorado, Arizona and California, combining this vocation with the collecting of botanical and biological specimens. In 1868, he gave up his medical career to devote himself to collecting in Arizona, California and Mexico. His botanical collections were widely distributed throughout the United States and comprised an estimated 100,000 specimens, of which 2,000 were new to botanists from regions hitherto unvisited by collectors.

He was a serious student of Western Indians and their way of life and a collector of Indian artefacts, which have proved amongst the most valuable sources of information on the ethnology of these now-vanished tribes. *A List of Plants Collected by Dr Edward Palmer* was published in 1875, and Palmer published *A List of Plants Collected in S. W. Chihuahua* in 1885.

Plants collected by Palmer in Mexico are now in the collections at the Royal Botanic Gardens, Kew.

Papworth, John, Buonarotti (1775–1847). Architect and landscape architect. Although Papworth's greater fame derives from his achievements as an architect with a wide and successful practice, he finds a place in this DICTIONARY as a landscape architect of unusual versatility.

He was born in Marylebone in London, the second son of John Papworth, the most eminent stuccoist of his day, and was intended for the medical profession, but,

217

Tented garden seat 'designed as an embellishment to the lawn or shrubbery', illustrated in Designs for Rural Residences *by John B.* **Papworth** *(1818).*

Garden seat beneath an oriental-style umbrella, reproduced from Designs for Rural Residences *by John B.* **Papworth** *(1818).*

Suggested design for a villa and garden for an artist, reproduced from Designs for Rural Residences *by John B.* **Papworth** *(1818).*

Design for a fishing-lodge for a country estate, reproduced from Designs for Rural Residences *by John B.* **Papworth** *(1818).*

John Buonarotti **Papworth** *(1775–1847).*

influenced by Sir William Chambers' high opinion of the young Papworth's facility as a draughtsman, he began training as an architect under John Plaw (later at the Royal Academy Schools) and acquired a practical knowledge of structural methods by apprenticeship to a builder. He showed an early authority and skill, designing his first house when he was eighteen, and within a few years he was the prolific head of an established practice, specializing in the building of and alterations to country houses. His exceptional and continuing ability as an artist and draughtsman undoubtedly led him to take a leading part in the fashionable interest of landowners in the laying-out and embellishment of their estates. Apart from his published designs for villas, cottages and rural residences of all kinds, he also published elevations and plans for decorative and practical garden buildings, plus a wide range of designs for furniture and domestic ware.

His practice as a landscape gardener was extensive and miscellaneous, mainly for a number of rich private patrons. These included a comprehensive garden plan, with conservatories, cottages, coach-houses and a gothick summer-house for Prince Leopold and Princess Charlotte at Claremont in Surrey; a seven-arched bridge and temples in the Greek and gothick styles for the Earl of Shrewsbury at Alton Towers in Staffordshire; plans for the Duchess of St Albans at Holly Lodge, Highgate; the Brockwell estate for John Blades (including completely rebuilding Brockwell Hall) and the Montpelier Estate at Cheltenham in Gloucestershire for Pearson Thompson.

Papworth was also a prolific writer on architecture, engineering design and landscape gardening. Amongst his most notable works were *Designs for Rural Residencies,* consisting of a *Series of Designs for Cottages, Small Villas and other Buildings,* 1818; *Hints on Ornamental Gardening,* 1823.

Papworth was one of the twelve founder-members of the Institute of British Architects and vice-president on several occasions. He added Buonarotti to his name in 1815 when submitting a drawing (rejected) to the Royal Academy to commemorate the Duke of Wellington's victory at Waterloo. John Papworth moved to St Neot's in Huntingdonshire in 1846 and died there a year later.

(Opposite) Six aquatints from Hints on Ornamental Gardening *by John B.* **Papworth,** *published in 1823 and typical of the small books on cottage and villa architecture being produced around that time. (Left) Three designs for fountains, the centre one including a plan. (Top right) A low, sheltered plantation seat with bronze pillars. (Centre right) An ice-house, tool-house and garden seat. (Below right) An apiary.*

Mungo **Park** *(1771–c. 1806), explorer and botanist, and (right) an engraving of the Shea, or Butter Tree, reproduced from his book* Travels in the Interior Districts of Africa, *which was published in 1799.*

Portrait of John **Parkinson** *(1567–1650), herbalist, gardener and author, and (right) Spiderworts. Both engravings are reproduced from his book* Paradisi in Sole Paradisus Terrestris *(1629).*

Park, Mungo (1771–1806). Explorer, botanist. Park was born at Foulshiels in Selkirkshire, Scotland. He was apprenticed to a surgeon and took a surgeon's diploma at Edinburgh University in 1791. Thanks to an introduction from his brother-in-law to Sir Joseph Banks, President of the Royal Society, he was appointed assistant-surgeon in the *Worcester* bound for the Far East. His interest in natural history was shown on the conclusion of this initial passage by a paper which was read to the Linnean Society, dealing with eight Sumatran fish unknown to the West. In 1794 Park was appointed by the African Association to explore the River Niger.

During the many delays he took the opportunity to draw examples of plant life that existed on the edge of the desert and in the Niger region. After a hazardous two-year journey, which included four months' imprisonment by a Moorish chief and the loss of all his baggage and equipment, he returned to London. The account of his travels, vicissitudes and discoveries were published in *Travels in the Interior of Africa* (1799), a classic among the records of eighteenth-century explorers.

After five years passed in practice as a doctor in Scotland, Park was again invited to lead a further expedition to the Niger. This well-equipped expedition was doomed from the beginning: several members of the expedition died before reaching the Niger, and Park and the remaining members were attacked from the river banks and either killed or drowned.

Parkinson, John (1567–1650). Herbalist, gardener, author. Little is known of Parkinson's early years, but he is generally thought to have been born in Nottinghamshire. He presumably came to London towards the end of the sixteenth century or at the beginning of the seventeenth, for he was appointed apothecary to James I. The royal connexion was continued by Charles I who gave Parkinson the title of Botanicus Regius Primarius following the publication of his compendious volume *Paradisi in Sole Paradisus Terrestris* in 1629.

The book opens with an introduction on *the Ordering of the Garden of Pleasure* which is followed by the *Garden of Pleasant Flowers*, comprising copious notes which form the main section of the book. Chapters on the kitchen garden and orchard complete a remarkable 600-page book with observations concerning a thousand plants then under cultivation in various parts of the nation. The book was embellished with almost 800 woodcuts.

Parkinson's garden in Long Acre, where he grew many of the flowers he described in his book, was famous. Here he practised what he termed 'the purest of human pleasures'. His prose was simple, effective and persuasive. Of anemones he wrote:

> 'so dainty, so pleasant and so delightsome flowers that the sight of them doth enforce an earnest longing desire to be a possessoure of some of them at the leaste'

After the death of Matthias de Lobel (1538–1616), the French author, physician and gardener who had settled in Highgate and was superintendant of Lord Zouche's garden at Hackney, Parkinson acquired his unpublished records and notes. He made considerable use of the papers in his *Theatrum Botanicum; the Theatre of Plants; or an Universal and Complete Herbal*, which was published in 1640. The book describes nearly 4,000 plants, but is of more interest to herbalists than to gardeners. Parkinson's renown continued throughout the rest of his life; he was buried in St Martin-in-the-Fields, the author of the first great British gardening book.

Parkinson, Sydney (c. 1745–1771). Botanist and artist. Parkinson was born in Edinburgh, the younger son of an unsuccessful Quaker brewer of that city. He was first apprenticed to a woollen-draper, but, on the basis of his rare skill in drawing fruit and flowers, he travelled to London. There his talent gained him commissions from botanists and natural historians. Sir Joseph Banks was one of his chief patrons, entrusting Parkinson with the task of copying on vellum a collection of drawings brought back by Governor Loten from Ceylon. Parkinson's intelligence, industry and character led to his selection as botanical and natural history draughtsman on the *Endeavour* expedition under Captain Cook (qv), which was sent by the Government to Tahiti in order to further British astronomical science and with the specific object of studying the transit of Venus in 1768. Banks was appointed to accompany the expedition as scientific observer.

Parkinson was employed as a draughtsman in Banks' 'suite' at a salary of eighty pounds a year. Throughout the voyage Parkinson worked extremely hard and, in one period of fourteen days, according to Banks, made ninety-four sketch drawings, 'so quick a hand has he acquired by use'.

Parkinson died from the effects of a direful wave of dysentery which killed several others in the ship in January, 1771.

His drawings were of high quality and accuracy and are now in the British Museum.

Parry, (Admiral Sir) William Edward (1790–1855). Sailor, explorer, botanist. Parry was born at Bath, the son of an eminent physician. He received his early education at the Grammar School in the city, but when he was twelve years old joined the *Ville de Paris*, flagship of the Channel Fleet, in blockading duties off the French coast. After an

Watercolour drawing, Winterana aromatica, *made by Sydney* **Parkinson** *(right) whilst aboard the* Endeavour *on its expedition under Captain Cook to Tahiti to study the Transit of Venus in 1769.*

adventurous introduction to a naval career in the Napoleonic wars, Parry was appointed in 1817 to the command of the discovery ship *Alexander* which sailed in company with the *Isabella* for the purpose of exploring Baffin Bay and the possibilities of a north-west passage to the Pacific. In all, Parry made three voyages of discovery to the Arctic. Apart from his geographical explorations, he made extensive botanical collections, which were listed in detail by Professor W. J. Hooker in the appendices to Parry's *Journals of Voyages for Discovery of a North-West Passage.*

Following his third arctic voyage, promotion and knighthood, Parry was appointed a Commissioner of the Australian Agricultural Company and spent five years in Australia. On his return he was appointed an assistant Poor Law Commissioner and Comptroller of Steam Machinery at the Admiralty, and in 1852 Captain-Superintendent of the Royal Naval Hospital at Haslar. He died at Ems in Germany whilst seeking recovery from an attack of cholera.

Parsons, Alfred (1847–1920). Floral artist. Parsons was born at Becking-ton in Somerset and, although showing early signs of artistic talent, received no formal art instruction. He became a clerk in the Savings Bank Department of the Post Office at the age of eighteen. After two years of this work, however, Parsons decided to devote himself full time to painting.

His flower paintings gradually began to gain public interest and critical attention and were commissioned privately for magazines and books. He illustrated *The Bamboo Garden* by A. B. Freeman-Mitford (1896) and *Genus Rosa* by Ellen Wilmott (1910–1914) (qv) as well as

William Edward **Parry** *(1790–1855) and an engraving from his* Journal of a Third Voyage for the Discovery of a North-West Passage.

THE HYBRID CRENATE CACTUS
(PHYLLOCACTUS SPECIOSISSIMO-CRENATUS)

several books of poems and travel books. He was elected President of the Society of Painters in Water-Colour in 1905 and became a Royal Academician in 1911.

Pasley, Anthony du Gard (1929–). Landscape architect. Pasley was born in Surrey and began practising gardening seriously as a child, greatly encouraged by his family. His interest continued throughout his schooldays. After a spell in the army he became a pupil of Brenda Colvin (qv) and studied under Professor Youngman at University College, London. He started work as landscape designer for the nursery firm of R. W. Wallace in Tunbridge Wells, and subsequently became assistant to Sylvia Crowe and Associates, leaving to start his own practice in 1970.

Pasley's landscaping work has ranged from projects for barracks and reservoirs to forestry programmes for country estates, from layouts for small town gardens to designs for conservatories. He prefers to work for private clients and specializes in the restoration of country gardens, in Britain and abroad, which have become unworkable under modern conditions. He also lectures extensively to students of architecture, town planning and landscape design as well as to the lay public.

Paxton, (Sir) Joseph (1803–1865). Landscape gardener and architect. Paxton, the seventh son of a farmer, was born at Milton Bryant, near Woburn in Bedfordshire. His first job was as a gardener at Battlesden, the seat of Sir Gregory Page-Turner, and by the time he was nineteen he had already constructed a lake, his first outstanding work. In 1823 he moved to the newly-opened gardens of the Horticultural Society, leased from the 6th Duke of Devonshire (qv), adjoining Chiswick House in Middlesex. There his inventiveness and industry attracted the attention of the Duke and, within two years, he was offered the position of head gardener at the Duke's seat at Chatsworth in Derbyshire.

Paxton's own description of taking over his new job is well worth retelling and indicates the calibre and character of the young man:

> I left London by the Comet Coach for Chesterfield and arrived at Chatsworth at half-past four o'clock in the morning of the ninth of May, 1826. As no person was to be seen at that early hour, I got over the green-house gate by the old covered way, explored

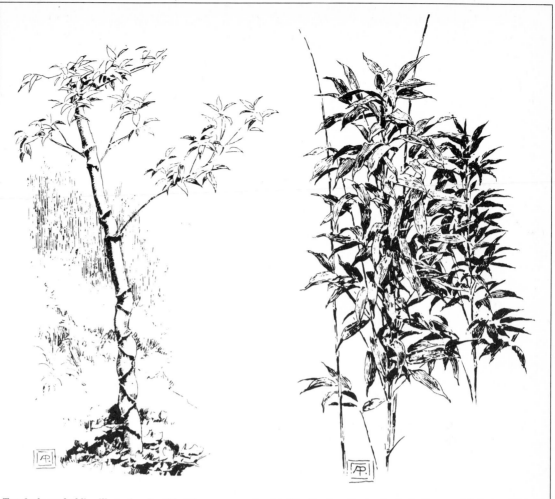

Two finely-worked line illustrations by Alfred **Parsons** *reproduced in* The Bamboo Garden *by A. B. Freeman-Mitford, published in 1896.* (Left) Phyllostachys heterocycla *and* (right) Bambusa marmorea.

the pleasure grounds and looked round the outside of the house. I then went down to the kitchen gardens, scaled the outside wall and saw the whole of the place, set the men to work at six o'clock; then returned to Chatsworth and got Thomas Weldon to play me the water works and afterwards went to breakfast with poor dear Mrs Gregory and her niece, the latter fell in love with me and I with her, and thus completed my first morning's work, at Chatsworth, before nine o'clock.

Within a short time the Duke was relying more and more upon Paxton's knowledge and authority. Thanks also to his marriage in 1827 to the highly intelligent and resourceful Sarah Brown, a mill-owner's daughter from Matlock in Derbyshire, who took much of the more mundane detail work off his shoulders, Paxton was enabled to extend his activities throughout the vast Chatsworth domain, until finally he became the Duke's agent. In the gardening sphere, Paxton, between 1835 and 1844, laid out the Chatsworth arboretum, designed rock gardens on a grand scale, constructed the Emperor Fountain, with the then-highest jet in the world, plus the attendant lakes and conduits. His ingenuity as a structural engineer was shown in a remarkable group of glazed and iron buildings erected in the Chatsworth kitchen gardens, and their success brought him a wide renown as propagator and botanist as well as designer of remarkably efficient structures. Between 1836 and 1840 he designed and supervised the

(Opposite) The Hybrid Crenate Cactus, Phyllocactus Speciosissimo-crenatus, *one of the plates from* Paxton's Flower Garden *by Sir Joseph* **Paxton** *and John Lindley, which was published in three volumes between 1850 and 1853.*

Garden with trellis and pergola, designed by Anthony du Gard **Pasley** *(1929–), seen above.*

223

Sir Joseph **Paxton** *(1803–1865).*

Part of the waterworks at Chatsworth, designed by Sir Joseph **Paxton**, *with the Emperor Fountain in the distance.*

building of the Great Stove which enclosed what was virtually a tropical landscape under glass. In designing a suitable conservatory for the propagation and flowering of the giant water lily *Victoria amazonica* in 1849, Paxton mastered the technical demands which were involved in the construction of an iron and glass building. This expertize led him to his enormous success in designing the 1851 Great Exhibition building in London.

Coincidentally with his remarkable achievements in gardening and the design of garden structures, Paxton also had engaged in rebuilding three entire Chatsworth villages: Edensor, Pilsley and Beeley.

Paxton's successes at Chatsworth brought him numerous commissions for the design of large-scale public gardens. Amongst those for which he was responsible were Princes Park, Liverpool (1842), Birkenhead Park (1843), Coventry Cemetery (1843), The People's Park, Halifax (1855) and Hesketh Park, Southport (1864) and, above all, the grounds of Crystal Palace on Sydenham Hill (1852–56), to which the Great Exhibition buildings were removed, with their Italian formal gardens and English informal gardens, lakes, terraces, statuary, temples and cascades.

In 1854, Paxton was elected to Parliament and became deeply involved in parliamentary committees and controversies concerning various metropolitan improvements then under discussion. He was also increasingly involved in the Sydenham project. Finally, overwork and ill-health caused his retirement from Parliament in 1865, the year of his death.

Perry, Frances (1907–   ). Horticulturist and garden author. Frances Perry was trained at Swanley Horticulture College in Kent and started her professional life at Perry's Hardy Plant Farm, Enfield. Here she took an active part in the study and growing of water plants, perennials and hardy bulbs.

After her marriage to the elder son of the owner she became horticultural adviser and, in due course, senior administrator for Middlesex County Council. Later, Frances Perry became Principal of Norwood Hall College of Horticultural and Agricultural Education.

She is a prolific writer and contributes to many papers and magazines. She is gardening editor of *The Observer* and has written fifteen books, including *Flowers of the World* and *Water Gardens*. She is also a regular broadcaster, has appeared in many television programmes and lectured in the United States of America, New Zealand, Canada, Australia and South America. She was the first woman elected to the Council of the Royal Horticultural Society in 1968 and has lately become its first lady Vice-

Monumental rock works and (right) the aqueduct at Chatsworth, Derbyshire, both designed by Sir Joseph **Paxton**.

Frances **Perry** *(1907–   ).*

*Two designs by Harold **Peto**. (Left) Canal-garden leading to the lake at Buscot Park, Oxfordshire, and (right) water-garden at Hartham Park, Wiltshire.*

President. Frances Perry also holds the Royal Horticultural Society's Victoria Medal of Honour.

Peto, Harold Ainsworth (1854–1933). Architect and landscape designer. Peto was the son of Sir Samuel Morton Peto, Bt, a leading railway contractor. After schooling at Harrow he spent two years in a Lowestoft joinery workshop before being articled to a London architectural practice. In 1876 he set up in partnership with Ernest George. Peto became increasingly interested in what he deemed to be the architect's complete *oeuvre*: exterior, interior and garden.

As his architectural interests were mainly classical and traditional, based on Renaissance Italy, the gardens of that period became the models for his extensive work. Such exercises in classicism might seem to have run counter to the considerable influence of Gertrude Jekyll and William Robinson, then in the heyday of their popularizing of the 'natural' or wild garden. Yet, such was the simplicity and logic underlying Peto's essentially architectural framework for his garden designs, that the results were greatly admired by Miss Jekyll, who included illustrations of various designs by Peto in her book, *Garden Ornament*. Inevitably, with such a background, Peto's garden schemes featured colonnades (usually of Ionic columns), terraces and statuary. His designs were never dominated by these architectural elements, however, for he was a plantsman of rare understanding and knowledge.

These qualities were seen in their most charming form in the garden he designed for himself at Iford Manor, near Bradford-on-Avon, in Wiltshire, a small stone manor-house, which he bought in 1899. The house lies in the deep valley of the River Frome below a well-timbered hillside. Here, Peto designed a garden of terraces, courtyards and colonnades. He also assembled his remarkable collection of garden ornaments, including a beautiful eighteenth-century pavilion which housed Greek, Roman and medieval French sculpture. This evocation of an Italian Renaissance garden seemed as natural to the English West Country as it would be in the Italian *campagna*.

Peto's practice as a designer was wide-ranging and eclectic. At Easton Lodge in Essex he was responsible for the revival of interest in the once-popular use of *treillage*, and at Buscot Park in Oxfordshire he designed the beautiful water-garden. He was also responsible for the remarkable garden design on Garinish Island, Glengariff, Ireland, now owned by the Commissioners of Public Works. His advice on garden design was greatly in demand, both in this country and abroad, and he designed several gardens on the French Riviera.

*Harold Ainsworth **Peto** (1854–1933).*

*Arched treillage at Easton Lodge, Essex, designed by Harold Ainsworth **Peto** (1854–1933).*

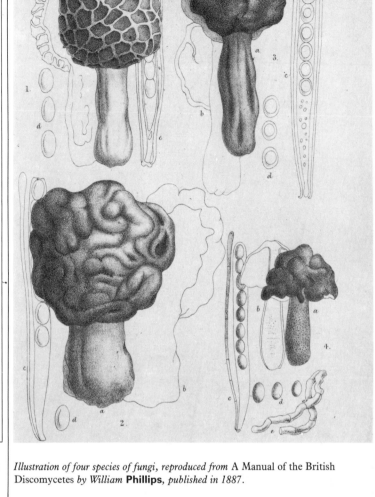

FLORA HISTORICA:

OR THE

THREE SEASONS

OF

THE BRITISH PARTERRE

HISTORICALLY AND BOTANICALLY TREATED;

WITH

OBSERVATIONS ON PLANTING,

TO SECURE A REGULAR SUCCESSION OF FLOWERS, FROM THE COMMENCEMENT
OF SPRING TO THE END OF AUTUMN.

TO WHICH ARE ADDED,

THE MOST APPROVED METHODS OF CULTIVATING BULBOUS AND OTHER
PLANTS, AS PRACTISED BY THE MOST CELEBRATED FLORISTS
OF ENGLAND, HOLLAND, AND FRANCE.

BY HENRY PHILLIPS, F.H.S.

AUTHOR OF " POMARIUM BRITANNICUM," " HISTORY OF CULTIVATED
VEGETABLES," AND " SYLVA FLORIFERA."

——— " FLORIDA QUISQUAM
HIC SIBI SERTA LEGET NITIDIS NECTENDA CAPILLIS."

IN TWO VOLUMES.
VOL. I.

LONDON:

PRINTED FOR E. LLOYD AND SON, HARLEY-STREET;
AND ARCHIBALD CONSTABLE, AND CO. EDINBURGH.

MDCCCXXIV.

Title page of the first volume of Flora Historica: or the Three Seasons of the British Parterre *by Henry* **Phillips**.

Illustration of four species of fungi, reproduced from A Manual of the British Discomycetes *by William* **Phillips**, *published in 1887.*

Phillips, Henry (1779–1840). Horticultural writer. Phillips was born at Henfield in Sussex, but little is known of Phillips' early life, although he is said to have been a schoolmaster and to have lived in Bayswater in London and later in Brighton, where he died. He was a prolific writer on many aspects of gardening, and his books, directed towards the growing ranks of domestic gardeners, were extremely popular.

Phillips, William (1822–1905). Botanist. Born at Presteigne in Radnorshire, Wales, Phillips was one of ten children of a farmer. After early schooling locally, he was apprenticed to an elder brother, a tailor. He also joined the Shrewsbury volunteers, became a colour-sergeant and a renowned marksman. In his late thirties, he took up the serious study of botany and began to specialize in fungi. Within ten years he was a leading authority on cryptogams, contributing notes on rare British fungi to specialist publications. He was also an authority on ferns, on which subject he was a frequent contributor to the *Transactions* of the Shropshire Archaeological and Natural History Society (which he helped to found). In 1878, he pub-

lished a *Guide to the Botany of Shrewsbury*, and in 1887 published his most important work, *A Manual of the British Discomycetes*. A genus of fungi, *Phillipsia* commemorates his name.

Pitcairn, William, M.D. (1711–1791). Physician and botanist. Pitcairn, the eldest son of David Pitcairn, a Scottish minister, was born at Dysart in Fifeshire. He studied at the University of Leyden, but took his M.D. at Rheims. Thanks to family connexions he became private tutor to James, 6th Duke of Hamilton, was with him at Oxford and accompanied him on the Grand Tour in 1742. Pitcairn was also given the degree of M.D. by Oxford University at the opening of the Radcliffe Library in 1749. Soon after, he set up what was to prove a most successful practice in London, was elected a Fellow of the College of Physicians and, in 1752, was appointed Gulstonian lecturer. He was continuously President of the College between 1775 and 1785, as well as physician to St Bartholomew's Hospital for thirty years. Pitcairn lived first in Warwick Court in the City of London, later in the Treasurer's House at St Bartholomew's Hospital, but also had a

house, with a botanical garden of five acres, in what was then the rural area of Islington. As an enthusiastic botanist and plant-collector he was responsible, with Dr John Fothergill (qv), for commissioning Thomas Blaikie (qv), to collect alpine plants for them in the Swiss mountains. Blaikie's expedition in 1775 proved to be eminently successful

William **Pitcairn** (*1711–1791*), *physician and botanist.*

and he sent back to England over 400 packets of plants, specimens, seeds and cuttings.

Pitt, William, 1st Earl of Chatham (1708–1778). Politician, landscape gardener. Although William Pitt's greatest fame rests on his career as one of Britain's most illustrious Prime Ministers, he also has claim to figure in this DICTIONARY, for, in 1747, he bought the lease of the seventy-five-acre estate of South Lodge in Enfield Chase, Middlesex, where he immediately engaged in the major task of evolving what his friend, the Reverend Gilbert West, termed 'a little paradise opened in the wild'. As the property was already possessed of two lakes, one graced with a well-timbered island, rustic bridge and most of the other requirements demanded by practitioners of the Picturesque, he was able to begin his improvements on Nature almost immediately. His

(Opposite) Four views of the garden at Iford Manor, near Bradford-on-Avon, Wiltshire, designed for himself by Harold **Peto** *from 1899 onwards. It was laid out as a series of terraces with colonnades, sculpture and courtyards, reminiscent of an Italian Renaissance garden.*

226

*William **Pitt**, Earl of Chatham, (1708–1778), a successful landscapist as well as politician.*

*South Lodge, Enfield Chase, landscaped by William **Pitt**, Earl of Chatham, in the eighteenth century. The engraving, which dates from the early nineteenth century, shows mature specimen trees, presumably planted by Pitt.*

*Leonard **Plukenet** (1642–1706), physician, botanist and author of Phytographia (1691–2).*

skill as a landscape gardener was highly regarded by many contemporaries, and his work at South Park was equated with that of Shenstone, Hamilton and Lyttleton in their respective ideal 'landscapes'. Pitt was undoubtedly far too restless and avid for the political rough-and-tumble to be able to lead the kind of sequestered life needed for the complete cultivation and realization of an ideal landscape. Despite his acknowleged pleasure in designing and cultivating his sylvan retreat, William Pitt rarely stayed at South Lodge for more than a few days at a time, and after five years he decided to sell the estate.

Plukenet, Leonard (1642–1706). Botanist. Plukenet was educated at Westminster School and trained for a medical career, possibly at Cambridge but more probably abroad.

Certainly he began to practise as a physician in St Margaret Lane, Old Palace Yard, Westminster, where he established a small botanic garden. He also owned a small farm at Horn Hill in Hertfordshire.

Leonard Plukenet was the friend and regular correspondent of many other botanists, and published many botanical works at his own expense. In 1689, Queen Mary appointed him superintendent of the Royal Gardens at Hampton Court under the title of Royal Professor of Botany or the Queen's Botanist.

Plukenet was a prolific writer and his publications, mainly devoted to exotics, include *Phytographia* in four volumes (1691–6) and various books concerned with the cataloguing of his own herbarium, reputedly comprising some 8,000 plants. This herbarium was bequeathed to the

British Museum, which also preserves several of his manuscripts.

Pope, Alexander (1688–1744). Poet, satirist, landscape gardener. Pope was the son of a rich Roman Catholic linen-draper. Due to his religion and a severe illness when he was twelve, which left him crippled and stunted, he was educated privately. He spent much of his youth in the country showing rare precocity as student and poet. His *Pastorals* were published in 1709, and his *Essay on Criticism*, which appeared anonymously, two years later. Both publications attracted a good deal of attention amongst the *literati* of London and brought him the patronage of Steele and Addison of the *Spectator*, with the latter of whom he quarrelled bitterly, the first of many such feuds in his life.

As a result of the popularity of his

mock-heroic poem, *The Rape of The Lock* (1712–1725), and his profitable translations of the *Iliad* (1720–25) and the *Odyssey* (1725–26), Pope was enabled to take over the lease of a villa at Twickenham, where he began to indulge his passion for gardening. He brought to this interest a visual imagination of a high order; a profound understanding of the English countryside; a practical knowledge of horticultural matters; and a rare talent for poetic exposition. William Mason, in his poem *The English Garden*, has said that 'Bacon was the prophet, Millar the herald and Addison, Kent and Pope the champions of the true modern taste in gardening', the taste now generally known as The Picturesque. Certainty, Pope's championship was persistent, poetic and practical, for in his own small riverside garden at Twickenham he fol-

*Engraving showing the underground grotto-passageway designed by Alexander **Pope** (1688–1744) to link the lawn garden with the main garden which were separated by a public road. The walls were decorated with randomly-placed coloured stones.*

*Alexander **Pope** (1688–1744), poet, satirist and gardener.*

(Left) Contemporary engraving of Alexander **Pope's** *house at Twickenham, seen from the River Thames. The main garden was behind the house, reached by the underground grotto. (Right) Handsomely-rusticated and pedimented Pope's Seat commemorating the woodland landscape which was designed by the 1st Earl of Bathurst and Alexander Pope for the former's estate at Cirencester Park, Gloucestershire.*

lowed the precepts which had been introduced by Bridgeman and Kent at Rousham in Oxfordshire, where Pope was a regular visitor. Indeed, there is reason to suppose that Pope had a hand in the design of this highly influential garden.

Pope's views concerning garden design were clearly expressed both in his *Essay on Criticism*—'First follow Nature, At once the source and end and test of Art'—and in his vast correspondence with other keen gardeners, including Lord Bathurst, Charles Bridgeman (qv), Lord Burlington, Philip Miller (qv), compiler of *The Gardener's Dictionary*, Sir Richard Temple, later Lord Cobham of Stowe.

Although Pope's villa had a lawn which sloped down to the Thames, the garden which he began to design and embellish from 1720 until his death (with the help of his gardener John Serle, engaged in 1726) was separated from the villa by the Hampton Road. This area of some four acres was reached by an underground passage-way, which Pope transformed into a grotto, in which 'a thousand pointed rays glitter and are reflected' thanks to the walls being covered with rocks, shells and chips of glass. On emerging from the tunnel the visitor saw a Shell Temple, 'rought with shells, flints and iron-ore.' The garden was, literally, a landscape garden, echoing a typically Claudian scene, well-timbered but with walks and open areas.

The garden seems to have been about 200 yards long and somewhat under a hundred yards in width. A modest kitchen garden was planted along the south side with an adjacent vineyard, both being screened from the road by tall trees. The eye-catcher of the garden, terminating an axial walk, was an obelisk dedicated to the memory of Pope's mother.

According to Walpole, 'the passing through the gloom from the grotto to opening day; the retiring and again assembling shades; the dusky groves, the larger lawn, and the solemnity of the termination at the cypresses that led up to his mother's tomb, are managed with exquisite judgement.'

Pope, Clara (née Leigh) (c. 1768–1838). Botanical artist. Clara Leigh was the daughter of an artist, Jared Leigh, and at an early age married Francis Wheatley, the Royal Academician for whom she acted as a model, figuring in many of his most charming paintings. Two portraits of her were painted by Wheatley and engraved by Bartolozzi and Stainier. She was a highly competent artist and in 1796 began exhibiting at the Royal Academy, first miniatures and later rustic subjects. In 1801 she was widowed with four young daughters to support, but in 1807 she married Alexander Pope, a well-known actor and artist. In 1812 she began to submit flower paintings to the Royal Academy, which gained her a considerable reputation and which she exhibited annually from that time until her death. She illustrated Samuel Curtis's *Camellia* published in 1819 and made drawings for *Paeonia* published in 1812.

Prain, (Sir) David (1857–1944). Botanist. Prain was born at Fettercairn in Kincardineshire in Scotland. He was educated at Aberdeen Grammar School and Aberdeen University. After two years as a schoolmaster at

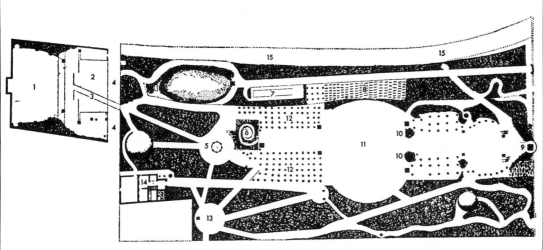

1 *Lawn between river and house* 2 *House* 3 *Underground grotto connecting lawn and main garden* 4 *Hampton Road* 5 *William Kent's Shell Temple* 6 *Large mound* 7 *Stoves* 8 *Vineyard* 9 *Obelisk* 10 *Small mounds* 11 *Bowling-green* 12 *Groves* 13 *Orangery* 14 *Garden house* 15 *Kitchen garden. The square symbols indicate urns and statues.*

(Left) John Serle's plan of 1745 showing Alexander **Pope's** *garden at Twickenham, begun some twenty-five years earlier. The miniature landscape was made in about four acres.*

Clara **Pope** *(c. 1768–1838) as depicted by her first husband, Francis Wheatley.*

Drawing by Clara **Pope** *for* A Monograph on the genus Camellia *(1819).*

Anne **Pratt** *(1806–1893).*

sale grocer of that town. Her youth was passed in Chatham, whence her father had removed, and she was educated at the Eastgate House School in Rochester. Due to her delicate health she spent most of her time in reading and writing and was encouraged by a local doctor to study botany. She quickly became proficient and knowledgeable in the subject and, thanks to the help of an elder sister who collected for her, she formed an extensive herbarium, making sketches of the specimens. These sketches afterwards formed the basis for the lithographs which embellished the series of copiously illustrated books which she wrote. The most important of these was *The Flowering Plants, Grasses, Sedges and Ferns of Great Britain*, published in 1855 in five volumes, written when she was living in Dover. She was also the author of several other books on subjects ranging from poisonous plants to ornithology. Although her books were written in a popular and unsophisticated style they were botanically accurate and helped to spread a knowledge of botany amongst a wide public. Their worth was recognized by a grant from the Civil List. In 1866 Anne Pratt married John Pearless of East Grinstead in Sussex.

Ramsgate in Kent, he returned to Scotland to study medicine at Aberdeen and Edinburgh Universities, gaining his M.B. in 1883. After several short-term academic appointments he entered the Indian Medical Service in 1884 and was attached to various native regiments. In 1887, he was appointed curator of the Herbarium and Library of the Royal Botanical Garden, Calcutta, becoming superin-

tendent in 1898 and also Director of Botanical Survey of India. In furtherance of the interests of the survey he undertook expeditions to Tibet and Burma as well as numerous journeys throughout India. He was also Professor of Botany at the Medical College of Calcutta from 1898 until 1905, in which year he was appointed Director of the Royal Botanic Gardens at Kew, remaining there until 1922. He was

a writer and editor of rare authority and industry. He edited the *Annals of the Royal Botanic Garden, Calcutta*, 1898–1904, and published the two-volume *Bengal Plants* in 1903 and edited the *Botanical Magazine* from 1907 until 1920.

Pratt, Anne (1806–1893). Botanist and author. Anne Pratt was born in Strood in Kent, the second of three daughters of Robert Pratt, a whole-

Price, (Sir) Uvedale, Bt (1747–1829). Essayist and landscape gardener. Price was a rich dilettante with literary ambitions and sufficient funds to be able to relate pen to practice as a landscape designer on his own estate at Foxley in Herefordshire. He was one of the foremost protagonists for the theories of the Picturesque, which exercised the minds and energies of a number of cultivated landowners in the late eighteenth century. He was the neighbour of another wealthy squire with literary inclinations, Richard Payne Knight (qv), with whom he made numerous garden-exploring excursions throughout England.

Price, friend of Gainsborough and Reynolds, developed his theories at somewhat inordinate length in his *Essays on the Picturesque*, published in 1794. In this prolix dissertation, Price took issue with the precepts and practice of Kent, Brown and Repton on the basis that they were at variance with all the principles of landscape-painting. He compared, to their detriment, what he deemed the monotonous nature of the landscaped parklands evolved by Kent and Brown with the romantic grandeur of the canvases of Poussin, Claude and Salvador Rosa. Kent's work, indeed, was tetchily dismissed as 'uncommonly mean, contracted, and perverse'.

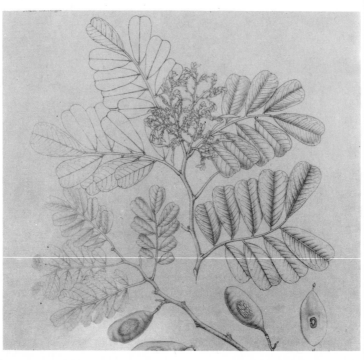

Sir David **Prain** *and (right) engraving of* Dalbergia congesta *reproduced from the volume on the* Species of Dalbergia of South East Asia *in the* Annals of the Royal Botanic Garden, Calcutta, *edited by Prain.*

(Opposite) Plates from the Flowering Plants, Grasses, Sedges and Ferns of Great Britain *by Anne* **Pratt** *(1855).*

*Uvedale **Price** (1747–1829) and (right) study of beech trees on Price's estate, at Foxley, Herefordshire, drawn by Gainsborough.*

*View of the gardens at Bodnant in Denbighshire, North Wales, whilst in the care of Charles **Puddle**.*

Much of the essay is devoted to a multiplicity of definition calculated to confuse anyone but a lexicographer. Picturesqueness, for example, 'appears to hold a station between beauty and sublimity, and on that account, perhaps, is more frequently and more happily blended with them than they are with each other'. Beauty is equated with smoothness and sublimity with roughness. And so on and on.

Price sought to capture something of these sublime effects in his own landscaped gardens which were evolved during the years of his friendship with his fellow-iconoclast, Payne Knight, author of a long-winded poem *The Landscape*, published in the same year as Price's *Essays*, and equally critical of Brown's landscapes. Gradually, however, the two neighbours fell out over their definitions of the Picturesque. Neighbourliness degenerated into a confrontation which Shelley likened to 'two ill-trained beagles snarling at each other when they could not catch the hare'. Knight ended his life an embittered man, reputedly poisoning himself.

Price, on the other hand, remained a buoyant and energetic extrovert.

Puddle family:

CHARLES PUDDLE (1917–   ). Horticulturist. Puddle was born at Scampston in Yorkshire during his father's time as gardener at Scampston Hall. He received his early training in the Manchester Corporation Parks Department before becoming a student at the Royal Botanic Gardens at Kew, where he remained until the outbreak of the Second World War.

Clipped hedges providing a backdrop for a seat and pair of statues at Bodnant, North Wales, tended by Charles **Puddle**.

William **Purdom** (*1880–1921*).

After military service, he joined his father at Bodnant and, on the latter's retirement, he became head gardener to Lord Aberconway and the National Trust, to which the greater part of the gardens were transferred in 1949. Puddle is also closely connected with the Royal Horticultural Society and received the Victoria Medal of Honour in 1962. For several years he acted as secretary to the International Camellia Society.

FREDERICK PUDDLE (c. 1877–1952). Horticulturist. Puddle was born at Sunninghill in Berkshire. He received his early horticultural training in the orchid nurseries of Sander of St Albans, later moving to Veitch's nursery in Chelsea. He then worked in the gardens of Hatfield House in Hertfordshire and later at Scampston Hall, near Malton in Yorkshire, where he remained for some twenty years. Soon after the First World War he was appointed head gardener to Lord Aberconway (qv), taking control of the renowned gardens at Bodnant in Denbighshire, North Wales, remaining there until his retirement almost thirty years later. Whilst at Bodnant he specialized in the cultivation of rhododendrons, but also bred orchids, *Clivias* and *Hippeastrums* with considerable success. Puddle was closely connected with the Royal Horticultural Society, receiving the Victoria Medal of Honour in 1937.

Purdom, William (1880–1921). Plant-collector. Purdom was born at Heversham in Westmorland and after training locally and at the renowned nurseries of James Veitch and Sons, he joined Kew in 1902, where he gained some reputation as a propagator and grower of hardwooded plants, later transferring to the Arboretum Nurseries. He left Kew in 1908 to undertake his first plant-collecting expedition to China in the following year. During this extended expedition he visited Inner Mongolia, Shansi, Kansu and the Tibetan borderland. In 1914 Purdom was elected as a Fellow of the Royal Geographical Society and in the same year set off to China once again as travelling companion and aide to the wealthy plant-collector Reginald Farrer (qv), who recorded their adventures in his book *On the Eaves of the World*, which was dedicated to William Purdom as 'an absolutely perfect friend and helper'. This Chinese expedition sent back rich collections of plants, many of which now have a permanent place in British gardens.

In 1915 Purdom was appointed to the Chinese Government Forestry Commission, and was employed in planning railway forestry. In pursuance of these schemes Purdom spent most of the last five years of his life living in a railway car in remote areas. Purdom had much success to show in his tremendous task despite lack of funds, changes of government and limited facilities. He died in the French Hospital in Peking, as a result of a breakdown, attributed to hardship and exposure during his arduous work in the Chinese interior, and following a comparatively minor operation.

Early-morning start during the Himalayan plant-hunting expedition of William **Purdom** *and Reginald Farrer.*

*(Left) Sir Thomas Stamford **Raffles** (1781–1826), colonial governor and patron of Chinese flower-painters, and (right) contemporary engraving showing Suffolk House, Penang, which was visited by Raffles in 1810.*

*Government House, Benculen, an official residence of Sir Thomas Stamford **Raffles** when colonial governor.*

Raffles, (Sir) Thomas Stamford (1781–1826). Colonial governor, patron. Raffles was the son of a captain in the West Indies trade and was born at sea. He was educated at a school in Hammersmith but left at an early age to join the East India Company as a clerk. He was a diligent employee and an assiduous scholar out of office hours, acquiring a sound knowledge of French. In 1805 he was sent to Penang and with his talent for languages became fluent in Malay. He was appointed secretary to the governor in 1807. Thanks to his friendship with Dr John Leyden, doctor and orientalist, he was brought to the notice of Lord Minto, who relied greatly upon Raffles' advice in the British seizure of Malacca, Batavia and Java, of which island Raffles was made lieutenant-governor in 1811. He proved himself an able, farsighted and energetic administrator, despite continuing ill-health. On the restoration of Java to the Dutch in 1816, Raffles returned to England where he wrote his *History of Java*. This was published in the following year, when he was appointed Governor of Benculen in Sumatra. These ceaseless travels about the islands enabled him to combine his botanical and philological interests with his administrative duties. On one of his journeys he discovered the enormous flowering fungus, *Rafflesia Arnoldi*, named after him. Fearful of Dutch determination to extend their possessions in the Far East, the British government appointed Raffles to begin the development of Singapore as a British base, an island already selected by Raffles as a dominant point in the control of Far Eastern politics. Raffles took over in 1819. During his tenure Raffles also discovered the *Nepenthes Rafflesiana*. Despite his ever-increasing official duties, Raffles continued to supervise his anthropological, zoological and botanical collections. In furtherance of this last interest, he commissioned native artists to make records of indigenous flowers and plants. Over 2,000 of these drawings were lost in a fire at sea in 1824, as well as his maps and records prepared for his projected history of Sumatra and Borneo. He returned to England in the same year and retired to a house at Barnet and founded the Zoological Society of which he was the first president. He died in 1826. Thousands of botanical drawings deriving from Raffles' patronage are now housed in the India Office Library.

Ray, (Reverend) John (1627–1705). Botanist. Ray was the son of a blacksmith and was born at Black Notley in Essex. Thanks to the patronage of the Vicar of Braintree, a nearby town, Ray was enabled to study at Cambridge University, entering Trinity College in 1644. Five years later he was elected a Fellow, and Tutor in 1653. In 1660 he was ordained in Lincoln Cathedral, having, in the intervening years, served in a succession of academic posts at Cambridge. Indeed, he seemed destined for a lifetime of modest

*(Opposite) Watercolours of oriental flora commissioned by Sir Thomas Stamford **Raffles** while colonial governor in the Far East and carried out by Chinese artists. (Above) Durio Zibethinus Murray (Bombacaceae), Durian Tree; (below) Anacardium occidentale (Anacardiaceae), cashew nut tree.*

234

South Front, with east front in perspective. an Elevation a little richer.

Scene, near the Temple, with a hint of the house on the Site proposed. distant about 3/4 of a Mile.

Sketch by **Repton** *for alterations to Woburn, Bedfordshire.*

Bath House at Corsham, embellished by **Repton** *and J. Nash.*

Sir John **Richardson** *(1787–1865).*

Drawing by Humphry **Repton**, *showing proposed alterations to the park at Longleat, Wiltshire, originally planned by Brown.*

The view (above) from Endsleigh House on the river Tamar in Devon, and (below) proposed improvements to the landscape by Humphry **Repton**, *reproduced from his* Fragments on the Theory and Practice of Landscape Gardening *(1803).*

gave him a unique and fashionable standing. His method of presenting his proposed schemes was by means of the now-famous Red Books, in which watercolours showing 'before' and 'after' versions of his plans (frequently with movable flaps) were augmented by manuscript recommendations. Drawings and text were bound together as a slim and persuasive volume in red morocco leather and presented to the flattered would-be patron. The Red Books are now collectors' items and on the rare occasions that they appear in the auction rooms they command formidable bids.

Repton generally followed the theories advocated by 'Capability' Brown, and it has been well said that he took over at the point where Brown left off. Yet his schemes were rarely as extensive as those planned by Brown. He favoured rather more abundant plantations and recommended a noticeably greater variety in the selection of trees and shrubs than his mentor. He also favoured terraces and balustraded walks. He was undoubtedly influenced by the theories of the Picturesque movement, although he later fell out with Richard Payne Knight (qv), following sharp criticisms in *The Landscape* published by Knight in 1803.

Repton also established an impressive reputation as an architect in his own right after first working with William Wilkins, and, from 1796 until 1800, with John Nash. His most notable architectural achievements were at Welbeck Abbey, where he was responsible for remodelling the east and west fronts, and at Sheringham Hall in Norfolk, where his designs for both house and garden were carried out almost to the letter. House and

Setting up camp in Canada, during the expedition on which Sir John **Richardson** *was doctor and botanist, sketched by G. Back.*

Henry Nicholas **Ridley** *(1855–1956).*

garden survive as lasting testimony to Repton's skills as both landscape designer and architect.

In 1811 Repton was involved in a carriage accident which made him something of an invalid for the remaining seven years of his life. He was buried at Aylsham in Norfolk. His practice was continued by his eldest son, John Adey Repton (1775–1860), a pupil of William Wilkins, who had collaborated with his father in 'the architectural department'. J. A. Repton was a skilful draughtsman, a cultivated gothicist but something of a recluse, owing to early deafness.

Richardson, (Sir) John (1787–1865). Naturalist and plant-collector. Richardson was born at Nith Place, Dumfries, Scotland, the eldest of the twelve children of a JP and provost of that city. He was educated at the local grammar school and at Edinburgh University where he studied medicine. After various junior medical appointments he qualified as a member of the Royal College of Surgeons and was appointed, in 1807, assistant surgeon to the frigate *Nymphe*, which was at the bombardment of Copenhagen. As surgeon in other men o' war, he was involved over several years in an adventurous and wide-ranging active service career in the Atlantic and the Mediterranean. After some years afloat he retired on half pay in order to return to Edinburgh University to further his medical studies and the study of botany and mineralogy. After marriage and practising, without notable success, as a physician in Leith, Richardson joined Sir John Franklin's polar expedition as surgeon, naturalist and botanist. As a result

of this appointment, he met Sir Joseph Banks (qv). The expedition covered vast areas of northern Canada, as well as the arctic regions. Richardson's *Journal* of the explorations, published in 1851, has been described as 'a model of a journal by a scientific traveller'.

On account of his age, he was disappointed in his wish to be appointed medical director-general of the navy. He therefore retired to Grasmere in Westmorland, and spent the rest of his long and energetic life in literary and scientific work, finding time also to act as beneficent physician to the local poor, a magistrate and an assiduous gardener. He also continued to travel widely in Europe, visiting art galleries. On the death of his first wife he married a niece of Sir John Franklin, by whom he had four sons and two daughters. His second wife died in 1845, he married again in 1847. He was elected FRS in 1825, was knighted in 1846 and received the Society's Gold Medal in 1856.

Richardson, Richard (1663–1741). Botanist, gardener. Richardson was born at North Bierley in Yorkshire, the elder son of a Yorkshire landowner, and was educated at Bradford Grammar School and University College, Oxford, and afterwards studied law at Gray's Inn. He then switched his interests to botany at Leyden University in Holland, studying under the eminent Professor Paul Hermann, but on his return to England began to practise as a doctor, mainly gratuitously, although botany remained his predominant interest. As a man of ample means he was able to travel widely in search of botanical specimens, and he also acted as patron

towards less materially privileged botanists. He also corresponded with numerous foreign botanists. His own garden on the family estates in Yorkshire was considered to be the most interesting garden in the North of England, being unusually well-stocked with native and exotic plants, and he was reputed to have built the second hot-house constructed in England. He also formed an unusually comprehensive botanical library, and contributed articles on botany and arborology to various scientific journals. His correspondence is amongst the Sloane manuscripts in the British Museum and documents in the Royal Society. He has been ranked with James Sherard (qv) in importance in the enlargement of the listing of native British plants and in establishing their natural habitats.

Ridley, Henry Ninholas (1855–1956). Botanist. Ridley was the son of a clergyman and was born at West Harling in Norfolk. He was educated at Haileybury and Exeter College, Oxford, where he studied science and was awarded a geological scholarship. After graduation he was appointed to the Botanical Department of the British Museum, and spent much of his leisure in the study of British flora and in plant-collecting in Norway and Switzerland. In 1887 he accompanied a small expedition to the Brazilian island of Fernando de Noronha to investigate the local flora, fauna and mineralogy.

In 1888 he was appointed Director of Gardens and Forests in the Straits Settlements. From his HQ in Singapore he made numerous expeditions throughout Malaya as well as visiting the Indonesian and the

Cocos Islands, sending back some 2,000 herbarium specimens a year to Kew. He also established a herbarium in Singapore, which quickly became recognized as one of the most richly endowed institutions of its kind.

Ridley's most notable botanical achievement was his discovery of a method of tapping the Para rubber tree, an event which, allied to his persuasive proselytizing amongst the planters, led directly to the foundation of the vast rubber industry in the East.

He retired officially in 1912, but continued to make further expeditions to the tropics, ultimately raising the total of his herbarium to 50,000 specimens. He also wrote prolifically on his subjects. Amongst his publications were *Spices* (1912); the five volumes of *The Flora of the Malay Peninsula* (1922–25); *Dispersal of Plants throughout the World* (1930). He received many honours and awards in Britain and abroad and the name *Ridleyella* was given to a genus of orchids. He was elected FRS in 1907.

Robinson, William (1838–1935). Landscape gardener, editor, writer. Although Robinson was born and spent his first twenty-two years in Ireland, his main career and influence were in England. Despite his later fame and prolific writings little is known of his childhood, for he remained extremely sensitive concerning his humble origins. He was probably born of Protestant parents either in Co. Leix or Co. Dublin, and was, presumably, educated at the local parish school. He was then apprenticed as a garden-boy to the Reverend Sir Hunt Henry-John Walsh, a clerical baronet and Vicar

*Upper part of the water-garden landscaped by William **Robinson** at Gravetye Manor, near East Grinstead, Sussex, seen in an engraving based on a photograph taken in August 1896 by Sir Henry Thompson and reproduced in Robinson's book on* The Flower Garden.

*William **Robinson** (1838–1935), from an etching by Francis Dodd.*

*Engraved bookplate of William **Robinson** from* Gravetye Manor, or Twenty Years' Work Round an Old Manor House *(1911).*

of Stradbally, Co. Kerry. By the time he was twenty-one Robinson was in charge of the gardens, with control over a wide range of conservatories and hot-houses. Two years later, as the result of a violent quarrel with his employer, he decided to leave for Dublin.

Robinson went to the Royal Botanic Gardens at Glasnevin to work for the Director, Dr David Moore (qv), who later recommended the young gardener to Robert Marnock, curator of the Royal Botanic Gardens in Regent's Park. Robinson was engaged at a wage of nine shillings a week to look after hardy herbaceous plants.

These tasks first engendered in Robinson that love of wild English flowers which was to be the enduring passion of his life and they also first prompted his lifelong friendship with the curator. Marnock, indeed, sponsored Robinson's election – at the age of twenty-nine – as a

Fellow of the Linnean Society. Around this time Robinson left the Botanic Gardens to become horticultural correspondent to *The Times*, which he represented at the Paris Exhibition of 1867, and also representative of the famous firm of nurserymen, Veitch.

Robinson now entered upon the most productive and congenial tasks of his long life, for he was a natural reporter and writer. In 1868 he published his first book, *Gleanings from French Gardens*, followed by *Parks, Promenades and Gardens of Paris* and, after a walking tour of Switzerland, *Alpine Flowers for English Gardens*, published in 1870. This was a crowded year for him, for he also made his first visit to the United States, and published his widely influential book, *The Wild Garden*, his first plea for the planting of indigenous wild flowers in the garden in a natural state.

In the following year Robinson

founded *The Garden*, a weekly paper that, after initial setbacks, became a resounding success. He also founded a sister-magazine, *Gardening Illustrated*, in 1879. Both publications appealed to the great new army of suburban householders who were also enthusiastic gardeners.

In 1883 he published his most successful book, *The English Flower Garden*, which describes the most practical methods of cultivation of plants and how to place them most effectively in the garden. The revision of successive editions of this book was one of the major pleasures throughout the rest of his life.

Meantime, thanks to the success of his various publications and shrewd investments in London property, he had become a rich man. His wealth enabled him to buy, in 1884, the 200-acre estate of Gravetye Manor in Sussex, where he spent the rest of his long life,

improving both house and garden, writing his books, editing his magazines, and advising on other people's gardens. His advice in these matters was of the most practical order. He deprecated all paper plans and marked out his intentions on the site, insisting that each element in the composition must be governed by the configuration of the land, with existing trees, plants and buildings given their rightful place in the plan. That a garden should 'grow out of its site', and that a plan of a garden could be made only *after* its evolution and not *before*, were two of his firmest dicta.

One of the most successful gardens designed to his theories was that at Shrublands, near Ipswich in Suffolk, for Lord de Saumarez. Acres of bedded-out plants were replaced by lawns and simplified borders. Apart from Gravetye, this notable garden became the most resplendent example of his passionate advocacy for the wild garden.

Around this time his unusual and fruitful friendship with Gertrude Jekyll (qv) was also begun. He had first met her in 1875, and later advised on the planting of her new garden at her cottage at Munstead Wood in Surrey. The friendship flourished and in 1899 she took over the editorship of *The Garden* for two or three years.

Yet Robinson could not keep away from editing for long. Four years later, he started the most formidably ambitious of his periodi-

*(Opposite) Open vistas to and from the house at Antony, in Cornwall, where the park was originally landscaped and planted by Humphry **Repton** for R. Pole Carew, c. 1793–1803. (Antony, which is open to the public, now belongs to the National Trust.)*

*Four generations of Thomas **Rochford** of the world-famous firm of the same name, specializing in indoor pot plants: (from left) Tom I, II, III, and IV.*

cals, a monthly publication called *Flora and Sylva*, which was produced in a pretentious and expensive format ill-suited to its intended market. After two years the magazine was discontinued.

Robinson's activities at Gravetye Manor resulted in two unusual books. In 1911 he published a sumptuous volume on *Gravetye Manor, or Twenty Years' Work Round an Old Manor House* and, three years later, a successor, *Home Landscapes*, showing handsome pictures of the results he had achieved in Sussex, both books underlining the scale on which he planned and worked.

In character, Robinson was as contradictory in behaviour as in his gardening. He deprecated the formal garden yet in some ways fostered one at Gravetye. He fought local villagers over rights of way yet was influenced by William Morris's 'Olde England'.

Robinson caused a revolution in English gardening design and practice, yet he was essentially conservative in his way of life.

Much of what he fought for is now attributed to his protégée, Gertrude

Jekyll, but, at all times, Robinson was the true originator and propagandist.

He died, unmarried, his misanthropy allegedly deriving from an ill-fated romance in his early days in London.

Rochford family:

MICHAEL ROCHFORD (c. 1819–1883). Gardener, nurseryman. Rochford was born at Clandulla, Co. Clare, Ireland, the son of a local smallholder. He left Ireland for England in 1840. By 1848, the year of his marriage, he was working for Lord Nugent at Weedon, near Aylesbury, Buckinghamshire. In 1852, he left for Helmsley in Yorkshire, to become head gardener to Lord Feversham who, on buying the Oak Hill estate at East Barnet in 1856, appointed Rochford in charge. In 1857, Rochford bought a 2-acre market-garden in Tottenham and set up on his own. By 1861 he was employing five men and a boy.

THOMAS ROCHFORD (1849–1901). One of the five sons of the above. At the age of twenty-seven, after hav-

ing trained in his father's nursery, he joined the well-known nursery of James Sweet at Leyton. In the following year he set up his own nursery in Tottenham, near his parents but, due to the expansion of London, he decided to take over Turnford Hall, with 3 acres of garden, in the Lea Valley and there established the world-famous firm specializing in pot plants. By 1896 he had 22 acres under glass and had built thirty-nine houses for his considerable number of employees.

THOMAS ROCHFORD (1877–1918). Known as Tom II, he continued the business until his death at the early age of forty-one. He was succeeded in turn by:

THOMAS ROCHFORD (1904–). Known as Tom III. After schooling at Ampleford, he began to learn the business in 1922, being appointed a director five years later. Under his direction, the firm has expanded to become the largest business of its kind in the world. In 1969, he was awarded the RHS Victoria Medal of Honour. The firm has been awarded the Laurence Medal at the Chelsea

show twice in recent years, apart from many other awards. The family tradition is continued in the person of THOMAS ROCHFORD (1947–), known as Tom IV.

Rohde, Eleanour Sinclair (1880–1948). Gardener and gardening historian. Eleanour Rohde was born in India, the daughter of the agent to the Maharajah of Dravancore and Cochin. She was educated at Cheltenham Ladies' College and Oxford University and then became private secretary to Lord Curzon. She moved to her parents' home, Cranham Lodge, at Reigate in Surrey, where she made an unusual garden based mainly on uncommon herbs and vegetables. She also designed a herb garden for Lullingstone Castle in Kent. She wrote many books on historical aspects of gardening including *Oxford College Gardens* and *Old English Gardening Books*.

Romaine-Walker, William Henry (1854–1940). Architect. Romaine-Walker was educated at Lancing College, a contemporary of the architect George Street. In 1900, he set up an architectural practice with

*Eleanour Sinclair **Rohde** (1880–1948), garden historian.*

*Architectural elements in the formal garden at Luton Hoo, Bedfordshire, designed by William Henry **Romaine-Walker**.*

*Lanning **Roper** (1912–), garden designer and writer.*

*William **Roscoe** (1753–1831).*

Frances Besant, specializing in the alteration and decoration of grand town and country houses. His many commissions included work at Medmenham Abbey in Berkshire and at Chatsworth in Derbyshire. Romaine-Walker was also profoundly interested in the design of gardens and estate buildings, one of his most successful schemes being the terrace at Luton Hoo in Bedfordshire.

Roper, Lanning (1912–). Landscape gardener. Although born and educated in the United States, Roper has spent almost all his working life in England. Having left Harvard, where he took a degree in Fine Arts, he abandoned an intention to study landscape architecture and, after teaching and war service, came to England and studied at Kew and the Royal Botanic Gardens, Edinburgh, becoming assistant to the editor of the Royal Horticultural Society journal in 1951. From 1951–1975 he was garden correspondent to *The Sunday Times*. He is responsible to the National Trust for various gardens, such as Chartwell and Scotney Castle in Kent. He has designed many gardens including those for H. H. The Aga Khan at Chantilly and the New Art Buildings at Trinity College, Dublin. His publications include: *Town Gardening* (1957) and *The Gardens in the Royal Parks at Windsor* (1961).

Roscoe, William (1753–1831). Botanist. In a long life, Roscoe managed to combine banking, gardening, writing and politics in a career of rare diversity. Roscoe was born at Mount Pleasant, near Liverpool, the son of a market gardener who also owned a tavern and bowling-green. Roscoe was articled to a Liverpool attorney, studying Latin and Italian in his spare time. In 1773 he was one of the founders of the Liverpool Society for the Encouragement of the Arts, and in the following year was admitted as an attorney of the Court of the King's Bench. He pub-

lished studies on Italian religion and literature. In 1790, he was induced to become partner in a Liverpool banking house and took up the study of botany and was mainly responsible, with Sir James Edward Smith (qv), the eminent botanist, for founding the Liverpool Botanic Garden in 1802. He contributed various papers to the Proceedings of the Linnean Society of which he was elected a Fellow in 1805. He was also interested in agriculture and was involved in the reclamation of Chat Moss, near Manchester. He was elected MP for Liverpool in 1806 and was forceful in his advocacy for the abolition of slavery.

After various banking vicissitudes and the forced sale of his books and paintings, Roscoe spent the last years of his life at his house at Toxteth Park, Liverpool.

Rose, John (c. 1621–1677). Horticulturist, gardener. Little is known of Rose's young life, but he was apparently sent by the Earl of Essex to study under Le Nôtre, the great French gardener, then working at Versailles. On his return he was appointed 'Keeper of the Garden of Essex House, Strand', a position he relinquished on being appointed by Charles II as 'Keeper of St James's Garden'. In this position he employed both London and Wise (qv) as assistants. Rose specialized in the design of gardens in the formal manner. He is best known through the painting by Danckerts, usually entitled 'Rose, the Royal Gardener, Presenting the First Pine-Apple Raised in England to Charles II'. With the help of John Evelyn (qv), Rose published *The English Vineyard Vindicated* (1666) and *A Treasure Upon Fruit Trees* (1688).

Rothschild family:

English landscape gardening owes much to the influence of members of this wealthy, worldly family, particularly during the Victorian and Edwardian eras. The family's initial gardening interests were epitomized in the activities of:

BARON FERDINAND JAMES DE ROTHSCHILD (1839–1898). He settled in England in 1860 and between 1874 and 1889 built Waddesdon Manor in Buckinghamshire, designed in the French Renaissance style by the French architect Gabriel-Hippolyte Destailleur, whilst the gardens were laid out by another Frenchman, the landscape gardener, Laine. On the baron's death, Waddesdon passed to his sister; thence, in 1922, to James de Rothschild, son of Baron Edmund de Rothschild. When he died, in 1957, he bequeathed the house, gardens and its remarkable collections to the National Trust.

*Hillbarn, Wiltshire, planted by Lanning **Roper**, showing close-clipped, symmetrically-planted yews in a framework of low brick walls.*

Trees trained on an enfilade *of arches at Hillbarn, planted by Lanning **Roper**.*

*Detail of the painting by Danckerts showing John **Rose** presenting Charles II with the first pineapple raised in England.*

*Alfred de **Rothschild** (1842–1918) and (right) Halton, his chateau-like seat in Buckinghamshire, showing the domed winter-garden at right.*

*Leopold de **Rothschild** (1845–1917) and (right) circular beds and connecting paths in part of the formal garden at Ascott, his seat at Wing, Buckinghamshire.*

ALFRED DE ROTHSCHILD (1842–1918). In 1847 he took over Halton, a mansion in Buckinghamshire, and set about gardening in the grand manner, with fifty glass-houses and a garden staff of sixty. His great mansion incorporated a magnificent winter-garden crowned by two large and nine smaller cupolas.

LEOPOLD DE ROTHSCHILD (1845–1917). Although the owner of four town and country mansions, Leopold's main gardening interests were concentrated at Gunnersbury House at Acton, which was one of the show places of the country, renowned especially for fruits of all kinds. For the Royal Horticultural Society Exhibition of 1912, held on the grounds of the Royal Hospital, Chelsea, twenty vans were required to transport the Rothschild display of fruit trees which occupied almost

(Opposite) Herbaceous border at Gravetye Manor, Sussex, the one-time home of William **Robinson**. (The house is now a country club and hotel.)

1,400 square feet of the exhibition display space.

He also owned Ascott, at Wing, in Buckinghamshire, which he took over as a hunting-box with thirty acres of garden laid out under the direction of Sir Harry Veitch (qv), the Chelsea nurseryman, and the gardens remain as an outstanding example of the landscaping and horticultural interests of the period.

LIONEL WALTER ROTHSCHILD (2nd Baron) (1868–1937). Naturalist and landscape gardener. Rothschild a member of the banking family, established a magnificent garden at his seat at Tring Park, in Hertfordshire, and a notable zoological museum which housed over a quarter of a million birds (later sold to the New York Museum of Natural History). The house is now a college.

LIONEL NATHAN DE ROTHSCHILD (1882–1942). Landscape designer, botanist, horticulturist. Rothschild was the son of Leopold de Rothschild, the head of the banking firm

in England and a leading racehorse owner. The young Rothschild took an early interest in botanical studies and at the age of five was given a small garden on the family estate.

He was educated at Harrow and Trinity College, Cambridge, afterwards joining the family banking business. When he was thirty he married Marie Louise Beer, a descendant of Meyerbeer, and bought the modest estate of Inchmery, at the mouth of the Beaulieu River in Hampshire, which became their weekend retreat. During the First War, Rothschild, although a major in the Buckinghamshire Yeomanry was, much against his will, kept in Britain, his international banking experience being deemed essential to the allied cause. In 1917 his father died and he became head of the great banking house. At the end of the war he bought the nearby Exbury, an estate of 2,600 acres, and immediately set about transforming the gardens. He enlarged the house to provide a spacious latterday neo-classic mansion, but well before the house was finished Rothschild had

*Lionel de **Rothschild** (1882–1942).*

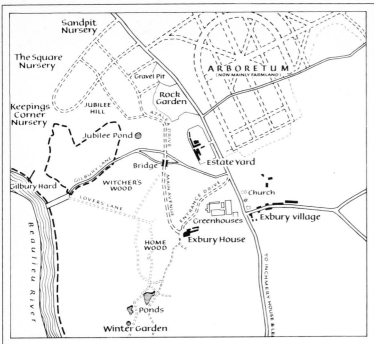

Plan of the gardens at Exbury, Hampshire, and (right) Edmund de **Rothschild** *(1916–).*

Exbury House, Hampshire, the home of Edmund de **Rothschild**, *and (below) rustic bridge in the woodland garden.*

had cleared over 200 acres for his new gardens. Needless to say, this project entailed an intensive use of man-power: a staff of sixty trained gardeners was employed in the woodlands, fifteen in the greenhouses, apart from a labour force of 150 men, known as 'the trenching team', which worked on various sites in the grounds in pursuance of Rothschild's grand plan for redevelopment. New houses for the regular staff were built in Exbury, ponds drained, woodlands cleared and two acres of greenhouses erected. Rothschild then began that cultivation of rhododendrons which was to make him and Exbury world-famous amongst horticulturists. To a collection of wild species he added his own flowering hybrids as well as new varieties raised by himself. Apart from the 250 acres devoted to rhododendrons, he also planted an arboretum, aided by the expertise of W. J. Bean (qv), curator of Kew Gardens and author of *Trees & Shrubs Hardy in the British Isles*. In this aboretum Rothschild aimed to plant every tree known to be hardy in England. He was also a notable cultivator of shrubs, including large plantations of cotoneasters, viburnums and hydrangeas. He also developed a Winter Garden, stretching down to the Beaulieu River. Here were planted further numbers of rhododendrons of his own raising.

Apart from rhododendrons (for which, in addition to other conventional greenhouses, he also built a special greenhouse suitable for growing small Javanese rhododendrons) Lionel Rothschild was an enthusiastic collector of many types of trees and shrubs. He was also a successful flower-grower, with a special interest in daffodils, primroses, bluebells, cyclamen, particularly in the Exbury woodlands. He became almost as famous for his orchids as for his rhododendrons, raising many new hybrids.

EDMUND DE ROTHSCHILD (1916–). After Harrow and Trinity College, Cambridge, Rothschild joined the family banking firm and also directed the post-war revival of the Exbury Gardens, which have been substantially reduced in size but redeveloped commercially so that they are now internationally renowned as one of Europe's leading nurseries, with an established and growing home market, especially for camellias, and sizable exports of rhododendrons and azaleas to the USA, Australia and Canada.

Roxburgh, William (1751–1815). Botanist. Roxburgh was born at Craigie in Ayrshire, Scotland, and studied medicine at the University of Edinburgh, becoming a surgeonmate in one of the East India Company's ships. After several voyages he joined the Company's Establishment in Madras in 1776. There he met the famous Danish botanist, Dr Gerhard Koenig, pupil of Linnaeus, and then in the service of the Nawab of Arcot. The two men became friends and combined in plant-hunting expeditions and research, until Koenig's death in 1785.

Between 1791 and 1794 Roxburgh sent over 500 plants to London, 300 of which were published in the three-volume *The Plants of the Coast of Coromandel*, the first volume of which was published in 1795 and the third and final volume posthumously in 1819. In 1793 Roxburgh was appointed Superintendent and Chief Botanist of the Calcutta Botanic Garden, succeeding Colonel Robert Kyd, the founder and first superintendent.

Roxburgh then set about building himself a house within the garden, but, due to ill-health (his 'constitution impaired by hard botanical work in the feverish jungles of the Carnatic', as his obituary recorded), he returned to England in 1797. After a stay of two years he returned to Calcutta, but, ill-health continuing, he was again in London in 1805, living in Chelsea for three years. After a final return to Calcutta and a further breakdown he took passage to the Cape of Good Hope, but continued homeward and died in Edinburgh in 1815. His book *Hortus Bengalensis* was published in 1814, and *Flora Indica*, in two volumes, posthumously between 1820–24. He also left over 2,500 coloured drawings made by himself, and now at Kew.

Royle, John Forbes (1798–1858). Naturalist and botanist. Royle was born at Cawnpore, in India, and studied medicine at Edinburgh University. At the age of twenty-one he joined the medical staff of the Bengal Army, but four years later was appointed superintendant of the East India Company's two hospitals at Saharunpur, in the Punjab, which also included supervision of the company's botanical garden.

This arduous dual task left little time for plant-hunting on his own account, but he trained natives to travel to Kashmir to collect plants for the garden. These were then drawn by the native draughtsman, Vishnuperasud, seconded to Royle by Dr Nathaniel Wallich (qv), head of the Calcutta Botanic Garden. The results of these activities was the sumptuous two-volume *Illustrations of the Botany and other Branches of the Natural History of the Himalayan Mountains*, published between 1833 and 1840, after Royle returned to London. He was also responsible for recommending the suitability of parts of the Himalayas for the cultivation of the Chinese tea-plant.

On his return to Europe, still a comparatively young man, Royle

William **Roxburgh** *(1751–1815).*

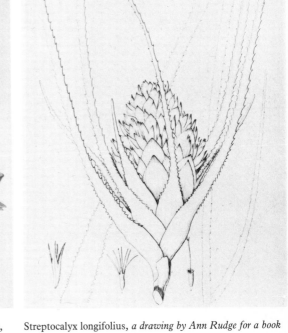

James **Russell** *and (right) Sunningdale catalogue cover when under his direction.*

Cotton-plants, a drawing commissioned from the Indian artist, Vishnupersud, by Dr John **Royle***.*

Streptocalyx longifolius, a drawing by Ann Rudge for a book by her husband, Edward **Rudge***.*

furthered his medical studies at Munich. In 1837 he was appointed Professor of Materia Medica at King's College in London. Whilst still in that appointment he was elected secretary of the Horticultural Society without his knowledge. John Lindley (qv), the vice-secretary, most favoured for the post, was passed over doubtless due to his somewhat masterful and outspoken ways. Royle served the Society ably during a particularly arduous time of growing indebtedness, although, during his tenure of the post, the Society's *Journal* became a monthly publication.

Rudge, Edward (1763–1846). Botanist. Rudge was born at Evesham, in Worcestershire, and was known as an antiquarian and amateur botanist. He was elected FRS in 1805. His chief claim to fame is that he was a motivating member of a syndicate which brought a collection of plants collected in Guinea by the French naturalist, Joseph Martin. The plants had been captured by British privateers and the collection sold to provide prize money for the crews. In 1805 Rudge began what was projected as a serial publication of *Plantarum Guineanae Rariorum*, but only the first volume was completed,

with illustrations made by his wife, Ann.

Russell, James Philip Cuming (1920–). Horticulturist, landscape gardener. Russell was educated at Eton and intended for an army career but decided instead to study botany at Cambridge, having been fascinated by plants from an early age. (He had even attempted the cultivation of onocyclus iris in his Eton window-box.) He spent the year following this decision in travelling in Europe, becoming greatly influenced by the historic Italian gardens, notably at Villa

Sander family group, photographed at Bruges in the eighteen-nineties. Behind Sander père *are (left to right): Fred, Fearnley and Louis. Seated at right is William Watson, then curator of the Royal Botanic Gardens, Kew.*

at Weimar, where he earned a high opinion from his employer for his intelligence and reliability. From Weimar he later moved to another nursery, but, whilst in his teens, decided to emigrate to England. He arrived, he later said, with only half a crown in his pocket. Making his way to London he got work in a nursery garden but soon afterwards moved to Carters, the well-known seed merchants, then at Forest Hill in South London. Here he met another German, Benedict Roezl, the famous botanist and plant-hunter. The meeting exercised a decisive influence on Sander's life, determining his life-long passion for orchids. Within a comparatively

short time he was corresponding on friendly terms with Professor Reichenbach, the foremost orchidist of the time.

Towards the end of the 1860s Sander moved to a nursery in St Mary Cray in Kent, and in 1870 married the daughter of a prosperous Kentish paper-maker. With the support of his wife, Sander took over the old-established seed business of Joslings of St Albans, then specializing in agricultural seeds. In 1860 he sent out Ralph Arnold to South America to collect plants and five years later had completely moved away from agricultural seeds to become exclusively devoted to the collecting, importing and selling of

orchid plants. Within a few years he was sponsoring over a score of expert orchid collectors throughout the world. His nurseries, with their enormous glass-houses, required their own railway siding. In the 1890s Sander established an offshoot of his St Albans firm on a large tract of land at Summit, New Jersey, outside New York, but in 1896, having set up a large orchid nursery at St André, near Bruges, sold the American subsidiary, concentrating all his efforts on his European interests.

Between 1886 and 1894, Sander produced his monumental *Reichenbachia*, an authoritative monograph on orchids and one of the most lav-

ish gardening books ever published, with drawings by Henry Moon (who married Sander's daughter, Dederika) reproduced by wood blocks and chromolithography, many of the plates needing twenty colour printings. All four volumes were printed in four languages. The project reputedly cost Sander over £7,000 (probably £150,000 by today's values), which he could ill-afford.

Such ambition and passion for orchids always meant that he was dangerously over-stretched financially, especially in his commitments to his plant-collectors. His Bruges nurseries prospered, frequently underwriting the losses incurred by the St Albans nurseries. In the First World War, however, when Belgium was overrun, the Bruges nursery was greatly diminished, although it was continued under a Swede. In the post-war years the nursery was reconstructed and rationalized under Sander's sons. Sander died in 1920.

The Bruges nursery was continued under the direction of Charles Fearnley Sander (1874–1957) and Louis Sander (1878–1936). After the Second War, the once-great nurseries fell into sad decline. Those at St Albans were demolished in 1953 and the business transferred to Selsfield, near East Grinstead in Sussex, under the direction of Sanders's grandson, David Sander (d. 1975). The Bruges nurseries were transferred to Roger Sander, a nephew of Frederick Sander.

Sanders, Thomas William, FLS, FRHS (1855 –1926). Horticulturist and horticultural journalist. Sanders was born in the village of Martley in Worcestershire. He had no formal education beyond that provided by the village school, but continued his education by 'self-instruction', as he termed his further studies.

Whilst still in his teens, Thomas Sanders gained a sound, practical training in gardening and farming, activities which he put to sound use in his later career as the prolific author of some forty books on subjects as various as roses and mushrooms, rustic ornaments and rock gardens. In 1887 he was appointed editor of *Amateur Gardening*, retaining that position until his death almost forty years later. He gained many honours and awards and, in 1906, following his leadership of a party of experts to inspect the agricultural industries of Sweden, he was made a Knight of the Order of Vasa. He continued his botanical interests throughout his life.

Saunders, William Wilson (1809–1879). Horticulturist. Saunders was born at Wendover in Buckinghamshire, and was intended for a military career. He was educated at the East India Company's Military

Henry Frederick Conrad Sander ('The Orchid King') (1847–1920).

Thomas William Sanders (1855–1926), horticulturist and author.

William Wilson Saunders (1809–1879), specialist in succulent plants.

Academy at Addiscombe in Surrey, and, joining the Royal Engineers, proceeded to India in 1830, but resigned a year later. Yet, even in his comparatively brief sojourn in India, he managed to make a substantial collection of plants and insects which he brought back with him to England.

In London, Saunders joined Lloyd's as an underwriter, but continued with his entomological and horticultural interests. At his home in Wandsworth, he made a large herbarium whilst his insect collections continued to grow until they were amongst the largest in the country. He was an early member of the Entomological Society, and edited and published *Insecta Saundersiana* (1850–1869).

After his marriage, Saunders moved to Reigate where he cultivated succulent plants, many of lesser-known provenance, which he featured in the five volumes of his *Refugium Botanicum* published between 1869 and 1873, drawing many of the plates himself. He also edited *Mycological Illustrations* (1871–72).

Following a severe financial setback in his underwriting business, Saunders sold his considerable collections of insects and herbarium specimens and he retired to Worthing where he became even more deeply involved in his horticultural interests.

Saunders was elected a Fellow of the Linnean Society in 1833 and of the Royal Society in 1853.

Savill, (Sir) Eric Humphrey (1895–1980). Landscape architect. Savill was the son of Sir Edwin Savill, head of the well-known family firm of chartered surveyors, Alfred Savill and Sons. He was educated at Malvern College and Magdalen College, Cambridge, and served throughout the First War as an infantry officer. He returned to join the family firm, becoming a partner in 1926. In 1931

Two views of the Savill Garden, Windsor Great Park, named after Sir Eric **Savill** *(1895–1980). (Left) A path away from the lake, through the woodlands. (Right) The interior of the greenhouse.*

he was appointed Deputy Surveyor of Windsor Park and Woods, the Crown Estate, then comprising some 15,000 acres.

At the time of his appointment there were no gardens in this considerable acreage, the royal gardens at Windsor being within the castle precincts and at Frogmore in the Home Park. One of the earliest of Savill's proposals was that a woodland garden should be established on the east side of the Great Park. The suggestion was enthusiastically backed by King George V, and Savill went ahead to establish what has become one of the most charming and interesting woodland gardens in Britain.

During the Second War, the garden received but minimal attention yet was little impaired and was quickly restored to its former glories in the post-war years. After the war, the Valley Gardens were also planned and developed, primarily based on plantings of magnolias, azaleas, rhododendrons and Japanese maples, many presented by a commercial firm in Slough, no longer requiring its unusually well-stocked gardens.

In 1951 a further garden was established a mile away from the Valley Garden and the renowned Rhododendron Species Collection. By command of King George VI this garden was named The Savill

Garden and it remains one of the most beautiful of all British gardens now open to the public.

Altogether, the Windsor gardens designed, established and fostered under Savill's direction total over 400 acres. He was knighted in 1955, and in 1958 appointed Director of Forestry to the Crown Estate. He retired in 1970, continuing to live in the Royal Park.

Schröder, (Baron, Sir) Henry (1824–1910). Orchidist and benefactor. Schröder, a merchant banker, was an eminent orchid grower, owner of the finest private collection in Britain at his home in Egham in Surrey. He was also one of

Sir Eric Humphrey **Savill** *(1895–1980), surveyor of Windsor Park.*

Looking towards the rose-garden of the Savill Garden, Windsor, named in honour of Sir Eric **Savill** *who was Director of Forestry to the Crown Estate.*

Baron Sir Henry **Schröder** *(1824–1910), orchidist and benefactor.*

257

Design for a formal garden reproduced from Garden Craft, Old and New *by John* **Sedding** *(1890).*

the most munificent benefactors of the Royal Horticultural Society, and chiefly responsible for the acquisition of the Society's present headquarters and hall in Vincent Square, Westminster. In 1902, he gave £5,000 towards the site, the 994-year lease of which he had acquired, on his own guarantees, from the Ecclesiastical Commissioners. The building, designed by Edwin J. Stubbs, was completed in 1904, and the Society's first show in its new hall was held in the same year. Schröder is justly remembered in the annals of the RHS as 'the Father of the Hall'.

Schröder's passion for orchids was such that he was prepared to pay vast sums to outbid rivals for rare species. In 1906, for example, he paid £1,250 for a single plant.

Scouler, John (1804–1871). Botanist. Scouler, the son of a Glasgow calico printer, was educated locally and at Glasgow University, where he studied medicine. He was appointed surgeon and naturalist to the Hudson's Bay Company's ship *William and Mary*, which explored the Columbia River. On this voyage he made friends with David Douglas, the botanist (qv). After a further voyage as surgeon on the *Clyde* for Calcutta, by way of the Cape of Good Hope and Madras, Scouler returned to Glasgow and set up in medical practice. In 1829, however, he was appointed professor of geology, natural history and mineralogy in what was then the Andersonian University. Five years later he

moved to Dublin as professor of geology, zoology and botany to the Royal Dublin Society. Although his principal study was geology he was a keen botanist and *Scouleria*, a genus of plants, was named after him.

Sedding, John Dando (1838–1891). Architect, gardener, author. Sedding was trained as an architect in the drawing-office of G. E. Street, and later joined the practice established by his brother, Edmund, in Penzance. On his brother's death, in

John Dando **Sedding** *(1838–1891).*

1868, Sedding took over the practice but, finding little prospect of enlarging his clientele, moved to London where he set up home and office in Charlotte Street in Bloomsbury, having meantime married a daughter of a Canon of Gloucester. As his practice (mainly in restoration) grew, he moved to a country house in West Wickham in Kent, where he remained until his death. Sedding specialized in ecclesiastical architecture, much of his work being in the West Country, although he also

William **Shenstone** *(1714–1763).*

designed Holy Trinity in Sloane Square, London, which William Morris considered 'the best modern interior of a town church'.

Sedding's preoccupation with garden design was a somewhat late interest, but swiftly became a passionate hobby, deriving from a considerable understanding of plants and gardens, exemplified in his book *Garden-craft Old and New*, published the year before his death, a modestly thoughtful book, still worth consideration and a pleasing contrast to the dogmatism of William Robinson (qv) and Reginald Blomfield (qv).

Shenstone, William (1714–1763). Poet and landscape gardener. Shenstone was the elder son of Thomas Shenstone, owner of a small farming estate, The Leasowes, near Halesowen, near Birmingham. He was educated at Solihull School and Pembroke College, Oxford, where he was a contemporary of Samuel Johnson. Both at school and university he made friends with whom he was to correspond throughout his life.

At Oxford he made no academic mark, although his first poems were published whilst he was still an under-graduate. He left the university without a degree, retiring to what he termed 'solitude and the country' at the Leasowes, which he had inherited, together with £300 a year, on his father's death in 1724. He proceeded to transform this modest property into an idyllic landscape garden, making up for his limited means by inventiveness, imagination and a rare feeling for the *genius loci*. In the words of his publisher, Robert Dodsley, 'the hand of art is no way visible either in the shape of the ground, the disposition of trees, or (which are here so numerous and striking) the romantic fall of the cascades.' There were, in fact, 'fourteen falls in a short line', a fact duly noted by James Boswell on his visit to The Leasowes with Samuel Johnson some years after Shenstone's death.

Although The Leasowes extended to little more than 30 acres, Shenstone's dedication to its embellishment made it the subject of considerable curiosity to his contemporaries, and he was visited by an impressive list of the notabilities, including William Pitt, Horace Walpole, Oliver Goldsmith, and his neighbours, the Lyttletons, from Hagley. Several of his visitors were improving their own gardens and estates and regarded Shenstone's *ferme ornée*, as he termed his essay in the Picturesque, as the ideal for

(Opposite) Woodland and lakeside planting in the Savill Garden, Windsor Great Park, established by Sir Eric **Savill** *and named after him by command of King George VI.*

FLORA
GRÆCA
Sibthorpiana.

CENTURIA TERTIA.
1819.

FLORA
GRÆCA
Sibthorpiana.

CENTURIA NONA
1837.

PHYSCUS

Sir Hans **Sloane** *and (right) his statue in the Chelsea Physic Garden.*

Alfred **Smee** *(1818–1877).*

rod and binoculars, seeking to embody in his plans his own highly individual visions of light and shade.

Sir George recorded many of his gardening experiences, theories and memorabilia in a book, *The Making of Gardens*, published in 1909, which remains a fascinating record of one man's absorbing passion.

Sloane, (Sir) Hans (1660–1753). Physician, plant-collector, author, philanthropist. Sloane was born and educated in Killyleagh, Co. Down, Ireland, youngest of seven sons of Alexander Sloane, receiver-general of taxes for Co. Down. From his earliest years Sloane took a keen interest in the study of plants. After a severe boyhood illness Sloane went first to London to study medicine and botany, thence, after four years, to Paris to continue his studies under the eminent Monsieur Tournefort. On his return to London he was taken up by Dr Thomas Sydenham, the most famous physician of

the day, and became his assistant, but in 1687 went to Jamaica as physician to the Governor, the Duke of Albemarle.

Sloane remained in Jamaica for about two years, finally returning home with 800 plants, most of which he distributed to John Ray (qv) and other botanists. Some twenty years after the visit, Sloane published a two-volume account of his sojourn, *The Natural History of Jamaica*, with illustrations by the Reverend Garrett Moore.

After his return to England, Sloane lived in the Bloomsbury mansion of the Duchess of Albemarle (who, after the Duke's death, had married Ralph Montagu). Here, Sloane began to build the reputation which made him one of the most fashionable—and wealthy—physicians in London. He was consulted by Queen Anne and Prince George of Denmark, the Queen's consort, he was a leading advocate for inoculation against smallpox, and was widely regarded

as one of the most able of London's medical profession, freely giving his services to the poor.

Sloane had been elected to the Royal Society in 1685 and his connexion with benefactions to the Society lasted until his death.

Thanks to his continuing success as a fashionable physician and his marriage to a wealthy widow in 1695, Sloane was able, in 1712, to purchase the manor of Chelsea from William Cheyne, 2nd Viscount Newhaven. He was made a baronet, one of the first physicians to be so honoured, by George I in 1716. In 1722 he bought the freehold of the garden of the Apothecaries' Society in Chelsea, where he had studied as a young man, letting the garden to the Society for an annual rent of £5, with the promise that they should send fifty specimens of plants to the Royal Society each year. In the same year Philip Miller (qv) was appointed Gardener, no doubt due to Sloane's influence. The marble statue of Sloane by Michael Rys-

brack was erected in the garden in 1737.

Sloane died in his ninety-third year. His collections formed the nucleus of the present British Museum, which was established partly on the basis of Sloane's bequest, together with the Harleian collection, and partly on the proceeds of a lottery aiming to raise £100,000. From these sums, Montagu House was acquired, the house in which Sloane had resided after his return from Jamaica and within a stone's throw of his own one-time house in Bloomsbury Square.

Sloane's achievement was perhaps best summarized in *Jardine's Naturalists' Library* (1843): 'as a naturalist, it is true, we cannot place him in the highest rank; but as the patron of natural history, the encourager of science, the promoter of every charitable work, he obtained the unanimous applause of his contemporaries, and deserves the grateful esteem and respect of posterity. As the founder of the British Museum, he merits the admiration of every one to whom the national progress in literature, science and art is dear.'

Smee, Alfred (1818–1877). Surgeon, scientist, gardener, author. Smee was born in Camberwell, the second son of William Smee, accountant-general to the Bank of England. He was educated at St Paul's School, completing his medical studies at King's College, London. He began his medical career at St Bartholomew's Hospital, specializing in surgery in relation to diseases of the eye. Even during his student days he was demonstrating his unusual skill as an inventor of a new form of plaster splint and the use of electrical means to locate the presence of needles in the body.

He married in 1840 and began to practise as a consulting surgeon in Finsbury Circus. In 1841, at the behest of the directors, he was

Two illustrations from My Garden: Its Plan and Culture *(1872) by Alfred* **Smee** *(1818–1877), surgeon as well as gardener and author.*

*Nineteenth-century engraving of the house and terraces at Tresco Abbey, Scilly Isles, laid out by Augustus **Smith**.*

*Augustus **Smith** (1804–1872).*

appointed surgeon to the Bank of England. His interest in electrical science led to various inventions in the printing of cheques and notes for the Bank, and he was one of the leaders in the early study of electro-metallurgy. In later life he became deeply interested in horticulture, having acquired a large garden at Wallington in Surrey. He published the results of his experiences and experiments in *My Garden: Its Plan and Culture* (1872), a book as unconventional as its protean author, who, as surgeon and inventor as well as gardener, was possessed of rare scientific curiosity and enormous physical energy. *My Garden* is a learned and discursive book, illustrated by well over 1,000 wood engravings, touched throughout by a kind of innocent delight in the splendours and wonders of gardening and garden-making. From an account of the geology and history of his garden, Smee proceeds to description of plants and planning, garden tools and garden-making as well as notes on the birds, animals and insects.

Smith, Alfred William (c. 1855–1927). Market gardener. Smith left school at the age of nine, and began work with his father, a market gardener in Feltham, Middlesex. He was paid no wages and given no holidays, a harsh regimen which he was to assert when he became an employer. He started on his own with the lease of forty acres of fruit at Bedfont. On the retirement of his father he took over the parental nursery, paying his father £3,000 by instalments. By shrewd leasing of land, intensive labour and concentrating on supplying the right produce to the Covent Garden market, he built up a market garden organization of over 1,000 acres and a remarkable reputation for honesty and reliability. His labour was prodigious: he worked all day supervis-

ing the workers in his gardens yet was on his stand at Covent Garden by 3am. His produce was taken up by the big stores such as Harrods and the Army & Navy.

He had a natural genius for the cultivation of vegetables, both in the open and under glass, and was a pioneer of early raising. He specialized in cabbages, being known as The Cabbage King, cauliflowers, brussels sprouts, kale and broccoli. He also cultivated mushrooms, defying horticultural convention by planting in unheated glasshouses, yet producing record crops. Smith was also a pioneer in the growing and marketing of tomatoes, building some twenty glasshouses for their production.

Smith, Augustus (1804–1872). Landowner, botanist, landscape gardener. Augustus Smith was born in London. At the age of thirty he became enamoured of the charm of the Scilly Islands, forty miles off the coast of Cornwall, and in particular of Tresco, the second largest of the group. He leased the islands from the Duchy of Cornwall, thus making himself Lord Proprietor of the Isles of Scilly. He built a house on rocky ground above the ruins of the twelfth-century Benedictine Tresco Abbey, and began to establish the gardens which were to become internationally renowned. Having studied the climate of the Scillies, and with a firm belief in the influence of the Gulf Stream on the island's horticultural potential, Smith built walls and planted windbreaks, so that the rare plants he intended to cultivate would be well-protected. His collections grew. Plants were sent from Kew, while ships' captains calling at the Scilly Isles brought seeds and roots from distant parts of the world.

The garden he ultimately made comprises about twelve acres, sloping to the south. The garden is

divided in three: the Top Terrace, a shorter Middle Terrace and the Long Walk, the main axis of the garden, traversed by the Lighthouse Walk, which leads to the Neptune Steps and a bust of the god. These main axes of the garden are inter-connected by numerous paths cut from the local granite.

Within the confines of this garden are plants that are not grown elsewhere in Britain. As early as 1850, Smith was making note of his ixias, sparaxis and mesembryanthemums. Gradually, he introduced into his terraced gardens such plants as hebes, acacias, fuchsias, pelargoniums as well as numerous other plants needing greenhouse rearing in most of Britain.

Although so busy a man, Smith, who remained a life-long bachelor, represented Truro in the House of Commons, but still spent much time at Tresco.

All the rare plants cultivated by Smith over a century ago still flourish in the garden at Tresco, which is now owned by his great-great-grandnephew, Robert Dorrien-Smith, who in spite of labour shortages has managed to maintain it. On the East Rockery, a natural out-crop of rock below Tresco Abbey itself, grow some beautiful Ratas from New Zealand, *Metrosiderous robusta*, covered with coppery scarlet brushes of flower at the end of June. The rare Ratas are a feature of Tresco. Elsewhere in the garden grows *M. diffusa*, with rosy scarlet stamens, as well as what is probably the largest specimen of *M. tomentosa* in Europe: the Maori name for this tree is Pohutukawa and it is a splendid sight when it flowers in July. Near the first group of *M. robusta* is an extraordinary plant from Mexico, *Furcraea longaeva*, like a large yucca, which after many years preparation throws up a flower spike, about twenty feet high, of cream and green bell-shaped flowers.

In a part of the garden called Mexico, numerous rare succulents are grown, but perhaps the most unusual of the plants grown there are the echiums, the giant borages from the Canary Islands and Madeira, which flower in many brilliant shades of blue. *E. 'Scilloniensis'* is a natural hybrid which originated in the Isles of Scilly.

Smith, (Sir) James Edward (1759–1828). Smith was born at Norwich, the eldest child of a wealthy wool merchant. He was educated at Norwich Grammar School and at Edinburgh University where he studied medicine, specializing in botany under John Hope (qv), one of the earliest protagonists for the Linnean method. His further studies in London led to an introduction to Sir Joseph Banks (qv), President of the Royal Society, who, on the death of the younger Linnaeus (qv) in 1783, persuaded Smith to buy—for one thousand guineas—the library, manuscripts, herbarium and natural history collections of the great Swedish botanist.

In the following year Smith took apartments in Chelsea where the Linnean collections were housed on their arrival in London from Sweden. Smith now became wholly devoted to the study of botany and began, with Banks' help, the systematic study of the Linnean collection. In 1786 he set out on an extended European tour, meeting many eminent scientists, botanists and medical men, and visiting botanical libraries. He published a three-volume account of his tour in 1789. On his return to London he took a house in Great Marlborough Street in which the first meeting of the Linnean Society was held and of which Smith was elected President. Here, too, Smith lectured on botany, and he also became lecturer in botany at Guy's Hospital.

In 1790 he began publication of

Sir James Edward **Smith** *(1759–1828).*

Thomas **Smith** *(1857–1955).*

Sir William **Smith** *(1875–1956).*

Lilian **Snelling** *(1879–1972).*

his remarkable work, the thirty-six-volume *English Botany*, which contains 2,592 plates of all known British plants (except fungi) drawn by James Sowerby (qv). On his marriage in 1796 Smith returned to live at Norwich, returning to London only to deliver an annual series of lectures at the Royal Institution.

He was a prolific writer on botanical subjects. Amongst his books were *Flora Britannica* (1800–1804); and his *Introduction to Physiological and Systematic Botany* (1807) which went through several editions in his lifetime. As well as writing over 3,000 botanical articles for Reed's *Cyclopaedia*, he completed his most important work, *The English Flora*, during the last seven years of his life. He was knighted in 1814.

Smith, Thomas (1857–1955). Horticulturist. Smith was one of five children of a Lancashire tinplate worker, and started work at the age of nine, becoming apprenticed to a

Manchester printer. He started his own successful printing business but in his late thirties decided to set up as a smallholder on 12 acres at Mayland in Essex. In co-operation with Joseph Fels, a well-to-do American expatriate, he became an early exponent of what was known as French gardening, or the intensive cultivation of vegetables. In 1909, he published a book on his methods and, later, *The Profitable Culture of Vegetables* (1911), one of the most influential of all books on commercial horticultural methods. He was awarded the RHS Veitch medal in 1950.

Smith, (Sir) William Wright (1875–1956). Smith was born at Lochmarben in Dumfriesshire and was educated at Dumfries Academy and at Edinburgh University. When he was twenty-seven, he was appointed lecturer in botany at the university, leaving to take charge of the Government Herbarium in the Royal

Botanic Garden in Calcutta where he gained valuable experience in the administration of a large scientific garden. He remained in India until 1911, carrying out a number of botanical expeditions as Director of the Botanical Survey of India, and gaining a wide knowledge of the flora of India and Burma. On his return to Britain, he was appointed Deputy Keeper of the Royal Botanic Garden, Edinburgh. He became Regius Keeper in 1922 and Regius Professor of Botany in Edinburgh University. During the First War he was seconded to the Timber Supply Department and gained a considerable insight into the work and problems of the Forestry commission in Scotland.

Even as Keeper and Professor, Smith found time to continue teaching and helped to train new generations of botanists. He also continued with his work in classifying Sino-Himalayan plants, mainly concerned with the great plant collec-

tion assembled and sent back to Edinburgh by George Forrest (qv). He made descriptions for over 500 new species. In the course of these interests he became one of the foremost authorities on primulas and, later, rhododendrons. Smith was knighted in 1952 and he received many honours and awards, both from British and oversea societies and universities.

Snelling, Lilian (1879–1972). Artist and lithographer. Born at St Mary Cray in Kent, Lilian Snelling studied lithography under Morley Fletcher. She was employed by the Royal Botanic Garden, Edinburgh, from 1916–1921, before becoming one of the leading illustrators for Curtis's *Botanical Magazine*, published by the Royal Horticultural Society in London. Between 1922 and 1952, she illustrated most of the plants in the *Magazine*. Lilian Snelling also illustrated the supplement to Elwes' *Monograph of the Genus Lilium* (1934–40) and F. Stoker's *Book of Lilies* (1943), but some of the finest examples of her work are to be seen in F. C. Stern's large-format *Study of Genus Paeonia*, published in 1946. Miss Snelling's work combined a rare delicacy with botanical accuracy, making her one of the foremost botanical artists of recent times.

Solander, Daniel Carl (1733–1782). Botanist. Solander was born in Norrland, Sweden, the son of a clergyman. His aptitude for botany was noticed at an early age by the great Swedish botanist, Carl Linnaeus, who, in 1756, gave Solander the task of editing his *Elementa Botanica*. In

Paeonia Clusii *and* Paeonia emodi, *drawn by Lilian* **Snelling** *for the* Study of the Genus Paeonia *by F. C. Stern.*

(Opposite) The gardens at Tresco Abbey, created by Augustus **Smith** *from 1834 onwards. Thanks to the clement climate of the Scilly Isles, the gardens support many plants which could not survive elsewhere in the British Isles.*

Pæonia corallina.   Entire-leaved Pæony.

Two views of the remarkable chalk garden at Highdown, Sussex, established by Sir Frederick **Stern** *(1884–1967) seen in the portrait above.*

contributed many papers to learned journals, and has written numerous books on botanical subjects for a wider public, including *Wild Flowers of Greece* (with C. M. Goulimis, 1968); *Introduction to the Species Plantarum of Carl Linnaeus* (1957); *Botanical Latin* (1966); *Gardener's Dictionary of Plant Names* (with A. W. Smith, 1972). He was awarded the RHS Veitch Memorial Medal in 1964 and the Victoria Medal of Honour in the following year. He was elected President of the Garden History Society in 1977, President of the Linnean Society in 1979, and made Commander of the Royal Order of the Northern Star in 1980.

Stern, (Sir) Frederick Claude (1884–1967). Botanist and gardener. Stern was born in London, the younger son of James Stern. After Eton and Christ Church, Oxford, he entered banking, but throughout his life was an enthusiastic gardener, and established a remarkable chalk garden at his home at Highdown, Goring-on-Sea, Sussex. He was elected a Fellow of the Linnean Society in 1925, and from 1941 until 1958 was also Treasurer to the Society. He was Chairman of the John Innes Horticultural Institution 1947–61. He was knighted in 1956. In addition to many articles in botanical and horticultural journals he published *Study of Genus Paeonia* (1946), *Snowdrops and Snowflakes* (1956) and wrote an account of his own gardening life in *A Chalk Garden* (1960). He was awarded the VMH in 1940.

Strutt, Jacob George (fl. 1825–1850s). Artist. Little is known of Strutt's early life, although he is known to have studied in London and, between 1819 and 1855, contributed drawings and paintings to the Royal Academy and British Institution. He seems at first to have engaged in portrait painting, but then switched to landscapes, specializing in forest and woodland scenes. In 1822 he published his best-known work, a series of etchings collected under the title, *Sylva Britannica, or Portraits of Forest Trees.* Six years later he published *Deliciae Sylvarum*, which depicted a series of handsome trees in England and Scotland. At some time in the early 1830s Strutt left London and settled in Rome, where he produced *Sylva Italica* (1844).

In 1851 he returned to England, but few details are recorded of his later life.

Sudell, Richard (c. 1900–1968). Landscape gardener. Richard Sudell was the son of a Lancashire farmer and at an early age decided to become a landscape gardener. In 1915 he was a student gardener at Kew, leaving to join a firm of landscape contractors. In 1927, following an informal meeting at the Chelsea Flower Show, Sudell and others decided to found a British Institute of Landscape Architects. Sudell was appointed chairman and in 1929 the Institute was formally constituted with Thomas Mawson (qv) as the first president. From his office in Gower Street, Sudell began publication of the *Journal* of the Institute.

In 1955 Sudell was elected president of the Institute. His work was highly regarded abroad and he received many commissions for work in America. He died in Kuwait whilst visiting projects in the Middle East and Pakistan. He wrote copiously and amongst his books were *Landscape Gardening*, 1933; *Herbaceous Borders and the Waterside*, 1938; *Town and Suburban Garden*, 1950; *Garden Planning*, 1952.

Sutherland, James (c. 1639–1719). Botanist. Of Sutherland's youth and upbringing, virtually nothing is known, although, according to Sir Robert Sibbald (qv), he had attained a 'great knowledge of plants' whilst still young. He makes his first appearance in Scottish botany as the keeper, or 'intendant', of a garden established by Sibbald and Sir Andrew Balfour (qv) in Edinburgh in 1675, which was superseded by the establishment, five years later, of what was to become known as the Physic Garden. He was plainly a man of considerable energy, assiduity and ambition. Within eight years of his appointment, he published the *Hortus Medicus Edinburgensis*, a catalogue of plants in the garden.

In 1695, a special Chair of Botany was created for him at Edinburgh University. In the same year he added to the two existing gardens part of the Royal Garden at Holyrood (known as the King's Garden) for the cultivation of medicinal herbs and vegetables. In 1710, he was made Regius Professor of Botany. By that time he had established the renown of the gardens he had founded. During the siege of Edinburgh in 1689, however, the King's Garden was flooded, a catastrophe which caused the loss of all the more tender plants. Sutherland devoted his fading energies to the reclama-

Engraving taken from the title-page of Sylva Britannica *by Jacob George* **Strutt,** *published in 1822.*

Garden design incorporating stone sundial, reproduced from The Town and Suburban Garden *(1950) by Richard **Sudell** (c. 1900–1968).*

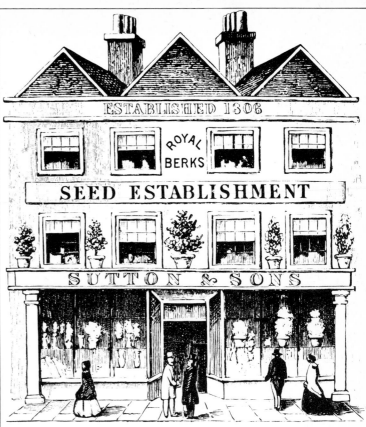

*The seed shop in Reading, Berkshire, which was started by John **Sutton** in 1806, and on which the firm's subsequent success was based.*

tion and restitution of the garden. In 1699, Sutherland was appointed King's Botanist. The last years of his life were shadowed by reprimands from the Edinburgh Town Council for neglect of his duties. Sutherland retired to spend more time on his other great interest, the study of coins and medals. He seems to have died in obscurity.

Sutton family:

JOHN SUTTON (1777–1863). Little is known of the early years of the man who founded the famous firm of seed merchants, Sutton and Sons, in Reading, Berkshire, in 1806. That he was a man of unusual business acumen is proven by the success of the firm which, in its early days, dealt in flour, agricultural seeds and products, and seems to have prospered from the beginning. But the main impetus to the firm's remarkable expansion came from John Sutton's second son:

MARTIN HOPE SUTTON (1815–1901). He was born in Reading and showed a deep interest in botanical studies during his boyhood years. After leaving school in 1828 he joined his father and even at that tender age showed a determination to add flower and vegetable seeds to the main agricultural side of the business. He made many of his exploratory journeys to other seedsmen on foot and once walked seventy miles on a round trip to various Thames Valley nurseries.

His practical botanical knowledge

was greatly respected by Queen Victoria and he advised frequently on the royal gardens at Windsor and Osborne. He was also responsible for starting the mail order side of the Sutton seed business, which was to make the firm's name known nationally. In these business operations he was aided by his brother ALFRED SUTTON (c. 1818–1897). The expansion of the family firm was continued under the third generation:

MARTIN JOHN SUTTON (1850–1913). He was born in Reading, son of Martin Hope Sutton, and entered the family business when he was sixteen. On coming of age he became a partner in the business and in 1887 became head of the business. He not only directed the ever-expanding seed business, including the development of a considerable overseas business, especially to Australia, New Zealand and the East, but wrote the authoritative *Permanent and Temporary Pastures* published in 1886. He was an active member of agricultural societies and a considerable philanthropist.

Other partners in the family business were his two brothers: ARTHUR WARWICK SUTTON (1854–1925), an early horticultural plant breeder and selector of domestic vegetables, who was responsible for producing many varieties of peas and beans (important papers on food-crops were read to the Linnean Society); LEONARD GOODHART SUTTON (1863 –1932), a specialist in flowers, with a particular interest in annuals.

*John **Sutton** (1777–1863).*

*Martin Hope **Sutton** (1815–1901).*

*Arthur Warwick **Sutton** (1854–1925).*

*Martin John **Sutton** (1850–1913).*

Ichnographia Ruftica :
OR, THE
Nobleman, Gentleman, and Gardener's
RECREATION.
CONTAINING

DIRECTIONS for the Surveying and Diftri-
buting of a Country-Seat into Rural and
Extenfive Gardens, by the Ornamenting and
Decoration of diftant Profpects, Farms, Parks,
Paddocks, &c.

Originally calculated (inftead of inclofed Plantations)
for the Embellifhment of Countries in general ;
as alfo for an Introduction to a General Syftem of

Agriculture and *Planting.*
ILLUSTRATED

With above Fifty Copper Plates, done by the beft
Hands, which, though firft publifhed above twenty
Years ago, has given rife to every thing of the
kind, which has been done fince.

The SECOND EDITION, with large Additions.

VOL. I.

By STEPHEN SWITZER, Seedfman and Gardener at the Seedfhop in *Weftminfter-Hall.*

Huc ades, inceptumque una decurre laborem :
O Decus ! O Fama ! merito pars maxima noftra,
Mæcenas pelagoque volans da vela petenti. Virg. Georg. 2.

LONDON :

Printed for J. and J. Fox, in *Weftminfter-Hall* ; B. and B. BAR-
KER, in the Bowling-Alley, *Weftminfter* ; D. BROWNE, without *Temple-Bar* ; and F. GOSLING, in *Fleet-ftreet.* 1742.

The frontispiece and title-page of Ichnographia Rustica *by Stephen* **Switzer**, *published in 1718.*

LEONARD NOEL SUTTON (d. 1965) wrote the *Cool Greenhouse* (1935).

In 1912, Suttons took over the old-established nurseries of Veitch and Company of Langley in Buckinghamshire.

In 1976, the business was transferred from Reading to specially-designed buildings in Torquay, Devon. Most of the seed crops are grown abroad, mainly in France, Italy and California, where harvesting conditions are more certain.

Sweet, Robert (1783–1835). Horticulturist, nurseryman, author. Sweet was born at Cockington, near Torquay in Devonshire. He joined his half-brother James Sweet, a gardener near Bristol. Subsequently, he had several jobs in gardening and in London nurseries. In 1812 he joined Colvills, the famous Chelsea nursery, having been elected a fellow of the Linnean Society. Whilst there, he was accused of receiving plants stolen from the royal gardens at Kew but was acquitted after being tried at the Old Bailey in 1824. He left the nursery in 1826 and during the next five years produced a number of botanical works, as well as cultivating (and selling from) a small nursery in his Chelsea garden. In 1831 he had a serious mental breakdown, although, judging by the dates of his various publications, he continued with some literary work.

His books include: *Hortus Suburbanus Londinensis*, 1818; *Sweet's Hortus Britannicus*, 1826; *Florist's Guide*, 1827–32, two volumes; and *British Flower Garden*, 1823–38, seven volumes.

Switzer, Stephen (1682–1745). Landscape gardener, horticultural writer. Switzer was born at East Stratton in Hampshire. Although the family's circumstances were plainly limited, Switzer wrote later that his education was 'none of the meanest for one of my profession', adding, however, that he early experienced 'the meanest labours of scythe, spade and wheelbarrow.' Whilst still young he started to work for London and Wise (qv), the lead-

Patrick **Synge** *(1910–   ).*

ing metropolitan gardening experts of the time, and in 1706 seems to have assisted London in the great task of laying out the grounds at Blenheim Palace. He is also thought to have worked as kitchen-gardener in the royal gardens at St James's Palace, and it is possible that he was also commissioned either to supply designs or to supervise his own designs in various Scottish gardens. Certainly, a century later, John Loudon purported to find traces of the Switzer manner in gardens in the Edinburgh region. From 1724 onwards, Switzer is known to have worked for various members of the aristocracy, including the Earl of Orrery, to whose help he later made fulsome acknowledgement in his published works. The latter were undoubtedly begun under the aegis of his lordly patron, for Switzer states that his greatest help in preparing his narrations had been by means of 'the library of my very worthy, learned and noble friend and master, the Earl of Orrery'. His first book was entitled, logically enough, *The Nobleman, Gentleman and Gardener's Recreation*, which was originally published as one volume in 1715, but reissued three years later, in three volumes, as *Ichnographia Rustica*. In 1724 he published *The Practical Fruit Gardener* and three years later, *The Practical Kitchen Gardener*.

Meanwhile, he had set up as a nurseryman on Millbank, Westminster, and, backed by his patri-

cian patrons, initiated a short-lived monthly horticultural journal, *The Practical Husbandman and Planter*, which ran between 1733–34.

His books display pronounced skills as a draughtsman, and despite his pretensions to a rich literary style (embellished with Latin passages, doubtless to substantiate his claims to have enjoyed an education in the classics), they found considerable favour, went through several editions, and reputedly led him to advise both Lord Brooke and Lord Bathurst on their horticultural projects. He also wrote upon agricultural improvements and tanning.

Synge, Patrick (1910–   ). Botanist, plant-collector and author. Synge was born in London, son of Edward Synge, artist and engraver. He was educated at Rugby and Corpus Christi College, Cambridge, where he studied Natural Sciences. After leaving Cambridge, he was appointed assistant botanist and photographer to the Oxford University Sarawak expedition (1932–33) which was responsible for the discovery of over a score of new species of orchid. He then joined the British Museum expedition to the mountains of East Africa where giant lobelias and senecios were collected. In 1937, he became a director of Lindsay Drummond, publishers. During the Second War he served in North Africa and Italy. In 1945, he was appointed editor of the *Journal* and other publications of the Royal Horticultural Society, a task which also included the preparation and publication of four separate yearbooks annually, in addition to the completion of the Society's *Dictionary of Gardening* and a supplement to that publication. From 1952–1970 he was President of the Horticultural Club, after Sir Frederick Stern (qv). He was a member of the Council of the Linnean Society, 1952–54. He was awarded the Royal Horticultural Society Veitch Memorial Gold Medal in 1957, the Lyttel Lily Cup, 1965, and the Victoria Medal of Honour, 1969. His major interests have been in trees and shrubs, especially magnolias and rhododendrons, also in bulbous plants and alpine flora.

His more recent publications have included: *Collins Guide to Bulbs* (1961), *In Search of Flowers* (1973), *Flowers and Colour in Winter* (1974), *The Gardens of Devon and Cornwall* (1977).

(Opposite) Cover and typical pages (originals measuring 11 inches by 9 inches) reproduced from the Amateur's Guide in Horticulture for 1887 which was issued by **Sutton** *and Sons, Reading. The early Sutton's catalogues were liberally embellished with these handsome lithographic plates depicting flowers and vegetables.*

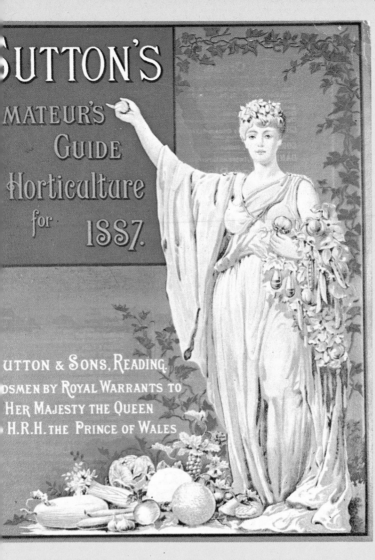

SUTTON'S
AMATEUR'S
GUIDE
Horticulture
for
1887.

SUTTON & SONS, READING.
SEEDSMEN BY ROYAL WARRANTS TO
HER MAJESTY THE QUEEN
& H.R.H. THE PRINCE OF WALES

SUTTON'S MOSS-CURLED LILAC PRIMULA. SUTTON'S MOSS-CURLED WHITE PRIMULA.
SUTTON'S DOUBLE WHITE PRIMULA.
SUTTON'S DOUBLE SCARLET PRIMULA.

SUTTON'S DOUBLE PETUNIAS.

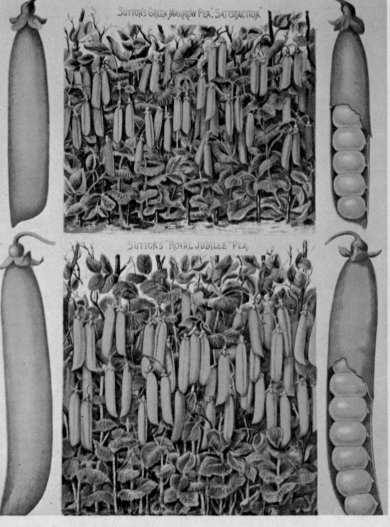

SUTTON'S GREEN MARROW PEA, SATISFACTION.
SUTTON'S "ROYAL JUBILEE" PEA.

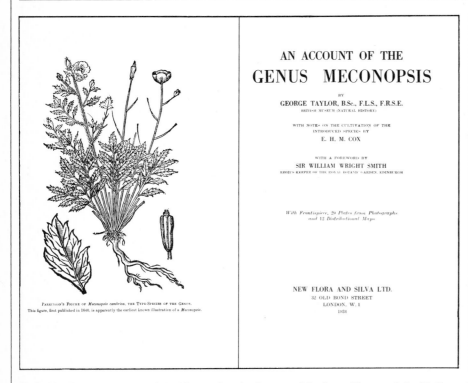

(Left) Meconopsis cambrica *and the title page from* An Account of the Genus Meconopsis *by Sir George* **Taylor**, *published in 1934. (Right) The Queen with Sir George Taylor (1904–   ), Director of Kew Gardens 1956–1971, walking through the Palm House in the Botanic Gardens.*

Taylor, (Sir) George (1904–   ). Botanist. Taylor was born in Edinburgh and educated at George Heriot's School and Edinburgh University, where he gained first-class honours in Botany. In 1927, he made the first of his botanical expeditions: to Rhodesia and South Africa. This was followed by his joint leadership of the British Museum expedition to the mountainous regions of East Africa (1934–35) and to south-east Tibet and Bhutan in 1938. After the Second War in which he served in the Air Ministry he was appointed Deputy Keeper of Botany at the British Museum, succeeding to the Keepership in 1950, which he relinquished in 1956 to become Director of the Royal Botanic Gardens at Kew. He remained at Kew until his retirement in 1971. He was editor of Curtis's *Botanical Magazine* from 1962 until 1971. He has served on many advisory committees concerned with botanical and landscaping interests. He has received numerous honours and awards, including the Royal Horticultural Society Veitch Gold Medal in 1963. He has contributed to many horticultural publications and published his *Account of the genus Meconopsis*

in 1934. He was knighted in 1962.

His directorship of the Royal Botanic Gardens at Kew was notable for enterprising innovations, perhaps the most memorable of which was the design and laying-out of the Queen's Garden, formerly known as the Dutch Garden, a skilful evocation of the formal gardens of the seventeenth century. There is a parterre with a central fountain embellished with five carved stone heads, each on its own pedestal. To the west of the parterre is a sunken garden encompassed by a raised walk with a laburnum *allée*. In this sunken garden is a traditional camomile-turfed seat.

Taylor, George Crosbie (1901–1962). Botanist, author. Taylor was born in Edinburgh and educated at Edinburgh University. He showed early talent for communicating his enthusiasm for gardening to a wide readership. In 1927, he published (with F. P. Knight) *Propagation of Hardy Trees and Shrubs*, followed by *Garden Making by Example* (1932), *The Modern Garden* (1936). His true *metier*, however, was as a gardening editor and journalist. He was gardening editor of *Country Life* for some years and gardening corre-

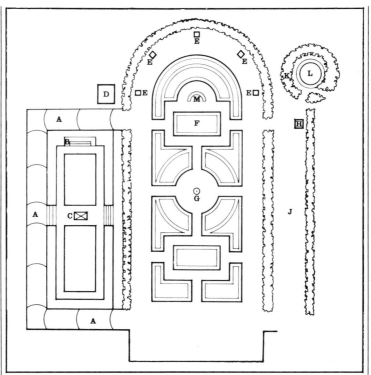

Plan of the Queen's Garden at Kew, laid out under the direction of Sir George **Taylor**, *1964: (A) Laburnum allée; (B) Camomile-turfed seat; (C) Wrought-iron pillar; (D) The gazebo; (E) Five stone heads on pedestals; (F) 'Boy with a Dolphin'; (G) Venetian well-head; (H) 'Satyr with a flute'; (J) Pleached hornbeam alley; (K) The Mount; (L) The Rotunda; (M) Stone seat.*

*Two illustrations by Gordon Davies to illustrate a feature by George Crosbie **Taylor** on gardening by the sea* (House & Garden, *August, 1960*).

spondent of the *Observer* and of *House & Garden* from 1950 until 1960, writing features on all aspects of gardening, including plants for the sea-side, gardening under glass and so on.

Taylor, Simon (1740–c.1796). Botanical artist. Little is known of the early life of Taylor, although it is established that he studied at William Shipley's recently-founded Drawing School. Shipley was also a leading light in the formation of the Royal Society for the Encouragement of Arts, Manufacturers and Commerce in 1754, from which the young Taylor gained a succession of prizes for his draughtsmanship between the years 1756 and 1761. When he was about seventeen his talents brought him to the notice of Lord Bute (qv) who commissioned him to paint a series of botanical subjects. This patronage became virtually a life-long service, for a contemporary memoirist records that Taylor was still working for Lord Bute in the 1780s.

This work did not, however, preclude carrying out commissions for other patrons, and it is known that Taylor worked for the Duchess of Portland in the 1770s. (Several of Taylor's drawings, presumably made at Bulstrode, Gerrards Cross, the Duchess's home, were sold at auction when the Portland Museum was dispersed in 1786.)

Taylor also carried out numerous commissions for John Fothergill (qv), the successful physician and botanist, whose remarkable collection of drawings by the most eminent botanical artists of his time was later sold to the Empress of Russia. His work was also commissioned by John Ellis, the naturalist, who, in writing to Linnaeus following the death of the great Danish botanical artist, Georg Dionysius Ehret (1708–70) (qv), spoke of Taylor as 'a young man who draws all the rare plants at Kew Garden for Lord Bute; he does it tolerably well'.

Simon Taylor also made many flower drawings on vellum for another noted patron and collector, Ralph Willett, who lived at Merly, in Dorsetshire.

Telfair, Charles (1778–1833). Surgeon, botanist. Telfair was born in Belfast and became a naval surgeon. He served during the 1810 blockade of the island of Mauritius and decided to settle there. At first he practised medicine but was soon given a number of official posts, including that of Private Secretary to the governor.

In spite of representing an occupationary force, Charles Telfair was very popular with the local inhabitants. He had always shown an interest in botany and, in 1826, established a botanic garden on the island. He also established a second botanic garden on the comparatively nearby island of Reunion. Telfair corresponded with many important scientists and botanists then working in Europe. He sent plants to Kew, as well as seeds, animals and shells to his friend, Robert Barclay (1751–1830), who had a large garden at Bury Hill in Surrey. He also sent back the celebrated double coconut from the Seychelles, the *Lodoicea maldivica*, plus a variety of plants from the African mainland as well as from other islands in the Indian Ocean.

Telfair's wife, Annabella (d. 1832) corresponded with Sir William Jackson Hooker (qv), and made drawings for the *Botanical Magazine*.

Temple, (Sir) William (1628–1699). Statesman and garden designer. Temple was born at Blackfriars, the son of Sir John Temple, an Irish landowner and Privy Councillor. Whilst he was still young his mother died and the boy was brought up by Dr Henry Hammond at Penshurst in Kent. He was educated at the local day school and at Emmanuel College, Cambridge, and was sent on the Grand Tour. Before embarking, however, he met Dorothy Osborne, daughter of Sir Peter Osborne, a Royalist leader, with whom he fell in love. The couple were married, after many vicissitudes, in 1654.

Temple's career was almost exclusively concerned with affairs of state and the building of the league against Louis XIV despite Charles II's vacillations and subservience to the French king. He became a member of the King's Council. Meantime, he had bought a small property at West Sheen in Surrey and, between his frequent travels

*Charles **Telfair** (1778–1833).*

*The botanic gardens on Mauritius, established by Charles **Telfair** in 1826.*

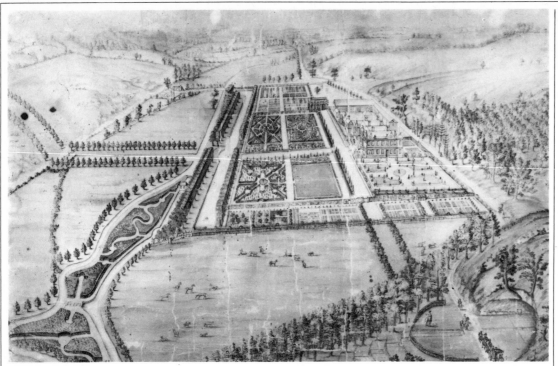

Bird's-eye view showing the elaborate formal gardens at Moor Park, Surrey, the home of Sir William **Temple** *(1685–1699).*

Rose rust, an illustration by Frances Bunyard for The Enemies of the Rose *by Frederick* **Theobald** *(1908).*

and residence abroad, cultivated the garden. He wrote to a friend, Lord Lisle, from Brussels, where he was ambassador, explaining that he was 'contriving how a succession of cherries may be compassed from May till Michaelmas and how the Sheen vines may be improved by half-a-dozen sorts which are not yet known here.'

During a period when the policies he advocated were unwanted by the King, he spent three years at Sheen, improving the small estate. He finally retired from his diplomatic career in 1681, following the intrigues attendant upon the Treaty of Nimeguen the previous year. In 1685, following violent disagreement with a Sheen neighbour, Lord Brouncker, he moved to Moor Park, at Farnham in Surrey, which was no mean translation considering that the Temples were by that time both

well into their late fifties.

Although no innovator in garden design, Temple undoubtedly cultivated a most unusual retreat. Philip Miller refers to the delicious quality of Temple's apricots in *The Gardener's Dictionary*. A young Swiss writer, one Muralt, after visiting Moor described Moor Park as 'the ideal of a pleasant retreat . . . the air wholesome, the soil good, a little stream making the only sound to be heard . . . cultivated by the master himself.'

Lady Temple died in 1695, followed four years later by Sir William. 'With him', wrote Jonathan Swift, Temple's one-time secretary, 'died all that was good and amiable among men.'

Theobald, Frederick Vincent (1868–1930). Botanist, entomologist. Theobald was born at Kingston-on-

Thames and educated privately and at St John's College, Cambridge. He was one of the earliest members of the SE Agricultural College and was later put in charge of the Economic Zoology section of the British Museum. In 1900 he was appointed Professor of Agricultural Zoology in the University of London. He wrote copiously upon various aspects of insect life in relation to agriculture and botany. Amongst his publications are *Enemies of the Rose* (1908); *Insect Pests of Fruit* (1909); *Insect Enemies of the Allotment Holder* (1918) and the three-volume *Plant Lice or Aphididae of Great Britain* (1926–29). Frederick Theobald died at Wye in Kent.

Thiselton-Dyer, (Sir). William Turner (1843–1928). Botanist, author. William Thiselton-Dyer was born in Westminster and educated in London. In 1864 he entered Christ Church, Oxford, where he studied natural history and mathematics.

At the age of twenty-five he was appointed professor of Natural History at the Royal Agricultural College, Cirencester. From there he went to Dublin, where he was Professor of Botany at the Royal College of Science, returning in 1872 to become Professor of Botany at the Royal Horticultural Society.

In 1875, Thiselton-Dyer became Assistant Director of the Botanic Gardens at Kew. From his earliest days there, he proved to be an invaluable help to the then Director, Sir Joseph Hooker (qv). One of the major tasks he was given was to deal with the ever-increasing work-load connected with the colonies. In 1877, Thiselton-Dyer married Hooker's eldest daughter, Harriet, a botanical artist who contributed drawings to the *Botanical Magazine*. On Hooker's retirement, in 1885, Thiselton-Dyer became director and set about establishing Kew as the botanical centre of the world. Several buildings, including the Alpine House, the Jodrell Laboratory, were constructed or completed in the gardens under his auspices.

In 1896 Thiselton-Dyer compiled a great work on *Flora Capensis* and, a year later, on the *Flora of Tropical Africa*. He was also responsible for initiating the *Kew Bulletin of Miscellaneous Information* which was first published in 1887 as a permanent record of work carried out at Kew, particularly that which was con-

(Opposite) Looking down from the Mount in the north-east corner of the Queen's Garden at the Royal Botanic Gardens, Kew, laid out in 1964, in the seventeenth-century style, with authentic planting, under the auspices of Sir George **Taylor,** *who was director at Kew from 1956 until 1971.*

Sir William **Temple** *(1628–1699).*   *Sir William* **Thiselton-Dyer.**   *Lady Harriet* **Thiselton-Dyer.**

Two views (1925) of the gardens at Rotherfield Hall, Sussex, showing (left) the north end of the terrace and (right) the garden-house at the north-west corner of the parterre, designed by F. Inigo **Thomas** *(fl. 1890s) who favoured an element of formality in garden design.*

cerned with the economic botany of the new worlds.

After his retirement as Director of Kew in 1905, Thiselton-Dyer continued to take an active interest in horticulture and, on the occasion of his eightieth birthday, his services to botany were acknowledged by the leading botanists of the day who sent him a congratulatory and appreciative address.

Sir William Thiselton-Dyer became a fellow of the Linnean Society in 1872, a Fellow of the Royal Society in 1880. He was vice-president of the Royal Horticultural Society from 1887–1889.

Thomas, F. Inigo (fl. 1890s). Garden designer, artist. Little is known of Inigo Thomas' young life and education. He is remembered as a latterday enthusiast for the formal style of gardening. In furtherance of this enthusiasm he contributed a series of drawings and reconstructions of early gardens for a book on *The Formal Garden in England* by Sir Reginald Blomfield (qv), published in 1892. This was probably the first attempt to associate the word 'formal' with an earlier fashion in garden design. The book was written as a counterblast to the notions of the 'natural' school of

gardening advocated by William Robinson (qv), who vehemently disapproved of the practice of topiary, rigidly symmetrical design and the lavish use of stonework, gravel paths and so on.

As well as being an artist of considerable skill, Inigo Thomas was a practising garden designer, producing semi-formal, somewhat architectural schemes for many large country gardens, including Athelhampton, Dorset (with Blomfield), and Rothersfield Hall, Sussex.

Thomas, Graham Stuart (1909–). Horticultural artist, author, lec-

turer, adviser. Thomas's horticultural training began, in 1926, at the University Botanic Garden, Cambridge, where he spent three years studying gardening, botany, ecology and geology. From there he moved on to the famous nursery of Clarence Elliot (qv), near Stevenage, in Hertfordshire, where he developed his interest in alpine plants. In 1931, Thomas joined the wholesale firm of T. Hilling & Co, a holding of some 300 acres at Chobham, in Surrey. Immediately after the war, he started his unique collection of old roses which he has been developing ever since. In 1956

Drawing by F. Inigo **Thomas** *for the* Formal Garden in England *(1892) written in conjuction with Sir Reginald Blomfield as a counterblast to the 'natural' school of gardening.*

'Nevada' rose, drawn by Graham Stuart **Thomas** *and illustrated in his book,* Shrub Roses of Today *(1962).*

Graham Stuart **Thomas** *(1909–   ), and a view of the recently established canal-garden at Sezincote, Gloucestershire, where Thomas has acted as garden-adviser. Sezincote and its landscape setting were designed in 1804–5.*

Illustrations from The English Flower Garden *by William* **Thompson**.

he became manager and, later, Associate Director of Sunningdale Nurseries, also in Surrey. By this time, Thomas was Garden Adviser to the National Trust, a post which he held until 1974 when he became the Trust's Gardens Consultant. Under his aegis, many new plantings in historic gardens have taken place, including a Victorian-style rose garden at Shugborough, in Staffordshire, a garden of old roses at Mottisfont, in Hampshire, and the formal garden at Knightshayes, in Devon. He also advised on the canal and planting of the water-garden at Sezincote, in Gloucestershire, and the restoration of the garden at Claremont, in Surrey.

As well as being a garden author, Graham Thomas is one of Britain's leading flower artists and his books are illustrated with his own watercolours, drawings and photographs. He specializes in hardy trees, shrubs, plants and bulbs and their uses in garden artistry; the history of garden design and history of plants. But, as the leading authority on roses, probably his best-known works are *Old Shrub Roses* (1955), *Shrub Roses of Today* (1962), *Climbing Roses Old and New* (1965).

An active member of the Royal Horticultural Society and Royal National Rose Society, Graham Stuart Thomas was awarded the VMH in 1968 and the RNRS Dean Hole Medal in 1976. He received an OBE in 1975.

Thomas's collection of old roses is established in beds of his own design at the Royal National Rose Society in Hertfordshire and at Mottisfont.

Thompson, Robert (1798–1869). Pomologist. Thompson was born in Echt, Aberdeenshire, Scotland, the son of a farmer. When he was fourteen he became assistant to his uncle, a gardener at Skene, although he seems to have been enabled to continue part-time at school. When he was twenty he went to work in the gardens of the Earl of Aberdeen's seat at Haddo House and afterwards for Lord Kennedy at Dunnottar. After further work at Raith, in Sir Robert Ferguson's gardens, he was recommended by his employer to the Horticultural Society and began work at Chiswick in 1824, where he

Plate from The Gardener's Assistant *by Robert* **Thompson**, *(1859).*

specialized in the study of fruit, resulting, two years later, in a revised nomenclature in *The Catalogue of Fruits Cultivated in the Garden of the Horticultural Society of London*. This was revised and reissued in 1831 (by which time Thompson was in charge of the Fruit Department) when 1,400 apples, 219 cherries and 677 pears were listed, and again in 1842. In 1877 he contributed to the first issues of *The Pomological Magazine* and was also largely responsible for the fruit sections in a new edition of John Loudon's (qv) *Encyclopaedia of Gardening* reissued in 1835. He

William **Thompson** *(1823–1903), author of* The English Flower Garden.

also wrote monographs for the Society on the apricot, gooseberry and cherry.

His lasting renown, however, rests on his book, *The Gardener's Assistant*, published in 1859. He made innumerable contributions to gardening magazines and was widely consulted as one of the foremost authorities on fruit, although his retiring manner was undoubtedly the reason for his receiving no honours and awards of consequence despite his life-long labours and high professional renown.

Towards the end of his life a subscription raised amongst gardeners in tribute to his services to horticulture reached £400. An editorial obituary to Thompson speaks of the debt that John Lindley (qv) owed to Thompson's knowledge.

Thompson, William (1823–1903). Botanist and horticultural writer. Thompson was born at Ipswich in Suffolk, and at an early age became interested in scientific studies, especially chemistry. He was also an enthusiastic photographer—one of the first to use the daguerreotype method of photography—travelling widely in East Anglia in search of picturesque subjects.

He also became interested in botanical studies and the cultivation of plants and whilst still in his twenties had begun to collect, exchange and sell seeds of rarer species. The small garden which he had started at his home in Ipswich was extended; and he issued his first catalogue in 1855. The specialities of his nurseries, which soon gained a reputation

David **Thomson** *(1823–1909).*

Joseph **Thomson** *(1858–1894).*

Dr Thomas **Thomson** *(1817–1878).*

Typically elaborate design for a series of flowerbeds, forming a colourful parterre, reproduced from The Handy Book of the Flower Garden *by David* **Thomson**, *published in 1868.*

'A glimpse of camp life', an illustration from a biography of Joseph **Thomson**, *plant-collector, African explorer and geologist, written by his brother, the Reverend James B. Thomson and published in 1897.*

extending far beyond Suffolk, were herbaceous and alpine plants, and he imported many species from the Western regions of the United States and from Western Australia. In 1861 he introduced *Helipterum manglesii*, which became a favourite amongst professional florists, as did the rarities of columbine, which he afterwards marketed. His nurseries, which had grown enormously by the end of the nineteenth century, acquired an international renown and were visited by botanists and horticulturists from all over the world.

His literary endeavours were more variable in their success. A monthly journal, *The English Flower Garden*, which he started in 1852, did not flourish, but his *Gardening Book of Annuals*, first published in 1855, and its supplement the following year, were reissued some years later. He was awarded the RHS Victoria Medal of Honour in 1897.

Thomson, David (1823–1909). Gardener and author. Thomson was born at Torloisk on the island of Mull, Scotland, the son of a steward, and received little schooling. When he was fourteen he began to work in the gardens of Carstairs House in Lanarkshire, and later at Bothwell Castle under Andrew Turnbull, one of the foremost plant-growers of the day. In 1844, he joined the Royal Botanic Gardens in Regent's Park, leaving to work as assistant to his elder brother, William Thomson (qv), at Wrotham Park in Hertfordshire. After other appointments, including the remodelling of the gardens and grounds at Dyrham Park in Gloucestershire, Thomson returned to Scotland to work at Archerfield in East Lothian. There, given a free hand and adequate means, he established both his own renown and that of the gardens. He left Archerfield to take charge of the Duke of Buccleuch's gardens at Drumlanrig, one of the largest private gardens in Britain,

where all types of gardening were practised, including fruit and orchid cultivation under a vast area of glass. Thomson was in charge at Drumlanrig for almost thirty years. After contributing for some years to *The Scottish Gardener* he became editor from 1854 until its closure in 1882. His books included *A Practical Treatise on the Culture of the Pineapple* (1866), *The Handy Book of the Flower Garden* (1868) and *Fruits under Glass* (1881). He was awarded the Neill Prize, the Veitch Memorial Medal and the Victoria Medal of Honour by the RHS.

Thomson, Joseph (1858–1895). Plant-collector. Thomson was born in the village of Thornhill, Dumfriesshire, the son of a stonemason, who later combined farming with quarrying. He showed an early interest in geological and other scientific studies. After working for a short time for his father, he entered Edinburgh University to study geology and botany, gaining medals in geology and natural history. In 1878, he was appointed naturalist and geologist to an expedition under Alexander Johnston, sponsored by the Royal Geographical Society for the exploration of East Central Africa. Following the death of Johnston from malaria, Thomson became leader of the expedition. In 1882 he published *To Central African Lakes and Back*, an account of the expedition. This remarkable journey, from which he sent back a collection of plants from equatorial Africa, was followed by one of a quite different and abortive order: a commission from the Sultan of Zanzibar to find coal in the island. More to Thomson's taste was a request from the Royal Geographical Society to open up a route between the eastern seaboard of Africa and the northern shore of Lake Victoria. Here again Thomson showed rare resolution in making his way through the dreaded warlike Masai country and succeeding in his mission, despite ill-health and manifold hazards. Thomson made further expeditions, mainly for Cecil Rhodes, but his health had been seriously undermined by his exertions, and despite recuperative sojourns in Southern Africa and Southern France, he died in London at the age of thirty-seven.

Thomson, Thomas (1817–1878). Botanist and author. Thomson was born in Glasgow and educated at the High School and University in that city, graduating in medical studies in 1839. Although influenced by the

(Opposite) Flower-paintings from a series of delicately-executed botanical watercolours by Simon **Taylor** *(1740–c.1796), now housed in the Library at the Royal Botanic Gardens, Kew.*

HELIANTHUS *Caroliniana Amer. Species.* 348

CISTUS *Laurifolius Sp. Pl. 736.* 342

MAGNOLIA *Acuminata Sp. Pl. 756.* 376

AMARYLLIS *Undulata Hort. Kew. 552.* 356

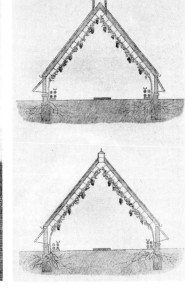

Illustration from Western Himalaya and Tibet: a Narrative of a Journey, 1847–48, *an account of his travels by Thomas* **Thomson**.

William **Thomson** *(1814–1895) and his proposal for a glass house from* A Practical Treatise on the Cultivation of the Grape Vine, *published in 1862.*

lectures of Sir William Hooker (qv), he gradually turned his attention towards botanical studies. After graduating he joined the Honourable East India Company as assistant surgeon, a decision which was to lead to an unexpectedly adventurous career, culminating in half a lifetime of ill-health, stoically borne.

On his arrival in Calcutta in 1840 he was appointed curator of the Museum of the Asiatic Society, but almost immediately was put in charge of a party of recruits *en route* to one of the many Afghanistan campaigns fought sporadically on the North-West frontier. The journey took over a year to reach Kabul, where Thomson was enabled, for a short time, to explore the regional flora, before becoming actively involved in the campaign. During the winter of 1841–42 the British expedition was imprisoned in Ghazni by the Afghans. Losses were high and after surrendering they were first imprisoned and then taken to Kabul, destined to be sold as slaves. But by bribing their captors they succeeded in reaching a relief force. He returned to Calcutta.

In 1847 Thomson was appointed one of three commissioners to determine the boundary between Kashmir and Chinese Tibet. Thanks to inevitable delays and misunderstandings between the two sides Thomson was enabled to engage in a number of botanical investigations in the Western Himalayas. Once again, however, he was involved in war, this time the Second Sikh War. In 1849, Thomson met up with J. D. Hooker (qv) who had been exploring and collecting in the Eastern Himalayas. They spent over a year exploring and botanizing in the Sikkim mountains and the Khasi forests, returning to Britain in 1851. In the following year, Thomson

published his *Western Himalaya and Tibet: a Narrative of a Journey, 1847–48*. Back in England, Thomson and Hooker began the monumental task of cataloguing and distributing the plant specimens they had both collected. Despite Thomson's continuing ill-health they published jointly *Flora Indica* in 1855, but, due to lack of funds, only a single volume was issued.

In 1854 Thomson was appointed Superintendent of the Calcutta Botanic Garden and Professor of Botany at the Medical College. Seven years later, he returned once more to England, broken in health. Five years later he returned briefly to India as interpretor for an Eclipse Expedition. For the rest of his life he divided his time between Kew and his home at Maidstone. He was

elected Fellow of the Linnean Society (1852), of the Royal Geographical Society (1854) and of the Royal Society (1855).

Thomson, William (1814–1895). Gardener and author. Thomson was born at Bowden in Roxburghshire, but was brought up on the island of Mull. He served his gardening apprenticeship on the Penrhyn estates in Wales. He then moved to Bothwell Castle, Lanarkshire, then to Wrotham Park in Hertfordshire, where he remained for sixteen years gaining the considerable horticultural experience which prepared him for his appointment in charge of the Duke of Buccleuch's gardens at Dalkeith in 1855. There he became a leading authority on the grape vine, and published in 1862 his

manual *A Practical Treatise on the Cultivation of The Grape Vine* on its cultivation. After sixteen years at Dalkeith, Thomson left to establish the Tweed Vineyard at Clovenfords, near Galashiels. Apart from building up a considerable knowledge in the large-scale production of grapes, he also established the firm in the successful cultivation of orchids and other high-class plants. He attributed much of his success to his production of an artificial manure which he also marketed. Between 1869 and 1882 he edited *The Scottish Gardener*, being succeeded in that position by his younger brother, David Thomson (qv).

Thornton, Robert John (c. 1765–1837). Botanist and publisher. Thornton was the son of Dr Bonnell

Frontispiece and title page for The Temple of Flora *published in part-form by Robert* **Thornton**, *1799–1807.*

Two views (1925) of the gardens at Chequers, Buckinghamshire, as laid out in the early part of this century by H. Avray **Tipping** *(1855–1933). (Left) Terrace and gateway to forecourt. (Right) The garden descending from terrace to grassway to sunk garden, looking west.*

Thornton, who had married a lady of some modest fortune. According to James Boswell, Thornton was agreeable, lively and odd. Whilst still at school he showed considerable interest in natural history. He studied medicine at Cambridge and Guy's Hospital and set up in practice in London in 1797.

After the death of his mother, the inheritance of her fortune and the growth of his practice, Thornton began to speculate upon the possibilities of writing a notable book on some important aspect of medical botany. He was vacillating in his choice of subject and title and inclined to a somewhat earnest and pompous approach to literature. His projected work, in three volumes, was first tentatively entitled *Philosophy of Botany* but finally issued as *Botanical Extracts; or The Philosophy of Botany* in three folio volumes. What is now internationally famous as *The Temple of Flora* was the third volume of the triad and heavily entitled *A New Illustration of the Sexual System of Carolus von Linnaeus*, first announced in 1797 and completed in parts by 1807. Amongst the artists he commissioned were Peter Henderson, Philip Reinagle, Abraham Pether and Sydenham Edwards (qv), not one of whom has any great renown outside that gained from *The Temple of Flora*. Needless to say, this immense undertaking, involving the commissioning of a considerable number of paintings and drawings, and the payment of engravers and printers for the expensive colour plates, made serious inroads into Thornton's fortune. His outgoings were further multiplied by the setting up of the Linnean Gallery in New Bond Street in which the paintings in progress were exhibited.

Thornton set out to recoup his losses by a lottery with original paintings as prizes, but the project was a desperate failure and Thornton was forced to return to his medical practice. He died in conditions of genteel poverty.

Threlkeld, (Reverend) Caleb (1676–1728). Botanist. He was born in Kirk Oswald, Cumbria, and was educated at Glasgow University before becoming a non-conformist preacher. He afterwards graduated as a doctor from Edinburgh University. He then moved to Dublin with his wife and six children and after some years combining sabbatical preaching with a weekday medical practice he joined the established church.

Meantime, Threlkeld had become a knowledgeable and keen student of botany and made several journeys of botanical enquiry throughout Ireland. In 1727, he published *Synopsis Stirpium Hibernicarum*, describing over five hundred plant species and the districts in which he had found them, from Co. Wicklow to the north, together with their scientific and Irish nomenclature. The book had some success but Threlkeld's knowledge of the Irish language seems to have been somewhat superficial for the task he had undertaken. His botanical knowledge, on the other hand, was soundly based on the wide-ranging, first-hand observations which he made in his own Dublin botanic garden.

Thrower, Percy (1913–). Gardener, broadcaster. Thrower was the second son of the head gardener on a large Buckinghamshire estate. He left school at fourteen to work under his father, a strict taskmaster. At the age of eighteen, at his father's instigation, he moved to the Royal Gardens at Windsor, where he

Percy **Thrower** *(1913–).*

began as an improver. After jobs with the Parks Departments, he was appointed superintendent at Shrewsbury. In 1948 he started on his long broadcasting career in a programme which soon became known as *In Your Garden*. This continued until television began in 1951. Since then he has become the best-known of all gardening experts who appear on television. In 1967, Thrower was asked to advise on the setting-up of a garden centre at Syon and became a director of the initial enterprise, but in 1970, in conjunction with Duncan Murphy, he bought the 40-acre established nursery of Murrells of Shrewsbury, an enterprise which has proved a considerable success. The nursery raises over 150,000 roses a year, 100,000 shrubs and 40,000 conifers, and also includes a garden centre.

Percy Thrower was awarded the Victoria Medal of Honour by the Royal Horticultural Society in 1974.

Tipping, H. Avray (1855–1933). Garden designer, author. Tipping was educated at Christ Church, Oxford, where he obtained a first class honours degree in Modern History. For many years he was a contributor to *Country Life* and garden correspondent to *The Morning Post*. His extensive knowledge of horticulture and garden design, combined with a profound interest in architecture, made him one of the most influential writers on garden design of his time. His books included *In English Homes* (with photographs by Charles Latham) and *The Garden of Today* (1933). In addition to his work as a prolific writer on gardening matters, Avray Tipping gained a considerable renown as a garden designer, laying out extensive gardens at Brinsop Court, Herefordshire, and Chequers, Buckinghamshire, and supervising the construction of many others.

Tobin, (Rear-Admiral) George (1768–1838). Botanical artist. Tobin was the second son of James Tobin of Nevis, an island in the West Indies. He was born at Salisbury in Wiltshire. He entered the navy at the age of twelve and made his first voyage on board HMS *Namur* and was in action two years later in the West Indies. His appearance in this DICTIONARY is due to his service as artist-naturalist on board HMS *Providence* during 1791–3, under Capt. William Bligh (qv), in voyages to Tahiti and the West Indies. Tobin's botanical journal and drawings, made during his voyage under Captain Bligh, are now in the Mitchell Library at Sydney.

Tradescant, John (The Elder) (c. 1570–1638). Gardener and botanist. Tradescant was the son of a Suffolk yeoman who moved to London. Little is known of Tradescant's early life, and the first reliable information concerns his enrolment as a gardener to the Cecils, both at Salis-

John **Tradescant** *(The Elder) (c. 1570–1638) and (right) The Ark, the Tradescants' home in Lambeth, then a village south-west of London, from 1626 until 1678. Here was assembled the extraordinary collection of rarities and antiquities which later formed the basis of the Ashmolean Museum, Oxford.*

bury House in the Strand and at Hatfield House in Hertfordshire, where formal gardens were laid out in the French manner.

In the effort to introduce fresh varieties of fruit and vegetables into England, Tradescant was sent on European journeys, and as well as bringing back black mulberries from France (with the aim to promote the silk-weaving craft in England) he is also reputed to have introduced the cos lettuce into England from the Greek island of that name, and to have sponsored the introduction of a vast number of vines from France for the establishing of a vinery at Hatfield. On the succession of William Cecil to the earldom and to the Hatfield estate, Tradescant was again sent to France to collect roses. He seems also to have travelled in the Mediterranean countries and North Africa. In 1607, he married at Meopham in Kent, where he had a house and land. In 1614, Tradescant left Hatfield and took up residence at Meopham, but later moved to Canterbury to work for Sir Edward Wotton at St Augustine's Palace. In 1618, he travelled to Russia, the first English botanist to make the journey, in the company of Sir Dudley Digges, Ambassador. Tradescant kept a journal of his travels (now in the Bodleian Library) and records that amongst the plants, seeds and objects of more esoteric interest he brought back with him were cones for the first raising of the larch tree in England.

(Opposite) 'Tulips': a plate from Temple of Flora, *part of* A New Illustration of the Sexual System of Carolus von Linnaeus, *published between 1799 and 1807 by Robert* **Thornton.**

Tradescant left the Wottons' service in 1623 to take over the direction of the Duke of Buckingham's gardens at Newhall, near Chelmsford in Essex, and continued his travels with a journey to the low countries, and again to France for the wedding by proxy of King Charles I to Henrietta Maria. After the assassination of Buckingham, Tradescant was appointed Keeper of His Majesty's Gardens at Oatlands, between Walton and Weybridge. In 1626, he moved to Lambeth, then in Surrey, taking over a house which was originally known as Turret House. The garden quickly gained an impressive renown amongst botanists, while in the house, renamed The Ark, Tradescant began to assemble that 'Closett of Rarities', acquired during his travels, which was later to form the nucleus of the Ashmolean Museum of Oxford, the first public museum in Britain.

In 1637 Tradescant was also appointed Keeper of the newly-formed Oxford Botanic Garden, but could not take up the appointment owing to ill-health and in the following year he died.

Tradescant, John (The Younger) (1608–1662). Gardener and botanist. Tradescant, the son of John Tradescant (qv) was born at Meopham in Kent, and was educated at the King's School, Canterbury, where he was a Scholar. He left school in 1623 and began to work as his father's assistant. In 1627 he married Jane Hurte, who died eight years later. In 1634 he was made a Freeman of the Gardeners' Company.

Following the death of his father in 1638, Tradescant was appointed to succeed 'as Keeper of His Maj-

esty's gardens at Oatlands' at a salary of £100 a year. In the same year he married one Hester Pooks. He followed his father's proclivities for travel, making at least three plant-collecting journeys to Virginia in 1637, 1642 and 1654, and possibly an earlier expedition, judging from various plant importations noted in the Tradescants' plant list. On his return from his last voyage to Virginia, Tradescant published the *Musaeum Tradescantianum,* the first catalogue from a public museum to be printed and published in England. The catalogue also included a list of all the plants which had been introduced into the Lambeth garden by the Tradescants.

Tradescant's young son, John III, died in 1652, and the great collection of varieties which had been assembled by his father and himself, originally intended for the Crown, passed by devious means into the possession of one Elias Ashmole, a place-seeker and supposed friend of the family. He in turn bequeathed the collection to the University of Oxford as the Ashmolean Museum, with no acknowledgement to the Tradescants. This wilful omission will, to a degree, be rectified by the Museum in its centenary year, 1983,

A corner of the gardens at Hatfield House, Hertfordshire, where John **Tradescant** *(The Elder) was head gardener.*

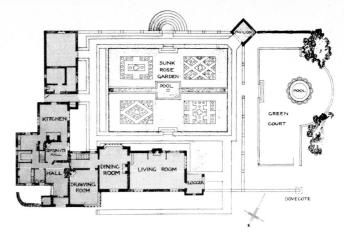

(Left) Garden designed by Inigo **Triggs** *for his own home at Little Boarhunt in Liphook, Hampshire. (Right) Plan showing relation of house and garden at Little Boarhunt.*

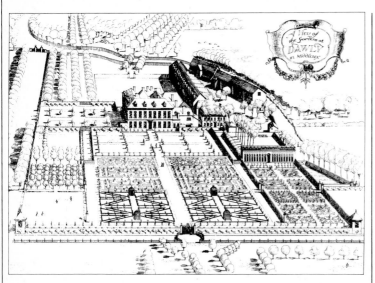

Illustration of Dawly in Middlesex, reproduced in The Formal Gardens in England and Scotland *by Inigo* **Triggs**, *published in 1902.*

Henry **Trimen** *(1843–1896), botanist and plant-collector.*

by the opening of a special Tradescant Room.

The Tradescants are credited with the introduction to Britain of hundreds of plants and trees, including the occidental plane (which was later crossed with the oriental plane to form the London plane tree, *Platanus x acerifolia*), the acacia and lilac.

Triggs, H. Inigo (1876–1923). Architect and garden designer. Triggs was born in Chiswick and educated first at the Godolphin School, Hammersmith, proceeding to the Schools of the Royal Academy, where he trained as an architect. He specialized in designing country houses, mostly in the south of England, and came to take an increasing interest in the laying out of their gardens. He was one of the earliest authorities on the history of the for-

mal style of gardening in Britain and wrote a comprehensive work on the subject. Although Sir Reginald Blomfield (qv) and Inigo Thomas (qv) had published their book, *The Formal Garden in England*, in 1892, Inigo Triggs' large-format book, *The Formal Gardens in England and Scotland*, published ten years later, was the first book to include a sufficiency of photographs and drawings of gardens, statuary, summerhouses, fountains to document his views and theories. Triggs' own designs for gardens reflected this interest in the formal school of landscaping.

Triggs' other books included: *Some Architectural Works of Inigo Jones* (written in conjunction with Henry Tanner, 1900); *The Art of Garden Design in Italy* (1906); *Town Planning, Past, Present and Future* (1909); *Garden Craft in Europe* (1913).

Trimen, Henry (1843–1896). Botanist, plant-collector. Trimen was born in London and educated at King's College School, where he began to collect plants and formed a herbarium. He began his medical

Three of the plates (much reduced) from the three-volume Handbook to the Flora of Ceylon *by Henry* **Trimen**, *published between 1893 and 1895.*

studies at King's College in 1860, and after a year at Edinburgh University, graduated MB at London University. Although he began to practise on graduation his inclination towards botanical studies led to an appointment in the botanical department of the British Museum. In collaboration with William Thistleton-Dyer (qv) (later Sir) he published *The Flora of Middlesex*, generally considered a model for such country records. Trimen became editor of *The Journal of Botany* in 1871, and between 1875 and 1880 published, with Professor Robert Bentley, the forty-two parts of *Medicinal Plants*.

In 1879 he accepted the post of director of the botanical gardens at Peradeniya, Ceylon, where he remained for the next sixteen years. Not only did he engage upon a re-arrangement of the gardens scientifically but sedulously explored the island, collecting material for a projected *Flora of Ceylon*. Three volumes were published between 1893 and 1895.

Failing health caused Trimen to retire and to return home in the latter year, although he continued with the compilation of his notes for further volumes of the *Flora*. He returned to Ceylon and died, at Peradeniya, the next year. The *Flora* was completed by two further volumes (1898–1900) edited by Sir Joseph Hooker (qv). Trimen was elected a Fellow of the Royal Society in 1888 and a Fellow of the Linnean Society in 1866. His name is commemorated in *Ficus trimenii*, a species of Cingalese fig.

Troup, Robert Scott (1874–1939). Botanist, silviculturist. Troup was born at Banbury in Oxfordshire and was educated at Aberdeen Grammar School and the University in that city. In 1897 he joined the Indian Forest Service in Burma, becoming assistant conservator of forests, a position he retained until 1905. He then joined the Forest Research Institute and College at Dehra Dun, until 1915.

During the First World War he was appointed Assistant Inspector-General of Forests to the Government of India, which he ran in conjunction with the control of timber supplies throughout India. In the early post-war years he was appointed Professor of Forestry in the University of Oxford, retaining that position until his death. In 1924 he was appointed Director of the Imperial Forestry Institute where he remained for eleven years. He was made CMG on his retirement.

He wrote prolifically upon silvicultural systems and his publications include *The Silviculture of Indian Trees*, published in three volumes in 1921; *Exotic Forest Trees in the British Empire* (1932); *Forests and State Control* (1938).

Tunnard, Christopher. (1910–   ). Landscape architect. Tunnard was educated in England, including a period at the Royal Horticultural Society, Wisley. After briefly working for Percy Cane (qv) he started his own private practice in 1934, and also contributed articles on landscape and garden design to various periodicals. In 1938, he published his influential book, *The Garden in the Modern Landscape*, in which he advocated his major premise that as a garden should be primarily designed for use, the recreational area should be maximized, with such activities as swimming and tennis readily accommodated and their requirements for space considered in the overall design. Tunnard considered the traditional, abundant, semi-wild Edwardian garden, romantic and sentimental, and he contended that a more objective attitude to nature, similar to that of the Japanese garden, was required. He designed several gardens, notably at St Anne's Hill, Chertsey, and at Halland, Sussex, for the house designed by Serge Chermayeff for himself. He received a special award for landscape design at the Paris Exposition of 1937. In 1939 he emigrated to the USA, concentrating on city planning, mainly in an academic capacity.

Turner, Dawson (1775–1858). Patron, antiquarian, collector, botanist. He was born in Great Yarmouth, where his father was a banker, and was educated at Pembroke College, Cambridge, where his uncle was Master. He intended to take Holy Orders but his father's death in 1796 caused him to forsake this ambition and to enter the family business. Under his direction, the business prospered and he was able to devote much of his leisure to his botanical interests. His other main interest at this time was the study of the antiquities of Norfolk. Later, he

Photographs from The Silviculture of Indian Trees *(1921) taken by the compiler, Robert* **Troup,** *who joined the Indian Forest Service in 1897.*

became a considerable collector, from botanical specimens to books, from pictures to manuscripts (now in the British Museum).

His books on botany include *Synopsis of British Fuci* (1802); *Muscologiae Hibernicae Spicilegium* (1804); *Botanist's Guide through England and Wales* (with L. Dillwyn, 1805).

Turner, Frederick (1852–1939). Botanist. He was born and educated in Yorkshire. In 1874, he joined the Queensland Government Service as a botanist and worked at the Brisbane Botanic Gardens where he was commended for his supervision of improvements to the gardens. He

travelled extensively in order to seek plants for the herbarium. He later became the curator of the Queensland Acclimatization Society's garden for which he collected a large number of plants of economic importance.

In 1890, Fred Turner became Economic Botanist to the newly-established Department of Agriculture in New South Wales. Turner had an exceptional knowledge of the inland areas of Queensland and New South Wales and was especially interested in indigenous grasses and plants which would be of economic value to agriculture. He also assisted in the laying out of the public parks

Dawson **Turner** *(1775–1858).*

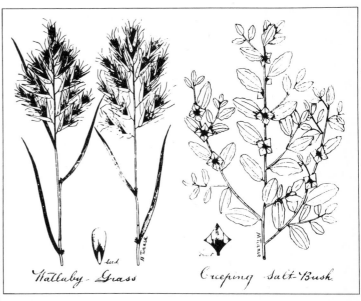

Drawings from Australian Grasses and Pasture Plants *by Frederick* **Turner.**

Sr. John Tradescant Junr.
in his Garden.

in Brisbane and Sydney. He wrote a number of books dealing with Australian plants.

Turner, (Reverend) Williams (c. 1508–1568). Physician and botanist. Born at Morpeth in Northumberland, the son of a tanner, he was educated at Pembroke Hall, Cambridge, at the expense of Lord Wentworth. After graduation he was appointed to a junior fellowship and to various collegiate appointments and took holy orders in 1537. He was deeply involved in the intense theological discussion and disputation of the time, prompted by the teachings of Hugh Latimer and Nicholas Ridley. Following two modest religious books, he published in 1538 his *Libellus de re Herbaria*, one of the earliest botanical books to come from Cambridge, where, he wrote, he was unable to learn Greek, Latin or English names for any herb or tree 'such was the ignorance in simples at that time'.

He left Cambridge in 1530 and seems to have spent some time at Oxford. His preaching, however, caused him to be imprisoned as he was unlicensed for such activities. On his release he travelled widely throughout Europe, in Holland, Germany, Italy and Switzerland, collecting plants throughout his travels. His botanical and medical knowledge impressed Conrad Gesner, the German naturalist, with whom he became friendly. In 1544, he was appointed physician to the so-called Erle of Emden, an area covering East Friesland and the off-lying islands of the North German coast. During this sojourn abroad he wrote several religious books which were so popular in England that they were proscribed by the authorities. He also completed his *Herball*, but delayed publication until 1551, after his return to England on the accession of Edward VI in 1547. He was appointed chaplain and physician to the Duke of Somerset and also seems to have become a Member of Parliament. He had a garden at Kew, continued his botanical studies and sought ecclesiastical preferment but was continuously disappointed.

Finally, after a further sojourn abroad, he was given the deanery of Wells. After further vexatious disappointments, frequently prompted by his resolution in propagating the tenets of a reformed church, he was suspended and lived until his death at Crutched Friars in London.

Turner was one of the innovators of scientific botanical studies in England and his *Herball* is one of the seminal botanical publications in British botany.

(Opposite) John **Tradescant** *(The Younger) (1608–1662) from a painting by de Critz.*

Turrill, William Bertram (1890–1961). Botanist and author. Turrill was born at Woodstock in Oxfordshire and educated at the Oxford High School and Chelsea Polytechnic. He entered Kew as a technical assistant in 1909 and became an assistant in the herbarium in 1914.

He remained at Kew for the rest of his life, becoming keeper of the herbarium and library in 1946, holding this position until his retirement in 1957. He wrote widely on his chosen subjects. His books ranged from *Plant Life of the Balkan Peninsula* (deriving from studies in the region and published in 1929), to *The Royal Botanic Gardens, Kew*.

He contributed many papers to the *Kew Bulletin* and other journals and edited the *Botanical Magazine* for the Royal Horticultural Society.

Tusser, Thomas (c. 1524–1580). Writer and poet. The exact year of Tusser's birth is uncertain although it is known that he was born at Rivenhall, near Witham in Essex. As a young chorister he seems to have moved from one place to another, singing and studying variously at Wallingford in Berkshire, Eton and St Paul's. He was elected to King's College, Cambridge, in 1543, but removed to Trinity Hall. Due to sickness, he left the University and became attached to the Court as a musician in the entourage of Lord Paget. Here he remained for ten years, leaving to marry and to farm at Cattwade in Suffolk. In 1557 he published his *Hundreth Poyntes of Good Husbandry* and this was amplified to *Five Hundreth Poyntes of Good Husbandry* in 1573. These homely verses have become classics of English literature, and in the words of Sir Walter Scott 'their rigid and minute attention to every department of domestic economy' deserved high praise. They have been reprinted in many varying editions throughout the centuries, although their success did little to alleviate the continuous misfortune which dogged Tusser's last years, thus sponsoring the contrast which is usually made between the shrewd practicality of his verses with his own lack of success, both as farmer and poet. This was succinctly expressed in the epigram composed by Henry Peacham in 1612:

Tusser, they tell me when thou wert alive
Thou, teaching thrift, thyself couldst never thrive;
So, like the whetstone many men are wont
To sharpen others when themselves are blunt.

He moved from one place to another in East Anglia and Cambridge, living frugally under the protection of various patrons, but dying, a prisoner for debt, in the Poultry in London.

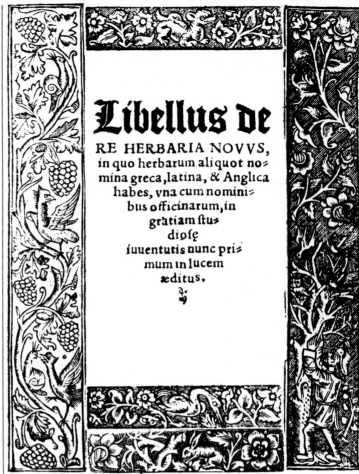

Title page from Libellus de re Herbaria Novus, *by the Reverend William* **Turner,** *one of the earliest botanical books (1538) published from Cambridge.*

Page from the original edition of A Hundreth Good Poyntes of Husbandry *by Thomas* **Tusser,** *published in 1557.*

U-V

Underwood, John (fl. 1780s–1834). Horticulturist. Little is known of Underwood's early life. He was born in Scotland, but, apparently, whilst still in his twenties, arrived in Dublin with his wife, Mary, and six children to become head gardener at what was then known as the Botanic Garden of the Dublin Society, which was established in 1796. Underwood was recommended by William Curtis (of Curtis' *Botanical Magazine*) and brought over to Ireland by John Foster, Lord Oriel, the last speaker of the Irish Houses of Parliament before the Act of Union. With Dr Walter Wade (the first professor of Botany to the Dublin Society) Lord Oriel was the prime mover in setting up the Botanic Garden. Between 1800 and 1804, Underwood published a catalogue of the collections at Glasnevin. He also published a series of annual weather reports.

In 1818 Underwood was held responsible for the loss of the Glasnevin specimen of the Norfolk Island Pine tree and fined. In fact, the loss was not entirely his fault as the structure that was being built to house the tree was not completed until November, by which time the tree had suffered from frost. The tree had been considered the finest in Europe. After that, the garden maintenance fell into a decline, possibly because Underwood lost enthusiasm. He retired in 1833 by which time he is said to have become senile. He died in 1834.

Uvedale, (Reverend) Robert (1642–1722). Horticulturist. Descendant of an ancient Dorset family, he was born in Westminster and educated at Westminster School and Trinity College, Cambridge, where he first studied divinity and, later, law. Whilst still in his early twenties he was appointed headmaster of Enfield Grammar School, then well outside the London area. He leased the manor-house in order to take boarders and began to enhance the social and academic standing of the school, whilst extending his lifelong botanical studies and experiments. Around 1670 he planted the cedar which was later to become something of a legendary landmark in the locality and stood until recent years. The boarding side of the school became so highly successful, with many boys from titled families

A view of the Botanic Gardens at Glasnevin, Dublin, which were in the care of John **Underwood** *between 1793 and 1833.*

The famous cedar tree in the gardens of the grammar school at Enfield, Middlesex, where the Reverend Robert **Uvedale** *was headmaster for over twenty years.*

enrolling as pupils, that Uvedale was criticized for neglecting the studies of the day-boys attending the school.

Uvedale's horticultural reputation was based on his skill in cultivating exotics and for his experiments as one of the earliest owners of hot houses. A contemporary account of gardens near London speaks of Uvedale as possessing an extraordinary art in managing plants and as 'a master of the greatest and choicest collection of exotic greens that is perhaps anywhere in this land. His greens take up six or seven houses or roomsteads. His orange-trees and largest myrtles fill up his biggest houses and . . . those more nice and curious plants that need closer keeping are in warmer rooms, and some of them stoved when he thinks fit. His flowers are choice, his stock numerous, and his culture of them very methodical and curious.'

After his death, most of Uvedale's plants were sold to Sir Robert Walpole and taken to Houghton Hall in Norfolk, and his herbarium, in fourteen volumes, containing plants from most of the great collectors of his time, was transferred to the Sloane Collection.

Vallentin, Elinor Frances (1873–1924). Botanist and botanical artist. Elinor Vallentin (née Ber-

Cochlearia officinalis, by Elinor **Vallentin** *(1873–1924).*

292

Garden wall terminating in a balustraded and quoined pavilion, designed by Sir John **Vanbrugh** *for the 1st Duke of Ancaster at Grimsthorpe Castle, Lincolnshire (1722–6).*

The Belvedere at Claremont in Surrey, built in 1715 to the designs of Sir John **Vanbrugh** *as an eye-catcher. (Photographed in 1977).*

trand) was born in the Falkland Islands where her parents had been living for two years. She showed an early interest in botany and studied at the Botanic Gardens, Kew. In 1904, she married Rupert Vallentin, also a botanist, and they returned to the Falkland Islands five years later. She was commissioned by Kew to make studies of the plant life of the Falkland Islands, in order to establish the extent to which the flora of the islands had changed since Sir Joseph Hooker's book, *Flora Antarctica*, was published in 1847. She produced an exhaustive study with many fine colourful illustrations giving full and accurate details. Her collections were presented to Kew. In 1921, she published *Illustrations of Flowering Plants and Ferns of Falkland Islands.* (The original drawings for this work are housed in the library at Kew.)

Elinor Vallentin and her husband returned to England in 1911 and settled at Plymouth, Devon.

Vanbrugh, (Sir) **John** (1664–1726). Architect, dramatist and landscape architect. Vanbrugh was born in Chester, the son of Giles Vanbrugh, a sugar-baker, and probably was educated at the grammar school in that city.

Between 1683 and 1685 Vanbrugh was in France where he may have received his architectural training, but in 1686 he received a commission in the Earl of Huntingdon's Regiment, becoming a captain

Sir John **Vanbrugh,** *designer of the Temple of the Four Winds at Castle Howard, Yorkshire. (Portrait, c. 1705, by Sir Godfrey Kneller.)*

in 1702. Before that, in 1690, Vanbrugh had been arrested in France and imprisoned at Vincennes and, later, in the Bastille. Whilst incarcerated Vanbrugh drafted the outline of what was to prove his most popular play, *The Provoked Wife,* although his first play to be given stage production was *The Relapse* in 1696. The former was staged at Lincolns Inn Fields in 1697 and the play's indecencies were such that a contemporary critic adjudged they ought to explode the play 'out of all reputable society'. But Vanbrugh was unperturbed by such criticism which undoubtedly helped to popularize his plays.

Vanbrugh's career as a playwright continued with other productions during the succeeding five years, but meantime he had become involved in architectural design of a most substantial order. In common with much else in Vanbrugh's life, the origins of this new and far-reaching interest are extremely obscure. What is known is that in 1701 he was commissioned by his friend, the Earl of Carlisle, to design a new house on the site of the ancient castle of Hinderskelf in North Yorkshire. The resulting house, or rather palace, was Castle Howard, not to be completed until 1714. Carlisle was plainly pleased with his new seat, for he was influential in having Vanbrugh appointed Clarenceux king-at-arms, despite Vanbrugh's cynical view of heraldry and its attendant pomp and circum-

*The **Veitch** family: from left to right (top) John (1752–1839), James (1792–1863), James (1815–1869), James Herbert (1868–1907); (below) Harry James (1840–1924), John Gould (1839–1870), Robert (1823–1885), Arthur (1844–1880).*

stance. In 1702 Vanbrugh had also succeeded William Talman as Comptroller of the Board of Works, a position he retained, against all intrigue, until his death. In 1705, at the special request of the Duke of Marlborough, Vanbrugh was appointed architect and surveyor of the great new palace which was to be erected at Woodstock in Oxfordshire, to commemorate Marlborough's victory at Blenheim and to be named after that battle. The first stone was laid by the architect in the same year, but the work proceeded slowly, due to uneven Treasury contributions and to the intervention of the formidable Duchess of Marlborough, with resulting lawsuits, which continued long after the duke's death in 1722.

The full story of Vanbrugh's playwriting and architectural talents is to be read elsewhere. As an influence on English landscape garden design he was remarkable more for his expressed attitudes than documented achievements. Those attitudes are most clearly evident at Castle Howard, where a wild and romantic countryside formed the perfect backdrop for the outworks which Vanbrugh and Hawksmoor intended and developed in consultation with Lord Carlisle.

At Blenheim (in conjunction with Henry Wise), at Stowe and Claremont, his recommendations were towards similar temples, bridges, grottos, pillars and statues integrated into romantic man-made landscapes.

In 1715 he was appointed by George I to the newly created post of 'Surveyor of the Gardens and Waters belonging to the Several Palaces within that part of Britain called England'. Vanbrugh's work was mainly concerned with the gardens at Hampton Court.

Vanbrugh's notions were rarely those of everyday life. He preferred palaces and palatial scale, seeking to give even a modest house a sense of grandeur and majesty. He also sought to give any garden a sense of scale well beyond its physical confines. As an architect, he was always desirous that the elaborate outworks he designed for his houses should be visually memorable, and always incorporated 'some plain but magnificent and durable monument' to his patrons.

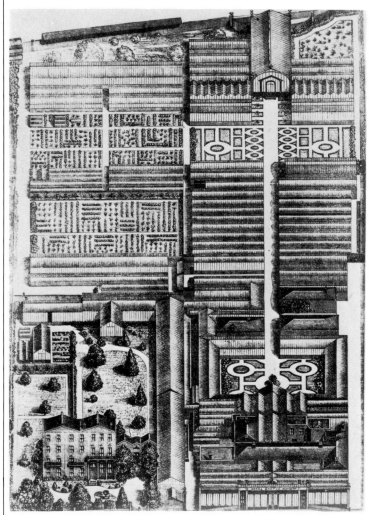

*The nursery in Chelsea, which was mainly the concern of James **Veitch** (1815–1869), and which became known as the Royal Exotic Nurseries.*

Veitch family:

JOHN VEITCH (1752–1839). Horticulturist. Nurseryman. Veitch, the founder of the world-famous firm of nurserymen, was born at Jedburgh in Scotland. At an early age he journeyed to England and began work in a London nursery. His abilities were soon recognized and within a short time, before he was twenty, he was asked by Sir Thomas Acland (qv) to lay out gardens at the family seat at Killerton in Devon, and he was soon acting as agent for all the Acland estates in addition to his work as a landscape gardener. By 1808 he had been enabled, with help from his patron, to set up his own nursery at Budlake, near Killerton. In 1832, in company with his son, James, he transferred the business to Mount Radford at Exeter, having found the distance from Killerton to Exeter a handicap. On his death, the business was transferred to his son.

JAMES VEITCH (1792–1863). Horticulturist. James, as son of the founder of the Exeter Nursery, was mainly responsible for the remarkable success of the Exeter venture. He was both a sound business man and horticulturist. In 1853, it was decided that the firm should have a base in London and the Knight and Perry's nursery in Chelsea was acquired, becoming known as the Royal Exotic nurseries. James Veitch remained in Exeter and his son, James junior, undertook the development of the Chelsea firm. On the death of Veitch *père*, the Exeter and Chelsea nurseries became separate enterprises, Robert, the younger son, taking over the Exeter branch.

JAMES VEITCH (1815–1869). Horticulturist. Under James, who was third in the dynasty, the Royal Exotic Nurseries in Chelsea flourished, becoming famous for orchids, stove and greenhouse plants. Other branches at Coombe Wood, Langley, Slough and Feltham were also set up in a policy of expansion, in which Veitch was ably and vigorously aided by his sons, JOHN GOULD VEITCH (1839–1870) who died a year after his father, and HARRY JAMES, the younger of the two brothers. After James' death, the Veitch Memorial Medal was instituted, and a portrait hung in

*(Opposite) The bridge at Blenheim, designed by Sir John **Vanbrugh** to span the stream (later enlarged by 'Capability' Brown to form a lake). (Below) Temple of the Four Winds at Castle Howard, Yorkshire, designed by Vanbrugh. The circular Mausoleum in the distance is by Nicholas Hawksmoor.*

the Council Chamber of the Royal Horticultural Society.

(SIR) HARRY JAMES VEITCH (1840–1924). Horticulturist. After the death of his father and brother within a year of each other, Veitch carried on the considerable enterprises of the firm alone. Having no sons, he took on two nephews and, in due course, retired, but under its new management the firm's fortunes declined and despite the return of Sir Harry (who was knighted in 1912) the firm was closed down in 1914. He was known as a skilful hybridizer of orchids and was author of a paper on the fertilization of *Cattleya labiata*.

The Exeter firm continued under descendants of the other branch of the family until 1969, when the business was sold. There are now no members of the family in the firm. Many notable horticultural manuals were sponsored by the House of Veitch, including *Hortus Veitchii* and those on orchidaceous plants and conifers.

The Veitch family's most lasting claim to gardening fame is their far-sighted sponsorship of plant-hunters, both in the Americas and the Far East, such as Ernest Wilson (qv) and William Lobb (qv).

Vines, Sydney Howard (1849–1934). Botanist. Vines was born at Ealing, the son of a schoolmaster. He received his early education in Germany and later entered Guy's Hospital to study medicine, but switched to physiology. After win-

*Sydney Howard **Vines** (1849–1934), Sherardian Professor at Oxford.*

*Charles Frances Annesley **Voysey** (1857–1941).*

ning an entrance scholarship he entered Christ's College, Cambridge, where he gained a first-class honours degree and was elected to a college fellowship. During his lectureship he virtually founded the scientific study of botany at the university, introducing laboratory studies after his own further tutelage under Julius von Sachs, the noted German botanist and scientist, at Wurzburg. Due to his energy and dedication, botanical studies prospered at Cambridge, and the course became so popular that a lab-

oratory was built. Vines was elected to the Sherardian professorship at Oxford in 1888, an appointment which included responsibility for the botanic garden and herbarium. His work at Oxford, although contributing largely to the furtherance of botanical studies at the university, was not on a comparable scale with his work at Cambridge. His intensive work there had undoubtedly undermined his health.

Vipan, John Alexander Maylin (1849–1939). Plant-collector. Vipan

was the son of John Maylin of Stibbington Hall, Wansford, Huntingdonshire. He was educated in Switzerland and at Sandhurst.

He spent most of his military service in India and Burma. During his periods of leave he cultivated, at Stibbington Hall, the orchids and ferns which he had collected on his travels in the Far East.

His mother was an enthusiastic supporter of his botanical interests and carefully cultivated the plants which he sent back to England, each consecutively numbered. She also kept him in touch with cultural experiments being carried out in England. Vipan sent home numerous plants to Sander and Company of St Albans (qv).

Two orchids were named after him: *Vanda vipanii* (1882) which was discovered by Vipan in Burma and the hybrid *Cypripedium x vipanii* raised at Stibbington Hall. Vipan was also well known as a skilful plant-photographer.

Voysey, Charles Francis Annesley (1857–1941). Architect, garden designer. Voysey was born at Hessle, near Hull in Yorkshire, the son of a vicar, but in 1871 his father was expelled from the Church of England and deprived of his living, owing to his unorthodox beliefs, and the family moved to London. Voysey was educated briefly at Dulwich but left in 1874 to take up apprenticeship to the architect, John Pollard Seddon, in whose office he remained for over five years before gaining further experience in other offices and setting up in private practice. The earliest influence of consequence in his life was that of Arthur Mackmurdo, who aided Voysey in his first essays in designing textiles and wallpapers. Voysey soon became interested in the tenets of the Modern Movement, influences of which were to be seen in his first house, designed in 1888, at Bedford Park.

Gradually, however, Charles Voysey moved away from these continental influences and began to design houses which, although strongly marked by an individual style, were in the long tradition of English country-house architecture. The main distinction of these designs lay in their sound proportions, the way in which they were characterized by high-pitched roofs, plain unfussy façades, emphatic bay windows, and practical interiors. Voysey's manner was widely copied—and debased—by hundreds of speculative builders between the wars. Inevitably, this interest in every aspect of domestic design led Voysey to the layout of the gardens of the houses for which he was responsible. Amongst these were Priors Garth at Puttenham, and New Place, Haslemere, both of which are in Surrey.

*John **Vipan** (1849–1939).*

*Garden at Shackelford, near Guildford, designed by Charles **Voysey**.*

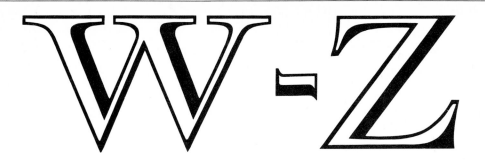

Rev. John **Walker,** *from* Naturalist's Library *by W. Jardine (1833–45).*

Walker, (Reverend) John (1731–1803). Botanist. Walker was born in Edinburgh, the son of the rector of the grammar school. After schooling under his father he proceeded to Edinburgh University to prepare for the Church. In 1758, he was ordained as minister of Glencorse, near Edinburgh.

At Glencorse he became interested in the efforts which were then being made by Lord Kames to further agricultural improvement, and in 1762 he was appointed to make a survey of the Hebrides, travelling over three thousand miles during his seven-month survey, collecting plants in addition to making his enquiries into the economy of the islands.

In 1779, Walker was appointed to the regius professorship of natural history at Edinburgh University, retaining his living at Moffat, Dumfriesshire. His lectures were extremely popular and he published exemplary syllabuses for his students.

John Walker cultivated a garden at Colinton, near Edinburgh, with particular attention to willows and other trees. He was a founder member of the Royal Society of Edinburgh in 1783 and published a paper on *Experiments on the Motion of Sap in Trees.*

Nathaniel **Wallich** *(1786–1854). A drawing by Alan Cracknell.*

Wallich, Nathaniel (1786–1854). Wallich, originally Nathan Wolff, in his native Denmark, was born in Copenhagen and studied medicine in that city. In 1807 he was appointed surgeon to the Danish settlement of Serampore, near Calcutta. This settlement was taken over by the British the following year, and Wallich's services were transferred to the Hon East India Company. The transfer seems to have caused no hardship or resentment to Wallich. He spoke and wrote in English and spent his leaves and retirement in London, and when his *Plantae Asiaticae Rariores*

Illustration from Plantae Asiaticae Rariores *(1830–2) by Nathaniel* **Wallich.** *The plates were engraved by Gauci after drawings by native Indian artists.*

was published in 1830–32, it seems to have been forgotten that the author was not British by birth. The book was hailed as a 'new glory to the British nation and the reign of George IV'.

By then, Wallich had become the director of the Calcutta Botanic Garden—known from 1817 as 'Wallich's Pet'—and from there sent vast numbers of plants, bulbs, seeds and specimens to England.

Wallich travelled extensively and collected in the East Indies and Burma and in several parts of India including Nepal and Assam, and he also made extensive use of native

collectors, particularly in Nepal. This resulted in some of the earliest introductions to gardens of hardy Himalayan plants—*Cotoneaster rigidus, Lilium (cardiocrinum) giganteum* and *Bergena ligulata.*

Wallich suffered a good deal throughout his life from ill-health, and in 1843 went for a holiday to the Cape of Good Hope; even from there he sent home plants, so that a species bearing his name need not necessarily come from India. But *Geranium wallichianum, Meconopsis wallichii* and *Lilium wallichianum* all resulted from his researches in the Himalayas.

(Left) Shell-design garden seat at Strawberry Hill, Middlesex, the gothick home (above) of Horace **Walpole**.

Horace **Walpole** (1717–1797).

He died in London. He was made a Fellow of the Linnean Society in 1818 and a Fellow of the Royal Society in 1829.

Walpole, (Horatio) Horace, 4th Earl of Orford (1717–1797). Politician, man of letters, architectural and landscape gardening dilettante. Walpole was the youngest son of Sir Robert Walpole, generally regarded as the first English Prime Minister. He was educated at Eton and King's College, Cambridge. In 1739, he set out with a school friend, Thomas Gray, on the Grand Tour, but returned to England after a quarrel with the poet. Two years later he entered Parliament, representing the Cornish borough of Callingford, and retained the seat until 1768, although his political achievements fell far short of his ambitions. He continued, however, to record the proceedings of both Houses in his memoirs. He showed an early interest in the then-fashionable study of the Picturesque. Whilst on the Grand Tour, he wrote of encounter-ing, 'precipices, mountains, tor-rents, wolves, rumblings . . . Salvator Rosa'. He continued to exercise these wildly romantic sentiments throughout his life.

In 1747 he took over the lease of a small three-storeyed Thameside villa at Twickenham, Middlesex, known as Strawberry Hill, and in the following year acquired the free-hold. Here he was able to indulge to the full his passion for the Pictur-esque—'I have two cows and a flock of Turkish sheep, all studied as becoming the view,' he wrote—and set about that transformation which was to turn the house into the most extravagant and charming of all essays in castellated eighteenth-century gothick.

Walpole was not only profoundly interested in the architectural aspects of his house, but also in the landscaping of his riverside garden. He also established a printing press in the villa, which he called Officina Arbuteana, on which various of his own and friends' publications were printed.

Walpole has been termed the 'best letter-writer in the English lan-guage' and in the course of a life-long, wide-ranging correspondence he showed himself to be the most percipient and practised of all com-mentators upon the considerable changes then taking place in English gardening taste and practice under the impact of Bridgeman, Kent and, later, Brown. Certainly there was much scope for such comment. As he wrote in one of the early issues of the periodical *The World* (1753–1756): 'There is not a citizen who does not take more pains to tor-ture his acre and half into irregu-larities than he formerly would have employed to make it as formal as a cravat.' These commentaries were encapsulated in his *Essay on Gar-dening*, first published in 1771. Although brief, the essay was undoubtedly the most effective and balanced of all critical and historical accounts of English gardening then available. Walpole clearly con-sidered that two men—Milton on the literary side and Claude Lorrain on the graphic side—provided the models for the English garden. He cited Kent as the founder of the Pic-turesque movement amongst land-scape gardeners. 'We have given the true model of gardening to the world,' he wrote, 'Let other coun-tries mimic or corrupt our taste, but let it reign here on its verdant throne, original by its elegant sim-plicity, and proud of no other art, than that of softening nature's harshness and copying her graceful touch.' He continued to enthuse rhetorically on his native school of landscaping: 'How rich, how gay, how picturesque, the face of the country! The demolition of walls laying open each improvement, every journey is made through a succession of pictures . . . Enough has been done to establish such a school of landscape as cannot be found on the rest of the globe. If we have the seeds of a Claud or a Gaspar among us, he must come forth. If wood, water, vallies, glades, can inspire a poet or a painter, this is the country, this is the age, to produce them.'

He died, unmarried, in his house in Berkeley Square.

Ward, (Dr) Nathaniel Bagshaw (1791–1868). Botanist and inventor. Few men have been responsible for so significant, practical and magnifi-cent a benefit to botany as Ward, the inventor of the Wardian case, which enabled plants to be transported across the world in a protected environment.

Ward was born in London and educated for the medical profession, thus following his father. He prac-tised for many years in the East End of London. As a result of a child-hood voyage to Jamaica and a brief sojourn in the island, a lifelong interest in botany was engendered. Throughout his medical studies he continued with his plant-collecting on the outskirts of London, and at his death his herbarium contained over 25,000 specimens.

Yet it was the invention of the Wardian case which immortalized his name amongst plantsmen and in botanical records. The discovery which underlay the invention was made by Ward in 1829, based on his observation of the healthy growth of fern and grass when placed on mould containing the chrysalis of a moth, all within a covered bottle. After further study and research, Ward announced his discovery to Dr W. J. Hooker (qv) in a letter published in the *Companion to the Botanical Magazine* and more com-prehensively in his own monograph, *On the Growth of Plants in Closely Glazed Cases*, published in 1842. As a result of his interest in giving microscopical soirées, the Micro-scopical Society was started in 1839.

These first close-glazed cases proved remarkably successful devices for the transport of living

Gothick gateway at Strawberry Hill, landscaped by Horace **Walpole**.

(Opposite) Garden at Portmeirion, North Wales, made by Sir Clough **Williams-Ellis** (1883–1978) from 1925 onwards.

plants from one country to another, protecting them from extremes of temperature and from salt spray which had doomed so many plants in the early days of plant-collection during their passage in sailing ships from the Far East to Europe. The Wardian case proved its worth on long-drawn ocean and overland journeys. Amongst the early successful transportations which were made possible by the invention of the Wardian case were the Chinese banana, *Musa Cavendishii*, which had been successfully cultivated by Sir Joseph Paxton for the Duke of Devonshire at Chatsworth in Derbyshire, sent first to the Samoan Islands, thence to the Friendly Islands and Fiji. Robert Fortune also sent 20,000 tea plants from Shanghai to the Himalayas by means of the Wardian case. Cinchona and rubber plants, from their native habitat in South America, were sent via Kew, for re-establishing in the Far East.

Plants growing in decorative Wardian cases later became popular in Victorian drawing-rooms.

Ward was an active member of the Apothecaries' Society, remaining the Society's examiner in botany for almost twenty years and taking charge of the Society's Chelsea garden with consequential improvements. In due course he became Master and Treasurer.

Ward was elected a Fellow of the Linnean Society in 1817 and of the Royal Society in 1852. His name is commemorated in *Wardia*, a genus of South American mosses.

Waterer family:

The two branches of this famous family of nurserymen descend from MICHAEL WATERER (1745–1827) founder of a nursery at Knaphill, near Woking, Surrey. In 1829, his two sons, JOHN WATERER and his brother HOSEA, started their own nursery at Bagshot, also in Surrey, specializing in the cultivation of rhododendrons for 'the Nobility, Gentry and others'. In 1844 the partnership was dissolved, John Waterer retained the Bagshot nursery, his brother taking over Knaphill.

The Bagshot nursery quickly became known as 'The American Nursery,' thanks to its remarkable stock of rhododendrons and other shrubs suited to the United States, whence thousands of plants were shipped every year.

The early success of the family firm during the Victorian era was based on the endeavours of three brothers, FREDERICK, JOHN and MICHAEL, who succeeded to the Bagshot nursery on the death of John Waterer in 1868.

Amongst the many rhododendrons sponsored by Waterers, the most famous was Pink Pearl, raised in 1890, and given an RHS

Nathaniel **Ward** *(1791–1868).*

John **Waterer** *(c. 1783–1868).*

Michael **Waterer** *(1824–1878).*

Award of Merit in 1897. Probably more than a million plants of Pink Pearl have been distributed during almost ninety years. Yet the plant nearly disappeared before it was a year old: the original, and solitary, plant was stolen from the Bagshot Nursery, but was subsequently found in a cottage garden a mile or so away. Much of this development was due to FRANK GOMER WATERER (c. 1868–1945).

In 1914 Waterers of Bagshot amalgamated with Bernard Crisp's Hardy Plant Nursery in Berkshire, thus adding herbaceous plants, irises, roses and fruit trees to the extensive collection of shrubs already grown. Shops and offices were opened in London.

Exhibits, particularly of rhododendrons, are staged annually at

Chelsea and other horticultural shows throughout the country. Particular emphasis has been given to the new strain of 'Exbury' type azaleas. At the Twyford nursery emphasis was given to the culture of bearded irises, many from the United States.

Hybridizing has long been a feature of Waterers: the most notable achievement in recent years has been the new range of dwarf *R. yakushimanum* hybrids, for which Percy Wiseman, nursery manager between 1925 and 1964, was mainly responsible.

In 1968 the Sunningdale Nursery (established in 1847) was taken over by Waterers, and, later, Dobbies of Edinburgh, thus making rhododendrons and azaleas, camellias and other shrubs more readily available

in Scotland. Waterers' production is now approximately 25,000 conifers, 30,000 azaleas, 45,000 rhododendrons, 30,000 trees and 300,000 shrubs annually, as well as 350,000 plants produced in soil-less compost. Waterers, which no longer has a member of the original family on the board of directors, also operates a large landscape design organization.

Meanwhile, the Knaphill nursery was continued under ANTHONY WATERER (1822–1896) and his son, also ANTHONY (1850–1924).

Watson, William (1858–1925). Horticulturist. Watson was born at Garston, Liverpool, and after modest schooling started work at an early age in a local nursery. In 1879 he went to Kew as foreman of the propagating department and in 1886 was appointed assistant curator, succeeding to the curatorship in 1901, a position he held until 1922. He worked under the directorship of Sir W. T. Thiselton-Dyer, with whom he collaborated closely in the revival of Kew as a horticultural as well as a botanical institute. Watson had a cyclopaedic knowledge and wide experience of growing plants under glass and his passion for and success with rhododendrons established the remarkable collection of these plants at Kew.

He was also a prolific writer on horticulture. He was, for many years, gardening editor of *The Field*, and virtually rewrote Robert Thompson's *Gardener's Assistant*. His other books included *Rhododendrons and Azaleas* (1911); *Climbing Plants* (1915) and, with W. J. Bean, *Orchids, Their Culture and Management* (1890). He also became the first editor of the Kew Guild's *Journal* and established the British Gardeners' Association. He was elected an Associate of the Linnean Society in 1904 and was awarded the

An example of a Wardian case, invented by Nathaniel **Ward** *in 1829 to facilitate the transport of plants over long distances.*

*William **Watson** (1858–1925) and an illustration of the* Mamilliaria Pectinata *from his* Cactus Culture *published in 1889.*

*John **Wedgwood** (1766–1844).*

Veitch Memorial Medal in 1892 and the Victoria Medal of Honour in 1916. He also advised on preparing the grounds for the British Empire exhibition at Wembley in 1924.

Webb, Philip Barker (1793–1854). Botanist, horticulturist, plant-hunter, writer. Webb was born at Milford, near Godalming in Surrey, the eldest son of well-to-do parents. He studied botany at Oxford, leaving in 1815, the year of his father's death. His patrimony made him financially independent and he decided to combine his interest in foreign travel with his passion for botanizing. His first voyage in 1818, however, was far more concerned with the attempt to solve problems of Homeric geography than with botanizing. He travelled to the Near East by way of Corfu, Athens and Constantinople, returning via Malta and Sicily. He travelled in Turkish costume, a garb which seems to have been much to his taste, for he commissioned his portrait to be painted thus attired. (One is in the National Portrait Gallery, London, another in the Hunt Library, USA.)

In 1825 Webb set out on the first of a series of botanical travels, spending much time collecting specimens in southern Spain, but his ambition was to explore Morocco, then a country forbidden to foreigners other than appointed ambassadors or recognized consular officials. Yet Webb, by strategic bribing, managed to become one of the first Europeans to climb the mountains of Beni Darsa and Beni Hosmar. He returned to Spain, especially to the Sierra Nevada and to the mountainous regions of Andalusia. He continued his botanizing in Portugal, which he found ideally suited to his pursuit, freed from the predatory bandits and peasants of Morocco and Spain. He later spent over two years in the Canaries. These travels resulted in various publications, including accounts of his collecting in Spain and Portugal, published in 1838 and 1839. His main claim to botanical renown, however, rests in the *Histoire Naturelle des Iles Canaries*, written in collaboration with Sabin Berthelot, the first volume published in 1835 and the third and final volume in 1860, four years after his death.

Wedgwood, John (1766–1844). Potter, horticulturist. Wedgwood was the eldest of the three sons of Josiah Wedgwood, founder of the renowned pottery at Etruria in Staffordshire. He was educated locally and in Lancashire, paying particular attention to the study of chemistry. He later entered Edinburgh University, specializing in mineralogy and chemistry. After a spell at the pottery, he travelled with his younger brother, Josiah, in Europe, making the Grand Tour. After their return they both worked in the pottery, but in 1792 John joined the London and Middlesex Bank as junior partner, relinquishing his partnership in the pottery. Two years later he married the sister of Josiah's wife and went to live in Devon, but later moved to London. Meantime, he had become deeply interested in gardening and in 1797 moved from London to a house at Westbury in Somerset, where he grew grapes, pineapples and peaches under glass, planted an orchard and cultivated a wide range of flowers, including azaleas, tulips and carnations.

During these years, the pottery, under the second Josiah, got into severe financial difficulties and John rejoined the firm. Consequently he spent much time in Staffordshire and on June 29, 1804, from Etruria, he wrote to William Forsyth (qv), gardener to King George III, beginning 'I have been turning my attention to the formation of a Horticultural Society, and have drawn up such heads as have appeared to me necessary for the first formation of the Society.' The letter was to result in the formation of the Society.

He spent much time in seeking to repair the fortunes of the pottery, but the bank, in which he had invested most of the fortune inherited from his father, failed and he was forced to sell his Somerset property and to make his home–or rather series of homes–in Staffordshire. Each home showed his passion for gardening and his *Garden Book*, now housed in the Lindley Library of the Royal Horticultural Society, gives details of his consistent cultivation of a wide range of vegetables and fruit, including, at one time, twelve different varieties of raspberries and thirty of strawberries, as well as an immense range of flowers.

The Horticultural Society of London was formed in 1804, the inaugural meeting being on March 19th of that year in the house of the bookseller, Mr Hatchard, seven men being present including Forsyth and Sir Joseph Banks. Wedgwood was Treasurer of the Society for the first two years. Unfortu-

*Philip Barker **Webb** (1793–1854) in oriental costume and (right) an illustration from* Histoire Naturelle des Iles Canaries, *written by Webb in collaboration with Sabin Berthelot (1838).*

Joseph Wells, head gardener to William **Wells** *at Redleaf in Kent.*

A view of the gardens at Redleaf in Kent, the home of William **Wells**. *The informal layout and planting were considerably in advance of their time. Reproduced from John Loudon's* The Gardener's Magazine, *1839.*

nately, his eyesight failing, he ended his gardening interests in 1843 and went to live with one of his sons at Tenby in Pembrokeshire, dying the following year.

Wells, William (1760–1847). Art collector and landscape gardener. Wells was a businessman who seems to have made a fortune whilst still comparatively young and bought the estate of Redleaf in Kent, adjacent to Penshurst. He was a genial host to a number of eminent artists and managed to acquire many of their works, including paintings by Landseer, as well as Old Masters. His main interest, however, was the transformation of the grounds at Redleaf and the making of a garden which was considerably in advance of its time, being wholly informal in feeling, embellished with several decorative buildings, and utilizing

what John Loudon (qv) termed 'the great leading natural features of the place'. He exploited the natural slope in the gardens to make a large rock garden, beds so formed being gaily filled with flowers. Trees and plants, many raised from seeds imported from abroad, were a feature of Redleaf. His head gardener was Joseph Wells (no relation), father of H. G. Wells, the world-famous novelist, to whom much of the credit for this remarkable garden is due.

Wells also started an experimental garden, and in 1825, according to Loudon, he raised the first dwarf dahlias. Loudon was equally impressed by the cottages which William Wells built for his gardeners, using local materials.

Whately, Thomas (d. 1772). Politician, gardener, writer. Although

Whately was an MP for eleven years, representing first Ludgershall, Buckinghamshire and then Castle Rising, Norfolk, until his death, little is known of his early life. He was appointed secretary to the Treasury in the administration of Lord Grenville and followed him into opposition. He lived at Nonsuch Park in Surrey, but whether his gardening activities there were of consequence is not known. His gardening reputation rests mainly upon the publication of his *Observations on Modern Gardening* which was published in 1770.

The book, which was widely praised for its 'beauty of style and justness of taste', was a typical exposition of the virtues of Nature and approbation of man-made essays in the Picturesque.

The book had its full share of typically high-flown eighteenth-century descriptive passages. He writes of craggy points of Middleton Dale, as 'a chasm rent in the mountain by some convulsion of nature, beyond the memory of man, or perhaps before the island was peopled', of the rocks at Matlock, Bath, as that 'scene of romantic magnificence; from such scenes, probably, was conceived the wild imagination, in ancient mythology, of the giants piling Pelion upon Ossa; the loftiness of the rocks, and the character of the Derwent, a torrent in which force and fury prevail; the cascades in it are innumerable'; and so on and so on; and of Dovedale with its 'air of enchantment; grotesque as chance can cast, wild as nature can produce—the monkish tombstones, and the monuments of benefactors long since forgotten, which appear above the green sward.'

Whately also included in his *Observations* accounts of visits to the landscape gardens at Blenheim, Painshill, the Leasowes, Hagley and

elsewhere, providing records of gardens since destroyed or altered.

White, (Reverend) Gilbert (1720–1793). Naturalist and gardener. White was born at Selborne, a village in Hampshire, the son of John White, a barrister of the Middle Temple, and his heiress wife, Anne, and was one of the eight surviving children of the marriage. Gilbert White was educated locally, probably at Farnham Grammar School, and at Basingstoke, entering Oriel College, Oxford, in 1740. In 1747, he took holy orders and was appointed curate to his uncle at Swarraton, near Alresford in Hampshire, at a stipend of £20 a year. In the same year he was afflicted with small-pox, but this seems to have had little effect upon his vigorous life as a traveller about England. He spent eighteen months as a curate at Durley, near Southampton, but, thanks to its proximity to Selborne, he was enabled to visit the family home frequently, sedulously compiling his *Garden Kalendar* during his visits. In 1751 he took over the curacy of Selborne, and in 1761 also took on the curate's nominal duties at Faringdon, two miles from Selborne. Two years later, on the death of an uncle, he inherited 'The Wakes', the place he was to make famous. He seems to have decided at this time to devote himself to the study of natural history. In 1767, Gilbert White met Thomas Pennant, the topographical writer and zoologist who, much struck by the originality of White's

The gardens at The Wakes in Selborn, Hampshire, as they are today, showing the sundial and ha-ha introduced by the Reverend Gilbert **White**.

(Opposite) Five plant introductions to Europe, sent from China by Ernest **Wilson**. *(Left, from top)* Magnolia wilsonii; *Clematis armandii;* Berberis wilsonae; *Davidia involucrata, the Dove or Handkerchief tree. (Right)* Acer griseum, *the Paper-bark Maple.*

observations on the natural history of the Selborne district, encouraged him in his endeavours, and also persuaded White to proof-read his own zoological papers. By this time White was an assiduous reporter, correspondent and journal-keeper. (He continued with his journals for over twenty-six years.)

Although latterday critics have suggested that White was an indolent clergyman, typical of his times, this is scarcely borne out by the entries in his journals. He rose at daybreak, worked early on his 'field diversions' and in his garden (in which he cultivated melons, grapes and apricots), conducted parish matters as well as a wide correspondence with other naturalists and botanists, including Linnaeus, as well as with friends made at Oxford, notably John Mulso, later Canon of Winchester. The Wakes estate also encompassed a small farmstead which also demanded White's supervision. Nevertheless, he continued steadily with the entries in his journal.

White's great work, *The Natural History and Antiquities of Selborne in the County of Southampton* was published in November 1789. The years following the publication of this original and unique book were as filled with observation as his earlier years. He remained, to the end of his life, a modest naturalist and botanist, despite the growing renown of his book. White died at Selborne in 1793.

White, John Ernest Grant (1901–). Landscape gardener. White studied at the Royal Horticultural Society at Wisley and subsequently lectured there and at Kew. In 1923 he was appointed landscape architect to the Wembley Exhibition, and was also responsible for turfing the stadium prior to the first Cup Final in 1923. For some years he was a horticultural contributor to *The Times*, and was one of the founder members of the Institute of Landscape Architects.

During half a century he has designed numerous gardens throughout the British Isles, including works at Dupplin Castle, Perth, for the late Lord Forteviot; at White Ladies Park, Ascot; Old Manor, Warnham; and at Royal Crescent, Brighton, for Lord Olivier. In recent years he has planned many courtyard gardens in London. His publications include *Designing a Garden To-day* and *Garden Art and Architecture*.

Wilks, (Reverend) William (1843–1923). Wilks was born at Ashford in Kent, and educated at Pembroke College, Cambridge, where, under the influence of Professor Charles Pritchard, he became keenly interested in botany in addition to his theological studies, which he con-

Reverend William **Wilks** *(1843–1923).*

tinued at Wells Theological College. In 1866 he became a curate in Croydon and in 1879 was appointed vicar of the nearby parish of Shirley in Surrey, where he was to remain for the rest of his life. There he established a beautiful garden and moved into the administrative side of horticulture. He became a member of the Floral Committee of the RHS in 1880 and was appointed Honorary Secretary in 1888. The Society was in a low state, financially and numerically. Fewer than a thousand members paid the subscription. Wilks' tenure of the position was an unqualified success. Membership rose to 16,000, an exhibition hall and offices were acquired, and a station for horticultural research established. Until the Society was re-established on a sound footing, Wilks took no renumeration for the onerous duties involved in this programme of reconstruction. He was

John Charles **Williams** *(1861–1939).*

awarded the Victoria Medal of Honour in 1912 and on his retirement in 1920 was elected to the Council. Much of the current authority of the Society is due to the dedication of Wilks.

Despite his combined clerical and horticultural tasks, Wilks found time to compile, with George Bunyard, two books: *Selected List of Hardy Fruits* and *Elementary Handbook of Fruit Culture* (1914). He also has an unusual claim to botanical fame. Since the seventeenth century the red poppy had been disfigured by the too familiar black spot. Wilks bred the Shirley poppy, which was wholly free from spot, and made his poppy available to the general public.

Williams, John Charles (1861–1939). Horticulturist. Williams was born at Caerhays Castle in Cornwall, and was educated at Rugby and

Trinity Hall, Cambridge. On the death of his elder brother he inherited the family's Cornish estates and spent the rest of his life at Caerhays, devoting his time to the cultivation and study of Chinese flora and to the affairs of his native county.

Williams showed outstanding enthusiasm, initiative and courage in his cultivation of plants from seeds, many of which were introduced into this country by such plant-collectors as George Forrest, Robert Fortune and 'Chinese' Wilson. His major floral interest was for rhododendrons and he was the first amateur grower to raise *Rhododendron calophytum*, which flowered in 1915. He showed the same foresight in appreciation and cultivation of other species of rhododendron and magnolias. Williams was MP for Truro from 1892 to 1895 and was appointed Lord Lieutenant of Cornwall in 1918.

Williams-Ellis, (Sir) Bertram Clough (1883–1978). Landscape architect. Williams-Ellis was born at Gayton in Northamptonshire, the fourth of the six sons of a clergyman. The family moved to Glasfryn in Carnarvonshire when the boy was quite young. He was educated at Oundle and Trinity College, Cambridge, where he read for a Science degree, but cut short his university career in order to study architecture. In the First World War he served in the Welsh Guards and was awarded the MC. As an architect he designed houses, hotels, clubs, apart from larger buildings in Britain, Africa and New Zealand.

In 1925, at the behest of a nearby landowner-uncle, he bought the estate of Aberia in North Wales, which he renamed Portmeirion, and set out to make an ideal holiday resort along the lines of an extended eighteenth-century folly, 'a gay, light-opera sort of approach' as he

The house and gardens at Portmeirion, in North Wales, designed for his own use by Sir Clough **Williams-Ellis** *(above).*

*Ellen Ann **Willmott** (1858–1934) and an illustration from her book,* Warley Garden in Spring and Summer.

termed the venture, encompassing architecture, landscaping, gardening and the use of colour. The result is the most unusual and delightful example of the Picturesque evolved in the twentieth century.

Sir Clough Williams-Ellis was appointed Vice-President of the Institute of Landscape Architects and the first Chairman of the first of the New Towns, Stevenage. He was knighted in 1972.

Willmott, Ellen Ann (1858–1934). Gardener, horticulturist. Miss Willmott was the descendant of a long line of wealthy gardeners resident at Warley Place in Essex, an estate once owned by John Evelyn (qv), diarist, during the period when he was writing *Sylva*. She began gardening at an early age and was especially interested in continuing the tradition of cultivating the *Cro-*

cus vernus and roses for which the garden was famous. In 1909 she published *Warley Garden in Spring and Summer* and in the following years commissioned the Royal Academician, Alfred Parsons, to make the drawings for her two-volume book *Genus Rosa* (1910–1914). Miss Willmott also made a garden at Tresserve at Aix-les-Bains. Miss Willmott was the first woman member to be elected to the Linnean Society. She was also a member of the RHS and one of the first three trustees appointed to supervise Wisley after Sir Thomas Hanbury presented the estate to the RHS. She and Gertrude Jekyll were the only women amongst the first recipients of the Victoria Medal of Honour instituted in 1897. She was known as an imperious and temperamental hostess and gardener, using her considerable wealth to achieve her hor-

ticultural ambitions. She was one of the subscribers to the expeditions of Ernest Wilson (qv) to China. The plants which she raised from the seeds brought back by Wilson were named to commemorate herself rather than the collector: *Ceratostigma willmottiae, Rosa willmottiae* and others.

Wilson, Ernest Henry (1876–1930). Plant-collector. Wilson was born at Chipping Campden in Gloucestershire, and at an early age was apprenticed to nurseries at Solihull in Warwickshire. By the age of sixteen, his talents were sufficiently evident for him to be recommended to the curator of the Birmingham Botanical Gardens. He spent his leisure in botanizing expeditions in the countryside and in evening study at the Birmingham Technical School, winning the Queen's Prize of the

School, before proceeding to the Royal Botanic Gardens at Kew in 1897, just before he was twenty-one. He soon made his mark as a practical botanist and as a student and entered the Royal College of Science with the objective of becoming a lecturer in botany. These ambitions were diverted to the work which was to make his name, for the renowned Veitch nursery requested the director of Kew, Sir William Thiselton-Dyer, to recommend someone suitable to the arduous task of collecting seeds and plants in Central China. Wilson was Sir William's nominee. He made his first journey in 1899, proceeding via the United States, meeting in Boston the eminent botanist, Professor Charles Sargent, director of the Arnold Arboretum in that city. This first expedition was so successful that, after his return to Britain in 1902, preparations were made for a second venture to another region of China. Between 1903 and 1905 Wilson made an even more successful trip and clearly established his renown as a plant-collector.

In 1906 he joined the Arnold Arboretum which sponsored two further expeditions to China, between 1906 and 1911, and to Japan in 1914 and again between 1917 and 1919. Much of the success of these expeditions was due to Wilson's skilful handling of his Chinese helpers. 'He was unusually sympathetic to the Chinese temperament,' wrote James Veitch. Reliable estimates have computed that Wilson's travels resulted in well over 3,000 species being discovered, of which over 1,000 were fresh introductions for cultivation in the West. Thanks to Wilson's endeavours, these introductions were soon grown in gardens throughout Europe and the United States.

In 1919 he set out on further travels to Australia, New Zealand, India and Africa, returning in 1921. In 1927 he was appointed Keeper of the Arnold Arboretum and from that time until his death spent most of his time in the United States.

Despite his manifold travels, Wilson was a prolific and authoritative writer. Due to his Directorship of the Arnold Arboretum, most of his books were first published in America. His first book, *A Naturalist in Western China*, was published in 1913 and other books followed in the intervals between his travels: *Cherries of Japan* and *Conifers and Taxads of Japan* (both in 1916) and so on. His finest book is undoubtedly *Lilies of Eastern Asia*, published in 1925.

Wilson was greatly honoured by horticultural societies and institutions in both England and the USA. He received the Victoria Medal of Honour in 1912, and an honorary MA from Harvard. Wilson (and his wife) died as the result of a motor-

*Ernest **Wilson** (1876–1930) and (right) one of Wilson's most successful introductions,* Lilium regale.

Ecklinville

Bramley's Seedling.

Duchess of Oldenburg

Ribston Pippin

Easter Beurré

Nouvelle Fulvie.

Olivier de Serres

car accident in America, a tragedy which cut short the life of a man who had become the legendary 'Chinese' Wilson before he was even forty years old.

Wilson, George Ferguson (1822–1902). Scientist, horticulturist. Wilson was born in Wandsworth, the son of a candlemaker and was educated locally. After a spell in a solicitors' office he joined the family firm and showed a considerable interest in the experimental side of the business, patenting in 1842 a process whereby cheap fats could be used in place of tallow for candle-making. As a result, the firm prospered and was sold and reconstituted to form the famous Price's Patent Candle Company. Prosperity did not dim Wilson's experimental curiosity and in 1854 he discovered a process for making pure glycerin. Even as an elderly man his scientific interests were still actively employed and he introduced the insecticide Gishurst Compound, widely used by gardeners.

His chief claim to inclusion in this DICTIONARY, however, derives from his purchase of an estate at Wisley, near his home, Heather Bank, at Weybridge in Surrey. Here he devoted himself to gardening on a considerable scale, specializing in the cultivation of lilies, winning many prizes at RHS shows, and the Victoria Medal of Honour in 1897. He was a Vice-President of the Society and was mainly responsible for introducing the guinea subscription. The now-famous garden he made at Wisley passed to the RHS.

Wise, Henry (1653–1738). Royal gardener. Wise was at pains to claim descent from well-established forebears in Warwickshire, but was apprenticed to George London (qv), to study horticulture at an early age, becoming partner in the highly successful Brompton Nursery, which he organized and cultivated with exemplary method and skill to judge from a report by John Evelyn. Soon after William III's accession, Wise was appointed deputy-ranger of Hyde Park and superintendent of the royal gardens at Hampton Court, Kensington and Windsor. Apart from their joint work concerned with the royal gardens, London and Wise held an incomparable position as gardeners to the aristocracy and were involved in works at Blenheim, Wanstead and Melbourne, where the gardens were remodelled in the French style by Wise, between 1704 and 1711, to include a *bosquet* and a 'waterpiece'. On the accession of Queen Anne, the care of the royal gardens was

Two coloured plates from the three-volume The Fruit Growers Guide *by John* **Wright**, *revised by Horace Wright (1924).*

A view of the water-garden at Wisley, originally landscaped by George **Wilson** *(1822–1902), seen above.*

Circular pond and formal paths at Melbourne, in Derbyshire, redesigned by Henry **Wise** *(1653–1738), seen above.*

handed over to Wise, yet, although disappointed by being superseded, London combined once more with Wise in the design of a garden in Nottinghamshire for Count Tallard, a French general captured by Marlborough in the battle of Blenheim. In 1714, Wise's appointment as Royal Gardener was renewed by George I. Wise's last years were spent on an estate in Warwickshire which he had bought as early as 1700. He died a rich man, reputedly worth £200,000, an enormous fortune in those times. Wise translated from the French of Louis Luger *Le Jardiner Solitaire*, adding certain of his own comments concerning his designs for Count Tallard. The book was published in two volumes in 1706. The renown enjoyed by Wise in his own time was signifi-

The yew tunnel at Melbourne, Derbyshire, where the gardens were redesigned in the French style by Henry **Wise** *between 1704 and 1711.*

cantly diminished by posterity: he was seen as the last practitioner in the more formal French and Dutch styles of landscape design which was ousted by the more naturalistic innovations of Charles Bridgeman and William Kent. His story has been most sympathetically narrated by David Green, historian of Blenheim, in *Gardener to Queen Anne* (1956).

Withers, Augusta Innes (fl. 1827–1864). Although she was known as 'Flower Painter in Ordinary to Queen Adelaide' and enjoyed a considerable renown as one of the leading botanical artists of her time, little is known of the early life of Mrs Withers, as she is consistently referred to in contemporary records. She contributed to several illustrated works of the mid-nineteenth century, making many drawings for the *Pomological Magazine*, over one hundred plates for *The Botanist*, and numerous drawings for *The Illustrated Bouquet*, which was published between 1857 and 1863. Yet it was her draughtsmanship (together with that of a Miss Drake) for the plates in one of the most magnificent (and certainly the largest-format) botanical books ever published, which established her reputation. This was James Bateman's *Orchidaceae of Mexico and Guatemala*, published between 1837 and 1843, for which the plates were lithographed by M. Gauci, the noted Italian artist. Mrs Withers' work as a teacher of botanical drawing was highly praised by Loudon in his *Gardener's Magazine*. Her work was regularly shown in the Royal Academy Exhibition between 1829 and 1846.

Wolseley, Frances Garnet (Viscountess) (1872–1936). Frances Wolseley was the daughter of the 1st Viscount Wolseley and succeeded her father in 1913, but died without an heir, the title thus becoming

One of the delightful drawings in Garden Form *by Frances* **Wolseley.**

extinct. She early showed a profound interest in gardening and before she was thirty had founded the Glynde College for Lady Gardeners. In 1908 she published the first of her several books, *Gardening for Women*. During the First War she was attached to the Ministry of Agriculture and, post-war, established at Haywards Heath a school for instructing women in the management of smallholdings for food production in their own homes. She wrote books on the history and domestic architecture of Sussex, and died at her home at Culpepers, Ardingly in Sussex.

Wotton, (Sir) Henry (1565–1651). Author. Wotton was born at Bucton Hall at Boughton Malherbe in Kent and educated at Winchester and Oxford. He went abroad to complete his education and to prepare himself for a career in diplomacy, and travelled widely in France, Germany, Spain and Italy. He had an

adventurous life and carried out many diplomatic commissions for James VI of Scotland, I of England. His frankness and wit, however, did not endear him to James I, and he was hard pressed to defend his casual definition of an ambassador as 'an honest man sent abroad to lie for his country'.

Apart from a few breaks, he spent much of his life between 1604 and 1624 as the King's representative in Venice, leaving only to act on the King's behalf elsewhere in Europe and to report to the Court. On his return to England he was appointed provost to Eton College, remaining there until his death. He makes an appearance in this DICTIONARY due to his acquaintance with European gardening thought and practice. He sent seeds and plants to the king and John Tradescant. In his book *Elements of Architecture* he wrote with percipience and foresight upon gardening: 'Gardens should be irregular, or at least cast into a very wild

regularity . . . I have seen a garden (for the manner perchance incomparable) into which the first access was a high walk like a terrace, from whence might be taken a general view of the whole plot below; but rather in a delightful confusion, than any plain distinction of the pieces. From this the beholder descending many steps, was afterwards conveyed again by several mountings and vailings, to various entertainments of his scent and sight, which I shall not need to describe (for that were poetical) let me only note this, that every one of these diversities was as if he had been magically transported into a new garden.'

Wotton's writings and his evocation of what has been termed a Jacobean Elysium had considerable influence on contemporary British gardening. He was an intimate friend of Isaak Walton.

Wright, John (1836–1916). Horticulturist, editor. Wright was born at Scawby in Lincolnshire, and started work at the age of eight. At twenty-four he was appointed head gardener at Branston Hall, Lincolnshire. Having become known as teacher and writer on horticultural subjects, he was invited to join the staff of the *Journal of Horticulture* in 1875, succeeding to the editorship twenty years later. Apart from his journalism, Wright wrote a series of elaborate guides to fruit and mushroom-growing for allotment holders and cottagers, as well as a manual of the *Culture of Chrysanthemum* 1883. The most significant of all his manifold contributions to gardening in Britain was undoubtedly his direction of a vast pioneer programme in Surrey for instruction in gardening in night-schools. In 1902 when the control of elementary education passed to county councils, the scheme encompassed over one hundred school gardens and two thousand plots in Surrey alone. Wright was also in considerable demand as a judge at fruit and flower shows. He had three sons who were also prominent in the history of horticulture:

Walter Page Wright (1864–1940), was born at Scawby, Lincolnshire, and after editing *The Gardener* became a prolific writer of popular gardening books, founder and editor of *Popular Gardening* and editor of *Cassell's Dictionary of Popular Gardening* (1902). He was also horticultural advisor to the Kent County Council and, due to the interest fostered by his father, he was a keen supporter of the allotment movement. In the production of his many guides and other gardening publications he was greatly aided by his brother, Horace Wright, editor of the *Journal of Horticulture* (d. 1915). The third son of John Wright was Frank Wright. He

The Librarian's Nightmare, *a cartoon by George Cruikshank drawn as a vignette for* The Orchidaceae of Mexico and Guatemala *(1837–41), with drawings by Augusta* **Withers.**

Sir Henry **Wotton** *(1565–1651), diplomat, author and correspondent of John Tradescant, by an unknown artist.*

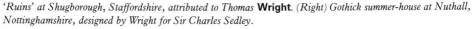

ARCHES.

A, a wide, rough ditch in the author's garden was divided in the centre by a bridge, over which an arch was placed. The two portions of the ditch made pretty dells, surrounded by a rustic fence.

B, an arch at the entrance to a Rose garden.

C, an arch in an herbaceous walk, rising from Lilies.

D, a triple arch ready for planting.

John **Wright** *(1836–1916).*

Rustic arches and fencing illustrated in a book by Walter Page **Wright** *(1864–1940).*

Samuel T. **Wright** *(1858–1922), fruit specialist.*

'Ruins' at Shugborough, Staffordshire, attributed to Thomas **Wright**. *(Right) Gothick summer-house at Nuthall, Nottinghamshire, designed by Wright for Sir Charles Sedley.*

Thomas **Wright** *(1711–1786), landscape gardener and artist.*

became superintendent of Victoria Park, London.

Wright, Samuel Thomas (1858–1922). Horticulturist, writer. Wright was born at Matlock in Derbyshire and started work at an early age at Snelston Hall in Derbyshire, moving on to Alton Towers and, later, Wood Seat, both in Staffordshire, followed by work in the gardens of other country estates, lastly at Glenston Court at Ross in Herefordshire, where he gained over 700 prizes at exhibitions. After that estate was sold in 1895, Wright was appointed superintendent to the gardens of the Royal Horticultural Society at Chiswick. He was thus responsible for supervising the transfer of the gardens to Wisley in 1903. He was a leading authority on fruit, especially on apples and pears,

and an indefatigable supervisor of the RHS fortnightly shows at Vincent Square as well as the transfer of the annual show, held first at Temple Gardens, and later at the present venue in the Chelsea Hospital Grounds.

Wright, Thomas (1711–1786). Landscape gardener, artist, writer. Wright was born at Byers Green, near Bishop Auckland, Durham, the son of a smallholder and carpenter. After an early life of vicissitudes, including service at sea, attempts at teaching mathematics and working for an instrument maker, an introduction to the Earl of Scarborough, who became his patron, enabled him to study astronomy and publish papers on the subject. Despite a certain impediment in his speech, wild notions

and absent-minded eccentricities Wright became something of a fashionable celebrity, and was retained by the Duke and Duchess of Kent as an instructor, not only for their children, but for themselves. They also introduced him to many of their aristocratic friends, for whom he made garden plans and drawings for garden buildings, strictly as an amateur. In 1762 he seems to have wearied of this life of sophistication and retired to a small house which he designed and built at his birthplace. This two-storied retreat overlooked a small garden which was embellished with 'Chinese and other seats' and various fancies. He also exercised his far-fetched skills as an architect for the Duchess of Kent at Windsor and for the Earl of Halifax in Northamptonshire, and, according to Eileen

A suggestion for a gothic grotto with cascades and wings, reproduced from Grotesque Architecture *by William* **Wright**, *1767.*

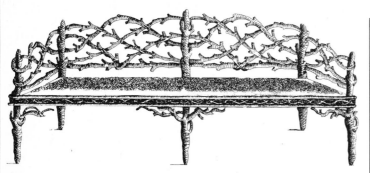

A rustic seat illustrated in Grotesque Architecture *by William* **Wright**, *1767.*

Harris (*Country Life*, September 1971), probably for Admiral Anson at Shugborough, where he certainly designed some of the remarkable garden buildings. Wright's most important building was Nuthall Temple (demolished in 1929) in Nottinghamshire which he designed for Sir Charles Sedley during the 1750s. Wright also devised the gothick summer-house at Nuthall.

Wright designed several other buildings for his various aristocratic patrons, including a root house, a mock-castle barn and castellated lodges and gothick cottages at Badminton; a miniature fortress at Wallington in Northumberland, and projects at Raby Castle in Durham. His most successful literary work was *Louthiana*, or an *Introduction to the Antiquities of Ireland* (1757); he

published *Six Original Designs of Arbours* (1755); apart from his astronomical and topographical books *Designs of Grottos* (1756).

Wright, William (fl. 1767). Although Wright styled himself 'architect', nothing seems to be known of his origins, life and achievements, and he is often confused with Thomas Wright (qv).

Although Wright's book is now rare, it must have had some influence on garden taste, for a second edition was published.

The book, published in 1767, was entitled *Grotesque Architecture or Rural Amusement*, consisting of *Plans, Elections and Sections for Huts, Retreats, Summer and Winter Hermitages, Terminaries, Chinese, Gothic and Natural Grottoes, Cascades, Mosques, Moresque Pavilions, Grotesque and Rustic Seats, Greenhouses, etc. many of which may be*

executed with *Flints, Irregular Stones, Rude Branches and Roots of Trees*. A second edition was issued in 1790. Wright may also have been responsible for the 25 plates illustrated in *Ideas for Rustic Furniture for Garden Seats, Summer Houses, Hermitages, Cottages*, which was published anonymously in the same year.

Wyatt, James (1746–1813) Architect. Wyatt was the sixth son of Benjamin Wyatt, a Staffordshire builder, and was born in Weeford in that county. Little is known of his boyhood or education, but when he was sixteen he travelled to Venice under the protection of a member of the Earl of Northampton's embassy in that city. He became a pupil of Antonio Visentini and was recognized as a highly accomplished architectural designer before he was twenty. After two years in Venice, Wyatt moved on to Rome, returning to England when he was about twenty-two. As an architect he was greatly influenced by the work of Robert Adam, despite his later contention that the Adam Brothers had 'corrupted public taste'. Wyatt's renown was early and firmly established by his designs for the Pantheon in Oxford Street, London, destined to be a 'Winter Ranelagh' and much patronized by fashionable society. He quickly established an enormously successful practice and became something of a celebrity as well as Surveyor-General to the Crown. Despite his feckless habits and unbusinesslike procedures, he was responsible for the design of more notable country houses than any architect of his time, although that same unreliability lost him as many more. Apart from his stylistic debt to the Adam Brothers, he was also an accomplished and successful gothicist and his designs for Sheffield Park, Lee Priory, Fonthill and Sandleford Priory were highly praised by Horace Walpole (qv), and established Wyatt as the first major architect of the Gothic Revival. Thanks to the fact that his gothic houses were built in already established settings, Wyatt has also been acclaimed as a master of the Picturesque, although he was scarcely accorded that renown by his contemporaries. Indeed, Joseph Farrington in his diary for January 22, 1798, recorded that:

'Wyatt acknowledged that he never passed the road through the gate which leads from Woodstock to Blenheim without being exceedingly struck with the general effect; and had often stood to consider to what cause it could be owing. It was not the buildings, or the grounds, or the woods or the walls singly, since none of these

(Left) Cassiobury Park, Hertfordshire, remodelled by James **Wyatt** *(1746–1813) for the Earl of Essex after 1800. Wyatt (above, from a drawing by George Dance) provided a castellated design for the house which reflected the then-fashionable taste for the Picturesque, both in architecture and landscaping.*

(Opposite) The Orangery at Heveningham Hall, Suffolk, designed by James **Wyatt** *for Sir Gerard Vanneck, 1788–99.*

*Sheffield Place, Sussex, gothicized by James **Wyatt** for the Earl of Sheffield between 1779 and 1791.*

*Richard **Yapp** (1871–1929).*

constituent parts were such as his judgment would approve entirely. Yet the whole makes a forcible impression.'

Not the attributes of a congenial landscape designer. Yet, thanks to his skills as a gothicist and the charm of many of the smaller gothic follies, dairies, pavilions which he designed for the sylvan settings in which his houses were so frequently sited, Wyatt's buildings undoubtedly furthered the cult of the Picturesque. He died deeply in debt and his widow was wholly dependent on a pension of £100 a year from Lord Liverpool, one of Wyatt's indulgent patrons.

Wythes, George (1851–1916). Gardener. Wythes was born in Worcester and after early training in various gardens in the Midlands he gained wide-ranging experience at Teddesley Park in Staffordshire. His reputation as a vegetable-grower recommended him to the Duke of Northumberland for the overseeing of the gardens at Syon House in Middlesex. He was head gardener there from 1888 until his retirement in 1906. For a time he combined this task with that of managing the Northumberland estate at Alnwick Castle. He was widely recognized as a skilful manager, cultivator and judge. He specialized in the raising of new varieties of vegetables, especially potatoes ('English Beauty' and 'Main Crop'), beans ('Progress' and 'Early Favourite') and cabbage ('St Martin'). His influence did much to improve kitchen garden crops in general. He was awarded the Victoria Medal of Honour in 1897. He wrote *A Book of Vegetables* in 1902, and was part-author (with Owen Thomas) of *Vegetable Growing Made Easy* (1913).

Yapp, Richard Henry (1871–1929). Botanist. Yapp was born in the village of Orleton in Herefordshire, and was educated locally. Following the death of his father, Yapp left school at fifteen to work in an office, but he was determined to enter the academic world. After attending lectures at University College in Nottingham he gained a scholarship at St John's College, Cambridge, in 1895. He proved a highly successful student and gained first class honours in botanical studies in 1898. (He was also captain of the university lacrosse team and a keen tennis-player.) In 1899 he was appointed botanist to the Cambridge Expedition to the Siamese and Malay States, and on his return was appointed Curator to the Cambridge University Herbarium. In 1902 he published papers dealing with his Malayan researches in the *Annals of Botany*. In 1904 he left Cambridge to become Professor of Botany at Aberystwyth. He travelled widely in South Africa, Canada and the United States. In 1919, Yapp was appointed Professor of Botany in the University of Birmingham, where he was responsible for the design of new botanical laboratories. His publications include a version of Maximov's *The Plant in Relation to Water* (1929) and a *Junior Book of Botany For Schools* (1923).

Yates, (Reverend) James (1789–1871). Antiquarian and botanist. Yates was born at Toxteth Park, Liverpool, the fourth son of John Yates, a Liverpool congregational minister with an outstanding reputation as a preacher. Yates was educated for the congregational ministry, first at Glasgow University and later at Manchester College (then at York) and Edinburgh University before returning once again to Glasgow. In 1813 he founded, with Thomas Southwood Smith, the Scottish Unitarian Association. He became an assiduous propagandist

*Syon House, Middlesex, where George **Wythes** (1851–1961), seen at right, was head gardener to the Duke of Northumberland from 1888 to 1906.*

*Reverend James **Yates** (1789–1871), antiquarian and botanist, who lived at Lauderdale House, Highgate (above).*

on behalf of Unitarianism, activities which continued, somewhat controversially, throughout his life. He finally left the ministry after further controversies, and reverted to the status of layman. He contributed largely to *The Dictionary of Greek and Roman Antiquities*, edited by Sir William Smith (1842), and to other learned publications but his significance for this DICTIONARY derives from his cultivation of cycas for which he gained the second prize at the International Horticultural Exhibition in 1866.

James Yates took the greatest delight in his garden at Lauderdale House, his home in Highgate in North London (now incorporated in Waterlow Park). He published notes on Cycadaceae in the *Proceedings of the Linnean Society* and on *Zamia gigas*.

He was also a fairly accomplished draughtsman; his plants and drawings were bequeathed to the British Museum.

Yeld, George (1845–1938). Botanist. After leaving Oxford University, Yeld became a schoolmaster at St Peter's, York, and became well known as an alpine climber, publishing in 1900 an account of his climbs, *Scrambles in the Eastern Graians 1878–1897*. Both in his own garden and in James Backhouse's Nurseries in York he began to specialize in the raising of irises and his experiments attracted considerable attention in the botanical world, and many enthusiastic gardeners followed his example and took up iris cultivation. In 1924, Yeld was elected first President of the Iris Society, and in the following year was awarded the Victoria Medal of Honour. He contributed numerous articles to the *Gardener's Chronicle* on the cultivation of irises and hemerocallis. On retirement from St Peter's School he moved to Orleton in Herefordshire where he continued to raise his favourite flowers until well into his nineties.

Young, William (1705–1785). Botanist. Young was the son of a small farmer living near Philadelphia in the United States, purveyor of a well-known nostrum known as Hill's Balsam, reputedly a product of John Hill, self-styled Botanist to their Majesties. Young seems to have come to London at an early age with seeds for Kew and to have made so considerable an impression on those in high places that in 1764 he was appointed Queen's Botanist. In London, Young studied botany under Hill, but seems to have left England in 1766 under something of a cloud. He returned to England in 1768 and established a nursery garden at Isleworth in Middlesex based on a cargo of plants which he brought with him. His reputation was somewhat controversial amongst collectors and gardeners in England, and he was accused of glutting the market with common plants and seeds, but he had more success in France, and in 1783 he published a

Catalogue d'Arbres, Arbustes et Plantes Herbacées d'Amerique. Young returned to Philadelphia and continued to send plants to Kew.

Zouche, Edward (c. 1556–1625). Horticulturist. The 11th Baron Zouche of Harringworth in Northamptonshire, was born at Molton in Lincolnshire, the only son of George de la Zouche, 10th Baron, and is said to have impoverished himself on more than one occasion by his passion for gardening. His early education was entrusted to Bishop Whitgift, then Master of Trinity College, Cambridge, but he did not take a degree. In 1586 he was one of the peers who tried Mary Queen of Scots, and was reputedly the only dissentient from the sentence of death imposed on her. In the following year he went abroad 'to live cheaply' as he said. After travelling in Germany, Austria, Italy and Turkey he returned to England in 1593. He sent seeds from Constantinople to John Gerard (qv), with whom he was on friendly terms. After carrying out diplomatic and commercial missions for Elizabeth in Scotland and Denmark, he left the country once again in order to conserve his modest fortune, this time to Guernsey, but remained for only a year. He was appointed President of Wales, retaining the position until 1615 when he became Lord Warden of the Cinque Ports. His passion for horticulture was exemplified in the cultivation of an extensive physic garden at his house in Hackney, where he engaged in serious botanical study under the tutelage of the superintendent of his garden, Matthias de Lobel (1538–1616), the eminent French-born botanist who was later appointed King's Botanist to James I. Patron and superintendent sponsored a number of plants but none commemorates the renown of Zouche.

*George **Yeld** (1845–1938).*

Title page of Catalogue d'Arbres *by William **Young**.*

*Baron **Zouche** of Harringworth (c. 1556–1625).*

Acknowledgements

Colour illustrations

8 Peter Coats; 13 Peter Coats; 16 Department of the Environment; 20 Edinburgh Botanic Garden; 25 High Commissioner for Australia; 28 Aminta Barton; 32 Woburn Estate; 37 Iris Hardwick; 40 Leonie Highton; 45 Leonie Highton; 49 Michael Wickham; 53 Leonie Highton; 56 Royal Horticultural Society; 60 RHS; 64 Edward Bawden (linocut), Peter Coats (photograph), British Architectural Library (Chambers' drawing); 69 RHS; 72 RHS; 76 RHS; 80 RHS; 85 Royal Botanic Gardens, Kew; 96 British Museum; 101 Peter Coats; 105 RHS; 109 RHS; 112 RHS; 116 RHS; 121 Alpine Garden Society; 125 RHS; 128 Michael Walpole; 132 James Mortimer; 136 Medici Society; 140 Peter Coats; 145 Peter Coats; 148 Roy Lancaster; 152 BM; 170 Leonie Highton; 175 Roy Lancaster; 178 Welbeck Gallery, London; 187 Peter Coats; 191 Royal Botanic Gardens, Kew; 195 Leonie Highton; 206 British Architectural Library; 211 Anthony D'Offay gallery, London; 214 William Macquitty/Royal Botanic Gardens, Kew; 222 RHS; 227 Iris Hardwick; 231 Royal Botanic Gardens, Kew; 235 India Office Library; 239 Basilisk Press; 243 National Trust; 246 A. F. Kersting; 250 Peter Coats; 255 Peter Coats; 259 Neville Poulter; 263 Royal Botanic Gardens, Kew; 267 Peter Coats; 271 Royal Botanic Gardens, Kew; 275 Sutton's Seeds, Torquay; 279 Peter Coats; 283 Royal Botanic Gardens, Kew; 283 Royal Botanic Gardens, Kew; 290 Ashmolean Museum, Oxford; 295 Peter Coats; 299 Peter Coats; 303 A–Z Botanical Collection; 311 Jasmine-Rose Innes, Peter Coats (inset).

Black-and-white illustrations

Most of the early views and portraits are reproduced from prints and books in private collections or in the libraries of the Royal Botanic Gardens, Kew, the Royal Horticultural Society, London, and the Linnean Society. Recent photographs, plans, etc, were supplied mainly by the gardeners themselves or by their families, or were specially taken by *House & Garden* photographers. Additional acknowledgements are made to the following:
10 (pagoda) Francis Machin; 14 (Lady Amherst portrait) Amherst College, Massachusetts; 26 (Banks portrait) National Portrait Gallery; 34 (Dukes of Bedford portraits) NPG; 58 (bridge at Hagley) Sabin Galleries, London; 59 (Capel family) NPG; 66 (Queen Charlotte portrait) NPG; 73 (Cobham family) Marquess of Bath; 80 (Cooper portrait) Royal Botanic Gardens, Edinburgh; 94, 95 (views of West Wycombe) Sir Francis Dashwood; 97 (pineapple painting) Fitzwilliam Museum, Cambridge; 104 (Douglas Fir) Forestry Commission; 123 (Forrest portrait) Royal Botanic Gardens, Edinburgh; 126 (Fothergill portrait) Royal College of Physicians; 139 (Haddington portraits) Scottish Portrait Gallery; 142 (Hamilton portrait) Simon Wingfield Digby, Sherborne Castle; 142 (Painshill temples) Patrick Matthews; 153 (Convent in the Woods) Edwin Smith; 174 (Langley portrait) British Museum; 193 (Lutyens portrait) NPG; 207 (Claverton Down Castle) A. F. Kersting; 242 (Robinson portrait) Peter Herbert; 293 (Vanbrugh portrait) NPG; 296 (Voysey garden) Duncan McNeill; 301 (Webb portrait) NPG.

Index to people

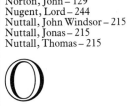

Index to places